Best Practice in Accessible Tourism

ASPECTS OF TOURISM

Series Editors: Chris Cooper (*Oxford Brookes University, UK*), C. Michael Hall (*University of Canterbury, New Zealand*) and Dallen J. Timothy (*Arizona State University, USA*)

Aspects of Tourism is an innovative, multifaceted series, which comprises authoritative reference handbooks on global tourism regions, research volumes, texts and monographs. It is designed to provide readers with the latest thinking on tourism worldwide and push back the frontiers of tourism knowledge. The volumes are authoritative, readable and user-friendly, providing accessible sources for further research. Books in the series are commissioned to probe the relationship between tourism and cognate subject areas such as strategy, development, retailing, sport and environmental studies.

Full details of all the books in this series and of all our other publications can be found on http://www.channelviewpublications.com, or by writing to Channel View Publications, St Nicholas House, 31-34 High Street, Bristol BS1 2AW, UK.

Best Practice in Accessible Tourism

Inclusion, Disability, Ageing Population and Tourism

Edited by

Dimitrios Buhalis, Simon Darcy and Ivor Ambrose

CHANNEL VIEW PUBLICATIONS
Bristol • Buffalo • Toronto

Library of Congress Cataloging in Publication Data
A catalog record for this book is available from the Library of Congress.
Best Practice in Accessible Tourism: Inclusion, Disability, Ageing Population and
Tourism/
Edited by Dimitrios Buhalis, Simon Darcy and Ivor Ambrose.
Aspects of Tourism: 53
Includes bibliographical references.
1. People with disabilities–Travel. 2. Older people–Travel. 3. Social integration. 4.
Tourism–Social aspects. I. Buhalis, Dimitrios. II. Darcy, Simon, 1964- III. Ambrose, Ivor.
HV3022.B47 2012
338.4'791087–dc23   2011048931

British Library Cataloguing in Publication Data
A catalogue entry for this book is available from the British Library.

ISBN-13: 978-1-84541-253-1 (hbk)
ISBN-13: 978-1-84541-252-4 (pbk)

Channel View Publications
UK: St Nicholas House, 31-34 High Street, Bristol BS1 2AW, UK.
USA: UTP, 2250 Military Road, Tonawanda, NY 14150, USA.
Canada: UTP, 5201 Dufferin Street, North York, Ontario M3H 5T8, Canada.

The policy of Multilingual Matters/Channel View Publications is to use papers that are
natural, renewable and recyclable products, made from wood grown in sustainable
forests. In the manufacturing process of our books, and to further support our policy,
preference is given to printers that have FSC and PEFC Chain of Custody certification.
The FSC and/or PEFC logos will appear on those books where full certification has been
granted to the printer concerned.

Typeset by The Charlesworth Group.
Printed and bound in Great Britain by Short Run Press Ltd.

Contents

Editors

Dimitrios Buhalis
Professor Dimitrios Buhalis is a Strategic Management and Marketing expert with specialisation in Technology and Tourism. He is currently Established Chair in Tourism and Deputy Director of the International Centre for Tourism and Hospitality Research (ICTHR) at the School of Tourism at Bournemouth University, and Professorial Observer at the Bournemouth University Senate. Professor Buhalis is leading the eTourismlab and is working with the Bournemouth team for introducing technology in all aspects of tourism research and teaching. He represents Bournemouth University at the United Nations World Tourism Organization. He is a Fellow of the International Academy for the Study of Tourism and the President of the International Federation for Information Technologies in Travel and Tourism (IFITT).

Simon Darcy
Associate Professor Simon Darcy is a strategic planning and policy expert with a specialisation in developing inclusive organisational approaches to diversity groups at the UTS Business School, University of Technology Sydney. He is Convenor of the Cosmopolitan Civil Societies Research Centre and is a member of the Disability Council of New South Wales, which is the Ministerial Advisory to the Department of Family and Community services. Over the last 25 years, Simon's work has spanned the built environment, transport, tourism, sport, arts and events industries where the hallmark of his work is his active engagement in changing industry and government practice through implementing the outcomes of his research. Simon was the recipient of the 2010 World Leisure International Innovation Prize for his work on developing a collaborative marketing approach to quality accessible tourism experiences with stakeholders from the private, not for profit and government sectors. As a power wheelchair using person with a spinal cord injury, Simon brings an insider's perspective to the ongoing challenges of the everyday experience of living with a disability.

Ivor Ambrose
Ivor Ambrose is the Managing Director and co-founder of ENAT, the European Network for Accessible Tourism, a non-profit association of organizations working in tourism development, disability, education, research and access consulting. With a background in Environmental

Psychology he has worked for over 30 years as a researcher, project manager, development and policy advisor in the fields of building design and evalua-tion, public housing, accessibility and assistive technologies for disabled and elderly people and information systems. He has previously held positions at the European Commission Directorate General DG, the Information Society in Belgium, the Danish Building Research Institute and the University of Surrey, UK. He now acts as an international consultant on accessible tourism development projects for regions, destinations, enterprises and funding programmes of the European Union.

Contributing Authors

Bruce Cameron is Director of Easy Access Publishing Australia. He has a Bachelor of Economics Degree (1980) and he is a Certified Practising Accountant (CPA). Following an extended trip to the United Kingdom and Europe in 1992, he left the finance industry to research, write and publish Easy Access Australia, Australia's only travel guide for people with a disability.

Andrew Daines gained an honours degree in Business and Tourism Management, and spent two years working for Hayes and Jarvis, Inghams, and car rental broker Holiday Autos. In 1997, Andrew joined the British Tourist Authority / English Tourist Board (trading as VisitBritain from 2003) where he spent almost 14 years. During that time, Andrew worked in a number of areas of the organisation, including information management, tourism technology and overseas operations. Andrew also represented VisitBritain on the European Travel Commission's Marketing and Technology Network where he held positions of both vice-chair and chair. Andrew left VisitBritain in March 2011, and is now undertaking freelance work within the travel and tourism sector for a broad range of organisations in the UK and overseas.

Arno de Waal is Sales Director of Adaptamos Group, Spain. Arno has a degree in Tourism and Leisure management from the Netherlands Institute of Tourism and Transport Studies. His career started in The Netherlands where he established a travel agency for people with special needs. In 1999 he developed a small holiday resort in Spain for people with a handicap, and has worked since then as an accessibility consultant in The Netherlands and Spain.

Tracey J. Dickson is Associate Professor within the Centre for Tourism Research at the University of Canberra, Australia. Her research focus is in alpine tourism, on diverse topics such as snow sport injury prevention, tourist satisfaction, seasonal workers' employment and living conditions and accessible tourism in alpine areas, with the overall aim of developing quality alpine tourism experiences that are sustainable for people and place.

David Edwards is Senior Research Fellow in the Employment and Social Exclusion (EASE) Research Group, School of Psychology, Deakin University, Australia. EASE research focuses on socially and economically disadvantaged groups, including: people with disability; people with mental illness; older workers; and people with a criminal history. Dr Edwards has a specific interest in psychiatric disability and employment and education. He is committed to research and teaching about the impact of social exclusion on the well-being of individuals and society.

Yuka Fujimoto is a Senior Lecturer in the School of Management and Marketing, Deakin University, Australia. Her research interest lies in the area of diversity-oriented participation, social inclusion and human-oriented human resource management education for current and future managers. She acts as a regular reviewer for *Human Resource Management* and serves on a Reviewers Panel of the *Research and Practice in Human Resource Management (RPHRM) Journal*. She is also a co-author of *Human Resource Management Education* book.

Georgia Fyka is qualified as a social worker and administrator, and holds a MA in Disability Studies. Working with the Greek NGO, Disability Now, she has extensive professional experience in disability support. She has managed numerous European and National projects in the field of independent living, assistive technology and accessibility, social inclusion, accessible tourism, training, education and employment for people with disabilities.

Pieter Ghijsels obtained a master's degree in Communication Sciences at the University of Leuven, Belgium. Since 1999, he has been working in the field of accessible tourism, first for the disability organization KVG, later as coordinator of the Accessible Travel Info Point and staff member for Accessibility Policy for the Tourism Administration for Flanders–Brussels.

Janet Haddock-Fraser is a specialist in organizational environmental sustainability, with a particular focus on societal agents as drivers of organizational change. In terms of application, she has worked on the role of customers and the media in this respect, as well as investigated multi-stakeholder drivers within tourism domains – particularly with respect to dive tourism. She is a member of the Centre for Tourism in Islands and Coastal Areas (CENTICA) at the University of Kent, UK.

Mark P. Hampton is Senior Lecturer in Tourism Management in Kent Business School at the University of Kent and Director of CENTICA in the UK. He has a PhD in Development Studies from the University of East Anglia and is a Fellow of the Royal Geographical Society. Dr Hampton specialises in tourism to Less Developed Counties, particularly island and small-scale tourism. He has published widely and has extensive fieldwork experience in South-East Asia, the Caribbean and the South Atlantic.

Jesús Hernández Galán is a qualified Forestry Engineer, Master in Business Management, Master in Environmental Management, anda graduate in General Management from IESE, Spain. He has been a consultant in accessibility to open spaces, and from 2000 to 2003 he was General Director and CEO of Fundosa Accessibility, Spain. In 2003 he was appointed Director of Accessibility of the ONCE Foundation. He is also Chairman of the Technical Committee of Standardization 170 of AENOR: 'Needs and adaptations for people with disabilities', Chairman of the technology platform Independent Living and Accessibility (eVIA), member of the Commission on Accessibility of the Spanish Committee of Representatives of People with Disabilities (CERMI) and of the Executive Committee of the European Institute of Design and Disability. He is also Vice-President of ENAT – the European Network for Accessible Tourism.

Philippa Hunter-Jones is Lecturer at the University of Liverpool Management School. Her research interests focus upon the relationships between tourism consumer behaviour and health. She is particularly interested in exploring the circumstances of those who travel with pre-existing health conditions (e.g. chronic, progressive and terminal conditions) and completed a PhD in 2001 in this area. Alongside this she has a general interest in the tourism consumer behaviour of other marginalized/hidden consumers (e.g. informal carers) in the wider field of travel-related illnesses and the relationship between charities and tourism.

Roland Krpata graduated from the TGM (Secondary School of Technical Industries), Austria. Since 1974 he has been Project Manager and Planning engineer in a lift and escalator business. He has been working since 1987 at Wiener Linien, as Project Manager for new underground construction and operation matters, and as Ombudsman for handicapped passengers at Wiener Linien. He has overseen the transition to right-hand traffic of the Stadtbahn (light rail system) and its transformation to a new underground line (U6) and the development of dispatching devices (mirrors). He has also worked on the lay out of the visual orientation system and creation of the tactile orientation system of the Wiener Linien and for the planning of barrier free station buildings (lift retrofitting program). Since 1991 he has participated in working groups at the Austrian Standard Institute and he has project-managed several research projects (Junction Flow, POPTIS, RAVE, MofA, ways4all).

Huong Le is a Lecturer in Management, School of Management and Marketing, Deakin University, Australia. She has conducted research projects and published on cross-cultural research in arts management, arts marketing, tourism marketing, inclusion, tourism and the arts.

Lilian Müller has worked as an accessibility consultant in Sweden since 1995, and is co-founder of the association Tourism for All in Sweden, the consultant company Svenska Equality and the Swedish network forum, Access Sweden. Lilian has developed methods to analyse accessibility and how to work successfully to improve accessibility in businesses and spatial planning. Lilian has also developed and holds training courses for accessibility auditors and staff in tourism and public authorities. Since 2008 Lilian has been the President of ENAT. Lilian holds a Masters degree in Political Science and Sociology from the University of Lund.

Susana Navarro Garcia-Caro is Managing Director of Adaptamos Group, Spain, specialising in tourism and leisure services for handicapped people. Her experience is in accessibility education and consulting. Susana Navarro has a Tourism degree from the University of Valencia, a Masters degree in Marketing and Sales from ESI University and a Masters in Tourism Planning and Management from the University of Valencia. She has delivered numerous training programmes and courses about accessibility issues and how to serve people with special needs. She has worked as a volunteer in a number of disability associations.

Peter Neumann is director of the consultancy NeumannConsult – Urban and Regional Development/Design for All, and Project Manager at the Department for Geography at the University of Muenster (Germany). He is also President of the European Institute, Design for All in Germany (EDAD), Board Member of Design for All Europe (EIDD) and Delegate of the Design for All Foundation. In addition he is member of the European Concept for Accessibility Network (EuCAN), ENAT, the Alliance of German Designers AGD) and the German DIN CERTCO Expert Group in the specific field of 'barrier-free planning, buildings and products'. Peter is Visiting Lecturer at the University of Lund (Sweden), University of Perugia (Italy) and Academy of Design at the HBZ Muenster (Germany). Since 1992 Peter has been working in the field of Accessibility and Design for All. He is specialist in the field of Design for All and tourism and housing, as well as urban and regional development.

Katerina Papamichail is a Greek architect who graduated from The National Technical University of Athens in 1978. She is Head of the Department of Architectural Studies at the Social Housing Organization, OEK, which is the government agency responsible for public housing, under the Greek Ministry of Labour. From 2001 to 2004, Katerina was seconded to the Athens Organizing Committee for the Athens Olympic Games 2004 (ATHOC) as Section Manager for the Olympic and Paralympic Villages, in charge of the accessibility of the combined facility. In this capacity she also worked on the accessibility of the city of Athens and other municipalities, as well as managing the architectural studies for several of the Media Villages. During the Games she was Deputy Site Manager of the Olympic Village and Site Manager of the Paralympic Village, overseeing the functions of the housing, national teams' offices and all related buildings and facilities. During the past 15 years, Katerina has participated in numerous European projects concerned with housing, tourism, disability and design. From 2005 to 2008 she was a member of the OSSATE and ENAT accessible tourism project teams.

Shane Pegg is a Senior Lecturer with the School of Tourism in the Faculty of Business, Economics and Law at The University of Queensland Australia. He has been involved in a wide array of research projects related to events and visitor services, therapeutic recreation, tourism access and inclusion issues, and the tourism and leisure behaviour of people with disabilities. He has an ongoing and active involvement in research related to the effective management of tourism events and leisure services, with accessibility issues a key area of inquiry. Shane has published in a wide array of professional journals related to leisure and tourism studies and is currently serving as an Associate Editor of the American Therapeutic Recreation Association's *Annual in Therapeutic Recreation*.

Mike Prescott works with governments and businesses to design, develop and deliver strategies that maximize accessibility and inclusion for all. He has a BSc in Kinesiology from the University of Illinois and an MBA from Simon Fraser University, with a focus on tourism partnerships. Mike leverages the science of dynamic social networks into his work, which included management of the accessible tourism strategy while at 2010 Legacies Now, Vancouver.

Ravi Ravinder (MBA, IIM Calcutta and M Com, UNSW) retired in 2010 as a Senior Lecturer in the School of Leisure Sport and Tourism at the University of Technology, Sydney, after 20 years of dedicated service. His areas of interest in teaching and research focused on tourism marketing, transportation issues and consumer choice processes. He also led a UTS team that worked with Ausaid support to set up Cambodia's first specialist tourism degree at the Royal University of Phnom Penh. He has undertaken consultancy work for Tourism Australia, Qantas and TAFE NSW.

Ruth Rentschler (PhD Monash) holds the Chair in Arts and Entertainment Management, School of Management and Marketing, Deakin University, Australia. Her special interest is in diversity, including publications on diversity management, the Aboriginal art market and women in management and the arts. She is widely published and has undertaken research projects with the Department of Planning and Community Development, the Australia Council, the Office of Multicultural Interests in Western Australia and the Australian Institute of Aboriginal and Torres Strait Island Studies. Ruth is deputy chair of the board of Multicultural Arts Victoria.

Sandra Rhodda is Director of Access Tourism NZ (http://www.access tourismnz.org.nz), which advocates for the development of accessible tourism in New Zealand. She is also Research Programme Leader in Access Tourism at the New Zealand Tourism Research Institute, Auckland University of Technology (http://www.nztri.org/). With a PhD in Zoology she has had a very varied working life, from research scientist to art gallery director and curator. She became interested in accessible tourism during a 2006 research project looking at tourism operator training. Appalled by the lack of accessibility in the built environment, and the kind of conditions that people with disabilities (PwDs) face, she has played an advocacy roll ever since, and has taken barrier-free assessment training to help her in her work.

Bodil Sandøy Tveitan worked at VisitOSLO in Norway from 2001 to 2009, the last few years as web editor for www.visitoslo.com. Bodil was responsible for the practical development and implementation of the

OSSATE project at visitoslo.com. Bodil has studied tourism at Oslo School of Management, and is now an independent consultant within tourism and technology.

Stephen Schweinsberg is a Lecturer in the School of Leisure Sport and Tourism at the University of Technology, Sydney, Australia. PhD considered the development of frameworks to assess the role of nature tourism as an agent of economic and social change in Australian rural communities. His PhD study was supported through a Sustainable Tourism Cooperative Research Centre (STCRC) Industry Scholarship, jointly funded by the Tourism and Transport Forum Australia and the Australian Sport and Tourism Youth Foundation. Stephen has published in a range of academic forums including *Australian Planner*, the *Finnish Journal of Tourism Research, Australasian Parks and Leisure* and *Geographical Research*. He has completed technical reports for the Australian Commonwealth Government and the STCRC and has graduate and undergraduate teaching experience in the School of Leisure Sport and Tourism (UTS), the Graduate School of the Environment (Macquarie University) and the School of Geosciences (University of Sydney).

Eleni Strati is a Sociologist, specializing in Disability Studies (MA) and Science and Technology Studies (MSc Research). Working with the Greek NGO, Disability NOW, she has conducted research in numerous European Union (EU) and National projects, in the field of independent living, assistive technology and accessibility, social inclusion, accessible tourism, training, education and employment for people with disabilities.

Norma Stumbo PhD, CTRS, is currently retired after being a professor at Illinois State University in Normal, Illinois, USA, since August 1984. She has also taught at the University of Queensland (Australia), the University of Western Sydney (Australia), and the Southern Institute of Technology (New Zealand). She previously served as the Associate Dean for Undergraduate Instruction and the interim director of General Education as well as the Recreation and Park Administration program director at Illinois State.

Antony Thornton is based in Liverpool, UK. He is a qualified teacher. He has almost eight years experience of organizing and leading residential camps for children and young people affected by serious illnesses for two charities based in the UK and Ireland. Tony was awarded the 2004 BT ChildLine Award for services to children and young people. He was nominated by a young person who came to camp. He has over six years experience of the education sector, most of them spent teaching in a residential school for emotionally damaged children, where he also looked after the school's farm. Recently, Tony has taught in a virtual school for children who are at risk of exclusion or have medical needs. Tony is passionate about facilitating experiences that provide fun, friendship and fulfilment.

Laurel Van Horn has specialized in accessible travel and transportation since 1987, working as a writer, educator, and consultant. Since joining

Open Doors Organization in 2004, she has developed their series of 'Easy Access' guides. as well as training programmes for hotels, airlines and, most recently, airports. Laurel holds an MA in economics from the New School for Social Research and resides in New York City.

Chris Veitch is an independent consultant with an interest in accessible tourism. After gaining a First Class degree in Tourism Management at London South Bank University, he was a policy executive in the English Tourism Council (ETC) managing projects to improve the accessibility of tourism in England. In 2003 he set up his own practice and has been involved in significant European projects to improve accessible information for consumers, as well as helping to produce online toolkits with a number of regions in England, encouraging tourism businesses to improve their accessibility.

Nikolaos Voulgaropoulos is founder and executive manager of Disability NOW, AUTONOMIA EXPO and web administrator of www. disabled.gr in Greece. Among other activities he has published books and articles, is system operator of online networks for disability, was the president of the International Conference 'People with disabilities and Mass Media', and chief editor of daily output on disability issues of the digital National TV channel.

Caroline A. Walsh is a PhD student at the University of Kent, UK. Her research area is disabled divers and Volunteer Tourism. Caroline has a BSc (Hons) in Environment Science and an MSc in Environmental Conservation. She is a Fellow of the Royal Geographical Society, the Zoological Society of London, the Royal Society of Arts and the Higher Education Academy. She has been diving internationally for the last 20 years and has travelled extensively. Caroline has been leading the NGO Access to Marine Conservation for All International (AMCAI), which she founded in 2001 advocating able-bodied and disabled people volunteering together in marine conservation activities and projects. AMCAI works to influence policy and practice alike. Due to her expertise Caroline is an observer on two All Party Parliamentary Groups for Marine and Coast and Disability, respectively.

Andy Wright had worked in the travel industry for 15 years, gaining expertise in both retail and business, when he was diagnosed with a rare neurological condition. Since becoming a wheelchair user he has utilised that expertise, combined with his insight into the world of disability, to develop Accessible Travel and Leisure (ATL) in 1997 in the UK. The company is dedicated to providing barrier-free holidays for all, whether clients use a wheelchair, have a modest impairment or just a temporary injury. ATL has since gained recognition with the British travel industry as the leading specialist arranging holidays for the disabled community. Andy has a regular 'Ask the Expert' spot in several journals and works closely with ENAT. He also operates in an advisory capacity to the Tourism for All UK Committee. Andy was a finalist for the RADAR Person of the Year Award 2009.

Acknowledgements

Like any project this book has a history that brought it to fruition. Back in 2005 Ivor Ambrose put a team together to work to improve the information provision for accessible tourism through the European project, One-Stop-Shop for Accessible Tourism in Europe (OSSATE). He included Dimitrios Buhalis as an information management expert in tourism and a handful of disability and tourism experts, many of whom had disabilities themselves and a passion to make a difference. As part of this project it was immediately evident that there was a body of research already in the area, primarily instigated by Simon Darcy and his collaborators. A couple of trips to Sydney and a few beers later, a close friendship and partnership was developed, fuelled by a passion for research on accessible tourism. A global network of friends/collaborators emerged rapidly to harness the best conceptual developments in the topic. Discussions were always about making a positive difference and taking this area forward and to the mainstream of academic enquiry and industry practice. As a result the idea of these books emerged as a way to achieve this and to assist the area to grow.

When we are discussing accessible tourism, all around the world, there is a realisation that several issues emerge immediately. People with access requirements are often frustrated with the lack of facilities and also of information that would make travel planning, and hence travelling, easier. They are dissatisfied with the public sector for the lack of regulation, control and implementation. They are also critical of the private sector for not understanding their needs as they would for any other consumer group and for being unwilling to invest in facilities that can improve accessibility. When discussing with tourism operators, especially in countries where accessibility is not at the forefront of legislation and practice, they express an inability to understand the complexity that is inherent to disability and access. They want simple practical guidelines and worry about the extra cost they will bear to adapt their facilities. In the centre of this mismatch in the marketplace, there are a number of misunderstandings or misconceptions from both sides that prevent the development and the implementation of accessible tourism.

This book complements the companion volume, *Accessible Tourism: Concepts and Issues*, by bringing together best practice and advice from around the world to show how accessible tourism can be developed and how existing facilities can be modified to become inclusive and accessible to all. Contributors from several countries and cities provide overviews of the political, cultural and technical challenges of accessible tourism and how these have been addressed in strategic and practical ways. The book demonstrates that often small changes and adaptation can make a big difference in providing access and a more inclusive tourism product. It aims to explain how to do accessible tourism and how this can bring benefits to stakeholders. Drawing on the experiences of leading practitioners, the book aims to support tourism operators and destinations in exploring how to improve their accessibility so as to reach new markets with a great potential and to improve their operational bottom line.

The editors were conscious of the need to make the material reflect industry practice and 'research driven' through a case study approach. Each of the contributing authors has attempted to honour the intent of the editors and we thank them for their collegiality and enthusiasm. As editors we also wanted to ensure the overall quality of the manuscript and subjected the chapters to refereed external review in addition to our own editorial processes. These processes have been important to ensure that the book has coherence and continuity in the development of the case studies.

The editors would like to express their gratitude to all our contributors for engaging in the debate and contributing to the project, and our publishers, Elinor Robertson and Tommi Grover, for their trust and support.

Dimitrios Buhalis, Simon Darcy, Ivor Ambrose
November 2011

Foreword

Best Practice in Accessible Tourism: Inclusion, Disability, Ageing Population and Tourism

As President of the World Travel and Tourism Council, the forum for CEOs and Chairmen of the world's leading travel and tourism companies, I am delighted at the publication of *Best Practice in Accessible Tourism: Inclusion, Disability, Ageing Population and Tourism*. The book epitomises the strategic vision of 'New Tourism' and demonstrates best practice in accessible tourism from around the world, highlighting how tourism destinations and organizations can learn from the innovators in serving this market.

As we outline in our *Blueprint for New Tourism*, 'New Tourism is a new sense of coherent partnership between the private sector and public authorities. It is geared to delivering commercially successful products – but in a way that ensures benefits for everyone. New Tourism looks beyond short-term considerations.' The book presents a powerful argument for just this, creating commercially successful products that are based on a foundation of including all people no matter what their access needs are.

This approach makes clear business sense. Travel and tourism businesses and destinations not only need to cater for the needs of growing markets, but must also operate within international conventions and national legislation in order to be sustainable. Inclusive design is a major step in ensuring social as well as environmental sustainability.

Accessible tourism takes into account not only people with disabilities but also the increasing number of senior travellers who have access needs. While these groups form a market segment in their own right, they also fall into the whole range of existing segments such as backpackers, luxury seekers, 'Frequent Individual Travellers' (FITs) or business travellers. We therefore call upon strategic thinkers across the Travel and Tourism industry to take on board the powerful arguments presented by this book.

David Scowsill
President and CEO
World Travel and Tourism Council
15 November 2011

1 Introduction

Ivor Ambrose, Simon Darcy and Dimitrios Buhalis

Introduction

Accessible tourism is gaining momentum across many different areas and activities within the tourism sector for both its inherent sensibility as a human rights issue and for its growing recognition as an important contribution to the economics of triple bottom line sustainability amid the general recession. This collection of accessible tourism best practice chapters is the companion volume to the first book, *Accessible Tourism: Concepts and Issues* (Buhalis & Darcy, 2011). While *Accessible Tourism: Concepts and Issues* sets out to explore and document the current theoretical approaches, foundations and issues in the study of accessible tourism, the focus of this book is on policy and best practice, reflecting the 'state-of -the-art' as expressed in a selection of international study chapters. In the following 24 chapters, the invited authors from around the world relate how the paradigm of accessible tourism is increasingly influencing tourism policies and taking form in a multitude of tourism settings and offers.

This book bears witness to the many faces and perspectives of accessible tourism. It can be portrayed – and can be understood – from a number of perspectives. Typically, innovative developments in tourism take into account the roles and views of different stakeholders, including policy-makers, construction, tourism providers and visitors. In this respect this book is no exception. It is also evident that, increasingly, accessible tourism is not only about providing access to people with disabilities, but is also about creating universally designed, barrier-free environments that can support people who may have temporary disabilities, families with young children and the ever increasing ageing population, as well as creating a safer environment for employees to work (Darcy & Dickson, 2009). As outlined in the conclusion to *Accessible Tourism: Concepts and Issues, universal design* and *access for all* applying the principles of universal design not only enables tourism organizations and destinations to expand their target markets but also to improve the quality of their service offering, leading to greater customer satisfaction, loyalty and expansion of business (Darcy *et al.*, 2011). The principles also enable them to develop flexible, multi-use accessible spaces and also enhance their productivity and operational management, all of which directly influences their profitability.

This book has three defining elements. First, it is truly interdisciplinary, multidisciplinary and international, as it synthesises best practice from around the world in a number of areas. The authors come from a variety of tourism-related backgrounds, reflecting our deliberate choice to invite academics, business leaders, public sector officials and leaders of Non-Governmental Organizations (NGOs) in this emerging field to share their experiences from research and practice. They include educators and researchers (Buhalis, Darcy, Dickson, Edwards, Fujimoto, Huong Le, Neumann, Ravinder, Rhodda, Schweinsberg and others), destination managers, professionals in architecture, marketing and information managers and executives working in tourist boards (Sandøy Tveitan, Daines, Veitch, Papamichail), leaders of NGOs and disability advocacy groups (Ambrose, Müller, Walsh, Van Horn, Voulgaropoulos) and owners of tourism businesses (de Waal, Navarro, Wright). Many of the authors are people with disability themselves and have experienced best and worst practice first hand. This provides an insider's understanding of not only the lived experience but their understanding of the relative inclusiveness of their professional backgrounds. Just as important, whether the authors are people with disabilities or not, we all share a passion to make our environments and the tourism experience more accessible and our societies more inclusive.

Second, the authors work and live in different parts of the world – including Austria, Australia, Belgium, Canada, Germany, Greece, Norway, New Zealand, Spain, Sweden, USA and the United Kingdom – reflecting the international nature of this research as well as the value and necessity of exchanging experience across national and continental boundaries. Learning from global experience means that, increasingly, standardised processes and legislations can gradually emerge. not only to make design and implementation easier, but also to improve the development time-scales and reduce costs. The contributions also emphasise – some directly and others indirectly – how specific geographical, cultural, political and sectoral contexts influence the nature of tourism management and the accessible tourism visitor experience.

Third, a wide range of subject matter is addressed in these chapters, including tourism policy development at international level (e.g. Ambrose on the European Union), at national and regional levels (e.g. Ghijsels on Flanders, Belgium and Hernández Galán on Spain); strategic destination management (e.g. Prescott on Vancouver), customer relations (e.g. Veitch on the UK, Navarro *et al.* on staff training, and Wright on international travellers), architectural design (Papamichail on hotels), marketing, business networking (e.g. Sandøy Tveitan on web-based access information), project-based working methods, public–private partnerships and third sector involvement in accessible tourism (e.g. Walsh *et al.*). All case studies and chapters present *research-based evidence* and include references and further reading that will enable readers to research and explore these topics further and discover initiatives in their locality. They represent best practice and provide easily implementable actions that can increase the inclusiveness of facilities and destinations.

Universal Approaches to Accessible Tourism

Of course, this book shares a common perspective with the volume, *Accessible Tourism: Concepts and Issues,* where the premise of that book was based on the following definition:

> Accessible tourism is a form of tourism that involves collaborative processes between stakeholders that enables people with access requirements, including mobility, vision, hearing and cognitive dimensions of access, to function independently and with equity and dignity through the delivery of universally designed tourism products, services and environments. This definition adopts a whole of life approach where people through their lifespan benefit from accessible tourism provision. These include people with permanent and temporary disabilities, seniors, obese, families with young children and those working in safer and more socially sustainably designed environments (Buhalis & Darcy, 2011, pp. 10–11).

Central to this definition is that accessible tourism is part of collaborative processes that understand the heterogeneity of access requirements informed by different embodiments, where the creation of enabling environments is understood through universal design, as summarised in Figure 1.1 from the concluding chapter that drew together the chapters of the book. This figure represents the conjunction of understanding accessible tourism from the experience of the tourist and the interplay that the tourist has with the disabling or enabling tourism environment. Understanding the tourist with a disability is a complex issue in that the tourist experience must be inclusive of: (1) the type of disability/dimensions of access (mobility, hearing, vision, cognitive and others); (2) the level of support needs of the individual (from the independent traveller with a disability to those with very high support needs); (3) their socio economic circumstances; and (4) the previous tourism experiences. The needs of each individual will vary depending upon their positioning within these four interdependent and overlapping constructs and the particular situation.

The tourism environment encapsulates the systems approach together with the individual journey of the tourist with a disability through the stages of travel. As we learnt through a number of the chapters in *Accessible Tourism: Concepts and Issues* (Arola *et al.*, 2011; Foggin, 2011; Fullager, 2011;

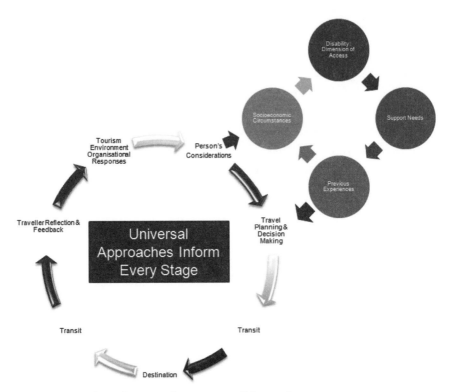

Figure 1.1 Universal approaches to accessible tourism
Source: Darcy *et al.*, 2011, p. 312 adapted from (Buhalis, Michopoulou,
Eichhorn, & Miller, 2005; Clawson & Knetsch, 1966; Leiper, 2003; Packer,
McKercher, & Yau, 2007; Small & Darcy, 2010)

Pegg & Patterson, 2011; Poria *et al.*, 2011; Small & Darcy, 2011; Veitch &
Shaw, 2011; Wang, 2011) what makes the tourist with a disability anxious
is that at every stage of the travel process accessibility is an unknown
variable that needs to be encountered with a series of constraints and barriers that the non-disabled tourist do not have to negotiate. As we saw with
the aforementioned chapters, the resultant experiences of travellers with
disability were some worst-case examples of dependency, despair, despond-
ency and indignity. Yet, when there is an enabling tourism environment,
visitors' experiences are independent, joyous, dignified and equitable. This
book provides examples of how the latter can be achieved for travellers
with disabilities, no matter what their disability or level of support needs. It
demonstrates that simple solutions and understanding of issues can make a
huge difference and open the destination to accessibility requiring markets
as well as improve operational efficiency.

Structure of the Book

In order to provide a guide for the reader, this section gives a short introduction to the key themes that are addressed in the five main sections of the book, namely:

(1) Policies and Strategies.
(2) Networks and Partnerships.
(3) The Accessible Tourism Value Chain.
(4) Destination Development.
(5) Accessible Tourism Experiences.

Significantly, all contributions point to the fact that accessible tourism cannot be delivered by means of a 'quick fix' or merely making cosmetic changes to information, a business or a destination. As the definition of accessible tourism used for *Accessible Tourism: Concepts and Issues* suggests, it needs to be part of a strategically planned for process, which specifically targets the market segment, and where the tourism industry groups work together to collaboratively-develop accessible tourism products and services. Hence, delivering *Accessible Tourism Experiences* typically depends on a process that incorporates the four interlinked sets of factors, as shown in Figure 1.2.

Starting with theme one, *Policies and Strategies* are basic requirements for initiating and implementing actions in support of accessible tourism. This is invariably true, whether they are complex and elaborate national plans

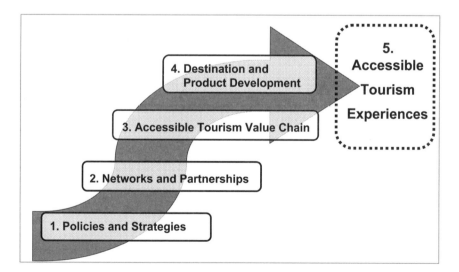

Figure 1.2 Structure of the book, based on a thematic approach

formulated in lengthy documents by politicians and bureaucrats, or decisions made among business partners in a destination or even by an owner–manager at a single venue. Only when a policy has been formulated and agreed is it then possible to assign resources to the new priorities, focus the necessary energy and move effectively towards the intended goal.

Successful businesses and destinations depend on building well-functioning *Networks and Partnerships* (Theme two). These must be composed of stakeholders and providers that are attuned to the needs of customers who require good access and who possess the capacity to collaborate with other market players in delivering products where and when they are needed.

Theme 3 addresses the *Accessible Tourism Value Chain* which denotes the set of transactions in the supply of the tourism product to visitors. The chain must be developed in each of its 'links', e.g. transport, attractions, accommodation, and there must be reliable connections between all links if the customer is to receive adequate services throughout the journey.

Destination Development (Theme four) focuses on the strategies, structures and activities which destinations must put in place to enable accessible tourism enterprises to thrive – and thus provide an overall experience which is satisfying to the visitor. Accessible hotels, restaurants, museums and other visitor attractions must not be isolated 'oases of accessibility' within otherwise inaccessible landscapes; they must be physically joined up by accessible routes and transport systems. Moreover, destination management organizations must advertise the existence of accessible facilities and attractions through regular marketing channels in order to attract customers.

Theme 5, *Accessible Tourism Experiences,* highlights *the visitor experience* as the objective of accessible tourism and the guiding factor in the design and development of tourism products. While mainstream tourism is starting to discover the importance of *the individual experience* in winning markets and commercial success, it is undoubtedly true that those providers who are successfully addressing the accessible tourism market have a great deal of expertise in understanding their customers' needs and finding ways to satisfy the particular demands of this sophisticated market.

Section 1: Policies and Strategies for Accessible Tourism

Section 1 explores how accessible tourism policies and strategies have been developed and implemented in contexts ranging from the European Union (EU), to USA, Australia and New Zealand.

Ambrose (Chapter 2) presents an analysis of European policies for accessible tourism over the last two decades, indicating that these have largely been made up of fragmented and short-term actions promoting access for disabled people to tourism services. European policies in tourism have generally lacked a sustained and purposeful trajectory, partly due to a lack of political authority on the part of the European institutions. With the new competences given to EU institutions by the Lisbon Treaty (European Union, 2009), there is now a possibility of a comprehensive policy approach, including political institutions, stakeholders and representative bodies of consumers, for concerted actions on accessible tourism in Europe. A road map is proposed which calls for integrated actions at EU, National, Regional, local and enterprise/SME levels, leveraging a range of EU funding programmes in order to finance the actions.

In a number of areas of the world accessible tourism is being facilitated by legislation, public sector orientation and a gradual understanding by and collaboration with the private sector. The accessibility of tourist services in Flanders, for example, as described by Ghijsels, (Chapter 3) is an integral and major part of the Flemish policy on tourism, following the principle that travellers with a disability or impairment should have access to the same tourist offers as other visitors. Through dedicated funding programmes the authority has worked over the past decade to provide reliable information on the accessibility of tourist facilities through regular channels. It has introduced an accessibility label based on assessment of venues and has developed programmes for sensitization, training, design, visitor reception, guides and accessible infrastructure.

In Germany, Neumann (Chapter 4) begins from the observation that accessibility is a civil right and its establishment is based on the currently applicable legal provisions and standards. Neumann examines the political, organizational and business implications of this right, citing convincing empirical evidence that the market of accessible tourism must be addressed more firmly and more widely if the group of travellers with mobility or activity limitations is to be properly served by the German travel industry.

In their contribution, Voulgaropoulos, Strati and Fyka (Chapter 5) give their perspective on Greece's accessible tourism development policy, as shown in relation to the subject of Beaches and Bathing for All. Describing the general policy framework, they note that the issue of accessible tourism has been dealt with in a rather piecemeal fashion, and although state initiatives have resulted in some good practices in the past, it has been inconsistent in encompassing accessibility in mainstream strategies for tourist development. There is also a need, they note, for setting standards, monitoring and evaluating accessible tourism policies and practices in order to deliver a better product for tourists with disabilities and reduced mobility.

Laurel Van Horn, (Chapter 6) addressing the US market of travellers with disabilities gives a thorough review of survey and market data. The findings indicate that, despite long-standing legislation and policies in support of Americans with disabilities, there are still many barriers which restrict the frequency of travel and the types of long distance travel which individuals with disabilities are willing to undertake. Despite the very large size of the disability travel market, both in terms of numbers and market value, persons with disabilities report that their travel is very much hampered by physical barriers and poor service levels.

Darcy, Cameron and Schweinsberg's examination of Australia (Chapter 7) highlights the role of government as an agent of change. After mapping and analysing the policy initiatives and measures taken by government and private players, it is evident that there is a lack of credible, reliable and accurate information, especially in respect to accessible accommodation. Therefore, there is a need for an overarching national approach to accessible tourism marketing, promotion or information provision. To date, the Australian government has failed to deliver such a system as it does for mainstream tourism product.

Rhodda, (Chapter 8) gives an account of the recent history of accessible tourism in New Zealand, which is a relatively under-developed area, moving gradually towards wider recognition and acceptance both in policy-making and among stakeholders. The evident lack of awareness about access needs for disabled and other visitors and the readiness to meet these are lacking both in the public and private sectors. Tourism websites also show little attention to the market and information needs of older and disabled travellers. Rhodda points out that, as Baby Boomers age and become more prone to disability over the next several decades, this market will continue to expand. In its current state of development, New Zealand requires more research studies and plans to meet this demand, as businesses and governmental authorities come to terms with this complex and interesting market.

Section 2: Networks and Partnerships

The chapters in Section 2 of this book show very conclusively that networks and partnerships are necessary for the successful implementation of accessible tourism initiatives. Groups of enterprises and public–private partnerships in cooperation can access the market more readily than isolated players, by combining their skills and developing new products and services that will serve these clients better. Participating in global knowledge networks helps enterprises and tourist boards to avoid 're-inventing the wheel', saving them time and effort.

Prescott's exploration of 'Universal Tourism Networks' (Chapter 9) applies network analysis to define and measure the capacity to deliver a seamless travel experience for the market sector that requires accessible facilities, transport and services. Travelling for disabled people starts from a different perspective because everyone's disabilities, and therefore needs, are different. There is very little that can be packaged together in advance – one

size definitely does not fit all. The gaps between supply and demand are
mapped through the identification of *assets*, (such as businesses or features
in the environment that serve as travel experiences such as a hotel, restaurant, monument, store, or beach), *connections* between the assets in the
form of accessible paths, routes and transport services, and *networks* which
are clusters of related assets. The density of the networks, the strength of
connections and centrality of certain assets represents an interesting and
powerful way to understand the destination environment for people who
have accessibility needs. It is evident that the more 'seamless' the travel
experience, the more the venue, service and destination will attract visitors.
Consideration of the specific needs at each stage of the holiday journey,
from the decision-making process right through to after-sales support, is
critical to achieve that. This is, indeed, reflected in all the cases examined in
this book.

Huong Le, Fujimoto, Rentschler and Edwards (Chapter 10) investigate
access and inclusion for people with disabilities, providing a policy-systematic
analysis conducted at a state level and a case study of tourism in Victoria,
Australia. Adopting a stakeholder perspective, they conclude that despite
the impressive State-wide policy of community oriented inclusion, those
policies need greater recognisable impact on the ground. In particular,
while much the tourism practice and research still imagines physical accessibility equates to inclusion, this study illustrates there is a need for wider
community social oriented inclusion.

Müller (Chapter 11) shows how marketing through stakeholder
networks has been a mobilising force for the development of accessible tourism in Sweden. There has been a shift in emphasis from the beginning of
the 1990s, when accessible tourism was focused on tourism for disabled
people, to the 21st century approach, which follows the principle that tourism should be accessible for all. The interplay between supply and demand
for visitors with access needs must be seen in relation to the underlying
changes in the society and disability policies, where more attention is now
being paid to rights of disabled people including the right to an independent
life.

Hunter-Jones and Thornton (Chapter 12) examine the role of the
charitable sector in holiday provision for vulnerable consumers. Highlighting the paucity of academic tourism research existing in this area, they have
investigated the fields of marketing and consumer behaviour research, as
well as practitioner and trade publications, in order to identify how these
networks and stakeholders are contributing to development in accessible or
disability tourism. While some studies have focused on the link between
charities and ethical/responsible dimensions of tourism at a community
level, the authors suggest that more useful insights might be gained in
future in relation to the contribution which this sector is making in terms
of health and wellbeing at an individual level. Their research points to the

importance of charities in providing accommodation, funding and signposting activities for people in need of accessible holiday offers. Yet they also identify one of the problems of the charity sector being somewhat divorced from mainstream tourism is the tendency towards 're-inventing the wheel'. The commercial tourism marketplace by its focus and sheer volume of operations is extremely well-placed to provide support to the third sector. Bridging the gap between these sectors represents a considerable challenge, yet one which also offers mutually beneficial opportunities to those prepared to think outside the box, they conclude.

Walsh, Haddock-Fraser and Hampton (Chapter 13) consider the potential for, and limitations restricting the incidence of volunteer tourism in the context of accessible dive tourism. Accessible dive tourism is described as an emerging sub-niche of dive tourism and has developed from disabled dive tourism. As discussed by the authors, this market has increased in recent years as more disabled persons and persons with disability are learning to dive. Volunteer opportunities within dive tourism for disabled participants, such as marine conservation work, are quite limited, yet this chapter shows how opportunities can be increased for developing volunteerism opportunities for disabled divers. It also makes recommendations that would enable the same participation for disabled divers in volunteer initiatives in marine conservation, natural resource management and poverty alleviation as able-bodied divers.

Inclusion is at the heart of the book, and this is a theme re-occurring frequently. There is a need at the policy level to acknowledge the gap in tourism inclusion practice and research which has been more focused on physical access and information than on community integration views and practices. It is evident throughout the book that people with disabilities need their voices to be heard, just as they need to participate in the development and implementation of inclusive policies and practices for the tourism sector.

Section 3: Accessible Tourism Value Chain

Section 3 points to the importance of considering all aspects of the Accessible Tourism Value Chain when catering for visitors who need good access. There is often a realisation that buildings, premises, public transportation, streets and squares often are insufficiently accessible to people with disability. Sometimes some elements may be accessible, but the route or the accessibility chain may be broken somewhere making travelling complex and difficult. Many inconveniences such as thresholds, the absence of a lift or an adapted bathroom often turn a pleasant trip into a major challenge. Hence, the important of seamless travel experiences is also evident throughout. In addition, accessibility information enabling people to make informed decisions about their travel plans is absolutely critical.

Travel entrepreneur Andy Wright (Chapter 14) explains his company's approach to providing organized tours for tourists with a disability, by taking into account all aspects of the journey, the destination and services that are involved. Beginning with a comprehensive account of holiday planning, transport and service provision, Wright also presents the franchising system which he has put in place, enabling persons with disabilities to work as travel agents in this specialised market segment.

Other contributors to the chapters in this section point out that *universal design* is a fundamental approach to the creation of environments, products and services that can be used by everyone. Accessibility is an easily reachable goal if simple standards and guidelines are followed, especially for new facilities. Universal standards that are communicated transparently to visitors will give them the confidence that they will be satisfied and that the facilities and services are suitable for their needs. Accessibility and universal design is not only for persons with disability.

Krpata (Chapter 15), writing about the accessible public transport system in Vienna, demonstrates how a series of actions and projects has contributed to provide an advantage for everyone. Citizens even without mobility restrictions appreciate a step-less access from all platforms to all vehicle floors. The dispatching time in all stop areas is shorter and enables more comfort and a quicker round trip circulation time on all lines. More comfort, quicker lines, more reliable time tables, shorter waiting times . . . a win–win–win situation for operators, citizens and tourists was the result of experiences in Vienna.

Darcy and Ravinder (Chapter 16) discuss examples from the airline industry and the so-called 'low-cost carriers' (LCCs) which demonstrate that there are several possible 'fail-points' in the service offered by LCCs to people with disabilities. In particular, these are related to fares (and baggage allowances), aircraft used, airport (ground) facilities and services and in flight services and facilities. Whilst there is a cost involved and a possible loss of efficiency in the provision of these services by LCCs, they may also be construed to be discriminatory. Hence this situation calls for a re-application of minimum standards in line with anti-discrimination provisions of the constitution and relevant legislation.

Papamichail (Chapter 17) focuses on hotel accommodation as one of the most important links in the accessible tourism value chain, showing how the application of universal design principles can provide appropriate and more cost-effective environments and facilities in new-build and renovations. Drawing on her practical experience and design studies for accommodation, including the 2004 Paralympic Village in Athens, this chapter gives a concise set of design guidelines for hotel owners, managers and designers who may be addressing the practicalities of achieving good access in their premises for the first time.

Section 4: Destination Development

Section 4 focuses on destination development, the key aspects of creating, promoting and marketing destinations that are accessible to all visitors. Information and communications are absolutely critical for accessibility, complementing architectural accessibility. Accurate, objective, media-rich information delivered through travel guides, specialised online services and as part of mainstream websites will enable disabled travellers to assess whether a particular product and facility is suitable and adaptable to their particular needs.

Cameron and Darcy (Chapter 18) discuss a number of issues on how to represent access information that describes destinations venues and facilities, in particular the use of icons in place of long text descriptions, the use of rating systems and issues concerning illustrations and formats. Moreover, innovative technologies such as real-time virtual reality and 3D photo imaging also provide an incredible wealth of information, allowing people to select destinations and facilities that they can visit, whilst having the potential to becoming a gateway to places for people who are not otherwise able physically to get there.

Pegg and Stumbo (Chapter 19), draw attention to how information and communication technologies could be more effectively utilised as an alternative mechanism through which tourism organizations and destinations became more accessible to visitors at tourism heritage sites.

Sandøy Tveitan (Chapter 20) recounts her experience in developing information about accessible tourism as a natural part of general tourism marketing of the city of Oslo, Norway. The VisitOSLO portal incorporates advanced information technology and multiple sources of content addressing people with special needs. VisitOSLO aims to reach new markets and attract more visitors to Oslo and uses universal design principles to communicate and market its tourism products.

Hernández Galán (Chapter 21) presents two case studies of accessible tourism initiatives from Spain: Arona in Tenerife and Madrid, showing how these destinations have developed their product and marketed themselves towards customers who rely on good access. In each case it is demonstrated how publications, design standards, publicity, business networking and service training can support accessible tourism and a number of guidelines for successful accessible destination management emerge.

Daines and Veitch (Chapter 22) give a detailed account of the efforts made by VisitBritain to provide reliable, accurate information for people with disabilities when they are planning a holiday, short break or a business visit. It is shown how this can make the difference between winning and losing customers for both tourism organizations and destinations.

Section 5: Accessible Tourism Experiences

Section 5 highlights accessible tourism experiences, which are seen as the central component of the transaction between the tourism organization, destination and visitor. Developing the goal to deliver *a comprehensive accessible experience*, taking in both stakeholder and visitor perspectives, is of paramount importance to improving customer care and satisfaction. This individual approach, however, does not lend itself to economies of scale, and is heavy on resources and manpower. However, cost is not necessarily the uppermost factor when disabled clients choose where and how to travel. Once trust has been gained and previous experiences have been satisfactory, disabled travellers will appreciate the extra value and typically return to the specialised operators and providers that offered the comprehensive accessible experience, increasing loyalty and profitability.

Dickson and Darcy (Chapter 23) examine the process and outcomes of a project on Alpine Accessible Tourism conducted in Australia from 2006 to 2008. This wide-ranging project was unique in that it sought to provide a systematic approach to accessible tourism across all alpine areas in New South Wales, Victoria and Tasmania, each area having its own state and local government jurisdictions, as well as separate protected area management agencies. The project was theoretically informed through social approaches to disability, the geographies of disability, destination management and the experience economy. The research design sought to reveal the users' perspectives and experiences of alpine tourism by applying a participatory action research framework using questionnaires, in-depth interviews and workshops. This produced a systematic account of accessible tourism within each of the destination precinct areas and led to the development of an accessible tourism resource kit, disability awareness training, accessible accommodation audit template and way-finding map.

Navarro, de Waal and Buhalis (Chapter 24) show how staff training for serving disabled customers and addressing their special requirements is of paramount importance in ensuring an accessible tourism experience. This chapter emphasises that raising the knowledge and awareness about disabled people's needs is more complex than just talking about physical access, requiring a wider and deeper understanding of accessible tourism from the point of diversity, design for all and customer-oriented management.

It is evident from best practice from around the world, that universal design, management, training, site access and equipment each play a role in enabling destinations and enterprises to deliver accessible tourism experiences. Proposals for European and global industry standards for accessibility and appropriate training at multiple levels and for multiple stakeholders are recognised as a potential source of improvement. Such standards need to be developed through participatory approaches involving disabled travellers, policy makers and local tourism providers.

The concluding chapter of the book by Ambrose, Darcy and Buhalis (Chapter 25) revisits some of the main themes of accessible tourism, looking at emerging definitions and terminology, the balance between market interest and social responsibility and the growing importance of the accessible tourism experience as a driving force for change in the tourism sector.

Moving Forward

One of the main purposes of this book is to increase awareness of universal design and access for all principles to a wider audience. It also provides a tool base by serving as a resource for those who are teaching or learning, either in academic institutions or within the field of continuing professional development and training. Another target group for this book is the growing number of tourism policy-makers, professionals and providers who are looking for information, insights and tested ideas that can help them improve their understanding and feed into better strategies and products for the accessible tourism market. In addition, the book aims at offering tourism professionals in the various sectors of the industry, such as hotels, airlines, ground transport operators and attraction managers, clear guidance through the demonstration of best practice and excellent implementation. These readers, whether driven by initial inquisitiveness or a more pragmatic determination to capture market share, should not be disappointed, given the wealth of material presented here in research reports, case studies and expert analysis. The book adopts an approach that encourages inclusive design when new facilities are built, taking advantage of legislation from around the world, and mild adaptations in existing structures that can enhance accessibility and operations in ways that are efficient and cost-effective.

Through the varied experiences and results revealed in this book it is important to emphasise that, at the end of the first decade of the 21st century, accessible tourism is still a 'work in progress', even in those countries and regions where it already appears. Moreover, it is still not widely known or practiced in the vast majority of countries. For this reason, whatever motivation the reader may have for opening this book, every example, every success and every failure recorded in these pages should be considered as a case for study and learning and as a possible signpost to the pathway of improvement.

References

Arola, E., Cooper, C. and Cooper, R. (2011) Encounters of disabled customers on the tourism stage. In D. Buhalis and S. Darcy (eds) *Accessible Tourism: Concepts and Issues* (Chapter 8, pp. 139–148). Bristol: Channel View Publications.

Buhalis, D. and Darcy, S. (eds) (2011) *Accessible Tourism: Concepts and Issues*. Bristol: Channel View Publications.

Buhalis, D., Michopoulou, E., Eichhorn, V. and Miller, G. (2005) *Accessibility Market and Stakeholder Analysis – One-Stop-Shop for Accessible Tourism in Europe (OSSATE)*. Guildford: University of Surrey.

Clawson, M. and Knetsch, J.L. (1966) *The Economics of Outdoor Recreation*. Baltimore: Johns Hopkins Press.

Darcy, S., Ambrose, I., Schweinsberg, S. and Buhalis, D. (2011) Conclusion – universal approaches to accessible tourism. In D. Buhalis and S. Darcy (eds) *Accessible Tourism: Concepts and Issues* (Chapter 19, pp. 300–316). Bristol: Channel View Publications.

Darcy, S. and Dickson, T. (2009) A whole-of-life approach to tourism: The case for accessible tourism experiences. *Journal of Hospitality and Tourism Management, 16*(1), 32–44.

European Union (2009) The Lisbon Treaty. Available from: http://www.lisbontreaty2009.ie/

Foggin, B. (2011) Tourism in the leisure lives of people with disability. In D. Buhalis and S. Darcy (eds) *Accessible Tourism: Concepts and Issues* (Chapter 6, pp. 98–122). Bristol: Channel View Publications.

Fullager, S. (2011) Travelling with and beyond depression: Women's naratives of recovery and identity. In D. Buhalis and S. Darcy (eds) *Accessible Tourism: Concepts and Issues* (Chapter 7, pp. 123–137). Bristol: Channel View Publications.

Leiper, N. (2003) *Tourism Management* (3rd edn). Sydney: Hospitality Press.

Packer, T.L., McKercher, B. and Yau, M. (2007) Understanding the complex interplay between tourism, disability and environmental contexts. *Disability and Rehabilitation* 29(4), 281–292.

Pegg, S. and Patterson, I. (2011) Ageing travellers: Seeking an experience – not just a destination. In D. Buhalis and S. Darcy (eds) *Accessible Tourism: Concepts and Issues* (Chapter 11, pp. 174–188). Bristol: Channel View Publications.

Poria, Y., Reichel, A. and Brandt, Y. (2011) Blind people's tourism experiences: An exploratory study. In D. Buhalis and S. Darcy (eds) *Accessible Tourism: Concepts and Issues* (Chapter 9, pp. 149–159). Bristol: Channel View Publications.

Small, J. and Darcy, S. (2010) Tourism, disability and mobility. In S. Cole and N. Morgan (eds) *Tourism and Inequality: Problems and Prospects*. Wallingford: CABI.

Small, J. and Darcy, S. (2011) Understanding tourist experience through embodiment: The contribution of critical tourism and disability studies. In D. Buhalis and S. Darcy (eds) *Accessible Tourism: Concepts and Issues* (Chapter 5, pp. 72–96). Bristol: Channel View Publications.

Veitch, C. and Shaw, G. (2011) Disability legislation and empowerment of tourists with disability: The UK case. In D. Buhalis and S. Darcy (eds) *Accessible Tourism: Concepts and Issues* (Chapter 4, pp. 62–72). Bristol: Channel View Publications.

Wang, Y. (2011) Ageing travel market and accessibility requirements. In D. Buhalis and S. Darcy (eds) *Accessible Tourism: Concepts and Issues* (Chapter 12, pp. 191–200). Bristol: Channel View Publications.

Section 1

Policies and Strategies for Accessible Tourism

Chapters in this section are:

2 European Policies for Accessible Tourism

Ivor Ambrose

Introduction

This chapter examines a range of policy initiatives addressing Accessible Tourism that have taken place in Europe over the past two decades. It provides a review of past initiatives and a roadmap for the future. It concludes with a proposal for a new 'Road Map' for accessible tourism policy, which was developed by the founding partners of the European Network for Accessible Tourism (ENAT). The chapter is based on an extensive Policy Study, published by ENAT (2008), which has been supplemented with some more recent information and analysis for the present chapter.[1]

There is a pressing need for policy makers in the European Union to adopt and implement a comprehensive 'Road Map for Accessible Tourism', as tourism services and facilities across the Member States are generally neither adequate nor consistent in terms of their accessibility. The variation in access standards and provisions between countries can be a source of considerable annoyance and inconvenience to many disabled travellers, in particular. It can also cause uncertainty about offers and value-for-money. The prevalence of inconsistent access provisions between countries and lack of access for some groups of visitors creates distortions in the single European market and it leaves EU citizens and visitors to Europe without suitable protection or guaranteed levels of service.

After almost two decades of initiatives with only limited progress in this area, a concerted and substantial effort is now needed to improve tourism accessibility across all EU member states. This is more urgent than ever, due to three emerging factors:

Firstly, tourism destinations in Europe are facing increasing global competition in terms of price and quality. Tourism enterprises and organizations, with the support of the public sector, must seek ways to adapt to new market conditions, so as to renew their competitive advantage and gain market share. *Improving accessibility* can be a way to enhance the overall quality of tourism. Better accessibility can broaden the customer base, opening up destinations and attractions to more visitors; it can contribute to long-term sustainability and enhance the quality of visitors' experiences. Some tourism providers have already realised the economic benefits of improved access but most have yet to reap the financial rewards.

Secondly, the demographic ageing of western industrial countries demands appropriate changes in the tourism sector. The European tourism market is ageing now and will continue to do so in the future. With increasing age the incidence of disabilities in the population rises. So, in order to anticipate and meet the demands of this market evolution, tourism providers must address *accessibility for older and disabled tourists* as a primary strategic concern in every part of their business.

Accessible tourism is not a niche market. Older people, (who increasingly want – and are able – to travel), will soon make up 25% of the European population. Added to this are around 50 million people with disabilities in Europe who wish to enjoy holidays with their family and friends. Thus, it is estimated that as many as 130 million people in Europe alone[2] will benefit from improved access to travel and tourism services. Making tourism accessible for all is a rational response to a foreseeable demographic trend, and a massive economic opportunity for the tourism sector.

Thirdly, the rights of persons with disabilities to equal participation in society are being strengthened throughout the world. This will inevitably bring increased demand for accessible tourism offerings and it will necessitate changes in tourism products and services. The ratification of the UN Convention on the Rights of Persons with Disabilities (2006)[3], as well as some recent initiatives at European level and by individual EU Member States are driving forward an *equal access agenda*, based on the principles of non-discrimination and equal participation of persons with disabilities. Providing equal access to goods and services will be a 'must', also in the tourism sector. Therefore, public and private providers need to be equipped with the confidence and the ability to meet their legal responsibilities under existing and possible future legislation. Actions to support tourism providers in becoming more accessible must be taken at all levels and with the participation of all stakeholders.

During the past 20–30 years, a small but growing number of businesses, organizations and individuals have worked very hard to make tourism in European countries more accessible for people with disabilities, older people, families with small children and those who have chronic health conditions. Local, regional and national initiatives have been established, sometimes in an *ad hoc* fashion and at other times in more structured ways, contributing a wealth of experience to the sector and creating some good examples that deliver credible and much-needed accessible infrastructures, facilities, transport and services to this diverse group of visitors.

Yet the goal of achieving accessible tourism for all throughout Europe is far from accomplished. For this reason, in 2006, ENAT was established by nine organizations that were experienced in tourism, disability and access consulting, within the context of a two-year, EU-supported transnational project.[4] As part of their work programme, the ENAT partners made an analysis of European policies in accessible tourism, leading to a series of recommendations for future tourism policy.[5]

The report is made up of four main sections:

(1) Objectives for accessible tourism policy.
(2) Review of the policy background and tools for change.
(3) Future needs and policy targets.
(4) A 'Road Map' for development of policies and the spread of good practices in Europe.

Some conclusions for future policy initiatives in Europe can be drawn.

Objectives for Accessible Tourism Policies in Europe

It may be posited that policies in any area tend *not* to be implemented successfully if there is no common vision or purpose among the stakeholders. The first section of the ENAT policy study presents, therefore, *a vision of accessible tourism for all*, and a series of concrete *objectives for accessible tourism policy*. The vision proposed highlights two areas where policies on accessible tourism must be focused and coordinated. These are:

- *Rights:* addressing the protection of citizens' and especially disabled and elderly persons' rights to enjoy tourism.
- *Access:* addressing the promotion of accessibility measures and guaranteed standards of access quality in the tourism sector.

Regarding citizens' rights, it must be emphasised that public authorities are ultimately responsible for promoting and safeguarding the rights of citizens and tourists, at home or abroad. Organizations of disabled people and individuals can cite a multitude of examples of discrimination against disabled tourists, including unavailability or refusal of service, poor levels of service and difficulties in obtaining redress when a service is denied or inadequate. ENAT's policy objective on rights is *to strengthen existing policies related to the rights of disabled people and the rights of all consumers, as tourists*. These rights should include the right of access to tourism venues, facilities and services, and full legal protection for disabled as well as non-disabled tourists.

Regarding the second area, *access*, greater efforts are required within the tourism sector to deliver truly accessible facilities and services. ENAT's policy objective on access is *to support the implementation of measures to meet the access requirements of persons with disabilities and others, in information provision, in transport, at destinations and at the level of the individual tourism enterprise.*

While the development of accessible tourism is clearly a necessity for tourists who are disabled, policy-making in this area is not only concerned with disability issues. The drive towards tourism accessibility must also take into account the conditions of the tourism industry and the interests of those who own and manage tourism enterprises in Europe. The tourism industry as a whole must be made aware of the necessity of making its offers accessible for everyone, and one of the major ways of doing this is to point out the business advantages which can be gained from improving access.

Policies must strengthen, on the one hand, the rights of disabled citizens to travel and enjoy tourism on an equal basis and, on the other hand, the ability of tourism providers to deliver accessible services and facilities in an effective, profitable and sustainable way.

It is not unreasonable to suggest that Europe still has the opportunity to become a world leader in accessible tourism. So far, it is not too late to realise such an ambition – if indeed, policy makers would have such ambitions – but the relative advantages that Europe has built up in this sector may not last for long.

European tourist destinations include exceptional cultural, heritage, natural, architectural, sporting and other attractions, which attracted over 460 million inbound tourists, making Europe the world's Number 1 tourism destination. European countries have certain advantages over other world regions in that accessibility standards are developed to some degree in all member states. However, access regulations need to be improved *and enforced*, and there must be significant progress 'on the ground' in tourist accommodation, venues and attractions before one can speak of the whole of Europe being a truly 'accessible destination'. All regions of the world have a long way to go to achieve accessibility for all, and those which move the quickest in meeting the demand are likely to reap the benefits earlier. It is also quite possible that the early adopter regions and countries which have the best policy frameworks, will maintain their lead over the long-term.

To take the lead, public tourist boards and private enterprises alike must first recognise that they are in the 'accessible tourism race' and that this race has, in fact, already begun. Taking just one example, the cruise industry has shown signs of marked expansion in Europe in recent years. Here the core market is made up of older and retired people with larger disposable incomes, who are relatively untouched by the global economic crisis. In the cruise industry, the *accessibility of shore-side transport and attractions within striking distance of cruise ports* is of key significance for passengers who may have reduced mobility. This makes good access and the availability of suitable services critical factors for the local tourism economy in the vicinity of cruise ports.

In order for European destinations to succeed in accessible tourism, the tourism sector as a whole must be made aware of the necessity of making its offers accessible for everyone. Public policies have an important role to play in this task by pointing to the visitors' needs and showing the business advantages which improved access will bring. Public policies must direct resources and information to all those who deliver tourism products and services.

To live up to a vision of accessible tourism for all, public sector bodies at all levels must ensure that public buildings, spaces, infrastructure and services are accessible, as these are used by both locals and tourists alike. An access upgrade of public transport vehicles and infrastructure will benefit all travellers whether they are local commuters or visitors. For example, taxis and mini-cabs that are accessible to wheelchair users are still quite rare, even in the major European towns and cities. The public authorities which issue taxi licences should take into consideration the need for a greater proportion of accessible taxis, to serve both local citizens and tourists with reduced mobility.

Given the general lack of access provisions, improvements in all areas are needed within as short a time-frame as possible. Public agencies have the authority and the means to promote accessibility measures, for example, by:

- Developing and distributing information on access requirements to tourism enterprises.
- Planning, setting priorities.
- Provision of financial incentives.
- Coordinating the implementation of accessibility measures, actions and projects.
- Establishing financial support programmes for enterprises targeting the removal of access barriers.
- Applying regulations which govern minimum access requirements and framework standards in public and private sector tourism enterprises.
- Promoting staff training programmes.
- Developing employment-support measures addressing accessibility.
- Benchmarking progress.

In addition to improving access in general, policies are required for certain *positive actions* for disabled tourists, (such as specific support services at airports or disability guides for cities), to enable them to participate easily – and without additional cost – in tourist activities. There will also be a continuing need for dedicated tourism options for people who are severely disabled or have long-term, serious illnesses requiring medical or other support services at the venue.

Coordination of Accessible Tourism Policies

When setting objectives for accessible tourism policies in Europe it is necessary to consider the policy frameworks under which such policies might be addressed. One of the major difficulties for introducing change in the area of tourism is that 'tourism policies' in Europe have so far not been clearly defined as a single area of action with a fixed scope. The term, 'tourism sector' is a slippery concept with moveable components and boundaries. It is sometimes characterised as a 'sector of sectors', and as such it may be subject to many areas of policy making. One consequence of this is that businesses and other actors in tourism are not always consulted in advance of changes to policy or legislation which may directly affect them. This may cause unintended hardship to small and medium-sized businesses, which must already take heed of many regulations.

In addition, many – indeed most – of the policies which impact on tourism are devised and regulated at the level of the 27 individual EU Member States and not at EU level. Correspondingly, almost all the policies which impact on *accessibility in tourism* are *not* set at European level, falling instead under the legislative powers of individual EU Member States and levels of authority within these states. This has led to the phenomena of:

- differing planning laws and policies;
- differing financial incentives; and
- differing building norms and standards for accessibility

both between the regions and the Member States of the European Union, and among neighbouring (non-EU) countries.

The availability of expertise in planning and designing accessible infrastructure and services also varies considerably between countries. This situation gives rise to some confusion and lack of certainty when planning and developing accessible tourism facilities and services in Europe – either when upgrading or starting from scratch.

The policy objectives for accessible tourism must be pursued through a 'twin-track' approach, where 'disability rights' and 'access in the tourism sector' are addressed in parallel. ENAT takes the view that these policy areas must be far better coordinated in future, and actions must be maintained through a long-term and continuous plan, across the Member States, in order to deliver significant and measurable advantages to all tourists in Europe.

Only by establishing commonly agreed policy objectives and coordinating certain accessibility measures *across the internal borders of the EU* can tourists with disabilities and others enjoy the levels of service they require in *all* the Member States. The issue of coordinating and developing pan-European policies and actions for accessible tourism is taken up in more detail in the later sections of the ENAT policy report.

Furthermore, ENAT firmly believes that that *policy-making cannot take place in isolation from those who are affected by it.* At all levels from local planning to EU-wide regulation, policy-making frameworks and procedures must allow both providers and consumers to contribute to policy development. Input from stakeholders is essential, both with regard to the assessment of the present situation and in setting targets and implementation mechanisms for the future.

It is important to underline that tourism depends to a large degree on supporting the diversity and richness of local and regional cultures. Policies for tourism must embrace this fact and ensure the sustainability of Europe's tourism, following the maxim: *do not let tourism destroy what tourists come to enjoy.*

European Accessible Tourism Policies

The second section of the ENAT study includes a review of the policy background and tools for change, tracing a historical path over almost two decades of policy statements and initiatives at EU (transnational) level. Starting with the 'European Year of Tourism', 1990, the policy review examines no less than *32 key events and policy actions*, focusing on international, EU and member states' actions in the areas of disability rights and tourism. The section outlines the competences and activities of the various stakeholders and describes the policy instruments available to support action. It concludes by emphasising the role of *networking*, as a tool for building consensus and transferring good practices, which are two of the primary aims of ENAT.

Despite many bold policy statements and initiatives over the years, so far the prevailing legislation, market forces and individual initiatives by providers have not proved sufficient to remove the many access barriers in tourism which persist from earlier times in the EU Member States. Nor are there sufficient measures in place to prevent new access barriers from arising. Policy makers need to address the immediate and widespread need to remove access barriers in tourism. The key is to ensure *the implementation of appropriate policies.* It is of vital importance to find new ways *to go beyond mere words and to change actual practices.* In particular, where the public sector is responsible for removing access barriers, it must act decisively and in a coordinated fashion.

Private tourism enterprises must be encouraged to bring about significant improvements in accessibility within as short a time-frame as possible by making general accessibility for customers a priority, to be accomplished within the normal business cycle – and not relying solely on 'one-off' financial support measures.

Various countries, regions, public authorities and enterprises have taken significant steps towards making their tourism offers accessible. There are many examples of good practice, as described in the ENAT Study, 'Services and Facilities for Accessible Tourism in Europe'[6] and in the ENAT online resource centre.[7] However, these still represent a minute fraction of the offers that are present in the European tourism industry as a whole. An integrated, strategic policy approach is required which provides a clear political direction for improvements, incentives to enterprises, appropriate information for customers and monitoring mechanisms that can reliably measure progress across Europe.

Over two decades, a strong consensus about *the need for accessible tourism*, has clearly emerged among those bodies that lead public policy-making in Europe (the Council of Europe, the UN World Tourism Organization, European Parliament, European Commission, tourism ministers of the EU Member States and disability NGOs. However, policy identification and analysis has been predominantly focused on *customer needs and demands,* and much less effort has been expended to examine *conditions in the tourism industry and the capacity of enterprises to change and adapt* to make their offers and facilities accessible.

As a simple example of this relative lack of attention to industry needs, it can be noted that no EU study has ever been commissioned to quantify the economic costs and benefits of implementing accessibility measures in tourism enterprises of a given size or type across the whole of Europe. Such studies are surely of vital interest when creating equitable and fair policies for the EU tourism sector.

It appears, then, that *tourism policy makers* have become sensitized to the needs of disabled and other visitors for accessibility in tourism, and have taken up the call for access improvements in the supply chain. But there has been much less deep and lasting engagement with the tourism enterprises and their representative organizations in Europe to inform them and foster debate about access issues. This has given rise to a fundamental weakness in the policy sphere, with the tourism industry perhaps feeling that its needs were being ignored, and being forced to take the role of the 'villain', not delivering access quickly enough and always on the defensive.

A more productive policy approach is needed, requiring balance and inclusion of the provider's perspective. In the analysis stage of the policy cycle it is necessary to identify, analyse and illustrate how tourism providers can also benefit in concrete terms from engaging in accessible tourism, and policies must encourage changes which will enable the industry to move in this direction for compelling economic reasons.

The record since 1990 shows that policies for accessible tourism in Europe have been slowed or stalled in several ways. This are summarised as follows:

- Without a political mandate for tourism, (due to limitations in the EU Treaties), EU policy-makers have been unable to make decisions that are binding on the tourism sector across Europe. This has reduced the effectiveness of actions to support accessible tourism.
- Community resources could not therefore be allocated directly for sustained EU actions or programmes on tourism accessibility.
- Policy analysis and modelling for accessible tourism development has been only partial, due to a lack of appropriate market statistics and analysis at EU level.
- Good practices (e.g. at Member State, Regional or local levels) have frequently been used as reference points or examples of good practice for tourism providers to follow but these examples have only given a partial view of the tourism sector's capacity to adapt. There is no systematic approach to using good practice in enterprises as a means to inform the development of policy instruments and promote innovation. (As mentioned, ENAT maintains an EU-wide database of 'Projects and Good Practices' in accessible tourism but it is no longer supported by EU funding)[8].
- EU-wide consultation on accessible tourism policies has lacked an overall framework and incentives to encourage the long-term engagement of stakeholders. Industry stakeholders have been introduced to the ideas of accessible tourism in a somewhat *ad hoc* fashion, and the lack of policy follow-through after some consultations has left certain issues (or perhaps the whole issue of accessible tourism, for some) 'open' or unresolved.
- The formal committees and advisory organs on EU tourism policy lack formally appointed and qualified representatives of disabled people and experts with in-depth knowledge of accessible tourism provisions. This perpetuates an unfortunate distance between the tourism sector and the disability community which must be bridged if there is to be progress towards finding common ground.
- Lack of agreed minimum standards for accessible tourism facilities, tourism services and customer information is a key factor inhibiting the development of common approaches to accessible tourism in Europe. Without such standards, EU countries and regions will continue to create or re-invent a multitude of idiosyncratic definitions of accessibility and solutions, which confounds rational attempts at policy-making, implementation and evaluation of accessibility measures across the EU.

During the 1990s, European policies concerning the *rights of disabled people* have undoubtedly been strengthened. Disability rights policies have led to concrete implementation of laws in policy areas where Europe-wide legal authority is firmly established, such as in employment. Moreover, the recent UN Declaration on Rights of Persons with Disabilities is expected to have the effect of extending the areas in which disability rights are recognised in EU policy-making and regulation, as EU member states have committed to ratify the Declaration, with its binding consequences for governments.

Yet despite the 'push' which may be felt by policy-makers from the rising influence of disability rights, the tourism sector has been relatively shielded from this, partly due to the EU's lack of jurisdiction over tourism issues. The EU has not had the competence to make tourism policy until this was recently granted after alterations in the Treaty on The European Union (Lisbon Treaty, 2009). Until 2009, the EU did have the authority to regulate certain activities closely related to tourism, for example, transport (by air, rail, buses and coaches, and lately maritime transport – which is under consideration), but it was exclusively up to the EU's 27 member states to determine their own tourism policies.

Future Policy Needs and Targets for Accessible Tourism Policies

The third section of the ENAT Study concerns the identification of future policy needs and targets for accessible tourism. Thirty-nine policy targets are presented based on the results of workshops, Conferences and analyses by the ENAT project team and members. The wide range of policy targets reflects, therefore, the diverse backgrounds and perspectives of the tourism industry and various stakeholders, including public sector organizations and NGOs.

The proposed policy targets are listed according to their respective areas of application, covering Economic Development, Tourism Development, Regional Development, Environment, Urban Development, Spatial Planning and Design, Public procurement, Human Rights and Social Development, Goods and Services, Consumer protection, Employment, Health, Education, Training and Research, Communications and ICTs, Culture and Transport.

Within all the above areas, Disability Mainstreaming is essential in order to reach the goal of accessible tourism for all. Achieving 'sector responsibility' is widely regarded as the key to disability mainstreaming. The term implies that each 'sector' of the public authorities must formulate and implement policies which include provisions for people with disabilities. This entails that services must be developed and delivered in ways that are appropriate to all users, (and with all kinds of disabilities). Furthermore, where sector responsibility is practiced responsibly, it is an established principle that where there are additional costs related to the provision of equipment or services to overcome access barriers experienced by people with disabilities, these costs should be borne by the customers or users as a whole, rather than being passed on to the customers with the disabilities.

Experience shows that public authorities typically take a considerable length of time to adjust their thinking and their processes to this approach, and they require a large body of information about the needs of disabled customers in order to meet the challenges of disability mainstreaming. Authorities also require the expertise of professionals who can advise on how to meet the defined user needs, using technical, managerial and other means. Sector responsibility typically requires both organizational change and the integration of a substantive body of knowledge about disabled people's needs and requirements. There is a continuing need for research of all kinds (socio-economic, humanities and technology) in order to develop and update knowledge that is relevant to the operations of each policy sector.

The mainstreaming approach has been endorsed by the European Commission, in policies concerning disabled citizens, for example in the European Disability Strategy.[9] Mainstreaming requires that the public authorities takes up their responsibilities to initiate and coordinate actions to make their services accessible. Whether or not the force of EU law will be used to bring about the implementation of accessible tourism measures, *mainstreaming disability considerations in tourism policy* is the key method for ensuring that persons with disabilities have the same possibilities and access to services as those who are not disabled. The mainstreaming method for achieving equality involves thinking through and integrating the needs of disabled people in all policies and planning so that provisions for disabled persons become part of everyday practice.

A wide range of policy tools (or instruments) that may be used for promoting accessible tourism are referred to in the ENAT Policy Study. Essentially, each policy tool is used to solve a particular problem of policy-making. In the following summary table a list of policy tools is given. The tools are characterised according to their purpose, to whom they are mainly addressed, and their effects (see Table 2.1).

A Road Map for Accessible Tourism Policies in Europe

Aiming to realise the vision of accessible tourism in Europe, ENAT's 'Road Map' is designed for the development of policies and the spread of good practices in all countries. It sketches a plan of what needs to be done to fulfil the stated targets in a coherent and targeted manner, starting with short term actions, within the framework of a long-term strategy.

TABLE 2.1 Policy tools for accessible tourism

Policy Tool	Application Area/Target group	Effect
1. *Information/References*	Information needs of policy-makers	Quality Assurance (QA) of policy process and content
Policy Review	Information needs of policy-makers	QA
Examples of Good Practice	Information needs of policy-makers and enterprises	Innovation. Validation of objectives and targets
Business cases	Information needs of enterprises	Understanding the relation between accessibility measures and ROI
Statistics and finance analysis	Policy-makers	Impact assessment
Stakeholder consultations	Policy-makers	Gain all-round view, consensus-building
UN Standard Rules	Policy-makers	QA
Agenda 22 process	Policy-makers	QA
UN Convention art 30.	Policy-makers	QA
Universal Design Principles (Design-for-All)	Enterprises, suppliers	QA
2. *Policy Status and Monitoring tools*		
Open method of coordination	Member states/policymakers	Comparative analysis, target-setting, tracking performance, evaluation.
Accessibility benchmarking: - baseline, targets and achievements	Stakeholders/policymakers	Comparative analysis, target-setting, tracking performance, evaluation.
3. *Information and Marketing tools*	Enterprises, customers	Engaging with the market for accessible tourism
Access auditing	Enterprises	QA of tourism services
Accessibility action plans	Enterprises	QA of tourism services

TABLE 2.1 Continued

Policy Tool	Application Area/Target group	Effect
4. Standards		
Physical access standards	Enterprises, designers	QA of tourism venues
Service standards for tourism facilities	Enterprises, service partners	QA of tourism services
Research and Development	Project partners	Innovation, new solutions, products and services
5. Awareness and Training		
Awareness campaign/Training	General public, actors and stakeholders/Enterprises	Raise awareness, acquire skills, give confidence.
Networking (ENAT)	All stakeholders	Raise awareness, share expertise, partnerships
6. Local and Regional plans	Public authorities	
7. Regulation	Enterprises, suppliers	
Public procurement	Public authorities, enterprises.	Procurement of accessible infrastructure and services
Certification of services	Enterprises	Service level compliance.

Eight actions are foreseen to strengthen coordination and planning, to raise awareness and shape public opinion, as well as to engage the tourism sector more firmly in proposed actions.

The Road Map proposes integrated actions at EU, National, Regional, local and enterprise/SME levels, leveraging a range of EU funding programmes in order to finance the actions. As part of the Road Map, ENAT proposes to use its network to address the (2007) proposals of DG Enterprise and the European Parliament for Accessible Tourism, with actions to develop, *inter alia*, a European accessible tourism label, accessible tourism standards, and the dissemination of good practices.[10]

The ENAT Roadmap outlines priority areas for EU and Member States' actions on accessible tourism. No fixed time-frame for implementation can reasonably be given without appropriate consultation with the relevant bodies who may engage in this plan. However, it seems reasonable to assume that a 5- to 10-year period would be necessary to achieve significant progress in all areas.

The eight actions of the Road Map are:

(1) High-Level Policy Group for Accessible Tourism
  - Engage all relevant EU institutions, the tourism industry, specialists and consumer representatives in strategic planning and guidance for the future of European Accessible Tourism Policy.
  - Mainstream accessible tourism as a primary responsibility of every public tourism authority and agency in Europe.
  - Establish action plans aiming for the realisation of disability rights and competitive and sustainable development in tourism.
  - Establish an Accessible Tourism Benchmarking Action for Member States, using the Open Method of Coordination, engaging national and regional tourism authorities and relevant stakeholder groups.

(2) Awareness-raising Campaign
  - (Online/TV/EUTUBE/Press) in all EU Member States on Accessible Tourism for All, in collaboration with ENAT, European Travel Commission, European Commission and National Tourist Boards.
  - Show what consumers need and what providers can deliver in Accessible Tourism across Europe.
  - Make 'accessible tourism' visible and valued within the tourism industry and among the general public.

(3) Mobilise EU funding programmes and agencies (ESF, ERDF, PROGRESS, LEONARDO 2, RTD, ENTR, SANCO, TREN, EUROFOUND, EUROSTAT, etc) to support projects/initiatives for accessible tourism destinations and services. Financing, for example:

- Annual tourism statistics/satellite accounts: 'Accessible tourism demand and supply in EU-27.
- An EU training curriculum for (a) tourism managers, and (b) front-line personnel.
- eLearning programmes and Accessible Tourism Toolkit for enterprises.
- Local, regional and city initiatives for accessible tourism with transnational participation.

Studies and development projects, for example:

- Impact assessment of UK Disability Discrimination Act on the UK Tourism Sector.
- Impact assessment of EU Regulation on Rights of Disabled and Mobility Impaired Air Passengers.
- Diversity Management toolkit for the Owners/HR Managers in Tourism.
- ICT projects (e.g. Accessible Tourism in Inclusion Work programme).
- Targeted actions for SMEs in Accessible Tourism.

(4) *European Accessible Tourism Marketing.* For example:
  - *Registration of accessible* venues with www.EuropeforAll.com
  - National and City Guides support grants.
  - Creation of a Travelling 'Accessible Europe' Exhibition Stand; publicity and presentations at major European and International Tourism Fairs.
  - European Airports Access Guide.
  - Cruise Europe – Access Guides to Ports and Attractions.

(5) *Targeted National Action Campaigns* (EU-27) for stimulating Accessible Accessibility provisions in mainstream tourism. For example:
  - At least one wheelchair accessible room in every 4- and 5-star hotel in EU-27.
  - Adapted hire cabs (taxis) for wheelchair users in all EU cities over 250,000 inhabitants.
  - 'Disabled Access Action Plan' for top 5 National Heritage Sites in all EU-27. states (- to be continued over a second 5-year period).
  - London Olympics and Paralympics 2012. Study of 'spin-offs' for Accessible Tourism.
  - 'Exchange of Good Practices in Accessible Tourism': Dissemination and take-up actions between cities, regions and countries.

(6) *Employment Actions*
  - Targeting jobs in the tourism sector for people with disabilities: analysis of job profiles, requirements, recruitment.

- Return-to-Work measures to support long-term ill and disabled staff in the tourism industries.

(7) Targeted actions to create a knowledge base and actions for 'Specialised' Accessible Tourism offers for severely disabled visitors.

(8) ENAT-led actions: Building the Accessible Tourism Network for sharing experiences and enhancing knowledge.
- ENAT 'Code of Good Conduct' label for tourism enterprises (ENAT members).[11]
- CEN Workshop Agreement: 'Consensus Document on Standards for Accessible Tourism Services'.[12]
- Proposal for an audited 'European Label for Accessible Tourism' (following on from the CEN workshop).
- ENAT International Congress on Accessible Tourism for All: 2009, 2011, 2013, . . .(various venues in the EU).[13]

Conclusions

The above objectives and actions can certainly not be achieved without wide cooperation, as in many areas the actions require leadership by EU institutions, Member States, Tourist Boards, Regional or Municipal bodies or other players in the tourism industry. Partnerships between actors and stakeholders, based on common interest must drive future activities.

With a view to ensuring the best possible *vertical coordination* of actions under this Road Map, special attention should be paid to the composition of working groups, committees and projects, with representatives from different levels of authority and action, working together wherever possible. The formal competences of representatives and their informal networking capabilities should be employed to move the actions forward, gather information and disseminate results at all levels.

ENAT's proposed Road Map is intended as a framework for a new pact between the political institutions, stakeholders and representative bodies of consumers for concerted actions on accessible tourism in Europe. Future actions must be *bolder, more concrete and better coordinated* than those of the past, in order to bring about a critical mass of activities involving member states, regions and cities, enterprises, NGOs and citizens.

Acknowledgements

The author wishes to acknowledge the support of the European Commission (grant no. VS/2005/0675) and of ENAT members and partners in the preparation of ENAT Study Report no. 3, on which this chapter is based, and in the development of the ENAT Policy Roadmap outlined above.

Notes

(1)   ENAT Study Report no. 3. (2008) Towards 2010: *Disability Policy Challenges and Actions for the European Tourism Sector*. See: http://www.accessibletourism.org/¿i=enat.en.reports.512.

(2)   Figures cited in the OSSATE Report: Accessibility and Stakeholder Market Analysis (2005) http://www.ossate.org/doc_resources/OSSATE_MarketandStakeholder%20 Analysis_Public_Version_Fina..pdf.

(3)   See: http://www.un.org/disabilities/.

(4)   ENAT's founding sponsors are listed at: http://www.accessibletourism.org/¿i=enat. en.enatsponsors2006-2007.

(5)   ENAT Study Report no. 3. (2008) Towards 2010: *Disability Policy Challenges and Actions for the European Tourism Sector*. See: http://www.accessibletourism.org/¿i=enat.en.reports.512.

(6)   ENAT Study Report no. 2. (2008) http://www.accessibletourism.org/¿i=enat. en.reports.441.

(7)   ENAT website: http://www.accessibletourism.org/¿i=enat.en.enat_projects_and_ good_practices.

(8)   See: http://www.accessibletourism.org/¿i=enat.en.enat_projects_and_good_practices.

(9)   See: http://ec.europa.eu/social/main.jsp¿catId=429andlangId=en.

(10) See: European Parliament Puts Accessible Tourism on EU Agenda at: http://www. accessibletourism.org/¿i=enat.en.news.261

(11) The *ENAT Code of Good Conduct* scheme for tourism providers has been implemented since the ENAT Policy Study was completed. It was launched in October 2009. For details of the scheme see: http://www.accessibletourism.org/¿i=enat.en.enat-code-of-good-conduct

(12) ENAT proposed a CEN Workshop Agreement on Access Standards for Tourism in 2008, see: http://www.accessibletourism.org/¿i=enat.en.news.522 This work is delayed, due to lack of funds.

(13) ENAT held its second International Congress on Accessible Tourism for All in Vienna in 2009, see: http://www.accessibletourism.org/¿i=enat.en.enat-congress-2009

3 Accessible Tourism in Flanders: Policy Support and Incentives

Pieter Ghijsels

Introduction

In Flanders (the northern region of Belgium), tourist accessibility policy is in the hands of Tourism Flanders. Tourism Flanders is a Flemish governmental institution whose mission is to promote tourism in Flanders. The key task of Tourism Flanders is promoting and marketing Flanders as a tourist destination at home and abroad. Our foreign offices in the major European cities and beyond play a key role in this. Another important task is developing tourism products in Flanders. This is achieved through quality control and the issuance of permits and classification stars, and through product innovation by means of direct investment, co-funding or subsidies. The accessibility of tourist services in Flanders is a key part of the Flemish policy on tourism. People with a disability are an important target group for the tourist industry in Flanders, especially from a forward-looking perspective (see Figure 3.1).

A recent study by the University of Surrey (Buhalis *et al.,* 2005), puts the potential accessible travel market at more than 134 million people (or 27% of the EU population), with expected tourism revenues upwards of €83 billion for European travellers alone. Due to the strong increase of the ageing population, the number of persons with disabilities will increase significantly. This is a target group that cannot be ignored by the tourist policy. Not only the sheer size of this group, but also the way disabled people travel, is important for our tourist sector: they spend at least as much on travel and leisure as other people, they rarely travel alone and often dispose of more free time to travel and they prefer low season. Still, the above mentioned percentages are surprising. Disabled tourists are not an unknown phenomenon, but the importance of this target group is not visible yet in practice. Tourism Flanders wanted to know the reasons for this.

A first accessibility analysis of 100 hotels in Flanders (1999) showed disturbing results: only a minority of the screened hotels could be considered 'accessible with assistance'. For those who did not have any assistance, even fewer hotels were available. A further analysis of these results (2000) and a survey of the tourist sector and of people with different disabilities led to a

Figure 3.1 Enjoying the Flanders beach

number of recommendations that in turn led to an accessibility action plan for Tourism Flanders (April 2001). It concentrates on three essential points:

- Improvement of the physical accessibility of tourism products in Flanders through an extensive system of premiums and technical assistance.
- Sensitisation and training.
- Obtaining reliable information on the accessibility of current tourism products. The lack of reliable information on this subject has proven to be a major obstacle to people with restricted mobility taking a holiday or break in the region. The only information available to visitors used to be the international wheelchair emblem that was used in tourism brochures without criteria and checks being conducted.

The Accessible Travel Action Plan resolutely opted for an inclusive approach. It is based on the principle that travellers with a disability or impairment should have access to the same regular tourist circuit. In other words, the disabled traveller should be able to stay in a normal hotel, apartment or holiday residence – not solely in specially adapted social holiday centres. The tourist with a disability should also be able to find reliable information on the accessibility of tourist facilities through regular channels, such as the 'Visit Flanders' website and other tourist brochures. This approach is reflected in the concrete approach of the various accessibility projects explained below.

Accessibility of Tourism Infrastructure

Studies conducted in 1999 and 2000 clearly showed that Flanders had some catching up to do concerning the accessibility of its tourist infrastructure. A variety of subsidies for renovation and new construction work were developed to address this problem. Hotels, campsites, social holiday centres, youth hostels, tourist information offices and leisure projects can qualify for subsidies from Tourism Flanders to make their infrastructure more accessible. It is important to point out that these measures are not limited to specialised facilities for disabled persons; this policy applies to the entire tourist sector.

Also, within the framework of the coast action plan, a subsidy decree has been drafted, in order to subsidise initiatives to improve the accessibility of the coastal area. Apart from the subsidies given to the private sector, this is also an opportunity for the local authorities to adapt public areas (parking spaces, toilets, sea wall and access to the beach) as well as public transportation. The amount of the subsidy depends on the type of infrastructure and can amount to between 30% and 70% of the cost price of the adaptation. In this way Tourism Flanders annually invests €3–3.5 million in a more accessible environment. The results can be measured among other things via the new Flemish accessible tourism label (see below).

The accessibility adaptation has to be carried out correctly and provide for all types of disabilities, not only for wheelchair users. Clear accessibility criteria have been identified in association with accessibility experts, with a view to basic accessibility and independent use of infrastructure by all. These criteria have been adapted into practical information cards tailored to the situation of owners, architects and contractors. They offer detailed information with explanatory diagrams for each part of a building (parking, reception, bedroom, bathrooms, etc) and can be obtained free of charge from Tourism Flanders.

For more important alterations and new constructions, a prior accessibility opinion by one of the four certified accessibility agencies is required. Because significant wrong investments can be avoided this way, Tourism Flanders also subsidises this opinion. The opinion can take several forms. If it concerns the renovation of an existing building, it can be expedient to first conduct a feasibility study. Such a study provides an overview of the modifications required to make the building (more) accessible. The consultancy firm examines whether it is technically (and thus often also financially) feasible. If this results in concrete plans, the consultancy firm then checks whether all the applicable accessibility criteria were correctly integrated in the building plans. In the accessibility report it indicates the items in the plans that need to be corrected in order to realise optimum accessibility. After completion of the work, the consultancy firm performs a final check. Possible shortcomings must be corrected before Tourism Flanders pays the subsidy.

Infrastructure investments are often long term plans. It takes a long time to adapt everything and often it takes a long time for the results to be visible. Moreover, not every owner is convinced that such an effort is necessary. We often hear 'We never see any disabled persons, why should we adapt our infrastructure to them?' They often forget that this way they risk losing business from potential clients with a disability (and their friends, family, etc) because their facilities are not sufficiently adapted to the special needs. Breaking out of this circular thinking is not always easy. During the information sessions Tourism Flanders organizes for the tourist sector, this issue is tackled from two angles: design and reception.

Obviously, investing in accessibility has a price – even if for new constructions the additional cost is limited. However, for example less stairs and more ramps not only benefit wheelchair users but also senior citizens who are less mobile, parents with strollers, people lugging heavy suitcases and personnel with trolleys. It improves everyone's comfort and operational efficiency. 'Design for all' is therefore the golden rule when building, renovating or designing for a better accessibility. It is important for creative designers and architects to arrange spaces and rooms in such way that the adaptation does not create a 'hospital feeling', but that the building is perceived as useful yet attractive. Tourism Flanders regularly organizes 'design for all' courses for owners and managers from the tourist sector, as well as architects and designers.

Apart from the 'design for all' principle, the other aspect that determines to a large extent whether a disabled person sees the facility as accessible is whether he feels welcome or not. Every year courses are organized on client-friendliness towards disabled people. These courses are experience-oriented and very interactive. They deal with the 'mental accessibility' of the personnel, and aspect that is far less tangible and does not cost much, but that, in conjunction with the material adaptations makes sure that a tourist infrastructure is perceived as accessible.

Mental accessibility plays an equally important role in a guided tour. Guides who wish to make a visit interesting and relevant to the disabled can take advantage of specific additional training from Tourism Flanders.

Reliable and Available Information on the Accessibility of Tourism Infrastructure

Creating an accessible environment is a long-term project. Despite the efforts of the past years there is still a long way to go. A lack of clear information on the facilities on offer still stands in the way of people with a disability or limitation being able to explore unknown places. Buildings, premises, public transportation, streets and squares often are insufficiently accessible to disabled persons. Many inconveniences such as thresholds, the absence of a lift or an adapted bathroom often turn a pleasant trip into a big deception. In order to avoid these unpleasant surprises, reliable information about accessibility is necessary. On the basis of this information, a disabled person can better evaluate what he or she exactly can expect and whether he/she should take precautions or not. To help disabled persons find this information, Tourism Flanders took a number of initiatives.

The Accessible Travel Info Point (Infopunt Toegankelijk Reizen in Dutch) is a service of Tourism Flanders, which grew out of the cooperation with various organizations and services by and for people with disabilities. The Info Point provides disabled travellers with the necessary information and advice about their travel destination. The Info Point is intended for Belgians going on holiday in Belgium or abroad and for foreigners going on holiday in Belgium. A traveller with a disability or impairment can expect reliable information, tailored to his/her personal requirements, such as:

- 'I have a dust allergy, where do I find accessible accommodation?'
- 'Can I take my guide dog to the restaurant?'
- 'What bus companies have buses equipped with wheelchair lifts?'
- 'What precautions should I take when taking a plane?'
- 'What insurance policies should I take out?'
- 'Where do I find someone who can assist me when I go on holiday?'

An extensive travel library with relevant brochures, books, web sites and travel reports can be consulted in the heart of Brussels. The fully accessible office is located at the head office of Tourism Flanders, where it links up with the general tourist information desk. The Accessible Travel Info Point website in four languages – www.accessinfo.be – forms the virtual counter-part of the physical information office. The site offers a myriad of valuable tips to help the disabled traveller find a solution to most of his questions. As the information is continuously completed and updated, the website is gradually growing into an autonomous search tool. Naturally the website has been developed in accordance with national and international accessibility standards as well.

The Accessible Travel Info Point focuses on a fast and reliable service. In principle every question is for instance answered in detail within a week. Because travellers with a disability or impairment need reliable information, the quality of the information is given very careful attention. Preference is given to objective data obtained by specialised research on accessibility. These data can be complemented with the (subjective) experience of travellers who themselves have some kind of disability.

The Accessible Travel Info Point, as demonstrated in Figure 3.2, is not only aimed at travellers with a disability. As part of the broad mission of Tourism Flanders, the Info Point also helps owners and managers in the tourist sector with practical information on how to make their facilities

Figure 3.2 Accessible travel info point

more accessible and gives them information on specific advice and subsidies. The Info Point plays a crucial role in the awareness of the tourist sector.

At the intersection of well-being and tourism, the Info Point is also a meeting platform. A concrete result of the exchange of information is the Gulliver Award, an accessibility award for innovative initiatives in the tourist sector in Flanders. The Flemish Minister of Tourism has always been a supporter of this initiative and always personally presented the Gulliver.

The need for objective and detailed accessibility information is met by the objective measurement data of Accessible Flanders (Toegankelijk Vlaanderen in Dutch). This is the accessibility databank cum website of Flanders. It was developed in 2003 by vzw Toegankelijkheidsbureau, as part of the interregional project Libretto, together with a number of other partners. The databank was originally limited to the Benelux–Middengebied region, but it was extended to cover the whole of Flanders under the impulse of Gelijke Kansen in Vlaanderen (the equal rights' administration). Other Flemish accessibility agencies joined the project. The databank contains local government offices, sports facilities, swimming pools, cultural centres and museums, as well as hotels, camping sites, youth hostels and tourist sites. Every part of the establishment is evaluated by a specially trained accessibility agent and given a + (plus), +/- (plus/minus) or - (minus) rating, reflecting the accessibility level offered by the establishment. Different types of disability are being taken into account.

As a governmental tourism agency Tourism Flanders has participated in this project from the beginning by commissioning accessibility agencies to conduct evaluations of tourist accommodations. The service is provided free of charge to tourist providers. More than 350 tourism establishments have been evaluated. The aim is to fill the databank with a good sampling of tourism products in Flanders by 2009, based on a multi-year plan and budget. In addition to the benefits of objective and detailed information for visitors with restricted mobility the Toegankelijk Vlaanderen databank offers a number of opportunities:

- It provides a good picture of the accessibility of tourism infrastructure in the region. It shows the problems and weaknesses, on which basis the Flemish authorities are able to establish policy. A thorough analysis of the results allows a clear picture of accessibility in the tourist accommodation industry and the most important problems. It is essential information in the development and evaluation of the system of premiums, to know which weaknesses have to be tackled in the industry.
- The information in the Toegankelijk Vlaanderen databank is linked to the general tourism databank, because it is important that accessibility information is offered in an inclusive way to visitors through regular tourism promotion channels. Visitors looking for information about a given hotel can check the accessibility section on the Visit Flanders website to access the relevant page in the Toegankelijk Vlaanderen databank to gain accessibility info in an inclusive way.
- The databank also provides a report to the owner of the establishment about the accessibility of the premises in question. A distinction is made in this report between minor inexpensive adjustments the owner can make and things that demand a more structural approach. This can raise awareness among owners in the tourism industry of the situation on their premises and act as a stimulus to gradually improve this situation. It is part of Tourism Flanders' awareness-raising policy.

The assessments made by Toegankelijk Vlaanderen are thorough, as demonstrated in Figure 3.3. The average inspection (including on-site survey, entering the data in the database and reporting) takes three working days. In order to keep the price acceptable, the salary cost of those measuring the accessibility is subsidised via social employment projects. This socially meaningful work is performed by (specially trained) workers who would find it difficult to get a job elsewhere.

Development of a Label

The meaning of the International Symbol of Accessibility (ISA) differs greatly between the various countries. The well-known white wheelchair logo on a blue background is awarded by some authorities based on objective, verified criteria. In other places it is more a symbol of goodwill. In Belgium, where the label can be bought in supermarkets, the latter is usually the case. Experience teaches us that the ISA label is not considered reliable by most users in Belgium.

Figure 3.3 Detailed measurement of tourism facilities

For those owners who go through great lengths to improve accessibility to their premises, this is extremely frustrating. After all their efforts, there was to be no instrument available to distinguish themselves from their colleagues and competitors who wrongfully use the ISA label. Consequently, in January 2008 Tourism Flanders introduced a new label for accessible tourism. The concept was developed after examining existing labelling systems and detailed discussion at an international level. In line with European best practices, the choice was made for the combination of a label for first-line information with a databank-cum-website for a detailed evaluation (Toegankelijk Vlaanderen databank). It is a practical tool for selecting from the large body of information in a brochure or on a website those accommodations with a good accessibility level. You don't have to read all the accessibility reports in detail. This is a practical solution for visitors but also for tourism services, which have to field questions about the accessibility of hotels, for instance. In combination with the detailed information in the databank, the user is thus given a full palette of details.

Tourism establishments that obtain a good score on the essential aspects of their premises in the Toegankelijk Vlaanderen databank are now rewarded with an accessibility label. The focus lies on functions and components that are essential for the type of building.

When awarding the accessibility label to a hotel, youth accommodation or vacation centre, the following aspects are considered essential: the access walkway from the public road, the entrance and the reception area, the communal toilet, the restaurant or the dining room and the bedroom with corresponding bathroom. For group accommodations, also the accessibility of the multifunctional room is assessed.

For a camping area, we look at the parking facilities with access path, the entrance and reception area, and the sanitary facilities. Of course, we also assess the corridors between these components for all accommodations. Other facilities such as a swimming pool and sauna are discussed in Accessible Flanders, but have no effect on the labelling.

The Flemish label for accessible tourism distinguishes three levels:

Label A+ means that the holiday accommodation scores positive (+) on the components mentioned above. It satisfies strict accessibility standards and is accessible such that the visitor is comfortable and independent.

Label A means that the holiday accommodation scores +/- on the components above. This means that slight anomalies were found. Such accommodations are still usable for most people with limited mobility, but extra effort or a helper may be needed. We consider this accommodation to have basic accessibility. It is certainly advisable to read why a '+ score' was not obtained.

If a characteristic is detected that makes the building difficult or impossible to use for some people, even with help, then the holiday accommodation receives a negative score (–) for this component. In practice, this problem especially applies to wheelchair users. For visitors with a different type of disability or lighter motor impairment, the accessibility offered can still be adequate. These holiday accommodations are designated with the informative label (arrow in the circle), which only indicates that this building has been objectively examined.

When granting the label, deviations from the scores are possible since the objective measurements do not always take account of the concrete conditions. In case of doubt, we examine the actual situation again on site and test potential bottlenecks with a standard wheelchair. The results of the evaluation are presented to a committee especially established for this purpose. The label committee consists of representatives from the disability movement and the tourism sector. In the end, it is this committee that decides which label a building will be awarded or what conditions must first be fulfilled. We are able to present positive results after only a year. Of the 326 accommodation establishments that were subject to a label study in 2008, 71 obtained a level A and one address even obtained the A+ label. Tourism Flanders intends to perform as many screenings again in 2009, hopefully with a proportional growth in the number of accommodations with A or A+ label. At the end of 2009, we would then have examined 30% of the accommodation offerings in Flanders. Since the studies are always done on a voluntary basis, we feel this is an ambitious, but realistic target.

By dividing the label into three levels, we in fact have developed a tool with the power to raise awareness. That is, it is attractive for the accommodation sector to climb step-by-step to a higher level. Thus we also note a growth tendency within the label levels. Promotion of the labelled accommodations is done via various channels: inclusion of the label in the regular tourist brochures and websites, a digital newsletter with very wide distribution to travellers with a disability, organizations and facilities for the disabled as well as to the tourism sector. Finally, the labelled establishments are bundled in the brochure 'All-In – accessible accommodation in Flanders and Brussels', which is available in both printed and browsable digital versions.

In a next phase, Tourism Flanders will extend the label criteria to include recreational tourist projects and information offices. Bicycle and footpaths, museums and objects of interest are already being adapted to the standards; the awarding of accessibility labels should place these efforts in the limelight.

Conclusion

Tourism Flanders has developed many instruments to increase the accessibility of tourist offerings in Flanders. With the label as promotional instrument for those who have invested in accessibility, and as objective indicator of the success of the policy, the circle is complete. As time passes, we are seeing much in the tourism sector that is moving in the right direction. Yet we have by no means reached our goal. A sustained effort is needed in all areas (investments, awareness raising, providing information and promotion). In this, our focus must not be limited to accommodations alone. In order to speak of an 'accessible holiday', the entire 'holiday chain' must be accessible: public areas and transportation, travel and information offices, museums and recreational, cultural and sports facilities and so on. Thus, consultation and collaboration with all private and public partners will be major code words for the coming years. This should make it possible to make a major leap forward on the way to a society in which all can participate equally.

References

Buhalis, D., Eichhorn, V., Michopoulou, E. and Miller, G. (2005), *Accessibility Market and Stakeholders Analysis*. OSSATE project Guildford: University of Surrey.

Toerisme Vlaanderen (2001), *Actieplan toegankelijkheid voor de toeristische sector in Vlaanderen*, Toerisme Vlaanderen Brussels.

Toerisme Vlaanderen, *Jaarverslag*, jaargangen 2001–2007, Toerisme Vlaanderen, Brussels.

Vzw Toegankelijkheidsbureau (1999) Toegankelijkheid van logies in Vlaanderen onder de loep. Toerisme Vlaanderen. Brussels

Vzw Toegankelijkheidsbureau (2000) *Een toegankelijker toerisme in Vlaanderen? Probleemanalyse en mogelijke beleidsinstrumenten voor de logiessector*. Toerisme Vlaanderen Brussels.

4 Accessible Tourism for All in Germany

Peter Neumann

Introduction

In Germany, accessibility is a civil right and its establishment is based on the currently applicable legal provisions and standards. The German act on the equality of persons with disabilities (Behindertengleichstellungsgesetz, or BGG) of 1st May 2002 provides a statutory framework (see section below). The currently applicable DIN standards are also relevant to the implementation of accessibility. While they determine the technical standards, they have no direct legal or factual force. The legal force of DIN standards is defined by the respective construction codes or other ordinances of each federal state. The topic accessibility also becomes more important with regard to the demographic change because through the rise of the average age, the percentage of older and disabled people increases as well. The number of people aged 60 or older will double over the course of the coming years. Thus the number of people with mobility or activity limitations that nonetheless enjoy travelling, will increase considerably as well.

For politics, economy and administration these development trends mean that necessary conditions need to be created to enable all citizens to remain active parts of the society and to be able to maintain their independence for as long as possible. This also includes all areas of the tourism industry. In this regard, the study 'Economic Impulses of Accessible Tourism for All', commissioned by the Federal Ministry of Economics and Technology (Bundesministerium für Wirtschaft und Technologie, referred to as BMWi below), proved for the first time that the group of travellers with mobility or activity limitations is of great economic interest for the German travel industry. Currently, €2.5 billion are earned annually by holidays and short vacations of people with disabilities (BMWi, 2004).

However, huge parts of this economic potential still remain unutilised. The study disclosed that through more accessibility in the German tourism industry, €4.8 billion net sales and new full-time jobs in connection with that up to 90,000 could be created (the expenses for companions as well as one-day and business trips, conference and event trips as well as travellers from abroad are not yet taken into account). With the help of the BMWi study, it was possible to demonstrate that well suited accessible products and services need to be developed. An adjustment of the marketing methods of the tourist funding agencies and destinations is necessary. The German Tourist Board (Deutscher Tourismusverband – DTV) shared this opinion and urged quick expansion of accessible tourism in Germany in order to keep up with foreign destinations. This warning of the tourist umbrella organization is sound considering that, according to the BMWi (2004) study, 17% of all German travellers with mobility or activity limitations spent their holidays outside Germany, just because the accessible offers were more suitable or known there.

Stage of Development and Structures of Accessible Tourism for All in Germany

Pattern of Demand Regarding Accessible Tourism for All

Within a new study, commissioned by the German Federal Ministry of Economics and Technology (Neumann *et al.*, 2008), the analysis of the pattern of demand shows that holidays and travelling are basic needs for the majority of the German population. Individual characteristics like age or disability are hardly relevant. The precise comparison of people with mobility or activity limitations to the average German population shows that there are almost no recordable differences regarding the motives for travelling or the travel behaviour. That is why it is difficult to define people with activity or mobility limitations as a (homogeneous) tourism target group. However, regardless of all positive developments of accessible tourism in Germany – travelling is still a challenge for many people because of numerous obstacles. These obstacles result in low vacation intensity of people with activity or activity limitations. Compared to the average population – they have rather modest travel plans for the future.

Political Engagement and Coordination in the Field of Accessible Tourism for All

At national level the decision-making in tourism policy is incumbent on the Federal Ministry of Economics and Technology. As a cross-sectional task, tourism policy also affects other areas of responsibility like finance, education and research, work and social issues, building activities and transportation, environment, culture and foreign affairs. In order to better coordinate and conceptually develop the activities in tourism policy, the office of the Commissioner of the Federal Government for Tourism was created in 2005. In the field of tourism policy the tasks of the Federal Government are strengthening the corporate personal responsibility and improving the general conditions to enhance the competitiveness of small and medium sized companies. The support of the tourism infrastructure is one task within the scope of the federal competence which is shared with the states and municipalities. The Federal Government also devised supporting programs relating to accessible Tourism for All. Contrary to that precise planning, development and direct support of tourism is generally a responsibility of the federal states.

Many nation-wide interacting groups are especially active in the area of the Accessible Tourism for All. They provide advice or even some tourist offers for their members and are politically involved in integrating people with mobility or activity limitations into tourism. Also organizations like the German Hotel and Catering Association (Deutsche Hotel- und Gaststättenverband – DEHOGA) and the Hotel Association Germany (Hotelverband Deutschland – IHA) embrace accessible tourism on a nation-wide level. They develop qualification courses and merchandise already existing offers, for example in the German hotel guide. They are also important contact points for special interest groups, as shown by the example of the target agreement with the hotel and restaurant industry (see section below).

From the special interest groups' and self-help organizations' point of view, a key player on a nation-wide level is the Nationale Koordinationsstelle Tourismus für Alle e.V. (NatKo) founded in 1999 by eight nation-wide umbrella organizations of people with disabilities (the national office of coordination for Tourism for All – an incorporated society). The function of NatKo is to coordinate and tie the nationwide activities of the self-help organizations in the field of tourism for all. On top of the activities of the NatKo, the ongoing engagement of different special interest groups should be mentioned here, like the internet platform 'Barrierefreier Tourismus Info' of the Seh-Netz e.V., the 'Koordinierungsstelle Tourismus' of the Deutschen Blinden- und Sehbehindertenverbandes e.V. (the German Association of people with visual impairments), as well as several other activities of the Bundesarbeitsgemeinschaft der Senioren-Organizationen (BAGSO) e.V. (the nationwide association of organizations of senior citizens). In addition, the German General Office for Tourism (Deutsche Zentrale für Tourismus e.V. – DZT) is responsible for the international marketing and image boosting of the holiday destination in Germany. Next to marketing abroad, the DZT also conducts a supra-regional national marketing in cooperation with the marketing organizations of the federal states since 1999. The German Tourism Association DTV, amongst other things, coordinates the actions of its members as a voluntary association of tourism organizations in Germany. In 2003 the national competition 'Willkommen im Urlaub – Familienzeit ohne Barrieren' ('Welcome to your vacation – Family time without barriers') was conducted. The competition was supported by the

Federal Ministry of Family, Senior Citizens, Women and Youth. From the DTV's point of view the primary goal is to further strengthen the competences in the accessible tourism and to best use the existing potential with consumers and providers.

In addition to that, the German Railways (Deutsche Bahn AG – DB AG) has developed a program for accessible railroad traffic in 2005, after they had already founded an office for customer-related issues with disabilities in 2002. A task force comprised of representatives from the German Disability Council and the DB AG was founded in this regard to plan the actions.

The German Act on Equality of Persons with Disabilities (BGG) and the Instrument of Target Agreement

The achievement of accessibility in preferably all areas of life is one of the most important requests of the German act on the equality of persons with disabilities (BGG) which became effective on 5th January 2002. Next to a commitment of the organizations of public authority to accessibility and equality, the BGG contains a code of practices with which accessibility should be accomplished with regard to building, transportation, communication, the use of electronic media, and elections. To reach that goal, several federal laws and directives were enacted, for example in the areas of railroad and airway traffic as well as mass transit, in gastronomy, for universities and in information technologies. Furthermore the German sign language was accredited an independent language.

The instrument of target agreement plays a decisive role in the BGG. According to section 5 BGG, these target agreements are obligations under private law. Companies or federations of commercial or industrial enterprises should commit to it in cooperation with organizations of people with disabilities to achieve accessibility. An obligation to negotiations is regulated under public law but there is no audit obligation. The first and until today only nationwide target agreement according to the BGG was concluded within the scope of the ITB 2005 to register, evaluate and display accessible offers in the hotel industry and gastronomy. This focused on the huge variation of terms like 'wheelchair accessible', 'wheelchair suitable', 'barrier-free', 'limited barrier-free', 'disabled friendly' and the respective pictograms and symbols in Germany, which led to insecurity amongst the guests who depend on accessible offers with regard to the actual on-site situation. This target agreement aimed at achieving a minimum standard for the evaluation of accessibility of accommodations and gastronomy businesses on a valid, nation-wide level. The declared objective was to create standards that can also be realized in already existing businesses. The target agreement mentions precise criteria and standards for the evaluation of accessible accommodations and gastronomy in the following categories:

(A) Accessibility for guests with a walking impairment who could also occasionally depend on a non-motorized wheelchair or a walker.
(B) Accessibility for guests with walking impairments and are permanently depending on a wheelchair.
(C) Accessibility for guests with visual impairment.
(D) Accessibility for guests with hearing impairments.
(E) Accessibility for all guests with bodily or sensory impairments (categories A–D).

Each criterion is oriented on the currently valid and relevant DIN standards without taking them over completely. The appendix of the target agreement contains a checklist with the above mentioned criteria according to the named categories that allow self-assessment for the hotels and gastronomy businesses. If a business completely fulfils all requirements on the checklist, it may use a certain pictogram that marks it as 'accessible' in the respective category. Furthermore, the business will be credited as 'accessible' in the German hotel guide and on internet platforms www.hotelguide.de and www.hotellerie.de. The participating trade associations have also introduced the criteria for accessibility to the updated German hotel classification on a voluntary basis. Usually, the statements of the hotels are not checked. Introducing such instruments was amicably passed because of the financially and time-consuming registration. However, complaint management was introduced, and guests may complain about a hotel that has the respective pictograms without complying with the criteria.

Marketing Accessible Tourism for All

On the national level, the German Centre for Tourism (DZT) is responsible for the presentation of Germany as a holiday destination abroad. The DTZ devotes a special section, 'Barrierefreier Tourismus' to the Accessible Tourism for All in Germany on their official internet platform www.deutschland-tourismus.de. Accessible also offers tips for the planning of the vacation can be found there. On the DTZ's website there is also a link to the association Accessible Destinations in Germany (Arbeitsgemeinschaft Barrierefreie Reiseziele in Deutschland) which was founded during the realisation of the first recommendation of action of the BMWi study in 2008 (BMWi, 2008; Neumann et al., 2008). The founder members are six tourism destinations from all over Germany.

The transportation businesses have reacted to the rising demand of accessible offers and generate increasing user numbers in public transport. As an important public transportation business, DB AG for example has special offers for travellers with mobility or activity limitations and does specific marketing. The brochure *Mobil mit Handicap – Services für Reisende*

(*Being Mobile with a Disability – Services for Travellers with Mobility Limitations*) contains advice and information for travellers with mobility limitations. This information is also offered on an audio CD for people with visual impairments. Furthermore, there is specific information available on the DB AG website. The services are completed by a mobility service centre which has already been introduced in 1999, to make the vacation planning easier for travellers with mobility limitations. In the bus services area, the Federal Association of German Bus Operators (Bundesverband Deutscher Busunternehmer – BDO) has published a registry of accessible motor-coaches in Germany that has become very popular.

While the German Travelling Association (Deutsche Reise Verband – DRV) is sustainably supporting the topic Accessible Tourism for All in Germany, the big travel agencies active in Germany pass on advertising accessible products; none of them has designated a respective market segment. Only TUI and Thomas Cook refer to features that benefit guests with mobility or activity limitations in the description of their hotels. However, the market of elder travellers is better supplied lately. Beside the mainstream there are a couple of highly specialised travel agencies in Germany that provide customised offers and special catalogues for travellers with disabilities.

Qualification Courses in Accessible Tourism for All

Qualification courses are not only of exceptional importance to the decision-makers but also to the service personnel. They enable the tourism professionals to respond to the needs of different target groups and to improve the quality of the tourist offers. Qualification programs in Accessible Tourism for All are offered only in a few of Germany's federal states. Usually, they are related to the nationwide qualification project 'Gastfreundschaft für Alle' (Hospitality for all) supported by the Federal Ministry of Economics and Technology and which was conducted by NatKo and DEHOGA in cooperation with NeumannConsult in 2004 and 2005. The qualification courses were work-related and conveyed good practice examples and a very informative training film. This nationwide qualification initiative was mostly directed in hotel and gastronomy businesses and was offered in all of the federal states. In 11 states, the 30 model training sessions could finally be conducted, whereas after the completion of the project even follow up training sessions took place in Brandenburg and Baden-Württemberg (Nature Park of South Black Forrest).

The German Seminar for Tourism (Deutsche Seminar für Tourismus – DSFT) based in Berlin is the central institution of further education in the German tourism industry. DSFT, in cooperation with NatKo, offers regular seminars on accessible tourism that are addressed to tourism service providers and offer advice on accessible design and marketing of tourist products.

So far, these seminars only take place once or twice a year in different locations in Germany. Next to further education, apprenticeship plays an important part. However, one could remark that the topic accessibility is not established in any of the examination regulations on federal level. Merely some of the educational books in tourism deal with the topic (e.g. Becker *et al.,* 2003; Dettmer *et al.,* 2005). This indicates that the topic of accessible tourism for all is not yet mainstream.

Strategic approach on national and federal state level

Most of the activities in the Accessible Tourism for All are based upon individual initiatives and the topic is rarely strategically addressed and pursued on the basis of a long-term planning on the national or state level. The Federal Government tries to act supportively within its power and devotes one sub-chapter to the topic in the tourism-political report for the 16th legislative period (BMWi, 2008). In addition, the topic is included in the so-called 'German Federal Government Policy Guidelines on Tourism', stating that more attention must be paid 'to mainstreaming accessibility as a cross-sectoral task in all policy sectors (. . .) We need to grasp that accessibility is part of hospitality' (BMWi, 2009: 2).

At Federal state level, a strategic approach to the topic can be found especially in those states that have established institutionalised state-wide offices of coordination that can work and plan in the long run without depending on the honorary engagement of individuals. Currently this is only the case in the federal state of Brandenburg and Saxony. In Brandenburg, a project centre has been established within the scope of the EU-wide Equality Project 'Fairway' that was established in the state tourism association from 2005 to 2007. After the project had expired both full-time positions were permanently implemented into the Tourism Academy of Brandenburg, which belongs to the Tourismus-Marketing Brandenburg GmbH.

Based on the initial project 'Dresden barrierefrei' (Dresden accessible) initiated by the Dresden-Werbung and Tourismus GmbH, a full-time position at the Tourismus Marketing Gesellschaft Sachsen mbH has been established, supported by freelance/temporary employees if needed. This position deals with the registration and evaluation of accessible offers, the initial consultation of funding agencies and marketing. There are close contacts to the three coordination and information centres in the regional boards of Saxony. Since 2008 accessible tourism is an individual segment next to family and wellness holidays in Saxony.

Conclusion

Compared to 2002, accessibility has significantly gained influence in the German tourism industry (Neumann *et al.,* 2008). Not only against the background of demographic change, the topic 'Accessible Tourism for All' is increasingly attracting the interest of tourism decision-makers and funding agencies. The public interest in the topic 'accessible travelling' within Germany and abroad could be considerably increased through the first study commissioned by the BMWi which outlined the economical impulses for Accessible Tourism for All (BMWi, 2004). The development process of accessible tourism in Germany has advanced. However, Accessible Tourism for All is still treated as a sensitive subject only in the sense of 'tourism for people with disabilities' with the focus on 'wheelchair users' by the supply side with regard to development and marketing. On the level of the federal states and municipalities the topic 'Accessible Tourism for All' is usually integrated into the professional tourism structures as a special interest topic and heavily depends on funding.

A nation-wide sustainable strategic planning in Germany is still missing as well as the respective precise operative implementation of the arrangement of quotation, communication and retailing along the whole tourism service chain. Marketing methods still depend on the motivation and on the honorary post of decision-makers and funding agencies or associations of the people concerned. Brochures, for example, are often not integrated into the professional structures of the tourism associations or are just the result of a successful acquisition of subsidies but not of a sustainable strategy.

Despite the positive development trends in the accessible tourism in Germany, travelling still poses a significant challenge for many people because of the numerous obstacles. German tourist destinations can face these challenges if they see accessibility as a cross-sectional task and as a quality benchmark and if they develop and market suitable products and services. This also means that Accessible Tourism for All needs to be developed and marketed more by addressing it as a topic rather than addressing a specific target group. The procedure to start developing and marketing accessible tourist products and services especially suited for the demands of people with activity or mobility limitations in Germany was vital for the still young market of Accessible Tourism for All. This group has been strongly neglected until then. However, it is clear that a too strong orientation on tourist products and services for disabled people could lead to economic risks.

This risk can only be avoided if economy and politics orient themselves along the lines of the concept 'Design for All', according to the results of the BMWi study from 2003, that accessibility is essential for 10% of the population, for 30–40% it is necessary and comfortable for 100% and serves as a quality benchmark (BMWi, 2004). Design for All is not only a concept but describes a process for achieving universal access including environments, products and services that are designed in a respectful, safe, healthy, functional, comprehensible and attractive way (Aragall et al., 2008). To achieve this, everything that is designed and made by people to be used by people must be accessible, convenient for everyone in society to use and responsive to evolving human diversity (EIDD, 2004). The concept of 'Design for All' thus assumes a perspective that does not imply the possible deficiencies or limitations but is built upon the diversity of the users and on extensions and enhancements of the use of products and services. With this, a new corporate and economic dimension is opened up that generates innovations and added value.

References

Aragall, F., Neumann, P. and Sagramola, S. (2008) The European Concept for Accessibility for Administrations, available at: http://www.eca.lu/index2.php?option=com_docmanandtask=doc_viewandgid=10andItemid=26

Becker, C., Hopfinger, H. and Steinecke A. (2003) *Geographie der Freizeit und des Turismus: Bilanz und Ausblick*. München: Oldenbourg.

Bundesministerium für Wirtschaft und Technologie (BMWi) (2004) *Economic impulses of Accessible Tourism for All. Study commissioned by the Federal Ministry of Economics and Technology. Summary of results*. (Documentation No. 526). Available at: http://www.bmwi.de/English/Navigation/Service/publications,did=29680,render=renderPrint.html

Bundesministerium für Wirtschaft und Technologie (BMWi) (2008) *Tourismuspolitischer Bericht der Bundesregierung*. 16. Legislaturperiode. Berlin. Available at: http://www.bmwi.de/BMWi/Navigation/Service/publikationen,did=239558.html

Bundesministerium für Wirtschaft und Technologie (BMWi) (2009) *German Federal Government Policy Guidelines on Tourism*. Available at: http://www.bmwi.de/English/Navigation/Service/publications,did=292316.html

Dettmer, H., Hausmann, T. and Kloss, I. (2005) *Gästemarketing*. Hamburg: Handwerk und Technik

Design for all Europe (EIDD) (2004) The EIDD Stockholm Declaration 2004. Available at: http://www.designforalleurope.org/Design-for-All/EIDD-Documents/Stockholm-Declaration/

Neumann, P., Pagenkopf, K., Schiefer, J. and Lorenz, A. (2008) *Barrierefreier Tourismus für Alle in Deutschland – Erfolgsfaktoren und Massnahmen zur Qualitätssteigerung*. Berlin: BMWi. Available at: http://www.bmwi.de/BMWi/Navigation/Service/publikationen,did=269772.html

5 Accessible Tourism in Greece: Beaches and Bathing for All

Nikos Voulgaropoulos, Eleni Strati and Georgia Fyka

Introduction

Greece is situated in south-east Europe at the end of the Balkan Peninsula, lying inside the Mediterranean basin. Owing to its geographic locality as well as to a remarkable number of islands, Greece has the 10th longest coastline among countries in the world. In total, the Greek coastline adds up to 14,880 kilometres (9246 miles). Greece is a traditional sun and sea tourist destination, occupying the 15th place in the world classification of tourist destinations (National Statistical Service, 2002b). The major part of international tourist arrivals (94.3%) originate from Europe, of which 68.9% are from the EU15 (UNWTO, 2007). The country welcomes millions of international tourists yearly, while tourist international arrivals rise steadily each year. With 14,765 million international arrivals in 2005, tourism noted a 10.9% growth from 2004, and within a year a further 8.6% rise from 2005 to 2006 (WTO, 2007). The National Statistical Service of Greece measured 18,754,593 tourist visitors in 2007, an 8.5% increase, compared to 2006 (National Statistical Service, 2007a). The figures for 2008 remained at similar levels, yet this was seen as positive, given pressures on economy worldwide (Spiliotopoulos, 2008). In addition to international arrivals, the tourist sector in Greece is favoured greatly by domestic tourism, although there is no official record of this so far.

Overall, tourism is a significant factor of the national economy, accounting for almost 18% of the national GPD (National Statistical Service, 2007b). The National economy is boosted by 11.5 billion Euros per year from tourist income, and around 850,000 people live directly or indirectly from the tourist product (National Statistical Service, 2007b). In terms of competiveness in the travel and tourism sector, Greece occupies the 22nd place among 130 countries, according to the World Economic Forum report (Blanke & Chiesa, 2007).

In terms of accessible tourism, infrastructure and facilities feature in some beaches of Greece, however, this remain far from common practice.

Tourism policy and strategy are not always comprehensive of accessibility, and initiatives have been limited in number and continuity. This places direct limits on the freedom of choice and movement for disabled tourists, as well as on reaping benefits from economic revenue for tourist development and sustainability. 18.2% of the Greek population has a health problem or disability, half of which are people over 65 (National Statistical Service, 2002a). It is estimated that 50% of Greek people with disabilities or mobility problems due to ageing would travel more if accessibility was improved, while Greece would welcome 25.7 million visitors out of potentially 90 to 120 million people with disabilities or elderly people in Europe (JBR Hellas, 2006). This chapter seeks to present current policy and practice of accessible tourism in Greece and sketch out recommendations for mainstreaming accessible tourism.

Key Management Structures of Greek Tourism

The Ministry for Tourist Development in Greece is the primary actor in setting the strategies and policies for tourism and securing necessary resources to enable set goals. The Ministry is also required to take additional measures for implementation of such policies, as well as for monitoring, evaluation and update of policies in the light of national and international market development. Different aspects of the regulation and development of the tourist sector in Greece are shared with four further key agents supervised by the Ministry of Tourist Development. Firstly, the Hellenic Greek National Tourism Organization (GNTO) acts as the ruling state agency for ensuring quality control, through market supervision and consumer protection. Furthermore, the GNTO carries out research and makes recommendations to the Ministry, with regards to issues for development, increasing competitiveness, and promotional campaigns.

Secondly, the Tourism Development Company acts as a real estate asset manager, managing and administrating the state-owned tourism property with the aim to optimize tourism development through partnerships between the State and the private sector. The portfolio managed by Tourism Development Company numbers over 350 assets throughout Greece that cover a total area of about 70 million square metres and consists of business units, such as marinas, hotels, organized beaches, camps, and so on, as well as undeveloped sites and natural springs.

Thirdly, the Hellenic Chamber of Hotels operates as statutory adviser on matters related to tourism and particularly the development of the Greek hotel industry. By law all hotels operating in Greece are members. The Chamber is co-managed by elected hotel managers as well as representatives of the State. It provides consultation to all its members on economic, legal and social matters regarding the industry. Furthermore, it supplies statistical data and monthly reviews regarding the industry, and publishes an annual guide of the Greek hotels. It is worth noting, that the website of the Chamber contains a search engine for all hotels in Greece, including search criteria based on 'suitability for disabled people', listing 1834 results in 2009. However, precise information on accessibility of hotels is not available, and usually rests on self- identification on the part of each hotel, rather than common standards or certification by the Hellenic Chamber of Hotels. In reality, 50% of disabled tourists find that the information is not reliable and in the majority of cases accessibility is worse than anticipated (JBR Hellas, 2006).

Finally, the Organization of Tourism Education and Training (OTEK) is the state institution providing education and professional training in the field of tourism. The Schools of Tourist Professions and Tour Guides, operate in 17 cities and towns of the country, offering further funding opportunities for continuing professional training. However, scanning through the training programmes operating under OTEK it is evident that there is a lack of any training connected to accessible tourism, even as a complementary module.

National Strategies for Accessible Tourism

The issue of Accessible Tourism first rose prominently among the goals of the Ministry of Tourist Development in view of the Paralympic Games hosted in Greece in 2004. The initiative was supported by a technical study on accessibility standards and guidelines for 'Access for all to the sand', published in 2003 by the Ministry of Tourist Development. The same year the Tourism Development Company undertook the responsibility of making four beaches accessible for all, through the project 'Everybody on the Sand', which were completed by the summer of 2004 in time for the Athens Olympics and Paralympics. The guidelines cover accessibility stand- ards for parking spaces, pavement curbs, corridors for access to the beach and sea, wheelchairs and aids for access to sand and sea, safe staircases, ramps, mechanisms for level change, WC and changing rooms, and sign- posting for information, orientation and warnings. Standards are included for all kinds of disability- physical, sensory and cognitive, covering accessi- bility, usability and safety aspects of architectural interventions. Through- out, all standards are discussed in detail, in terms of suitable material and gradient, steepness, length and width, texture, easy use of mechanisms, colour- contrast, symbols and location of signs, and systems of audio and visual information.

The guidelines for access to the beach (Hellenic Ministry of Tourist Dvelopment, 2003) build on accessibility standards published previously by the Office for Studies on People with Disabilities of the Ministry of Environment back in 1996–2000 (Hellenic Ministry of Environment, 1996– 2000) for autonomous access and living of people with disabilities in the built environment. The guidelines provide accessibility standards for all aspects of exterior and interior spaces and buildings, many of which are equally applicable in tourist destinations (for instance, parking, ramps, facilities, WC).

In fact, the modification of the General Construction and Urban Planning Regulation (L 2831/2000) made obligatory the provision for accessibility in all new buildings, including ramps for access, elevators, and wide spaces in the interior (Official Gazette of Government, 2000). Restoring accessibility for buildings older than 2000 is a legal requirement only in the case of public buildings (Article 28 of Law 2831/2000). A step towards mainstreaming accessibility in the tourist sector in specific is the Presidential Decree (43/2002) which requires the provision of one room in every five to be suitable for people with reduced mobility (Official Gazette of Government, 2002). This requirement is reinforced as accessibility was introduced among the ranking criteria of hotels. Yet, this only applies for new hotels built after 2002. A subsidy also exists as an incentive to hotel owners to make their venues accessible to people with reduced mobility, run yearly by GNTO.

Conventional approaches to tourism and disability, established through law provisions, overwhelmingly lack a mainstream or holistic approach. 'Tourism for All' is translated mostly into funding or co-financing of stays in designated hotels as well as therapeutic tourism (natural or built landscapes) for disabled people, coordinated by the GNTO. However such provisions lack strategic consideration of accessibility. There is no explicit requirement of accessibility for candidate hotels to participate in the programme and the GNTO does not explicitly employ or disseminate accessibility standards. There is lack of information on accessibility features and status of hotels once approved and published in the form of guide for disabled participants and a lack of information about the accessibility of tourist destinations and facilities, including information about accessible public means of transportation, access to beach and sea, access to sightseeing and cultural activities, access to other venues, such as restaurants, shops or leisure, available medical assistance and social services.

New strategies by the Ministry of Tourist Development were included under the government plan for spatial planning and sustainable development in 2007. The strategies for tourism are based on improving quality, diversity and sustainability of tourist destinations, facilities and services. There is a particular aim for overcoming the highly seasonal character of tourist arrivals, by creating alternative forms of tourism utilizing (yet protecting and sustaining) the environment in different parts of the country, including city centres and mainland countryside. The quality of tourist services and facilities is similarly linked in with goals in tourist development, and in particularly the Minister of Tourist Development introduced two additional awards, traditionally given at the annual international exhibition 'Philoxenia' at Thessaloniki, for Corporate Social Responsibility and Environmental Awareness.

The accessibility of tourist destinations represents a third main axis in the plan. However, this is focused exclusively on transport to isolated destinations, rather than ensuring accessibility standards at tourist destinations and facilities. This is clear both through proposed measures as well as orientation of funding under the new community framework 2007–2013. The aim is upgrading infrastructure in all systems of transport – air, sea, rail and road.

Means of transport are undeniably a vital part in the chain of accessible tourism, while people with disabilities face particular barriers in using public means to reach destinations. It is not clear however whether the plan will ensure/restore accessibility to enable travel for disabled people. In addition, accessible means of transport are of little use if the tourist destinations remain overwhelmingly inaccessible. Overall, there is no open recognition or address of the benefits of accessibility in current strategies for tourist development. By contrast, initiatives for accessible tourism have performed in separate 'special' measures for people with disabilities, so practice has rather been patchy and discontinuous.

Accessible Beaches and Bathing in Greece

The first official initiatives to build access to the sand and sea were run under the project 'Access for all to the sand' launched in 2003 by the Tourist Development Company under the guidance of the Ministry of Development (Hellenic Ministry of Tourist Development, 2003). Four accessible beaches were created by the end of 2004, three in Athens (Voula, Varkiza and Vouliagmeni) and one in Thessaloniki (Agia Triada), mainly with the view to accommodate athletes and visitors of the 2004 Olympic and Paralympic Games. Still, the projects had an immediate impact at a local level, appealing to hundreds of Greek disabled people, who even reported that it was the first time they had the option to swim. The infrastructure built in all cases provided access to both the beach and the sea, through main corridors on the sand and a ramp entering the sea, as well as accessible facilities such as showers and WCs. All structures are permanent and can be used independently by people with disability. The beaches are also staffed with a lifeguard, or helpers, available to help in case they are needed. Unfortunately, a few years later, the infrastructure in Agia Triada was dismantled, as the Hellenic Public Real Estate Corporation (HPREC) ruled it as unlicensed construction – paradoxically, as this project was supervised by the Ministry of Tourist Development. There has been no initiative to restore access since.

Another beach in the coastline of Athens was made accessible in 2007, by the municipality of Palaio Faliro. On the local authority's initiative, a conference was organized on accessible tourism in cooperation with the French Embassy, presenting good practice in Marseille, with a view for the Greek local authority to implement. At the moment, the beach has only been equipped with a corridor for access to the sand and sea, but plans also include installation of equipment (e.g. wheelchair floating device) OK for access to sea, as well as a system of audio information throughout the beach, to inform visitors with visual problems of their position and choices to move in the space. The first initiative providing broad and holistic access to sand and beach was completed in 2008 in seven beaches in the municipality of Rodopi. The proposal was approved in 2007 under a funding programme run by the Ministry of Internal Affairs, within the framework of 'cultural infrastructure and activities for local development and environment protection', and specifically a line of action for 'combating social exclusion'. It was the only proposal submitted that related to accessible tourism. It is also worth noting that similar strands of funding for social inclusion are not available under the remit of the Ministry of Tourism.

It was also the first case that a project for making accessible beaches was designed and implemented jointly by the local authority and a disabled people's association 'Perpato' ('Walk'). The direct involvement of users in the design and evaluation of infrastructure has been key in meeting holistically the needs and expectations of visitors. The project included the placement of a network of main and complementary corridors for wide freedom of circulation on the beach as well as access to all available facilities. The project also made available special wheelchairs for access to sand and sea, accessible showers and chemical toilets, and foresaw the creation of resting places, kiosks and parking spaces all built according to accessibility standards for independent use.

The Need for a Strategy for Accessible Tourism

The issue of accessible tourism has been dealt in a rather piecemeal fashion, and although state initiative has resulted in some good practices in the past, it has been inconsistent in encompassing accessibility in mainstream strategies for tourist development. Despite existing guidelines for access to sea and the built environment there is weak commitment and investment in accessible tourism in practice. This shows slow progress and continuity in improving accessibility in more tourist destinations. Given the remarkable number of beaches all over the country, accessible beaches and bathing facilities are minimal in both number and location. There are several issues that need to be addressed so that accessible tourism accelerates and becomes a common standard. These basically tie in with levelling consideration to design for all among mainstream priorities in tourist development, and understanding the economic potential of tourists with disability or any mobility or health limitation.

Accessible tourism figures in patchy parts in public/political dialogue, and where it is addressed, it appears more as an issue of 'sensitivity'. Yet, accessible tourism is based on the same intrinsic principles and demands as for non-disabled tourists: free choice to visit any place at any time, independently, and opportunity to enjoy a wealth and quality of services and activities. Maintaining disability in a distinct category, as a 'vulnerable group', fails to meet this citizen right, and indeed benefit from the consumer demand.

The concept of accessibility is strongly connected to a social, rather than medical, understanding of disability, which focuses on *environmental* barriers to social participation. Firstly expressed by disabled people's movements (Union of the Physically Impaired Against Segregation and the Disability Alliance, 1976), this understanding is now widely and officially adopted as the appropriate response to disability on an EU level (European Commission, 2003; European Commission 2000) and worldwide (UNWTO, 2005) and has been reinforced by the UN Convention on the Rights of People with Disabilities, (United Nations, 2006), to which the European Union is a signatory. The task at hand is, therefore, to provide equally for all needs, rather than treat accessible standards as exceptional requirements. Unless this is genuinely realised, accessible infrastructure will be viewed as an added, specialised (and therefore expensive) intervention; rather than as proactive design method for all, which makes economic sense not only in terms of short-term cost, but even more so in terms of long-term revenue.

Accessibility is key to sustainable development: it provides safer, more liveable, more adaptable, more comfortable, and more user-friendly infrastructure and facilities (European Commission, 2003). By 2040, it is estimated that 30–40% of the EU population, including people with disabilities, older people, young children, and other people with mobility, functional or health limitations, will benefit from accessibility, with expected tourism revenues upwards of €83 billion for European travellers alone (ENAT, 2007). Unfortunately, the economic value of accessible tourism is not yet addressed in political dialogue and strategies for tourism in Greece. Equally, there is generally lack of awareness of the marketing value of accessibility among private owners. Research into tourism intensity and travelling profile/ needs among disabled people in Greece, as well as international tourists, could provide the grounds for estimating the financial potential of accessible tourism, and orient actions into necessary standards and preferred destinations and facilities.

Mainstreaming of accessible tourism also requires coordinated action cutting across all policy areas in the chain of tourism (information, including ICT systems, means of transport, spatial planning, buildings, goods and services and social policy). The exclusive focus on accessibility as an architectural issue for instance, weakens political commitment, as it is seen purely in technical terms and set outside their field of expertise. Similarly, there is a risk that conventional funding in social policies for tourism for disabled people in Greece override action in making accessible tourism common practice. Equally, on a practical level, the lack of accessible means of transport, or the lack of dissemination of information on accessible destinations, disrupts access to the destination in the first place.

Finally, there is a lack of mechanism in Greece for certifying, monitoring and evaluating accessibility standards. This is evident, for instance, with regards to the hotels listed under the Hellenic Chambers of Hotels which self-identify as accessible, or in the lack of publicised information about accessibility in hotels approved for funding of stay under 'Tourism for All' programmes. Another case is the award of the 'Blue Flag' for beaches, which foresees the fulfilment of 28 criteria. One of the criteria is that a minimum of one Blue Flag beach in each municipality must have access and toilet facilities provided for disabled persons. (Blue Flag program, 2008). 'Access', however, is left undefined and with no list of standards to be checked. Currently 38 municipalities have been awarded with Blue Flags, but this is far from meaning that awarded beaches have the necessary requirements to be accessible. In many cases 'accessibility' starts and ends with a placement of one ramp to reach the beach, but overlooks access for circulation on the sand or access to sea, as well as vital facilities such as accessible toilets, changing rooms and parking spaces. The close cooperation between state or local authority agents and users from the very first stages of design to implementation and evaluation of access to beach and seas captures all lessons for good practice. The involvement of disabled people gives a direct view of their rights, needs and expectations as citizens, users and tourist consumers. Disabled people are in the unique position to identify current barriers in all aspects related to the tourist chain, and can offer their knowledge and direct experience in building, testing and evaluating appropriate solutions from the user perspective.

Conclusion

In conclusion, the real goal at hand is that accessible tourism occurs as a given, as for the rest of the non-disabled population. It is necessary therefore to mainstream accessible tourism among the priorities for tourist development and investment. Otherwise practice will remain inconsistent and incomplete, effectively removing freedom in travelling and bathing for a significant part of the national population as well as international arrivals. Mainstreaming accessible tourism requires attention to all parts of the tourist chain, where accessibility is proactively and 'naturally' included among design standards. The object of design for all is not 'special requirements'. It is about simple, accessible, safe and friendly infrastructure and facilities, equally applicable standards for all users. On a practical side, investment in accessible tourism can only occur from an open and wide recognition of the benefits of accessibility in great revenue, as well as for sustainability and quality of services, so far overlooked in the country.

References

Blanke, J. and Chiesa, T. (2007) (eds) *The Travel and Tourism Competitiveness Report*. Geneva: World Economic Forum.

Blue Flag Programme (2008) *Blue Flag Beach Criteria and Explanatory Notes 2008–2009*. Available at: http://ec.europa.eu/ourcoast/download.cfm?fileID=1018

European Commission (2000) *Towards a Barrier-Free Europe for People with Disabilities*, Communication from the Commission to the Council of Europe, the European Parliament, the Economic and Social Committee and the Committee of the regions. COM 284 (2000). Brussels: European Commission.

European Commission (2003) *2010: A Europe Accessible for All*. Report from the Group of Experts set up by the European Commission. Brussels: ENAT Publiccations.

European Network for Accessible Tourism (ENAT) (2007) *Services and Facilities for Accessible Tourism in Europe*. Brussels: ENAT publications.

Hellenic Ministry of Environment (1996–2000) *Design Guidelines for Independent Access of Disabled People*. Athens: Hellenic Ministry of Environment, Office for Studies on People with Disabilities.

Hellenic Ministry of Tourist Development (2003) *Access for all to the sand*. Athens: Hellenic Ministry of Tourist Development.

JBR Hellas (2006) *Accessible Tourism*. Presentation at the *International Conference IMIC 2006: Marketing Destinations and their Venues*. http://www.gbrconsulting.gr/articles/Accessible%20Tourism.pps

National Statistical Service (2002a) *People with Health Problems or Disabilities (2nd quarter of 2002)*. Athens: The National Statistical Service of Greece, Ministry of National Economy.

National Statistical Service (2002b) *Tourism: Number of outbound trips (by country of destination)*. Athens: The National Statistical Service of Greece, Ministry of National Economy

National Statistical Service (2007a) *Arrivals of Foreigners in Greece*. Athens: The National Statistical Service of Greece, Ministry of National Economy.

National Statistical Service (2007b) *Gross Value added by Industry*. Athens: The National Statistical Service of Greece, Ministry of National Economy.

National Statistical Service (2008) *Evolution of Tourism Indicators 2005–2008*. The National Statistical Service of Greece, Ministry of National Economy

Official Gazette of Government (2000) Law 2831/2000: *Modification of Law 1577/1985 General Construction Regulation and other Urban Planning Regulations*. Athens: Official Gazette of Government 140A.

Official Gazette of Government (2002) *Star Ranking of Main Hotel Accommodation and Technical Standards thereof*, Presidential Decree (43/2002). Athens: Official Gazette of Government 43A.

Spiliotopoulos, A. (2008) Speech by the Minister of Tourist Development at 24th International Exhibition for Tourism 'Philoxenia', Thessaloniki, 30th October – 2nd November 2008.

Union of the Physically Impaired Against Segregation and the Disability Alliance (1976) *Fundamental Principles of Disability*. Summary of the discussion held on 22nd November, 1975, London.

United Nations (2006) *Convention on the Rights of Persons with Disabilities*. Available at: http://www.un.org/disabilities/

World Tourism Organization (UNWTO) (2005) *Accessible Tourism for All*. Adopted by resolution A/RES/492(XVI)/10 at the sixteen session of the General Assembly of the World Tourism Organization (Dakar, Senegal, 28 November – 2 December 2005), on the recommendation of the Quality Support and Trade Committee. Madrid: UNWTO.
World Tourism Organization (UNWTO) (2007) *Tourism Highlights,* 2007 Edition. Madrid: UNWTO.

Websites providing further information

Disability Now www.disabled.gr
Gerasimos Polis blog www.access2sea4disabled.blogspot.com/
Greek National Tourist Organization www.gnto.gr
The Organization of Tourism Education and Training (OTEK) http://www.ste.edu.gr/uk/ste_uk.htm
The Tourism Development Company http://www.tourism-development.gr/
The Hellenic Chamber of Hotels http://www.grhotels.gr/

6 The United States: Travellers with Disabilities

Laurel Van Horn

Introduction

Until 2002 when the Open Doors Organization (ODO) sponsored its first nationwide study on travel and hospitality among adults with disabilities (ODO, 2002), conducted by Harris Interactive, there had never been a major, statistically reliable survey on the US disability travel market. No one could say with any assurance what percentage of adults with disabilities were travelling, how frequently, what modes of transportation they used or how much they spent on transportation, lodging or dining. This meant that corporations in the travel industry had no data on which to base investment decisions and thus little incentive to do more than the minimum required under Title III of the Americans with Disabilities Act or the Air Carrier Access Act.

In 2002 the US Bureau of Transportation Statistics (BTS) carried out its own *Transportation Availability and Use Survey* (BTS, 2002) which explored not only travel by public transportation but also private vehicle. Its sample was divided evenly between disabled and non-disabled respondents of all ages. The motivation was the 'critical lack of information [on] transportation use by people with physical, mental or emotional disabilities' but the goal in this case was 'to create an information source for transportation planners and policy makers . . .' rather than the private sector (BTS, 2003: 3). While it focused primarily on local transportation, the BTS study also covered long distance travel. Findings from this survey have been released in several reports including *Freedom to Travel* (BTS, 2003) and *Travel Patterns of Older Americans with Disabilities* (Sweeney, 2004).

In 2005, ODO sponsored a second nationwide study which explored in greater depth the barriers facing travellers with disabilities in airports and airplanes as well as hotels and restaurants (ODO, 2005). The 2005 study also examined how these travellers planned and booked trips and identified which destinations are most popular in the continental US and overseas.

Taken together, these studies and reports corroborate and complement each other to provide a detailed portrait of the disability travel market in the US today including the barriers which may restrict the frequency of long distance travel. Indeed, Open Doors Organization projected that the market could easily double if these problems with service and facilities were resolved (ODO, 2002: 68).

Open Doors Organization (ODO) Travel Market Studies

Both studies by the Open Doors Organization were carried out by Harris Interactive using identical methodology so as to make trending possible. For the 2002 ODO study, the total sample included 1037 interviews with adults with disabilities: 534 interviews conducted online, using The Harris Poll Online Database, and 503 interviews conducted by telephone, using a pre-screened sample of adults with disabilities from The Harris Poll. In 2005, the total sample consisted of 1373 interviews among adults with disabilities: 871 online and 502 by phone. To develop the questionnaires, ODO held focus groups within the disability community in Chicago and conducted telephone interviews with business leaders from across the US.

Disability was defined as 'having blindness, deafness or a condition that substantially limits one or more basic physical activities such as walking, climbing stairs, reaching, lifting or carrying' (ODO, 2002: 5). Respondents were screened based on these criteria using a variation of the 2000 Census question. Fifteen percent of the general adult population (or more than 31 million adults aged 18 and older) define themselves as having one or more of these characteristics. This data on the incidence of adults with disabilities was obtained through The Harris Poll (The Harris Poll November 2002 and November 2005, cited in ODO 2002 and ODO 2005, respectively) and based on the 209,128,094 people aged 18 years and older in the US population, according to the 2000 US Census. The data was weighted to represent the populations with these disabilities aged 18 and older.

For the 2002 ODO Study, the key objectives were to: (ODO, 2002: 4)

(1) 'measure general travel behaviours including how often adults with disabilities are travelling, with whom, how much they spend, and on which sources of information they rely to make decisions';
(2) 'gauge experiences with airlines, cruise lines, restaurants, and hotels';
(3) 'determine how well the needs of adults with disabilities are being met by airlines and hotels';
(4) 'quantify the top services/products that would encourage adults with disabilities to fly and stay in hotels more often';
(5) 'estimate the current and potential economic impact of the disability community'.

For the 2005 ODO Study, the key objectives were to: (ODO, 2005: 4).

(1) 'measure general travel behaviours including how often adults with disabilities are travelling, how much money they spend, and which sources of information they rely on to make decisions';
(2) 'gauge experiences with airlines, airports, car rental agencies, hotels, and restaurants';
(3) 'determine the obstacles that adults with disabilities encounter with airlines, airports, hotels, and restaurants';
(4) 'estimate the current and potential economic impact of the disability community';
(5) 'compare 2005 findings to the 2002 study to uncover possible trends and differences over time'.

Travel Frequency and Overall Expenditure

The 2002 ODO study found that 71% of adults with disabilities, or more than 22 million people, travel at least once in a two-year period. This includes 5.6 million business travellers, 21 million pleasure/leisure travellers and 5 million travellers who combine business and pleasure. Overall, adults with disabilities take about two trips every two years, or approximately 63 million total trips, the majority of which are for pleasure (ODO, 2002: 7). Each trip generally lasts five days. There is also a subgroup of more frequent travellers: 20% of all adults with disabilities travel at least six times every two years (see Figure 6.1). 'While travelling, the typical adult with a disability spends US$430, which means travel expenditures among the disability population top US$27 billion over the course of 2 years' (ODO, 2002: 8). On an annual basis, adults with disabilities spend approximately US$13.6 billion on travel.

As Figure 6.1 shows, in 2005 the percentage of adults with disabilities travelling and the number of trips taken remained roughly the same as in 2002. Sixty-nine percent of adults with disabilities, or more than 21 million people, travelled at least once in the prior two years. The subgroup of more frequent travellers held steady at 20%.

Internet Use

When planning a trip, the internet is a key resource for adults with disabilities. In 2002, almost half of those who travel (46%) said they consult the internet for accessibility information. One-third (33%) of those who travel booked their trips most frequently online, which appears to be somewhat higher than the general population. According to the Travel Industry Association (TIA), 27% of travellers in 2002 used the internet for actually booking something related to their travel during the past year (TIA cited in ODO, 2002: 9). Word of mouth is also an extremely important source of information for adults with disabilities: '85% of those who travel said they

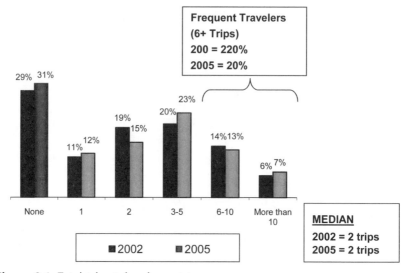

Figure 6.1 Total trips taken in past two years
Source: Open Doors Organization, 2005, p.21

share their travel experiences with others, indicating a powerful network among travellers with disabilities' (ODO, 2002: 9).

In 2005 half of those who travel (51%) used the internet to book their trips (see Figure 6.2), which once again appears to exceed usage by the general population. 'According to the Travel Industry Association, 40% of travellers in 2005 used the internet for actually booking something related to their travel during the past year (TIA, cited in ODO, 2005: 9). Almost half (43%) of travellers in the ODO sample said they consult the internet to support their disability-related travel needs. For these travellers, the top ways they use the internet are: finding and/or booking accessible hotels (57%); finding accessibility information about airlines (47%); and finding accessible activities, tours, and attractions at their destination (47%) (ODO, 2005: 9).

While internet use in planning and booking trips is on the rise, use of travel agents appears to be declining among travellers with disabilities. In 2002, 22% of ODO respondents stated that they booked most frequently with a travel agent. In 2005, only 16% had used a travel agent to book a trip during the two-year period. By 2005 booking via the pnternet had also surpassed direct calls to airlines and hotels (see Figure 6.2). This may be due in part to the surcharge that airlines now levy for non-internet bookings.

Air Travel

In the 2002 ODO Study, almost one-third (30%) of adults with disabilities, or 9.4 million air travellers in total, travelled by air in the previous two

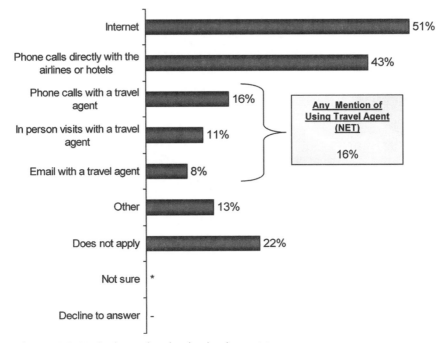

Figure 6.2 Methods used to book trips in past two years
Source: Open Doors Organization, 2005, p.30

years (see Figure 6.3). Air travellers typically took two flights every two years and spent US$349 per flight, which equates to US$3.3 billion per year for the entire airline industry. Air travellers said they would take two more flights per year if airlines were to accommodate their needs as a person with a disability. This translates into 18.8 million more flights and means that air spending by the disability community could more than double if airlines were to make necessary accommodations. The top features or services that airlines would need to offer to encourage more frequent travel are: '(1) more accommodating staff, (2) guaranteed preferred seating, and (3) a designated employee at check-in and arrival' (ODO, 2002: 10).

In 2005 the percentage of adults with disabilities travelling by air over the two-year period stayed at approximately the same level: 31% or 9.6 million air travellers in total. Air travellers typically took two flights every two years, as they did in 2002, and they spent US$302 on air travel per trip or US$2.9 billion per year for the entire airline industry (ODO, 2005: 12).

However, the vast majority of air travellers (84%) stated that they 'encounter obstacles when dealing with airlines' (ODO, 2005: 12). Topping the list were physical obstacles (67%), with cramped seating areas (52%) being the most common complaint. Problems with service/personnel were

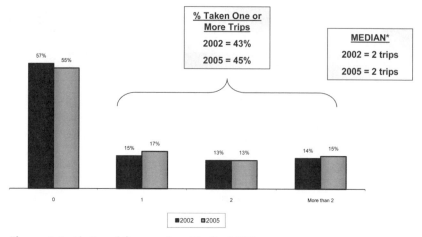

Figure 6.3 Air Travel for people with disabilities
Source: Open Doors Organization, 2005, p.38

also prevalent (60%), with long queues (42%) and problems reserving their preferred seat (20%) predominating. Respondents also reported expense-related obstacles (37%) and difficulties with communication (28%), including difficulty hearing announcements (17%). Four out of five air travellers (82%) also experience obstacles when they are at the airport, the most common being long distances to or between gates (63%) and long queues (48%). More than one in four (27%) mentioned communication-related obstacles in the airports (ODO, 2005: 13).

Other Modes of Transportation

Despite these obstacles, air travel was by far the most popular form of paid transportation. The 2005 ODO study found that only 11% of adults with disabilities had travelled by train or bus, making on average one such trip during the two-year period. Twenty percent of adults with disabilities, or 6.2 million people in all, rented a car over the course of two years. Car renters typically rent a car on one trip every two years and spend about us$40 per day (ODO, 2005: 14). To increase the likelihood of rental, the top features or services that companies would need to offer are: (1) pickup and delivery service, (2) global positioning system, and (3) lift-equipped vehicles.

The 2002 ODO Study, which included two questions on cruise travel, revealed that over a five-year period 12% of adults with disabilities took a cruise. This appears to be somewhat higher than the general population since, according to the Cruise Lines International Association (CLIA), only 8% of the US general population took a cruise during the same five-year period (CLIA *2002 Market Profile Study,* cited in ODO, 2002: 14). Among adults with disabilities, the repeat business for cruises may be particularly high: 59% of those who took a cruise in the previous five years say they plan to take another cruise within the next five years (ODO, 2002: 14).

Hotels

The 2002 ODO Study found that 55% of adults with disabilities had stayed in hotels in the previous two years (or 17.3 million hotel users). Hotel users typically stayed in hotels two times every two years (or 34.5 million visits) and spent US$241 per visit. So, total expenditures for the hotel industry among travellers with disabilities equalled more than US$8.3 billion for two years or approximately US$4.2 billion annually. In 2005 the percentage of adults with disabilities who stayed in hotels, motels or inns over a two-year period stayed roughly the same at 52% (or 16.3 million hotel users). Among travellers with disabilities, however, those who stayed in a hotel at least once increased from 64% to 76% (see Figure 6.4). The median number of hotel stays also increased to three stays every two years.

While satisfaction with hotels increased from 2002 to 2005, approximately three out of five hotel users (60%) still reported obstacles of the following types: physical (48%), service/personnel (45%) and communication-related (15%). Most prevalent among the physical obstacles were doors that are heavy or hard to open (36%), lack of room to manoeuvre in hotel

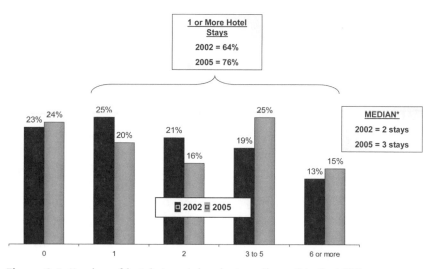

Figure 6.4 Number of hotel stays taken by travellers with disabilities
Source: Open Doors Organization, 2005, p.52

rooms and bathrooms (20%) and inaccessible shower or bath facilities (19%). The most common service/personnel obstacles were lack of availability of convenient rooms such as those on the first floor or near the elevator (36%) and personnel being unaware of services provided for people with disabilities (17%) (ODO, 2005: 16).

Restaurants

In both 2002 and 2005, ODO found that adults with disabilities generally patronize fast food restaurants once per week and casual dining and more formal restaurants less frequently. Patronage of the latter two declined somewhat between 2002 and 2005, while median expenditures increased (see Table 6.1). Typical personal expenditures in 2005 ranged from US$5 for fast food restaurants to US$20 for more formal restaurants (ODO, 2005, p. 17).

The 2005 ODO Study also queried how many travellers with disabilities ate at restaurants during their trips over the previous two years. Not surprisingly, the vast majority patronized restaurants during at least one trip (90%), with three trips being the median. Sixty-four percent of the adults with disabilities surveyed in 2005 encountered obstacles when dining out: physical (62%), personnel/customer service (27%), and communication-related (22%). Physical obstacles most frequently mentioned were lack of room between tables (40%), doors that were hard to open or manoeuvre through (33%) and steps at the entrance or within the restaurant (28%). The most common personnel/customer service problem was lack of availability of the seating wanted (20%). Lack of an online menu (9%) and problems in communicating with restaurant personnel topped the list of communication-related obstacles.

TABLE 6.1 Restaurant visits and expenditure

Restaurant type	% who patronize at least once a week		Median Personal Expenditures (of those who patronize restaurant)	
	2002	2005	2002	2005
Fast food	53%	50%	$5	$5
Casual dining (e.g. T.G.I. Fridays or Outback)	53%	42%	$9	$12
More formal	35%	22%	$15	$20

Source: ODO 2002, p. 15, and ODO 2005, p. 17

Destinations—Domestic and International

To encourage destinations to improve access and marketing to travellers with disabilities, the 2005 ODO Study also asked online respondents to identify which cities and countries they had visited. Most popular in the continental US were New York City (47%), Washington, DC (45%), and Chicago (44%), edging out Orlando, Las Vegas, and Los Angeles (all tied at 42%). Other top 10 destinations, in order, were San Francisco, Atlanta, Dallas, and San Diego (ODO, 2005, p.8).

Three out of five adults with disabilities (62%) who are online have travelled outside the continental United States at least once in their lifetime, the vast majority (85%) to other North American destinations including Canada (56%) and Mexico (52%). More than two out of five (44%) of those who have travelled outside the continental United States have been to Europe, mostly to Germany (28%), England (26%), and France (25%). Almost one out of three (31%) who have travelled outside the continental United States have visited the Caribbean (see Figure 6.5).

In the previous two years, 16% of online adults with disabilities travelled outside the continental United States. 'The typical international traveller spent almost US$1600 on this travel, which means current international travel expenditures among the disability population top US$7 billion over the course of two years' (ODO, 2005, p.8).

Finally, as noted above, the 2005 ODO study identified a segment of adults with disabilities who may be described as frequent or heavy travellers. One in five (20%) are frequent travellers, making six or more trips in a two-year period; 11% are heavy airline users, taking three or more flights over two years; 21% are heavy hotel users, staying in hotels four or more times in two years; 10% are heavy car renters, renting two or more cars in two years; and 7% are heavy international spenders, typically spending more than US$1000 on a trip outside of the continental US in a two-year period (ODO, 2005: 8, 35).

BTS 2002 National Transportation Availability and Use Survey

The BTS 2002 study involved 5019 interviews: 2321 with individuals who self-identified as having a disability and 2698 with non-disabled individuals. By surveying equal numbers of persons with and without disabilities, the BTS study sought 'to compare the two groups and identify common transportation uses and problems as well as uses and problems unique to each group' (BTS, 2003: 14). Persons of any age, including children, were eligible although proxy interviews were used for those under 16, 16–17 year-olds living with adults, and those unable to complete the interview due to their disability (BTS, 2003: 13).

By Continent/Region	Total
Base	603
	%
North America	85
Europe	44
Caribbean	31
Asia	16
Central and South America	7
Africa	6
Australia	5
Israel	5
New Zealand	3
Other	33

Europe	Total
	%
Germany	28
England	26
France	25
Italy	16
Switzerland	12
Holland	11
Scotland	10
Spain	9
Ireland	7
Greece	6
Portugal	4
Russia	2
Czech Republic	1

Asia	Total
	%
Japan	13
Thailand	5
China	4
India	2
Dubai	1
Malaysia	1

Africa	Total
	%
Egypt	3
Morocco	3
South Africa	1
Kenya	1

North America	Total
	%
Canada	56
Mexico	52
Hawaii	25
Alaska	16

Caribbean	Total
	%
U.S. Virgin Islands	17
Puerto Rico	16
Bermuda	11
Jamaica	9
Aruba	4

Central and South America	Total
	%
Costa Rica	3
Brazil	3
Argentina	2
Peru	2
Chile	1

Figure 6.5 Places travelled to outside the continental US
Source: ODO 2005, p. 26

Because the methodology, sampling and weighting techniques used in the BTS survey are complex, readers are referred to the *Freedom to Travel* report (BTS, 2003: 12–16) for a full description. Survey respondents were asked to 'self-identify disability according to several definitions, specifically: the Census 2000 definition, the 1990 Americans with Disabilities Act (ADA) definition, which considers disability as a 'physical or mental impairment that substantially limits one or more of the major life activities'; and if a child in the household received 'special education services" (BTS, 2003: 3). However, disability data presented in *Freedom to Travel* (BTS, 2003) and *Travel Patterns of Older Americans with Disabilities* (Sweeney, 2004) are only from respondents who self-identified using the Census 2000 disability definition in order to provide comparability with the Census.

Topics covered in the survey included: (BTS, 2003: 3)

(1) 'frequency of travel outside the home, including trip purpose, mode of transportation, frequency of use of different modes, need for assistance, and satisfaction with transportation services';
(2) 'availability of paratransit (curb-to-curb service) and respondent use of paratransit';
(3) 'motor vehicle ownership, use and safety issues, including vehicles modified for use by people with disabilities';
(4) 'experiences when using various modes of travel, including difficulties with public and private transportation'.

The focus here will be just on topics related to long distance travel and transportation.

According to the *Freedom to Travel* report, the 2002 BTS survey found that over a one-year period 60% of people with disabilities travel long distance (more than 100 miles one way) versus 76% of those without disabilities (BTS, 2003: 9). Among both groups, the two most frequently used modes of transportation for long-distance travel are personal motor vehicles and commercial airlines (see Figure 6.6). Among long-distance travellers, 31.5% with disabilities had taken a commercial flight, compared to 40% of those without disabilities. Other types of transportation were used much less frequently: only 5% or fewer of both disabled and non-disabled respondents used an intercity bus, private/chartered bus or Amtrak/intercity rail (BTS, 2003: 9).

A significantly higher percentage of air travellers with disabilities experience problems at airports than do their non-disabled counterparts: 55% versus 45%. The most frequently cited problems for both groups are schedules not being kept and restrictive security measures. However, these general issues were mentioned less often by travellers with disabilities than by the non-disabled. One in four travellers with disabilities (25.39%) complained of schedules not being kept compared to more than one in

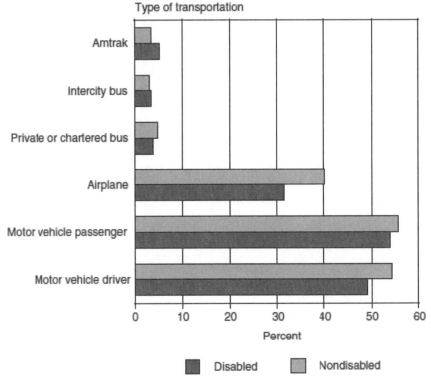

Figure 6.6 Transportation used for long-distance travel during past year
Source: U.S. Department of Transportation, Bureau of Transportation
Statistics, *2002 National Transportation Availability and Use Survey*.
Cited in *Freedom to Travel*, p. 9

three (37.66%) travellers with no disability. Restrictive security measures
bothered one in three (34.12%) travellers with disabilities versus almost one
in two (49.13) travellers with no disability (BTS, 2003: 9). Instead, those
with disabilities complained more often of staff assistance/poor sensitivity,
inadequate seating, too much walking and unavailable wheelchairs. More
travellers with disabilities also experienced problems on airplanes: 32.91%
versus 23.61% of those without disabilities. In each case, the biggest griev-
ance was inadequate seating: 68.61% among complainants with disabilities,
52.44% among those without (BTS, 2003: 36–37).

Discussion

As both the ODO Studies and BTS Survey show, the travel market
among Americans with disabilities is sizeable. Although one cannot strictly
compare their results since ODO excluded children and persons with

mental/cognitive disabilities from its samples, both reveal that the majority of Americans with disabilities are making long distance trips. In the BTS survey, 60% of respondents travelled within a one-year period, while 71% of the ODO respondents in 2002 and 69% in 2005 had travelled over a two-year period, making on average two trips. By referencing a two-year period in its surveys, ODO explicitly seeks to include that part of the market that travels less frequently, but nonetheless does travel long distance. Respondents taking one trip in a two-year period totalled 11% in 2002 and 12% in 2005 (see Figure 6.1).

Among those travelling long distance, 31.49% in the BTS survey used a commercial airplane (BTS, 2003: Table 29, p. 350), which equates to 10.2 million air travellers with disabilities per year. ODO's 2002 study found that 30% of adults with disabilities, or 9.4 million, had flown over a two-year period, making an average of two flights each. In ODO's 2005 study this increased to 31% or 9.6 million. Thus, the ODO and BTS estimates on air travel by persons with disabilities are very similar. So are their figures for long distance travel by bus and train. While BTS reports usage of 3.49% for intercity bus, 4.02% for private or chartered bus and 5.15% for Amtrak/intercity train (figures that may overlap) over a one-year period (BTS, 2003: Table 28, p. 34), ODO in 2005 found bus and train usage together to be 11% over two years. Paid ground transport is clearly much less popular than both airplanes and personal motor vehicles.

While the BTS and ODO studies both explore the problems facing long distance travellers with disabilities, the overall percentages and specific complaints vary significantly. In the 2005 ODO study, 84% of air travellers experienced problems with airlines and 82% with airports. By comparison, 33% of air travellers in the BTS survey experienced problems with airlines and 55% with airports. As noted above, these percentages were significantly higher than for their non-disabled counterparts. In both ODO and BTS studies, problems with onboard seating topped the list of complaints against airlines. One should note that in the BTS survey, 'schedule not kept' somehow wound up in the airport rather than airline tally. The issue of long queues, a major complaint among ODO respondents, was not a choice in the BTS survey (BTS, 2003: Tables 30–31, pp. 33–37). On the other hand, ODO did not include general issues affecting all travellers such as delayed flights.

Conclusion

Thanks to the studies referenced, we now know much more about American travellers with disabilities than we did prior to 2002. Rather than just a problem to be faced – although the above certainly indicates that many problems remain – travellers with disabilities now represent a real economic opportunity for the businesses who serve and market to them.

Although the old stereotype was that people with disabilities are too poor or incapacitated to travel, in actuality they represent a broad spectrum of wealth and ability. Yes, many individuals are not travelling long distance and may never leave their homes due to severe disability or poverty. At the other end of the spectrum are a significant number of frequent or heavy travellers making multiple trips per year and even spending heavily overseas. Internet use among travellers with disabilities, both to plan and book travel, may exceed that of the general travelling public. So may the percentage of Americans with disabilities taking cruise vacations.

As Baby Boomers age and become more prone to disabling conditions over the next several decades, the need for greater accessibility in travel and tourism will continue to expand. That trend alone should guarantee many more research studies to come, as businesses and governmental authorities demand yet more insight into this complex and evolving market. A follow-up market study by the Bureau of Transportation Statistics is due to be released in 2010, and the Open Doors Organization plans to commission a third nationwide survey among adults with disabilities in the near future as well.

Those interested in not only the current state of the disability travel market in the US but also the factors that led to its relatively advanced development may also like to read 'Toward A Global History of Accessible Travel' (Van Horn and Isola, 2006).

References

Bureau of Transportation Statistics (BTS) (2002) *Transportation Availability and Use Survey*. Washington, DC: US Department of Transportation. Available at: http://www.bts.gov/programs/omnibus_surveys/targeted_survey/2002_national_transportation_availability_and_use_survey/

Bureau of Transportation Statistics (BTS) (2003) *Freedom to Travel*, BTS03-08. Washington, DC: US Department of Transportation. Available at: www.bts.gov/publications/freedom_to_travel.

Open Doors Organization (2002) *Research Among Adults With Disabilities: Travel and Hospitality*. Chicago: Open Doors Organization.

Open Doors Organization (2005) *Research Among Adults With Disabilities: Travel and Hospitality*. Chicago: Open Doors Organization.

Sweeney, M. (2004) *Travel Patterns of Older Americans with Disabilities*, 2004-001-OAS. Washington, DC: US Department of Transportation. Available at: www.bts.gov/programs/bts_working_papers/2004/paper_01/

Van Horn, L. and Isola, J. (2006) Toward A Global History of Accessible Travel, *Review of Disability Studies*, 2(2), 5–23. Available at: www.rds.hawaii.edu.

7 Accessible Tourism in Australia

Simon Darcy, Bruce Cameron and Stephen Schweinsberg

Introduction

Over recent years there has been an increasing body of work on the intersections between disability, ageing and tourism. This research aims to provide a review of the last 30 years of the Australian accessible tourism industry. It has been completed in Australia (Darcy, 1998, 2000, 2002; Darcy & Daruwalla, 1999, 2000; Daruwalla, 1999; O'Neill & Ali Knight, 2000), Canada (Foggin, 2000), as well as in the USA (Burnett & Bender-Baker, 2001; Harris Interactive Market Research, 2003; Ray & Ryder, 2003), UK (English Tourism Council, 2000; Goodall, 2002), Israel (Israeli, 2002), Hong Kong (McKercher *et al.*, 2003), the Asia Pacific (Foggin *et al.*, 2004) and Finland (Arola, 2000). While the existing research base has done much to interrogate supply and demand issues relating to the disabled tourism market; to date there has been little attention paid to the role of government in tourism, particularly the role of government in accessible tourism.

There are a number of reasons why governments may seek active involvement in tourism planning. Veal (2002) notes that the size and multi-year time-frames of long term tourism strategies often mean that planning is beyond the individual capabilities of the private sector. Recent events such as Severe Acute Respiratory Syndrome. (SARS) have highlighted the need for active involvement of governments in tourism planning. McKercher and Chon (2003) note that it was an absence of centralised coordination amongst governments that was responsible for the 'sequential, country by country unveiling of reactive responses [to SARS]'. Within a capitalist market system of economic organization the rationales for intervening in the market are clearly defined (Parsons, 1995; Veal, 2002). Government roles in tourism generally involve planning, legislation and regulation, government as entrepreneur and stimulation (Mill & Morrison, 1985). However, in Australia apart from coordination of domestic and international marketing, these largely take place outside of the charter of the tourism departments and tourism marketing authorities, and are the responsibility of other government departments. In Australia, Tourism Marketing Authorities (TMAs) are statutory authorities charged with specific tourism charters under Commonwealth and State legislation (Davis *et al.*, 1993).

In dissecting the role of government in Accessible Tourism, this chapter provides a short history of the last 30 years of Accessible Tourism in Australia. It provides a review of policy initiatives and private industry activities in accessible tourism from the mid 1980s to 2009. The premise is that most significant achievements resulting in major steps forward have been at the hand of private initiatives, and as a result of the efforts of a few individuals who have 'driven' accessible tourism. However, those initiatives could not have occurred without a framework provided by legislation, infrastructure and public bodies such as TMA (or at least semi-public) body impetus.

This chapter considers the role of TMAs in promoting the industry and reviewing the 'priority' or otherwise afforded to Accessible Tourism. It takes a chronological approach to major accessible tourism developments in Australia developing a framework for guiding future accessible developments.

For the purpose of this chapter the following working definitions and acronyms shown in Table 7.1 have been adopted.

Rationales for Government Involvement in Tourism

In Table 7.2, the tourism industry sectors outlined by Leiper (2003) and Weaver and Oppermann (2000) have been combined into one list, and the relationship between the tourism industry (TI) and the tourism marketing authorities (TMA), as used in this chapter are indicated. Further, the table indicates the relative level of involvement of public sector and private enterprise in each sector, indicating that, despite significant public sector involvement, provision of tourism goods and services is overwhelmingly in the hands of the private sector. The table reflects the situation in Australia, whilst acknowledging that the pattern of public-private sector involvement varies considerably from country to country.

The approach that an STO or TMA takes to managing issues and stakeholder sectors is affected by their ideology. Ideologies in their simplest form can be thought of as sets of ideas about the way to organize the world (Veal, 2002: 20). Ideologies are constructed truths that become the basis for social action (Leach, 1993). Hall (1998: 88) identifies that tourism is largely a private sector industry. As a private sector industry, the tourism industry adopts the capitalist market ideology of the private sector. Tourism is seen as an industry organized, like any other industry, to maximise financial return. Further, as suggested by (Elliott, 1997), it is the tourism industry which has a primary role in developing tourism product: accommodation,

TABLE 7.1 Definitions and defining the tourism industry (TI) and tourism marketing authorities (TMA)

Term	Definition
Accessible Tourism	The meaning of accessible tourism has evolved over time and is best enunciated in work by Darcy (2005) and Darcy and Dickson (2009) reflecting the Sydney Olympic Coordination Authority's Access Guidelines for the Sydney 2000 Olympic and Paralympic Games, which defined accessible tourism as:
	'Accessible tourism enables people with access requirements, including mobility, vision, hearing and cognitive dimensions of access, to function independently and with equity and dignity through the delivery of universally designed tourism products, services and environments. This definition is inclusive of all people including those travelling with children in prams, people with disabilities and seniors.'
STO	State Tourism Organization, for example where TMA are State Government bodies such as Tourism New South Wales. STOs are regional bodies reflecting a local government input with local operator membership, such as Eurobodalla Tourism.
TMA	Tourism Marketing Authority refers to Tourism Australia, on a national level and State Government bodies such as Tourism New South Wales.
TI	Tourism Industry

TABLE 7.2 Defining the Tourism industry (TI) and tourism marketing authorities (TMA)

Sectors	TI or TMA	Public/private sector involvement		
		Private	Private and Public	Public
Travel authorities	TI	✓		
Carrier sector	TI		✓	
Accommodation sector	TI	✓		
Food and beverages	TI	✓		
Attractions sector	TI/TMA		✓	
Tour operator sector	TI	✓		
Merchandisers and miscellaneous sector	TI	✓		
Coordinating sector	TMA			✓

hotels and resorts, theme parks, travel agents and tour guides and transportation. This role was emphasised by the Australian Government's Committee of Inquiry into Tourism (1987) who noted that the provision of facilities and services to satisfy tourists should be done in a way to maximise financial returns. Even public sector operators, who have a primary function to serve local residents – for example, railways in the carrier sector and museums in the attractions sector – tend to adopt a market ideology when considering tourism.

Tourism and the Role of Government

In May 2008 the Australian Commonwealth Government announced the development of a steering committee to formulate a long term strategy for the Australian Tourism sector. This report, which has become known as *The Jackson Report* reported on a number of supply side/productive capacity issues influencing the Commonwealth's ability to maximise the net benefit of the tourism sector to the Australian economy. Supply side issues that were considered included: infrastructure development; research and statistics; labour and skills; digital technologies, distribution and market access; investment and leadership (Jackson *et al.*, 2009). Other policy documents including the *Tourism White Paper* (Australian Commonwealth Government, 2004) have placed considerable weight on demand side issues. As part of this strategy, the Commonwealth established Tourism Australia with the expressed charter of working with state agencies to 'vigorously market a revitalised Brand Australia in key global markets' (Australian Commonwealth Government, 2004: ix). These and other initiatives have done a lot to interrogate supply and demand issues relating to the national tourism industry. To date, however, there has been little expressed attention paid to the role of government in tourism planning and management, and particularly with respect to government involvement in the accessible tourism sector.

In 2003–2004 it is estimated that tourists with a disability spent a total of A\$8034.68 million. This amount comprises overnight tourism (A\$4822.39 million), day-tripper tourism (A\$1596.00 million), outbound tourism (A\$222.29 million) and inbound tourism (A\$1394.00 million) (Darcy & Dwyer, 2008). Tourism receipts form one of the core indicators of the success of a tourism industry when seen as part of a broader market economy. Within a capitalist market system of economic organization the rationales for intervening in the market are clearly defined (Parsons, 1995; Veal, 2002). Government roles in tourism generally involve planning, legislation and regulation, government as entrepreneur and stimulation (Mill & Morrison, 1985). However, in Australia these largely take place outside of the charter of the STOs and TMAs and are the responsibility of other government departments. STOs and TMAs are statutory authorities charged with specific tourism charters under Commonwealth and state legislation (Davis *et al.*, 1993). This section reviews the STO and TMA role as coordinator for the Australian tourism industry.

Government involvement in tourism has had a close relationship with the private sector as a way to improve the economic contribution of tourism to the host economies (Hall & Jenkins, 1995; Veal, 2002). This economic imperative is a consistent feature of national tourism policies across nations (Baum, 1994; Elliott, 1997). As Hall (1998) documents, this has been the situation in Australia at the Commonwealth and state levels. However, as Fayos-Solá (1996) argues, the strategies for achieving the economic imperative have changed from pure marketing to product development through market segmentation to maintaining competitiveness. Yet, as Goeldner *et al.* (1999) suggest, the success of tourism destinations and hence, tourism policies, involve both competitiveness and sustainability. The STOs and TMAs charged with tourism marketing for competitiveness have little understanding of planning for sustainability, and the areas of government charged with planning for sustainability of tourism tend to have little understanding of marketing. This poses questions as to where disability would be addressed within tourism policy: marketing or planning?

Table 7.3 presents represents two interpretations of the different rationales for government involvement in tourism planning. Veal (2002: 64–65) outlines the various rationales for state involvement in mainstream economic terms. Rationales are grouped under first order national defence and law and order rationales, as well as rationales related to market failure (incl. public goods and services, and option demand) and socio-political arguments (including equity or humanitarian measures). These rationales for government intervention are discussed in relation to the broader leisure industries. In contrast, Hall (1998) bases his analysis on Mill and Morrison's (1985) rationale for intervention in tourism with the addition of social

TABLE 7.3 Rationales for government involvement in tourism industries

Hall (1998)	Veal (2002)	Veal (2002)
Coordination	*Mainstream economic*	*Socio-political*
Planning	Public goods	Equity
Legislation/regulation	Mixed goods	Economic management
Entrepreneur	Merit goods	Tradition
Stimulation	Option demand	Incidental enterprises
and social tourism	Size of project	
	Externalities	
	Natural monopoly	
	Infant industries	

tourism. When reviewing the major state and Commonwealth statutory tourism authorities, the major rationales involve a combination of coordinating an industry wide approach to international marketing due to the potential 'invisible export' economic contribution that tourism can make to the economy. This is partly due to the competitive nature of the industry and a need to present a collaborative marketing brand to major international markets. The Australian Tourist Commission and its successors then the vast majority of their budget on these two rationales with relatively little engagement in other more environmentally or socially orientated rationales. This is largely left to other departments and other levels of government. This economic management rationale (Veal, 2002) is complemented by a coordination role in overseas marketing of tourism to Australia (Hall, 1998). In the Australian context, government has historically led the tourism industry by coordinating tourism marketing and market research (Hall, 1998).

The coordination role was seen as necessary because of the fragmented nature of the tourism industry. Coordination has been undertaken by STOs and TMAs established by Commonwealth and state governments with the specific charter to market international tourism into Australia. This role has changed little since the inception of the STOs and TMAs. Recently, a greater emphasis has been placed on domestic tourism due to the series of external shocks since 2001, including the September 11th attack on the World Trade Centre in New York, the Bali bombing, SARS and the Iraq conflict (Tourism Forecasting Council, 2003). The STOs and TMAs were deliberately established at 'arms length' from government to reduce bureaucratic control and promote a more 'marketable' corporate and, hence, private-sector approach (King & Hyde, 1989). This close relationship between STOs and TMAs and the tourism industry was reinforced in 2002 with government tourism responsibilities being incorporated into the Commonwealth Department of Industry, Tourism and Resources.

The government legislation establishing the STOs and TMAs encouraged them to adopt the ethos of the private sector tourism industry with whom they represent. The role of the STOs and TMAs has had an emphasis on marketing and market segmentation through the collective marketing of destinations and as the conductor of market research (Hall, 1998). Within these roles, STOs and TMAs are dominated by the private sector market ideology of yield where markets are segmented and chosen for the level of profit that is provided to the state per tourist captured (Hall, 1998). This has been reflected in the marketing strategies of all Commonwealth and state STOs and TMAs (Clark, 2002; Commonwealth Department of Tourism, 1995d). While economists may argue over methodologies and the best ways of strategically planning to maximise yield, little else is considered by national tourist offices in their decision-making criteria (Calantone &

Mazanec, 1991). Perceptions of yield have changed over time as research about market segments was undertaken. For example, in Australia in the late 1980s there was a concentration by Australian STOs and TMAs on Asian inbound markets. However, it was not until the early 1990s that there was a differentiation made between high yield (Japan) and low yield (Korea) Asian markets (Griffin & Darcy, 1997). Similarly, only after two significant research studies on the backpacker market (Loker, 1993; Pearce, 1990) did perception change to recognise the value of the backpackers (Commonwealth Department of Tourism, 1995a, 1995b, 1995c; Haigh, 1995).

A number of areas have been omitted in the examination of tourism as market and the role of government in tourism. These omissions may have implications for disability and tourism. Firstly, concerning whether or not the perceptions of market segments by the decision-makers within STOs and TMAs and the tourism industry affect the tourism policy decisions and industry practice. Secondly, while it is acknowledged that the tourism lobby in Australia exerts tremendous influence over government (Craik, 1991; Hall & Jenkins, 1995), little evidence exists of how this occurs in practice. Unfortunately it seems the accessible tourism market has yet to influence the TMA to the extent that it accepts responsibility for promoting and marketing accessible tourism on a domestic or international level.

Disability Tourism Initiatives

The next section of this chapter will present an analysis of disability-related tourism initiatives that have been enacted by the Commonwealth, State Governments and others. Comment will be made about the approaches of these policies and initiatives. Appendix 7.1 provides a summary of Commonwealth Government initiatives and Appendix 7.2, a synopsis of State initiatives. A commentary of the emergent themes follows.

Table 7.4 identifies a simplified Timeline for access related initiatives in Australia 1981 – 2009, drawn from the data in Appendices 1 and 2. It is colour coded to assist highlight three sources of initiatives: Commonwealth, State and Private. The two left hand side columns represent Commonwealth Departments or agencies and their outcomes while the two right hand columns represent State or Private agencies initiatives and their outcomes.

Considering Table 7.4, it can be inferred that State Governments have been the most proactive in improving the day-to-day accessible tourism inclusions for people with disabilities. This has not been driven not by TMA but by people with disabilities' desire to be fully participating citizens and a legal framework in which to achieve this outcome. Each state has its own anti-discrimination legislation and environmental planning framework in which discrimination and access related issues can be addressed. However, the Building Codes of Australia and the Australian Standards for Access and

TABLE 7.4 Timeline of access-related tourism initiatives in Australia 1981–2009

Commonwealth Responsible Agency	Outcome/document	Timeline	State or private responsible Agency	Outcome/document
		1981	NSW Department of Tourism	Tourism and disability stakeholder seminar – IYPD
Comm.Gov.	Accommodation Information	1982		
	Australian Standards	1986	AS1428 - Access & Mobility	(AS 1428)
Comm. Attorney General	Disability Services Act includes Tourism	1986	The Wheel Resort, Byron Bay, NSW (North Coast)	Accessible Accommodation – Resort Style
Comm. Dept. of Sport, Recreation and Tourism	Accessibility guide to tourist attractions in Australia			
Department of Aviation	Australian Airport facilities for people with disabilities	1987		
Australian National Parks Service	Park Access: Report Series No. 10			
	Comm. Disability	1992	Discrimination	Act
Dept. of Family and Community Services	NICAN Established, recreation and tourism			
Australian Tourist Commission	Fact Sheet – Travel in Australia for People with a disability	1994	Accessing Sydney Acrod NSW Div.	Access Guide to Sydney
		1995	Clark Bay Farm, Narooma, NSW (South Coast)	Accessible Accommodation – Resort Style
	Easy Access Australia – A Travel guide to Australia			Travel Guide

TABLE 7.4 Continued

Commonwealth Responsible Agency	Outcome/document	Timeline	State or private responsible Agency	Outcome/document
		1996	Accessing Brisbane	Access Guide to the City of Brisbane
		1997	Western Australian Disability Services Commission (WADSC)	Accessing New Markets: TI Think Tank Report
			Tourism Tasmania (TT)	Tourist information for people with disabilities
National Office of Tourism	Tourism for All Campaign	1998	ACT, Canberra Tourism and Events Corporation	Access Information
Bureau of Tourism Research.	National Visitor Survey		Tourism NSW (TNSW) Darcy (1998)	Anxiety to Access
		1999	Accessing Melbourne	Access Guide to the City of Melbourne
			(Toowoomba and Golden West Regional Tourist Association, 1999)	Access the best guide – Toowoomba
Dept. of Family and Community Services	Gold Medal Access Strategy		ACT, Canberra Tourism and Events Corp	Access Info Website Discovery, magazine
Australian Tourist Commission	Facts for the Visitor: Disabled visitors. Poor quality information		Queensland Tourist and Travel Corp	Accessible Queensland

TABLE 7.4 Continued

Commonwealth Responsible Agency	Outcome/document	Timeline	State or private responsible Agency	Outcome/document
			South Australian Tourism Commission	*Tourism Strategy for People with Disabilities ACCESSIBLE: Making it easier to discover South Australia* *Disability access audits*
		2000	Tourism NSW	*Disability Action Plan:1 January 2000 to 31 December 2002*
			Tourism Queensland (TQ)	*A Guide to Accessible Caravan Parks in Queensland* (J. Graham 2000)
			Tourism Queensland	*A schedule of service providers and accessible public infrastructure Accessible Queensland Images* *Accessible Queensland Website*
			O'Carrollyns at One Mile Beach,	*Accessible Accommodation – Resort Style*
			Easy Access Australia – A Travel guide to Australia, Ed 2	*Travel Guide*
	SYDNEY OLYMPIC	2000	GAMES	

TABLE 7.4 Continued

Commonwealth Responsible Agency	Outcome/document	Timeline	State or private responsible Agency	Outcome/document
Australian Tourism Data Warehouse (Aust Tour Comm)	NO access information provision	2001		
Comm. Department of Industry Tourism and Resources	Green and white paper Identified Access as a niche market segment			
		2002	Access Sydney	Ausralian Quadriplegic Association
Bureau of Tourism Research	National Visitor Survey incl. disability module	2003	STO and Commonwealth accessible tourism steering committee	STO and Commonwealth officers with the accessible tourism responsibility
Tourism Australia	Accessible drive tourism routes/day trips	2004		
Commonwealth	Games, Melbourne	2005	Accessing Melbourne, 2nd edn	Access Guide to the City of Melbourne
		2007	Tourism Victoria	Accessible Tourism Strategy (Commenced)
				Access Alpine Information to Alpine Areas
		2008		Sustainable Tourism Cooperative Research Centre Research - Accommodation, Precinct and Vision
				Australia for All website
			Tourism New South Wales	Sydney for all Web portal

Mobility apply across Australia, setting the benchmark for access to new developments and major renovations to the public built environment.

Importantly, all states are subject to the Federal *Disability Discrimination Act, 1992* (DDA). This Act has empowered individuals with disabilities to pursue individual cases of disability discrimination and seek satisfactory outcomes. While it is beyond the scope of his chapter to examine these outcomes, it can be seen from the Table 7.3 that post the DDA, important initiatives from the private sector became more likely.

It is also interesting to note there was a great deal of major activity in the lead up to the Sydney Olympic Games in 2000, with the major states of NSW, Victoria and Queensland all undertaking programs designed to attract visitors to the state. However, these initiatives didn't reflect any strategic approach to accessible tourism, rather an opportunistic effort to attract visitors pre and post Olympics and Paralympics.

Commonwealth Government initiatives

In its 1992 strategic policy statement, the Commonwealth Department of Tourism (Commonwealth Department of Tourism, 1992) identified the broad issues affecting disability and tourism in Australia. Some of the inherent problems and weaknesses in existing arrangements were identified as costs of providing facilities, staff training, information base, physical access and transport. Subsequent policy statements (Office of National Tourism, 1997, 1998a) moved away from an issues-based approach to identify disability as one of a number of emerging special interest market segments. This approach sought to publicise development of the arts, cultural, indigenous, sports and educational tourism as well as tourism for seniors and people with a disability. Environmental and rural tourism were also initiatives (Office of National Tourism, 1998a). This was the only mention of these policies in the 1998 document, which did not provide a strategic agenda to implement them. Yet, since 1992, policy and research initiatives had been undertaken for many of the other segments mentioned but not for people with disabilities. This superficial approach continued with the most recent federal government discussion paper that states:

There are also significant opportunities for tourism products aimed at particular groups in the community, for example, seniors tourism, tourism for people with disabilities, and tourism aimed at 'enthusiast' niche markets (Commonwealth Department of Industry Tourism and Resources, 2002: 70).

Appendices 7.1 and 7.2 identify the Commonwealth and state initiatives that are reviewed below to analyse the 'ableist' discourse inherent in the Commonwealth government actions and inaction. These initiatives are broadly categorised in Table 7.5 to provide an overview of the areas of Commonwealth and state initiatives and, together with the academic literature form the basis of the following analysis.

TABLE 7.5 Commonwealth and state government initiative comparison, 1990–2009

Initiative

	NICAN*	ATC/TA	Com Dept	ACT	NSW	NT	QLD	SA	TAS	VIC	WA	Total
a. Disability Tourism Strategy Strategy Strategy or	✓							✓				2
Disability Action Plan					✓					✓	✓	3
b. Industry awareness campaign			✓									2
c. Private Sector Initiatives												
Fact Sheet		✓	✓							✓	✓	4
Brochure – integrated						✓						1
Self reported/on-line info	✓				✓	✓					✓	4
Third party access audit					✓			✓				2
Market-specific information			✓				✓					2
Image Library							✓					1
d. Tourism Disability Research	✓				✓	✓				✓		4

Source:* Funded by Department of Family and Community Services

The review of the STO and TMA initiatives is based on a review of published and unpublished literature and Internet sources as checked against STO and TMA officer interviews.

Disability Tourism Strategies/Disability Action Plans

Three state-based examples exist of a developed strategic approach to tourism and disability:

(1) a strategic plan developed in South Australia;
(2) a Disability Action Plan developed in New South Wales;
(3) a Strategic Accessible Tourism Plan being developed (at the time of writing), in Victoria.

In 1999, the South Australian Tourism Commission produced its *Tourism Strategy for People with Disabilities* (South Australian Tourism Commission, 1999b), which sought four outcomes:

(1) ensure South Australia is positioned as an accessible tourist destination for people with disabilities;
(2) ensure people with disabilities are able to easily access the South Australian tourism product;
(3) ensure people with disabilities are able to make an informed decision on tourism products in South Australia;
(4) ensure the tourism industry is aware of the benefits and the need to be responsive to the requirements of people with disabilities (SATC, 1999a: 6–7).

Each outcome was assigned a series of performance measures. However, no timeframes or responsibilities were assigned to achieve the outcomes. The SATC produced an accompanying brochure (SATC, 1999a) outlining examples of accessible regional attractions and experiences but it included only passing references to the accessible features of the attractions and experiences listed. The SATC commissioned a selected audit of tourism products for people with disabilities (SATC, 2000; Porter, 2001). The audit employed an access consultant to assess a selection of tourism products identified by a State Tourism Access Forum established to oversee these initiatives. The forum included people with disabilities and tourism industry expertise. However, the project was only funded for 12 months and further funding was not forthcoming to implement the results (Porter, 2001). A member of the forum subsequently stated his dissatisfaction with the non-implementation of a project that the forum group had worked on for a year (Heath, 2002).

The DDA provided a mechanism for organizations to address systemic disability and access issues through Disability Action Plans (DAPs). Tourism NSW is the only STO or TMA to have lodged a DAP to date (Tourism New South Wales, 2000). DAPs set out a strategic agenda that includes timeframes and responsibilities for improving disability access to facilities, services and employment. The NSW response was brought about by the general NSW government requirement for all agencies to formulate a DAP, so it was not undertaken voluntarily by Tourism NSW. Despite the existence of the DAP, product development in NSW has remained dormant, even though the recommendations of the DAP identified product development as crucial to providing opportunities for people with disabilities to travel in NSW. Tourism NSW has, however, supported a number of third party information sources (Australian Quadriplegic Association, 2002; Cameron, 2000).

A further initiative that had the potential to lay the grounds for a strategic and national approach to disability issues was a 1999 meeting of Commonwealth and State Tourism Commission policy officers called to discuss disability and tourism issues, prompted by the Sydney 2000 Olympic and Paralympic Games (Douglas, 1999). However, nothing occurred as a follow-up to this meeting, although the minutes suggest that the group were aware of many of the key issues that have been identified in this research.

The Victorian approach was initiated by Tourism Victoria (Tourism Victoria, 2007) to develop a strategy following community and industry input. A consultant was engaged to run workshops, gather views and information and with the oversight of a managing committee, develop a strategy. This process has occurred and a draft document has circulated for public comment. However, final publication was delayed as a consequence of the King Lake bushfires 2009.

Industry Awareness Campaigns

Two projects have been identified aimed at increasing general industry awareness of disability as a tourism issue. Both were Commonwealth initiatives.

The Commonwealth Office of National Tourism (ONT), *Tourism Challenge: Access for All* (Office of National Tourism, 1998b) publication appeared in the form of a set of 26 pages of loose-leaf information sheets with both hard copy and internet distribution. The kit detailed marketing, accommodation, transport, contact information and training practices, together with an explanation of relevant legislation and good practice examples. The objective of the project was to assist the tourism industry to better address the needs of tourists with a disability. The project emphasised the economic benefits of providing services for people with disabilities. The rationale was that it would lead to the provision of more products by tourism industry and, hence, opportunities for people with disabilities. The project had no published objectives and there were no resources to implement the project beyond the hard copy and Internet distribution. No outcomes of the initiative are known.

In 1999, the Commonwealth Department of Family and Community Services (CDFACS) and the Office of the Prime Minister initiated the *Gold Medal Disability Access Strategy* (Commonwealth Department of Family and Community Services, 1999). In a similar vein to the above ONT initiative, this document was designed to raise industry awareness of the economic benefits of improving access to facilities, goods and services for people with disabilities. The documentation consisted of a 'launch kit' of four one-page fact sheets for each of four key areas: employment; premises; tourism; and transport. The sheets referred to previous data sources (ABS, 1998 and Darcy, 1998) but no new information collection was envisaged.

The strategy did not indicate objectives, outcome measures, timeframes or responsibilities. Apart from the demonstrated lack of accountability of the strategy, there were also problems with its conceptualisation. In the foreword to the strategy, the Prime Minister stated: '. . .in the lead up to the

Sydney 2000 Olympic and Paralympic Games, the demand for access to facilities, goods and services by people with disabilities will certainly increase, from Australian residents as well as from overseas' (CDFACS, 1999c). This appeared to dismiss participation by people with disabilities in the community unless these events occurred. This apparent view was reinforced by the fact that the program was only funded for one year up to the period of the 2000 Games.

The Olympic and Paralympic Games became the focus for government to be seen to be doing something about disability and access issues over a short time period. While the government made use of the strategy for publicity about disability and access issues, it had very little involvement from disability groups. There was no formal consultation process with the disability sector.

Private Sector Initiatives

Tourism or holidays for people with disabilities existed well before the timeline shown in Table 7.4. People with intellectual impairments housed in institutions were periodically able to go away on trips as respite. It was a small step to incorporate people with access needs on these trips, if the access was available (personal communication in Darcy et al., 2008).

The first major step forward from the private sector was taken by two ladies, both wheelchair users who established a resort near Byron Bay, on the north coast of New South Wales. The Wheel Resort was the first resort in Australia to be specifically designed and constructed to be accessible with cabins constructed with no steps, sliding doors, cooking facilities with knee space underneath, open plan offering circulation space and accessible bathrooms comprising wheel-in showers, grab rails, lever taps and hand held shower rose. The property also comprised ramped entry to reception, a swimming pool with gently sloping ramp entry and accessible barbecue. Additional services such as attendant care, equipment and transport could be arranged.

It wasn't until 1995, almost a decade later, when the next accessible resort was constructed. Clark Bay Cottages was opened in 1995 at Narooma, south coast, New South Wales. Clark Bay Cottages went a step further than The Wheel Resort by making the property accessible for the carers of people with high support needs. Features included gentle (5%) graded ramps to automatic sliding doors, large living areas, kitchen area with height adjustable bench top comprising sink, cook top, microwave and kettle. The bathrooms all were wheel-in with grab rails, lever taps etc. Importantly, a ceiling mounted hoist was available to assist carers move someone from the bed into the bathroom with out the need for a physical lift. A huge games room was accessed by ramp, the swimming pool was lift equipped, attendant care and equipment was also available.

The year 1995 was significant for the publication of *Easy Access Australia – A Travel Guide to Australia* (EAA) (Cameron, 1995). EAA took two years to research and write and was several years in the planning. The guide was based on a simple premise: a trip to any major tourist region in Australia was likely to be accessible because many people were already going there, the question about access had already been asked and resolved. The problem was the lack of information, which EAA sought to address. EAA took a philosophical stance to provide information to the user who could then make up their own mind to travel, or to ask additional questions of the relevant property manager/owner. Up until this point in time access information, particularly accommodation was rated either Access Independent or Access with Assistance – whatever either of those definitions meant (ACROD, 1994, 1999; National Roads and Motorists Association (NRMA), 1999). EAA offered a unique alternative for providing information to potential travellers: a floorplan showing circulation spaces and accessible bathroom layouts, combined with key measurements such as toilet and grab rail heights.

Following the publication, it was apparent that Australia had a substantial stock of accommodations, experiences and attractions and transport options which offered access to travel. For example:

- Large number of motels and hotels offered at least one access room.
- Systems were in place to transport people with disabilities throughout Australia.
- Transport providers were becoming more aware of access so taxis are available in every major city and town, access buses are becoming more prevalent (except, sadly, on long haul trips) and accessible hire vehicles were available from each state.
- Care and equipment were available for short term stays in each of the major tourist destinations.

1998 saw a major development in the TI with a significant step taken shifting the 'feel good' communal aspects of access provision to a more market-oriented approach upon which arguments of economics and demand could be argued to support the case for access provision to wide spread accommodation, transport, attractions and experiences. Until this time there had been no market research undertaken anywhere in the world. The research entitled Anxiety to Access – The Travel Patterns of people with a Physical Disability in NSW (Darcy, 1998), provided the TMA and disability movements with market information which until this time had been purely anecdotal. For instance it identified that:

- The majority of people with a physical disability travelled with between two to five people in their group (mean 4.1). In the majority of cases (87%) they were the only member of their group with a disability.

- In the previous year 77% respondents had undertaken at least one domestic trip. A large number of these respondents had undertaken more than one trip with the average number of trips being 4.3.
- On average New South Wales people with a physical disability spent eight nights away on their domestic trip. The majority of trips were within the 1–5 nights range.
- It is estimated the market generated expenditure in the order of A$472 million Australia wide.
- The day trip market generated expenditure of some A$304 million Australia-wide.

The research was further developed by Darcy (2005) and Darcy *et al.*, (2008).

Two events occurred in the year 2000, Sydney hosted the Olympic and Paralympic Games and O'Carrollyn's at One Mile Beach opened. O'Carrollyn's embraced the concept of Universal Design Principles (Center for Universal Design, 2003) in creating a relaxing resort holiday environment in a bush setting, by the sea. The resort encompasses nine cabins comprising car parking, accessible paths of travel to level entries, open plan living area including kitchen with access to bench and sink, reachable facilities, lever taps, internal sliding doors, open plan accessible bathroom with lever taps, roll-in shower, hand held shower rose and grab rails for the shower and toilet.

An accessible path of travel is provided around the facility with graded concrete pathways leading to the lake, bridge, lookout, and fishing spot. An accessible performance stage is adjacent to an undercover barbecue area with conference/meeting room that has accessible bathroom facilities. A heated swim and spa pool, equipped with a hoist. Shower chairs, commode chairs, hoists, hospital beds, monkey bars and bed sticks are also available. In addition to the accommodation offered, O'Carrollyn's provides accessible holiday experiences with a 4WD vehicle and beach-wheelchair access, while local fauna such as koalas and echidnas roam the site. Its website features the access provisions made.

The inherent difficulty in respect to facilitating an accessible tourism industry is the lack of information. As can be seen the TMA and Commonwealth bodies have been poor at developing the industry. Two exceptions are noted. One is the Tourism Queensland initiative of the late 1990s in promulgating access tourism information, the other is the initiative towards inclusive practices adopted by the City of Melbourne (City of Melbourne, 2006) which commissioned and published a suite of access documents designed to facilitate better access for its residents and travellers (Melbourne Mobility Map, Accessible Eating Guide and Access Melbourne). It is no coincidence that a major initiative occurred prior to the Commonwealth Games in 2006.

During the period 2003 to 2009 the State Government in Western Australia, via the Disability Services Commission Western Australia (DSC WA) has been extremely active developing a programme entitled You're Welcome WA Access Initiative. The initiative seeks to address access issues identified by people with disabilities as being of major concern to them.

The You're Welcome WA project is led through community consultation via a team of key stakeholder organizations including local government, people with disabilities and state government including Tourism WA. The project developed three objectives which resulted in strategies, which are particularly informative for this project:

(1) 'Collecting accurate access information so that people with disabilities know how to access local business and community attractions, services and facilities.'
(2) 'Developing and maintaining easy-to-obtain online access information to publicise community business and attractions.'
(3) 'Providing practical information to assist business and community groups expand their customer base by making their services more access friendly.'

It is important to note that information provision is a key plank in the strategy. In 2008 the project launched its website (http://www.accesswa.com.au/Default.asp) containing access information gathered around the state. The information is accessed by a search facility, while population of data is an ongoing exercise.

In 2007 a web-based database was launched, australiaforall.com, designed to allow 'tourists with disabilities and their families to obtain information about the accessibility of the accommodation and tourism venues which they wish to visit'. Information is provided 'that is reliable and can be trusted as it is based on a consensus regarding the criteria levels and standards for accessibility'.

The information provided is self assessed and/or photographically verified to meet criteria levels which are defined as: M1, M2 HS, H and V representing; people who are ambulant (M1), wheelchair users (M2), wheelchair users with high support needs (HS) (denoted by an icon of person in a sling!), and people with hearing (H) and vision (V) needs.

Tourism Disability Research

The Australian tertiary sector has been at the forefront of moves to raise the profile of the disabled tourism sector. In July 2005, a Sustainable Tourism Cooperative Research Centre Research (STCRC) workshop was held titled *Setting a Research Agenda for Disability and Tourism*. This event drew together approximately 45 key academic researchers, industry partners, community organizations and government representatives with the aim to (Darcy, 2005):

- Assess and critique the state of accessible tourism in Australia;
- Identify current research gaps and opportunities for necessary collaborative research, and;
- Establish a prioritised research agenda for accessible tourism in Australia for the STCRC.

From this workshop a number of recommendations were made to further enhance the sustainability sector nationally. One recommendation related specifically to the need for collaborative engagement of government in accessible tourism planning emerged to investigate an internal government driver of accessible tourism through cooperative Commonwealth and state government Tourism Ministers' Council (Darcy, 2006).

Table 7.6 provides a breakdown of the aims; methodologies and core outcomes of Australian based accessible tourism research since the 2005 research agenda meeting.

Conclusions

Australia has a quite long and varied history in the area of accessible tourism dating back to the early 1980s. The Commonwealth Government has had a substantial impact on accessibility with two initiatives which have served as a foundation upon which State Government and private organizations could develop an industry; The Building Code of Australia and the Australian Standards for Access and the Disability Discrimination Act 1992.

However, apart from programmes and initiatives such as creating and funding NICAN (which wasn't a specific tourism initiative) and Tourism Australia's Accessible Touring Routes, very little has been done by the Commonwealth to develop, foster and promote the accessible tourism industry. There certainly was a push in the lead up to the Sydney Olympic Games but primarily from the state based TMAs.

The private sector has seen the demand and requirement for the provision of access so it's not surprising this sector has made the biggest commitment to provision of product and information. Yet it is the lack of credible, reliable and accurate information, especially in respect to accessible accommodation, which continually surfaces during research into the needs of travellers with disabilities. Despite the market estimates (Darcy, 2008) and financial success of providers (and identified but unquantified inbound access market), there remains no overarching national approach to marketing, promotion or information provision.

TABLE 7.6 Post 2005 accessible tourism research summary

Title and Authors	Objectives	Methodology	Key Findings
'Tourist Experiences Of Individuals With Vision Impairment' Packer, Small and Darcy (2008)	This research aimed to understand the experience of travelling with vision impairment. Travelling with vision impairment is a poorly researched subject, so this research was the first step in a process designed to gain an understanding of whether a market exists and the potential of any vision tourism market.	The research approach was informed by a social constructionist approach to disability which views disability as a product of social relationships. This approach firmly places disability on the social, economic and political agendas rather than locating disability as the fault of an individual's impairment. Using an inductive, qualitative and iterative approach that drew on grounded and phenomenological traditions, the study explored the tourist experiences of people with vision impairment through in-depth interviews and focus groups. All were transcribed verbatim and content analysis was undertaken.	Enforcement of legislation was seen as the role of governments. Introduction of legislation mandating equal access (free entrance to companions, auditory and tactile safety features etc.) was suggested as ways for governments to improve equity of access.

TABLE 7.6 Continued

Title and Authors	Objectives	Methodology	Key Findings
'Accessible Summer Alpine Tourism' Dickson (2008)	The total project involve three phases: Assessing: facilities, conducting workshops to develop capacity to provide accessible tourism opportunities, and developing resources and marketing strategies	To achieve this, the research design involved four methods. 1. Access audit/Management Information Systems 2. Semi-structured interviews with key precinct stakeholders 3. Observation research of precinct areas 4. Workshops As stated, this research project developed an access overlay for precinct operations and the marketing of the precinct experience to people with access requirements. This involved taking complex technical information based on the Building Codes of Australia (1996) and the Australian Standards (Standards Australia, 1992, 1993, 2001) and transforming this information into spatial and experiential dimensions (for further information see Darcy et al., 2008)	In conclusion, this project has provided an excellent demonstration of the possibilities of a strategic approach to accessible tourism within clearly defined geographic areas (Darcy, 2006, Darcy et al., 2008). By specifically targeting the accessible tourism market and working in collaboration with others in the tourism destination area, accessible destination experiences can be promoted and branded to create a competitive advantage through a strategic approach to accessible tourism (Leiper et al., 2008). What stakeholders found empowering was that the project sought to build upon current infrastructure, abilities and product through providing a framework to interpret, present and disseminate access information that required no changes to the way that they operated. While the approach required time to attend the workshops and to work with the project team, there were no extra costs involved. Once this investment in time had been made it was efficient for the organizations as they could disseminate information permanently through their own websites and continuously through consumer enquiries. The destination approach then provided those involved with collaborative edge as the destination became an accessible destination area complete with infrastructure and experiences beyond their individual enterprises.

TABLE 7.6 Continued

Title and Authors	Objectives	Methodology	Key Findings
'Visitor Accessibility in Urban Areas' Darcy, Cameron, Dwyer, Taylor, Wong and Thomson (2008)	The research was designed to evaluate urban tourism environments in the context of universal design principles.	This research adopted an action research strategy. The overall approach was informed by universal design, the experience economy and a geographic hierarchy of accessible tourism, based on individual facilitators, access precincts and accessible touring routes. A management information systems audit was conducted. In addition, primary data were collected by means of in-depth interviews with industry stakeholders, observation and participant observation. As determined by the IRG the precinct study area is the main Sydney tourism precinct that incorporates: • The transport hub from Central Station to Circular Quay • East and West Circular Quay • The Rocks • Royal Botanic Gardens • Sydney Harbour environs and Sydney Harbour National Park • Manly Ferry, Manly boardwalk and North Head Lookout.	The web portal www.sydneyforall.com is an outcome from the Visitor Accessibility in Urban Areas research but deserving of a specific separate mention as it provides innovation to information delivery for visitor attractions and experiences. The web site is access information weighted but incorporates access provisions for people with vision and hearing impairment while the site is 'customisable to the users needs'. It won an award from Vision Australia for its functionality for people with vision impairment.

TABLE 7.6 Continued

Title and Authors	Objectives	Methodology	Key Findings
'Developing Business Case Studies For Accessible Tourism' Darcy, S., Cameron, B., Pegg, S. and Packer, T. (2008)	The objectives of the research project were to: • document the business case for accessible tourism through the development of business based case studies of successful operators • identify examples of 'best practice' in delivery of accessible tourism product • identify the key indicators or key result areas to measure the business case, social case and environmental case	Due to the relative lack of attention to accessible tourism business case studies within academic and business research, an explorative qualitative research approach is appropriate. Such an approach was employed using selected cases as the objects for study. The methodology was informed by case study approaches and the triple bottom line scorecard. The research design sought to expand the thinking in general business to consider performance more broadly than financial measures. The evaluation of environmental and social benefits has become part of core corporate practice. The preliminary work utilised a Delphi group to identify a range of high standard of accessible product, across states, segments and reflecting a range of ownership structures. The next stage involved developing a Business Case Instrument to 'capture' triple bottom line metrics. The metrics' work collected through reviews of management information systems, in-depth interviews with key informants and review of financial and performance information.	The research developed a BCI comprising a series of Key Indicators or Key Result Areas to reflect good business practice meeting the components of the Triple Bottom Line concept, reflecting a call for the tourism industry to adopt universal design principles as a foundation to achieving greater social sustainability as part of the triple bottom line: • Financial Report Card • Environmental Report Card • Social Report Card

TABLE 7.6 Continued

Title and Authors	Objectives	Methodology	Key Findings
	• develop and refine a Business Case Instrument to reflect the key result areas and facilitate data collection • collect information and document each business case, social case and environmental case • use innovative methods of information presentation to present the above measured information • develop an innovative format to present the case studies to industry to demonstrate the benefits to the triple bottom line for the provision of inclusive tourism practices		

TABLE 7.6 Continued

Title and Authors	Objectives	Methodology	Key Findings
'Accessible Tourism Accommodation Information' Preferences Working Paper 10 Darcy (2008)	The objectives of the research sought to: Provide information about accessible accommodations in the four currently available formats to people with disabilities to determine whether the information met their access needs; Ascertain which format was preferred; Determine whether the participants perception of the accessible information reflected the reality of the accessible room by conducting room inspections; Uncover the perceptions of hotel managers towards the accessible accommodation; and Establish the perceptions of non-disabled customers towards accessible accommodation.	Access audits were undertaken of 10 hotels with the accessible accommodation and this information was translated into the four information formats. One of these hotels was chosen as the basis for testing the four information formats. An online questionnaire was developed to: Determine the relative importance of access criteria identified under the Building Code of Australia to people with disabilities; Test the four formats of presenting access criteria; and Provide a profile of the respondents. A sample of the participants who completed the online survey inspected the rooms to judge whether there was a true reflection of the information provided. In-depth interviews with accommodation managers to ascertain their perceptions and practices towards accessible accommodation. With regard to the formats of information provision, the literature revealed that there were four ways accessible information was presented in Australia and overseas (Buhalis, Michopoulou, Michailidis, and Ambrose, 2006; OSSATE, 2005).	The research outcomes included a template for assessing accessible accommodation and this anecdotal suggestions that iconography or rating systems for accessible accommodation were misguided. Simplification of the high level of detail required by the Building Code of Australia and the Australian Standards for Access and Mobility is not possible in a rating system.

The most strategically focused model for developing an accessible tourism industry must be that evolving in Western Australia under the You're Welcome WA initiative. Any country seeking to develop its accessible tourism industry can draw on the Australian experience which lacks a national focus. A developing industry should seek to develop a national responsibility for the marketing and promotion of accessible tourism product. The acceptance of marketing responsibility will encourage the private sector to develop and provide accessible product.

Hopefully, the future will include a greater number of information websites designed to include attraction and experience opportunities for all travellers – much along the lines of SydneyforAll.

Resources

Disability Services Commission, WA, *You're Welcome WA Access Initiative*. Available at: www.disability.wa.gov.au/aud/yourewelcome.html.

Disability Services Commission (2008). *You're Welcome, a Western Australian Access Initiative*. Available at: www.accesswa.com.au/Default.aspx,

Sustainable Tourism Cooperative Research Centre: www.crctourism.com.au/

Disabled Wintersport Australia: www.disabledwintersport.com.au/index.htm

Australia For All Alliance Inc.: www.australiaforall.com.au

Canberra University, Centre for Tourism Research: www.canberra.edu.au/centres/tourism-research/projects

Disability Discrimination Act, 1992. Available at: http://www.austlii.edu.au/au/legis/cth/consol_act/dda1992264/

References

ACROD (1994) *Building Access – AAA Accommodation Checklist*. Canberra: ACROD.

ACROD (1999) Room 206 – Accommodating travellers with disabilities. Available at: www.acrod.org.au/access/room206.htm

Arola, E. (2000) The Encounters of Disabled Customers on the Stages of Tourism.

Australian Bureau of Statistics (1998) *Disability Ageing and Carers. Summary of Findings* (Cat No. 4430.0). Canberra: Australian Bureau of Statistics.

Australian Government Committee of Inquiry into Tourism (1987) *Report of the Australian Government Inquiry into Tourism – Volume 1* (Kennedy Report). Canberra: AGPS.

Australian Quadriplegic Association (2002) *Access Sydney: the Easy Guide to Easy Access* (1st edn). Sydney: Australian Quadriplegic Association.

Baum, T. (1994) The development and implementation of national tourism policies. *Tourism Management,* 15(3), 185–192.

Burnett, J.J. and Bender-Baker, H. (2001) Assessing the travel-related behaviors of the mobility-disabled consumer. *Journal of Travel Research,* 40(1), 4–11.

Calantone, R.J. and Mazanec, J. (1991) Marketing management and tourism. *Annals of Tourism Research,* 18(1), 101–119.

Cameron, B. (1995) *Easy Access Australia*. Kew, Victoria: Kew Publishing.

Cameron, B. (2000) *Easy Access Australia* (2nd edn). Kew, Victoria: Kew Publishing.

Canberra Tourism and Events Corporation (1999a) Access Info Website: www.canberra tourism.com.

Canberra Tourism and Events Corporation (1999b) *Access to ACT Venues Project – Checklist*. Canberra: Canberra Tourism and Events Corporation, ACROD and NICAN.

Canberra Tourism and Events Corporation (1999c) *Discover*. Canberra: Canberra Tourism and Events Corporation.
Center for Universal Design (2009) Universal Design Principles. Available at: www.design.ncsu.edu/cud/about_ud/about_ud.htm.
City of Melbourne (2006) *Accessing Melbourne*. Melbourne: City of Melbourne.
Clark, A.K. (2002) *Show Me the Money: A Market Segment Approach to Spending by International Travellers*. Canberra: Bureau of Tourism Research.
Commonwealth Department of Family and Community Services (1999a) *Better Information and Communication Practices*. Canberra: DFACS.
Commonwealth Department of Family and Community Services (1999B) *Better Physical Access*. Canberra: DFACS.
Commonwealth Department of Family and Community Services (1999C) *Gold Medal Disability Access Strategy – Information Kit* (Vol. 2000). Canberra: DFACS.
Commonwealth Department of Industry Tourism and Resources (2002) *The 10 Year Plan for Tourism – A Discussion Paper*. Canberra: Department of Industry, Tourism and Resources.
Commonwealth Department of Industry Tourism and Resources (2003) *Green paper: A Medium to Long Term Strategy for Tourism*. Canberra: Department of Industry, Tourism and Resources.
Commonwealth Department of Industry Tourism and Resources (2004) *Tourism White Paper: A Medium To Long Term Strategy For Tourism*. Canberra: Department of Industry, Tourism and Resources.
Commonwealth Department of Tourism (1992) *Tourism: Australia's Passport to Growth – A National Tourism Strategy*. Canberra: Department of Tourism.
Commonwealth Department of Tourism (1995a) *A National strategy for the meetings, incentives, conventions and exhibitions industry*. Canberra: Department of Tourism.
Commonwealth Department of Tourism (1995b) *National backpacker tourism strategy*. Canberra: Department of Tourism.
Commonwealth Department of Tourism (1995c) *National cruise shipping strategy*. Canberra: Department of Tourism.
Commonwealth Department of Tourism (1995d) *The Yield from inbound tourism*. Canberra: Department of Tourism.
Craik, J. (1991) *Resorting to Tourism: Cultural Policies for Tourist Development in Australia*. Sydney: Allen & Unwin.
Darcy, S. (1998) *Anxiety to Access: Tourism Patterns and Experiences of New South Wales People with a Physical Disability* (pp. 76). Sydney: Tourism New South Wales.
Darcy, S. (2000) Tourism Industry Supply Side Perceptions of Providing Goods and Services for People with Disabilities. Sydney: Report to New South Wales Ageing and Disability Department.
Darcy, S. (2002) Marginalised participation: Physical disability, high support needs and tourism. *Journal of Hospitality and Tourism Management,* 9(1), 61–72.
Darcy, S. (2005) Accessing All Areas: The potential of the Draft Access to Premises Standard. *Australasian Leisure Management,* 49(April/March), 44–46.
Darcy, S. (2006) *Setting a Research Agenda for Accessible Tourism*. Gold Coast: Sustainable Tourism for Cooperative Research Centre.
Darcy, S. (2008) Valuing Accessible Rooms: Understanding Accessible Tourism Accommodation Information Preferences. Paper presented at the Creating Inclusive Communities conference of the Association of Consultants in Access, Australia, Hyatt Regency, Adelaide.
Darcy, S. and Daruwalla, P. (1999) The trouble with travel: Tourism and people with disabilities. *Social Alternatives,* 18(1), 41–48.
Darcy, S. and Daruwalla, P. S. (2000) Tourism policy: disability, the invisible dimension. Paper presented at the Peak Performance in Tourism and Hospitality Research Conference, Mt Buller, Victoria, Australia.

Darcy, S. and Dickson, T. (2009) A Whole-of-Life approach to tourism: The case for accessible tourism experiences. *Journal of Hospitality and Tourism Management*, 16(1), 32–44.

Darcy, S., Cameron, B., Dwyer, L., Taylor, T., Wong, E. and Thomson, A. (2008) Visitor accessibility in urban centrespp. 75). Available at: www.crctourism.com.au/BookShop/BookDetail.aspx?d=626.

Darcy, S., Cameron, B., Pegg, S. and Packer, T. (2008) Technical Report 90042: Developing Business Cases for Accessible Tourism, STCRC technical report. Available at: www.crctourism.com.au/default.aspxg.

Daruwalla, P.S. (1999) Attitudes, Disability and the Hospitality and Tourism Industry. PhD Thesis, University of Newcastle, Newcastle, NSW.

Davis, G., Wanna, J., Warhurst, J. and Weller, P. (1993) *Public Policy in Australia*. Sydney: Allen & Unwin.

Dickson, T. and Hurrell, M. (Writers) (2008) Alpine Accessibility Tourism Toolkit [DVD]. T. Wn (Producer). Australia: Australian Tourism Development Program/Australian Federal Government Initiative.

Dwyer, L. and Darcy, S. (2008) Economic contribution of disability to tourism in Australia. In S. Darcy, B. Cameron, L. Dwyer, T. Taylor, E. Wong and A. Thomson (eds) *Technical Report 90040: Visitor Accessibility in Urban Centres* (pp. 15–21). Gold Coast: Sustainable Tourism Cooperative Research Centre.

Elliott, J. (1997) *Tourism: Politics and Public Sector Management*. London: Routledge.

English Tourism Council (2000) *People with Disabilities and Holiday Taking* (pp. 6). London: English Tourist Council.

Fayos-Solá, E. (1996) Tourism policy: A midsummer night's dream? *Tourism Management,* 17(6), 405–412.

Foggin, E. (2000) The Experience of Leisure Tourism of People with Disabilities. Thesis, Universite de Montreal, Montreal.

Foggin, S.E.A., Cameron, B. and Darcy, S. (2004) Towards Barrier Free Travel: Initiatives in the Asia Pacific Region. Paper presented at the refereed conference proceedings of *Developing New Markets for Traditional Destinations*, Travel and Tourism Research Association (TTRA) Canada Conference 2003, Ottawa.

Goeldner, C.R., Ritchie, B. and McIntosh, R.W. (1999) *Tourism: Principles, Practices, Philosophies* (8th edn). New York: Wiley.

Goodall, B. (2002) Disability discrimination legislation and tourism: The case of the United Kingdom. Paper presented at the Tourism and Well Being – 2nd Tourism Industry and Education Symposium, Jyvaskyla, Finland.

Graham, J. (2000) *A Guide to Accessible Caravan Parks in Queensland*. Brisbane: Tourism Queensland.

Griffin, T. and Darcy, S. (1997) Australia: Consequences of the newly adopted pro-Asia orientation. In F. M. Go and C. L. Jenkins (eds) *Tourism and Economic Development in Asia and Australasia* (pp. 67–90). London; Washington: Cassell.

Haigh, R. (1995) *Backpackers in Australia*. Canberra: Bureau of Tourism Research.

Hall, C.M. (1998) *Introduction to Tourism: Development, Dimensions and Issues* (3rd edn). Melbourne: Longman.

Hall, C.M. and Jenkins, J. (1995) *Tourism and Public Policy*. London: Routledge.

HarrisInteractive Market Research (2003) Research among adults with disabilities – travel and hospitality (pp. 66). Chicago: Open Doors Organization.

Heath, J. (2002) South Australian Tourism Access Forum process. In S. Darcy (ed.). Adelaide: Jeff Heath, Link Publications.

Israeli, A. (2002) A preliminary investigation of the importance of site accessibility factor for disabled tourists. *Journal of Travel Research,* 41(1), 101–104.

Jackson, M., Brown, C., Collins, K., Eslake, S., Hingerty, M., Hywood, G., . . . Lambert, J. (2009) *Tourism Australia, stop was Canberra*. The Jackson Report On behalf of the Steering Committee – Informing the National Long-Term Tourism Strategy.

King, B. and Hyde, G. (1989) *Tourism Marketing in Australia*. Melbourne: Hospitality Press.

Leach, R. (1993) *Political Ideologies: An Australian Introduction* (2nd edn). Melbourne: Macmillian.

Leiper, N. (2003) *Tourism management* (3rd edn). Sydney: Hospitality Press.

Loker, L. (1993) *The Backpacker Phenomenon II: More Answers to Further Questions*. Townsville, Queensland: James Cook University of North Queensland.

McKercher, B. and Chon, K. (2004) The over-reaction to SARS and the collapse of Asian tourism. *Annals of Tourism Research*, 31(3), 716–719.

McKercher, B., Packer, T., Yau, M.K. and Lam, P. (2003) Travel agents as facilitators or inhibitors of travel: perceptions of people with disabilities. *Tourism Management*, 24(4), 465–474.

Mill, R.C. and Morrison, A.M. (1985) *The Tourism System: An Introductory Text*. Englewood Cliffs, NJ: Prentice-Hall International.

National Roads and Motorists Association (NRMA) (1999) *Accommodation Guide May 1999–May 2000*. Sydney: National Roads and Motorists Association.

Office of National Tourism (1997) *Towards a National Tourism Plan: A Discussion Report*. Canberra: Office of National Tourism.

Office of National Tourism (1998a) *Tourism – A Ticket to the 21st Century – National Action Plan for a Competitive Australia*. Canberra: Office of National Tourism.

Office of National Tourism (1998b) *Tourism Challenge: Access for All*. Canberra: Office of National Tourism.

O'Neill, M. and Ali Knight, J. (2000) Disability tourism dollars in Western Australia hotels. [Yes]. *FIU Hospitality Review*, 18(2), 72–88.

Packer, T., Small, J. and Darcy, S. (2008) Technical Report 90044: Tourist Experiences of Individuals with Vision Impairment STCRC Technical Report Available at: www.crctourism.com.au/default.aspxg.

Parsons, W. (1995) *Public Policy*. Cheltenham: Edward Elgar.

Pearce, P.L. (1990) *The Backpacker Phenomenon: Preliminary Answers to Basic Questions*. Townsville, Queensland: James Cook University of North Queensland.

Porter, G. (2001) Access Audit of South Australian Accommodation and Attractions. In S. Darcy (ed.). Adelaide: SATC.

Queensland Tourist and Travel Corporation (1998) *Accessible Queensland*. Brisbane: Queensland Tourist and Travel Corporation.

Ray, N.M. and Ryder, M.E. (2003) 'Ebilities' tourism: An exploratory discussion of the travel needs and motivations of the mobility-disabled. *Tourism Management*, 24(1), 57–72.

South Australian Tourism Commission (SATC) (1999a) *ACCESSIBLE: Making It Easier to Discover South Australia*. Adelaide: SATC.

South Australian Tourism Commission (SATC) (1999b) *Tourism Strategy for People with Disabilities*. Adelaide: SATC.

South Australian Tourism Commission (SATC) (2000) Disability Access Audits Results – SATC. Adelaide: SATC.

Tourism Forecasting Council (2003) Forecasts Full Analysis including External Shocks. Canberra: Department of Industry, Tourism and Resources.

Tourism New South Wales (2000) *Disability Action Plan: 1 January 2000 to 31 December 2002*. Sydney: Tourism New South Wales.

Tourism Victoria (2007) DRAFT: *Victorian Accessible Tourism Plan*. Available at: www.tourism.vic.gov.au/images/assets/All_TXT/VicAccessibleTourismPlanAppendix1-2007Draft.txt.

Veal, A.J. (2002) *Leisure and Tourism Policy and Planning*. Wallingford, UK: CABI Publishing.

Weaver, D. and Opperman, M. (2000) *Tourism Management*. Milton Park, Queensland: John Wiley and Sons Australia Pty Ltd.

Appendix 7.1 Commonwealth Government Initiatives

Year	Originating Body/Author	Initiative/Report	Focus of policy
1980 ongoing	Australian Bureau of Statistics	Cat No. 3401.0 Short Term Arrivals and Departures	No disability module
1982	Dept. of Industry and Commerce	Accommodation for disabled travellers in Australia	Descriptive inventory of facilities availability
1986	Attorney General	Disability Services Act	Provide an equal level of government service provision for people with disabilities – includes recreation and tourism components
1986	Dept. of Sport, Recreation and Tourism	Accessibility guide for disabled travellers to tourist attractions in Australia	Descriptive inventory of facilities availability
1987	Department of Aviation	Australian Airport facilities for people with disabilities	Descriptive inventory of facilities availability
1987	L. Fraser Aust National Parks Service	Park Access: Report Series No. 10	Descriptive inventory of facilities availability
1992	Attorney General	Disability Discrimination Act	Eliminate disability discrimination in Australia
1992	Dept. of Tourism	Tourism: Australia's Passport to Growth, a national tourism strategy	Issues base – Helen McAuley's (ACROD) contribution
1992	Dept. of Family and Community Services	NICAN Established	Provide information on Arts, sport, recreation and tourism for people with disabilities
1993; 1995	Australian Tourist Commission	Travel In Australia for People with a disability	Factsheet
1997	National Office of Tourism	Towards a National Tourism Plan: A Discussion Report	Market segment/potential of people with disabilities
1998	National Office of Tourism	Tourism for All Campaign	Market segment/potential approach to people with disabilities Case studies of practical and useful tips for operators.

Year	Originating Body/Author	Initiative/Report	Focus of policy
1998	National Office of Tourism	Tourism- A ticket to the 21st century - National Action Plan for a Competitive Australia	Market segment/potential of people with disabilities
1998	Bureau of Tourism Research.	National Visitor Survey	Includes disability module
1998	Dept. of Industry, Science and Resources	Cooperative Research Council for Sustainable Tourism	No 'node' subprogram for disability issues. No disability study has been funded
1998 pre	Bureau of Tourism Research.	Domestic Tourism Monitor International Visitor Survey	No disability module
1999	Dept. of Family and Community Services	Gold Medal Access Strategy	Award and Symposium Series for organizations. Includes Tourism and Transport – focus on Olympics and Paralympics
1999	Australian Tourist Commission	Facts for the Visitor: Disabled visitors	Website Inaccurate, Poor quality information
1999	Tourism Minister's Council	National Forum on Tourism and Access	
2001	Australian Tourism Data Warehouse (Australian Tourist Commission)	One Small Step - One Joint Leap: Intelligent tourism distribution	Cooperative information provision on tourism services
2003-2005	(Commonwealth Department of Industry Tourism and Resources, 2003, 2005) – division of tourism	Green and white paper	Accessible tourism identified as a niche experience
2003	Bureau of Tourism Research	National Visitor Survey	Includes disability module
2004	STO and Common-wealth accessible tourism steering committee formed	STO and Commonwealth officers with the accessible tourism responsibility	Information exchange
2007	Tourism Australia	Accessible drive tourism routes	10 drive tourism routes and 5 accessible day trip experiences

Appendix 7.2 State and Local Government Initiatives

Year	STO	Policy and Initiatives 1990-2000	Focus
	Australian Capital Territory		
1998	(Canberra Tourism and Events Corporation, 1999b) (CTEC)	*Access Info*	Third party system of accommodation and attraction information
1999	(Canberra Tourism and Events Corporation, 1999a)	*Access Info Website*	Access information transferred to the website
1999	(Canberra Tourism and Events Corporation, 1999c)	*Discovery*	One-off magazine featuring stories on accessible experiences
	NSW		
1981	NSW Dept. of Tourism	*Tourism and disability stakeholder seminar*	IYDP seminar to improve tourism for the disabled (sic). Presented the different stakeholder positions
1998	Tourism NSW (TNSW)	Darcy (1998) *Anxiety to Access*	Reviewed previously
2000	Tourism NSW	*Disability Action Plan:1 January 2000 to 31 December 2002*	Disability action plan (DDA)
2008	Tourism New South Wales	Sydney for all Web portal	Prototype Web portal based on accessible destination experiences
	Queensland		
1999	(Queensland Tourist and Travel Corporation, 1998) (QTTC)	*Accessible Queensland*	Extended listing of services for people with disabilities
2000	Tourism Queensland (TQ)	*A Guide to Accessible Caravan Parks in Queensland* (J. Graham 2000)	A guide of caravan parks based on an individual's experiences
2000	Tourism Queensland	*A schedule of providers of services and accessible public infrastructure*	A detailed listing of services and accessible public infrastructure

Year	STO	Policy and Initiatives 1990-2000	Focus
	Australian Capital Territory		
2000	Tourism Queensland	*Accessible Queensland Images*	A CD of disability tourism images
2000	Tourism Queensland	*Accessible Queensland Website*	Website of previous publications
	South Australia		
1999	South Australian Tourism Commission (SATC)	*ACCESSIBLE: Making it easier to discover South Australia*	Policy document
1999	South Australian Tourism Commission	*Tourism Strategy for People with Disabilities*	Strategy from policy document
1999	South Australian Tourism Commission	*Disability access audits*	Third party disability access audits
	Tasmania		
1997	Tourism Tasmania (TT)	*Tourist information for people with disabilities*	Basic listing sheet of accessible tourism products/ disability contacts
			products/disability contacts
	Western Australia		
1997	Western Australian Disability Services Commission (WADSC)	*Accessing New Markets: TI Think Tank Report*	A report on TI think tank of providing services and facilities for people with disabilities
1999	Western Australian Tourism Commission (WATC)	*Accessible accommodation information*	Self reported information
2000	WADSC	*You can make a difference to customer service for people with disabilities*	A disability awareness training video
	Victoria		
1990	Tourism Victoria	*Disability Fast Facts*	Basic factsheet
2007	Tourism Victoria	Disability action plan	A strategic plan under the DDA to address accessible tourism initiatives within the organization

Appendix 7.3 Private Industry Key Initiatives

Year	Location	Activity	Description
1986	The Wheel Resort, Byron Bay, NSW (North Coast)	Accessible Accommodation – Resort Style	Cabins set in bush, with access features such as pool with ramp access, BBQ, access equipment.
1995	Clark Bay Farm, Narooma, NSW (South Coast)	Accessible Accommodation – Resort Style	Designed for people with high support needs. Automatic opening doors, ceiling hoist, large kitchens with height adjustable bench, hoist equipped pool.
1995	Easy Access Australia – A Travel guide to Australia	Travel Guide	Innovation in supply of information on accessible accommodation, transport, attractions and experiences.
1996	Accessing Brisbane	Access Guide to the City of Brisbane	
?????	Two others of note include Merindah Cottages, near Bairnsdale Vic, and Alvina Holiday Cottages Phillip Island Vic.		
1999	Accessing Melbourne	Access Guide to the City of Melbourne	
2000	O'Carrollyns at One Mile Beach, situated at Port Stephens NSW.	Accessible Accommodation – Resort Style	Designed and constructed employing the principles of Universal Design in a bush setting, hoist equipped pool, accessible transport to the beach, equipment supplied.
2000	Easy Access Australia – A Travel guide to Australia, Ed 2	Travel Guide	Innovation in supply of information on accessible accommodation, transport, attractions and experiences.
2005	Accessing Melbourne, Ed 1	Access Guide to the City of Melbourne	

8 Accessible Tourism in New Zealand

Sandra Rhodda

New Zealand Tourism

New Zealand is located in the southern Pacific Ocean and comprises two main islands (the North and South Islands) and many smaller islands. The combined total land area is about the same as the British Isles or Japan. It has a population of just over 4 million, and an economy heavily dependent on overseas trade. It is a member of numerous international bodies, and, of particular interest in the context of this essay, chaired the United Nations committee responsible for drafting the Convention on the Rights of Persons with Disabilities (http://www.un.org/disabilities/default.asp?id=259). For this and other reasons, New Zealand was presented with the Franklin Delano Roosevelt International Disability Award for making 'noteworthy progress towards the full participation of citizens with disabilities as called for in the Convention' (UN News Centre, 2008).

Tourists were coming to New Zealand as early as the 1850s (Collier, 2003). In 1901, New Zealand became the first country in the world to have a national ministry for tourism, and first recorded the number of people visiting (8050) in 1922. Currently (2008–2010), about 2.5 million tourists visit New Zealand each year. This represents about 0.26% of all world tourism, and 1.33% of Asia Pacific arrivals (Coventry, 2008).

While these proportions are small on a world scale, tourism is New Zealand's number one export earner. For the year ended March 2010, tourism expenditure contributed 18.2% to total New Zealand exports, generated 5.1% of gross domestic product, and directly employed 9.6% of the workforce (Ministry of Economic Development, 2010). The very size and importance of the industry to New Zealand means that any downturn in tourism will have an adverse effect on the entire economy.

One problem for New Zealand in international tourism is its geographical location. The country is a long way from its tourist markets, the largest and closest of which is Australia, at a distance of 2250 km (1400 miles). Its next most important market is the United Kingdom (19,200 km away), followed by the United States of America (9600 km). Other important markets are Japan, South Korea, China, Hong Kong, Taiwan and Singapore.

For able-bodied people, the time spent traveling to New Zealand is ordeal enough; for people with disabilities (PwDs) it imposes an extra burden.

Tourism New Zealand (TNZ), a Crown Entity, is the official tourism promotion agency (http://www.newzealand.com/International/). It develops, implements, and promotes strategies for tourism, and advises the Ministry of Tourism (now incorporated in the Ministry of Economic Development) and the industry on matters relating to these. It is responsible for marketing 'Destination New Zealand' offshore, but to date, neither TNZ nor the Ministry have targeted people with disabilities, and the accessible tourism market has not yet come in to clear focus in this country. For example, the Ministry and TNZ have not sent representatives to any of the numerous international events and meetings on accessible tourism held between 2000 and 2011, nor did they send representatives to the first New Zealand conference on accessible tourism held in October 2010.

Accessible Tourism in New Zealand

In 2005, Tai Poutini Polytechnic examined how well the tourism industry on the West Coast of the South Island catered for wheelchair users. The study looked at about 40% of all West Coast tourism businesses, and found that 62% of these were either difficult or impossible for a wheelchair user to access. However, about 86% of the businesses studied stated that their premises were wheelchair accessible. Of tourism information sites, more than half were impossibly difficult to access and use, although all stated they were accessible (Rhodda, 2007). This is surprising because some are run by the Department of Conservation, a government department supposed to adhere to guidelines on access. Some businesses that claimed they were accessible were further assessed for ease of use after entry. Only 30% were found to be truly accessible, and a further 31% were only accessible with difficulty.

While the study looked at only one region, tourism businesses in regions other than the West Coast that claim they are accessible are not always so. While some tourism businesses are accessible, reliable information concerning access is often very difficult or impossible to obtain. There are two guide books about accessible tourism, but one (Pickering, 2000) has been out of print since 2005, and the other (Jameson & Jameson, 2000) is more than ten years old and only available to purchase online.

Until March 2011 the Ministry of Tourism and TNZ have not included accessible tourism as part of their tourism strategy. The Ministry has only recently analyzed its own data on the age of international visitors. The analysis shows a slow but steady rise in the percentage of visitors coming to New Zealand who are 45 years old or older (Ministry of Tourism, 2008). In addition, over 70% of cruise passengers visiting New Zealand are in this age group (Rhodda, 2008). On the domestic tourism front, the Ministry has recognized that Baby Boomers (those born between 1946 and 1965) and seniors are New Zealand's largest market segment. They have also at last recognized the role that disability may play in travel by this group. A report prepared for the Ministry (Angus and Associates, 2010), shows that this group of older citizens comprises 22% of the New Zealand population, and is comparatively rich. However, the report also states that for this group, the *'major barriers to travel are health and disability (their own or that of a travelling companion) as well as lack of travelling companions'* (p. 30). The report reinforces the idea that it is a person's disability that is a barrier, rather than environments such as inaccessible transport and accommodation that are disabling, and which therefore reduce tourism and travel opportunities for PwDs (Rhodda, 2010a). No recommendations about improving access in tourism are given in the report. In spite of the recognition that our visitors are ageing and that disability is a factor influencing travel, there is no information available concerning the number of visitors coming to or travelling within New Zealand who have disabilities.

On a regional level, Wellington City has been proactive in terms of accessible tourism. The Wellington City Council, with Positively Wellington Tourism (the regional tourism organization funded by the city council and private sector partners), has listed in a small brochure and on the council website a few operator-self-assessed accommodations, sites, and activities (http://www.wellingtonnz.com/search/node/Accessible+Activities). To circumvent problems of inaccurate self-assessment, the City Council had planned to partly fund a Barrier Free NZ Trust (http://www.barrierfreenz.org.nz/) project to produce an accessibility checklist for Wellington accommodations, restaurants, and conference venues in the city. The checklist would have been tested at a number of businesses before refinement for general use as an audit tool. Thereafter, businesses that successfully completed the checklist would be able to promote their accessibility. It was hoped that the audit would become part of a national tourism business auditing system (Barrier Free NZ Trust, personal communication, November 11, 2008), but there has been no progress in this project to date. Positively Wellington Tourism has also demonstrated an increased awareness of the potential of accessible tourism by including for the first time in its tourism strategy accessible tourism objectives (Positively Wellington Tourism, 2008). These objectives include to advocate to the council and central government agencies for the development of infrastructure in the city that will offer universal access, to position the city as a universally accessible 'creative playground', and to improve awareness and understanding of the importance of universal access in tourism at all levels. However, there is no action plan yet in place, and Positively Wellington Tourism are limited by their funding, and therefore limited in what they can achieve apart from providing advice and support (Positively Wellington Tourism, personal communication, March 20, 2009).

These steps by Wellington made it the first municipality in New Zealand to at least include a mention of PwDs in their tourism strategy. In addition, a website concerning access in Wellington was in development for the Council. The website would have gone some way to providing the kind of information needed by PwDs planning a trip to or in Wellington, such as about accessible accommodation, transport, mobility scooters, ATMs, car parks, entertainment, and recreation. It intended to encourage consumer feedback and suggestions about suitable facilities. However, development of the site was stopped because the 'council does not have the resources to host and maintain such a website' (Wellington City Council, personal communication, March 20, 2009).

To ascertain the situation in municipalities other than Wellington and Auckland, a brief questionnaire was sent to 72 city, district, and regional councils enquiring about their plans for developing accessible tourism. Of the 22 that replied, 77% stated that they have no such plans (Rhodda, 2010c). Christchurch City Council said they were developing an access map of the city, but this map has to date (March 2011) not been available at the airport, nor at the main tourism information centre. Waitaki District Council replied with descriptions of access at some of the attractions in their region. However, a search of their tourism website (http://www.visitoamaru.co.nz/) provided no information about such access. The fact that the council does not provide such information on its site is fairly typical of the difficulties PwDs face in New Zealand in finding information about access to tourism products.

Nor is there much interest in or understanding of accessible tourism amongst those more directly involved in tourism. Regional Tourism Organizations (RTOs) such as Positively Wellington Tourism are responsible for promoting their region domestically and, in some cases internationally to consumers, wholesalers, retail travel agents, and the media. They work closely with TNZ and other tourism organizations, and are funded by their local councils, and/or by tourism business membership fees. To find out if RTOs knew about accessible tourism, all 29 RTOs were emailed a brief questionnaire. Fifteen replied, and their responses showed that, in their region, seven knew of accessible tourism businesses, three promoted those businesses as accessible, four leave such promotion up to the businesses concerned, five intend to encourage the development of accessible tourism, but only one has ever researched accessible tourism regionally (Rhodda, unpublished). No details about this research were given. These results are a further indication that the value of accessible tourism is not understood by most at industry level, although Positively Wellington Tourism and one other RTO did send a representative to the first New Zealand accessible tourism conference in October 2010.

The subject of tourism for PwDs is practically non-existent in tourism courses given in universities and polytechnics in New Zealand, at least if prescribed text books are anything to go by (Rhodda, 2007). In 2008, 23 educational institutes (universities and polytechnics) who teach tourism and travel courses were asked if accessible tourism was included in any course taught, or if there were plans to do so in future. They were also asked if any member of staff researched accessible tourism. Of the 15 that responded, seven do not include a consideration of accessible tourism in their courses, while the rest cover some aspects of accessible tourism, but these are not usually examined (Rhodda, unpublished). Only one institution replied that it had a staff member who had researched accessible tourism. However, this research considered whether the attitudes of hospitality students towards PwDs could be changed by exposure to the needs of those with physical disabilities, and did not research accessible tourism. No academic researcher in New Zealand other than the author focuses on accessible tourism, and only one refereed journal paper on the subject in this country (Lovelock, 2010) has been published to date. This paper explored the links between physical mobility, environmental values, and attitudes to the development of motorized access to the backcountry of New Zealand. People with mobility impairments expressed a stronger desire for enhanced access to these environments than did people without such impairments.

New Zealand is hosting one of the largest international sporting events in 2011. Rugby World Cup (RWC2011) kicks off on September 9th, and New Zealand is expecting upwards of 80,000 visitors to this event. Auckland, the main host city, did include a consideration of access in planning for this event. In early 2010, Tourism Auckland ran three, one-hour workshops on access for tourism operators. In addition, it commissioned the construction of a toolkit meant to inform tourism (and other business) operators about how and why they should improve access in anticipation of RWC2011 and for the long term. However, with just a few months to the games, this toolkit is not yet available. From the point of view of disabilities, there are other problems with RWC2011. For example, PwDs are asked to fill in 'special needs' forms, or to call for help long distance if overseas, and there is to date (March 2011), no information about access at any of the venues that is promised on the official website (Rugby World Cup, 2011).

One recent positive step has been the running of New Zealand's first Access Tourism conference in October 2010. The conference (http://www.nztri.org/podcasts-and-presentations-access-tourism-conference) was organized by the New Zealand Tourism Research Institute at Auckland University of Technology, and was attended by about 120 people from very diverse backgrounds. The Institute has since set up a Research Programme Area in Access Tourism (http://www.nztri.org/accesstourism).

Accessible Tourism Businesses in New Zealand

While Google searches using combinations of key words such as 'tourism', 'disability', 'disabilities', 'wheelchair', and 'New Zealand' conducted in New Zealand and in Australia show the first dozen or so entries to be almost entirely irrelevant or outdated, deep searching reveals about 14 tour businesses in New Zealand catering for PwDs. These businesses range from those dedicated to providing tours for PwDs and seniors to those that offer a variety of tours or services, including some catering for PwDs. An example of a tourism business that specialises in accessible travel in New Zealand is Ability Adventures (http://www.abilityadventures.co.nz/) (Department of Conservation (2007). They create custom itineraries based on customer needs, but also provide sample itineraries for the mobility, hearing, blind, and vision impaired, and for people with special medical needs. They also cater for older visitors.

It is difficult to find information about accessible accommodation in New Zealand, and even more difficult to verify the accuracy of any informa-tion given. Google searching for accessible accommodation brings up a number of sites, including umbrella sites. One such is the New Zealand Tourism Guide, which is part of the Yellow Pages Group. The Guide website has a regional map of New Zealand on an 'accessible accommodation' page (http://www.tourism.net.nz/accommodation/accessible-accommodation/). However, when the first region listed (Auckland Central) is selected, only one accommodation provider comes up. When that is selected, no information about accessibility is given.

In addition, the Tourism Guide website states that 'For travellers with visual impairment, it is important to check whether accommodations welcome your guide dog. . .'. This is in spite of the fact that under New Zealand legislation, guide dogs are legally protected from discrimination and denying access to a person with a guide dog is an offence under the law (Rhodda, 2010b). Examination of other accommodations listed as accessible in other regions on this site, and on other such sites shows that while accessibility is claimed (for example, by the use of the wheelchair symbol), information about access is not always provided, even on the home site of the accommodation provider. Some sites, for example Bed and Breakfast (http://www.babs.co.nz/04_access/new_zealand_si.htm), warn customers to check the extent of accessible facilities with operators listed. Recently, a website listing just accessible accommodation has been set up, but access at the listed businesses is assessed by the owner/operator. Several other such websites are currently being planned, but they all suffer from the fact that there is no independent reliable assessment of access, and as Rhodda (2007) showed, owner/operator assessment is often inaccurate. Some websites dedicated to disability information in general may also carry a little information about accommodations or other tourism information, but this type of informa-tion is very sparse. There are no websites dedicated to providing informa-tion to consumers about accessible tourism in New Zealand, in any of its regions, or in any of its municipalities. In contrast, web searches reveal many websites worldwide that are dedicated to accessible tourism. These websites have information about both commercial and non-commercial accessible tourism products in countries, regions, or municipalities, and/or discuss travel products, post opinion pieces, run forums, or cover other aspects of travelling for PwDs.

Why New Zealand Needs to Improve its Accessible Tourism Offer

The rationale for developing and ensuring a quality accessible tourism industry are well covered in other chapters of this publication. These include the moral imperative, the ageing of the Baby Boomer generation with its predicted rise in disability, the market (economic) imperative, and legal obligation. Finally, and compellingly, PwDs wish to experience tourism and travel.

In spite of these reasons:

- The seniors tourism market has not been researched and is rarely included in market targeting by TNZ.
- There is little indication that the Ministry of Tourism and tourism industry bodies in New Zealand have yet fully realized the connection between the ageing of the large Baby Boomer cohort and the inevitable rise in the number of PwDs.
- PwDs as visitors to or in New Zealand have not been the subject of research, and remain an unknown and untapped market. They are never targeted in TNZ advertising.

New Zealand is a long way from having any kind of accessible tourism strategy. To advocate for a more rapid appreciation of this market, a website – Access Tourism NZ (http://www.accesstourismnz.org.nz) – has been set up to focus attention on accessible tourism, and to highlight the economic benefits of developing this sector. Access Tourism NZ wishes to show that by supporting the development of accessible tourism, government and industry will achieve the two values described as central to the New Zealand Tourism Strategy 2015. These are:

- kaitiakitanga, a Māori philosophy describing guardianship, care, and protection, and providing *a basis for our approach to sustainably managing our natural, cultural, and built environment for current and future generations;*
- manaakitanga, which is *sharing exceptional and natural hospitality, knowledge, and beliefs, on the basis of mutual respect between host and visitor* (Ministry of Tourism, 2007).

New Zealand can only achieve its strategic goals of sharing our environment in mutual respect with current and future generations – which do of course include PwDs – by developing accessible tourism. Access Tourism NZ hopes to convince the Ministry and industry of this. To that end, an analysis of the Tourism Strategy and several other strategies has shown that the development of accessible tourism is a government obligation (Rhodda, 2008c).

Tourists with disabilities certainly experience difficulties in New Zealand. If these experiences are sensational enough, they may be reported in the local news. These news items are picked up by international websites (for examples, see Rains, 2008a, 2008b), and certainly bring to the fore the unfortunate state of accessible tourism in New Zealand. New Zealand needs to avoid the kinds of situations that lead to such reports.

Actions to Develop Accessible Tourism in New Zealand

If New Zealand is not to miss out on this growing, lucrative, and web savvy market, the various levels of government, industry organizations, and individual operators need to follow the lead of those in other countries who have begun to recognize and cater for tourists who are PwDs. In order to do this, New Zealand must:

- Recognize and appreciate the current and future potential importance of this market.
- Create, adopt, and champion national (central government) and regional (local government/RTOs) accessible tourism strategies and accessible tourism action plans.
- Promote and champion universal design.
- Survey and describe attitudes to accessible tourism amongst operators, central and local government, and communities, and define how any barriers can be eliminated.
- Incorporate training and education in catering for the needs of PwDs and seniors in tourism and hospitality courses.
- Earmark central government funding for the development of accessible tourism products, (such as through the Tourism Facilities Grants Programme – http://www.tourism.govt.nz/Funding/Tourism-Facilities-Grants-Fund/), and for accessible tourism training (for example, through Enterprise Development Grants – http://www.med.govt.nz/templates/MultipageDocumentPage____19932.aspx).
- Develop segmental models of best practice in accessible tourism.
- Encourage all tourism businesses to upgrade their facilities where at all possible in order to increase accessibility .
- Create – possibly through Qualmark – standards and guidelines that can be used to develop a rating system for accessible tourism businesses so that PwDs can rely upon those ratings. Qualmark (http://www.qualmark.co.nz/) is a TNZ (http://www.newzealand.com/travel/)

Automobile Association (http://www.aa.co.nz/travel/Pages/default.
aspx) star rating system. An example of such a rating system can be
found at Visit Dublin (http://www.visitdublin.com/pdf/Sleep.pdf).

- Provide a one-stop-shop web site featuring audited businesses so that
  PwDs can begin to visit New Zealand knowing which services are
  reliably accessible.
- Create through the Tourism Industry Association of New Zealand (an
  operator representative body, http://www.tianz.org.nz/) annual awards
  for accessible tourism businesses. An example of such and awards
  system can be found at Enjoy England (http://www.enjoyengland.com/
  corporate/corporate-information/excellence-awards/access-for-all.
  aspx).
- Create a research agenda, identify research gaps and opportunities for
  research collaboration, and dedicate funding for research in accessible
  tourism.
- Survey current tourists in New Zealand who are PwDs to ascertain trip
  motivational factors, pre-trip planning and information gathering, how
  they rate access and accessible tourism products, and perceived barriers
  to a successful accessible tourism experience.
- Survey potential tourists who are PwDs to ascertain what would
  encourage them to visit and the extent and nature of their needs.

Conclusions

New Zealand is disadvantaged in tourism in general because of the
distance from its major markets. It is disadvantaged in accessible tourism
because it has little awareness of the importance of this market and no
audited accessible tourism sector. However, the latter may be turned to
our advantage as New Zealand can learn from other countries that have
already started on the path of developing an accessible tourism industry. For
New Zealand to do the same, it will take commitment from all involved in
tourism.

References

Angus and Associates (2010) Domestic Tourism Market Segmentation Report. Prepared
    for The Ministry of Tourism. Available at: www.tourismresearch.govt.nz/
    Documents/Research%20Reports/DomesticMarketingResearch/DomesticTourism
    ReportApril2010.pdf.
Collier, A. (2003) Principles of Tourism: A New Zealand Perspective (6th edn). New Zealand:
    Pearson Education.
Coventry, N. (2008) Carriers still need 29,400 new aircraft, says Salter. Inside Tourism, 712.
    Available at: www.insidetourism.co.nz
Department of Conservation – Te Papa Atawhai (2007) Easy access walks. Available at:
    www.doc.govt.nz/publications/parks-and-recreation/tracks-and-walks/easy-access-
    walks-south-island/.

Jameson, A. and Jameson, A. (2000) *Accessible Walks*. New Zealand: Madyeti Publications.

Lovelock, B.A. (2010) Trains, planes and wheelchairs in the bush: Attitudes of people with mobility-disabilities to enhanced motorised access in remote natural settings. *Tourism Management,* 31(3), 357–366.

Ministry of Economic Development (2010) Tourism satellite account commentary. Available at: www.tourismresearch.govt.nz/Data--Analysis/Economic--Satellite--Data/Tourism-Satellite-Account-/Tourism-Satellite-Account-Commentary/.

Ministry of Tourism (2007) New Zealand tourism strategy 2015. Available at: www.nztourismstrategy.com/download.htm.

Ministry of Tourism (2008) Growth in senior international visitors, *Tourism Leading Indicators Monitor,* 2008(7), 2–3. Available at: www.tourismresearch.govt.nz/Documents/TLIM/TLIM%20Commentary%202008/Aug08-Growth%20in%20Senior%20International%20Visitors.pdf.

Pickering, A. (2000) *Accessible New Zealand*. New Zealand: McLaren Brown.

Positively Wellington Tourism (2008) Wellington Visitors Strategy 2015. Available at: www.wellingtonnz.com/files/uploads/About_Us/PWT_WGTN_Visitor_Strategy_2015.pdf.

Rains, S. (2008a) Blind hotel guests charged for guide dogs. *The Rolling Rains Report*. Available at: www.rollingrains.com/archives/002138.html.

Rains, S. (2008b) Follow-up story of trapped wheelchair users. *The Rolling Rains Report*. Available at: www.rollingrains.com/archives/002307.html.

Rhodda, S. (2007) Tourism for visitors to New Zealand with mobility problems: A West Coast perspective. Tai Poutini Polytechnic. Available at: www.tppweb.ac.nz/pdf/resreports/disability%20studyv2.pdf.

Rhodda, S. (2008) Accessible tourism for people with disabilities, the New Zealand tourism strategy, and other government strategies. Tai Poutini Polytechnic. Available at: www.tppweb.ac.nz/pdf/resreports/Report_Tourism2008.pdf.

Rhodda, S. (2010a) NZ Ministry of Tourism recognizes importance of Baby Boomer travellers and role of disability. Available at: www.accesstourismnz.org.nz/2010/04/nz-ministry-of-tourism-recognizes-importance-of-baby-boomer-travellers-and-role-of-disability/.

Rhodda, S. (2010b) Visitors told to check if guide dogs are acceptable in NZ accommodation, despite being legally protected. Available at: www.accesstourismnz.org.nz/2010/05/visitors-told-to-check-if-guide-dogs-are-acceptable-in-nz-accommodations-despite-being-legally-protected/.

Rhodda, S. (2010c) Access tourism and New Zealand councils. Available at: www.accesstourismnz.org.nz/2009/11/access-tourism-and-new-zealand-councils/.

Rugby World Cup (2011). Accessibility information. Available at: http://tickets.rugbyworldcup.com/info/accessibleinfo.aspx.

UN News Centre. (2008, May 6). Ban Ki-moon hails New Zealand's leadership on disability issues. Available at: www.un.org/apps/news/story.asp?NewsID=26585andCr=disabandCr1.

Section 2

Networks and Partnerships

Chapters in this section:

9 Universal Tourism Networks

Mike Prescott

Introduction

This chapter will introduce the reader to the challenge of assessing and monitoring the efficacy of universal tourism strategies. The proposed approach, network analysis, is a methodology that has been used extensively in the social sciences to map and measure the social relations between actors. The application of (social) network analysis to the tourism industry has just begun to emerge as the shift to a tourism planning paradigm that embraces '... no social exclusion, democracy, public participation, social justices and community development' (Costa, 2001: 434).

Research in this area has examined tourism policy networks (Pforr, 2002, 2006; Brandes *et al.*, 1999; Gibson *et al.*, 2005), partnership networks (Selin & Chavez, 1995; Selin, 2000; Buonocore & Metallo, 2004; Bramwell & Lane, 2000) travel pattern networks (Miguéns & Mendes, 2008), and tourism industry innovation networks (Novelli *et al.*, 2006; Borgatti, 2007; Jackson & Murphy, 2006). These studies provide valuable insights into new ways to collaborate and compete as well as understanding market dynamics between nations. This chapter offers a novel new application of network analysis to the physical layout of a travel destination. It is being leveraged to define and measure a region or district's capacity to deliver a seamless travel experience for a market sector, that is often neglected in traditional planning (Ray & Ryder , 2003). This approach will help destination marketing organizations (DMOs) take stock of the structure of their accessible and inclusive tourism assets, services and business practices in order to identify opportunities for strategic improvements to infrastructure and to improve their competitiveness (Buhalis, 2000; Scott & Cooper, 2008). These benefits can be passed on to DMO members, community or region, the tourism industry, or to the nation as a whole.

At a practical level, network analysis provides the tourism industry with simple tools to identify gaps between supply and demand from a systemic viewpoint. With a foundation in graph theory and visualization tools to support interpretation, network analysis makes it easier for decision makers in government and industry to understand the interdependent nature of the current product and service mix in their destination markets. In addition to this, it provides a consistent approach for communicating and marketing accessibility and inclusion information to potential travellers – a critical gap in its own right (Daniels *et al.*, 2005).

This idea of providing inclusive travel options for seniors, people with disabilities, families with strollers, and others with accessibility needs is relatively new to the tourism industry (Burnett & Bender-Baker, 2001). A key driver for this change has been government compliance legislation such as the Americans with Disabilities Act in the United States, the Disability Discrimination Act in the United Kingdom and in Canada, the Accessibility for Ontarians with Disabilities Act. In many cases, these policies are a culmination of human rights and advocacy efforts to create more egalitarian societies that have been decades in the making (Bickenbach, 2001). A rising undercurrent that is also at play is the economic opportunity available to broaden and deepen market share. The universal tourism market has been greatly underappreciated because of a lack of awareness about its potential. The reality is, however, that nearly one in eight people worldwide have a disability and they have purchasing power in excess of US$500 billion (Open Doors Organization (ODO, 2005). In Europe there are 46 million people with a market potential of 127 million (Buhalis *et al.*, 2005) with a disability and nearly the same in the United States where they spend US$13.6 billion annually on accessible tourism (ODO, 2005).

The tourism industry's initial response to these forces has varied – even within the same country. In Canada, for instance, the province of Quebec sponsored a disability organization (Stafford, 2001) to assess businesses in key travel districts and communicate this through their publications. Meanwhile, British Columbia (BC) has sought to leverage the 2010 Winter Games by investing US$1.14 million into a comprehensive accessible tourism strategy. By embedding accessible tourism into existing business infrastructure and taking advantage of mainstream marketing channels (2010 Legacies Now), BC hopes to establish a sustainable program well beyond the Games (unlike the abbreviated success following the Games in Athens). They have adopted the more traditional approach of setting up a range of accessibility levels and assessing businesses based on pre-defined standards.

Meeting the Challenge

Whichever approach is adopted, they all have their advantages and drawbacks which may differ depending on that market's dynamics. Despite there being no single way to address the challenge, *the industry needs to find ways to measure the success of the programs they adopt*. The viability and sustainability of existing and future programs will hinge on the tourism industry's ability to meet its objectives and communicate this effectively to stakeholders. To date, very little has been done to objectively tie the business case to actual results. Anecdotal evidence and limited market research appears to support the business case for accessible tourism so far, but this is not enough.

On top of this, each stakeholder in the system is going to have a different definition of success which has distinctive metrics tied to them. Government agencies funding accessibility initiatives are going to look for social, economic and political benefits. The tourism industry needs to broaden and deepen market share and spur innovation (Darcy *et al.*, 2008) and also through collaboration and community planning (Jamal & Getz, 1995). Communities and regions look for opportunities to promote themselves and search out employment opportunities for people with disabilities through improved access. People with disabilities and seniors desire more travel choices and opportunities to work in the industry. These are a diverse set of needs that are competing with a number of other programs for the public's attention. Adopting network analysis as a core tool will provide the industry with a competitive advantage and help sustain its position as one of the fastest growing sectors in tourism (OSSATE, 2006).

Accessibility Principles

While there is no agreed upon formula for developing a successful accessible tourism strategy, there are a few key principles that are emerging. Based on market research in tourism and in other areas, patterns have developed that should be accounted for in any strategy:

(1) Seamless experiences.
Understanding the travel experience from the perspective of the customer is not new. The '. . . satisfaction with travel and tourism services is the result of satisfaction with the services provided at each stage of this hybrid experience, namely it depends on satisfaction with pretrip services, satisfaction with services at the destination and satisfaction with transit route services.' (Neal & Gursoy, 2008: 60). For seniors and people with disabilities, gaps in accessibility and inclusion take on added importance to address. Whether it is a door that is not wide enough for a wheelchair, inadequate communication options for someone who is deaf or stigmatizing business policies that deter someone with a learning disability from participating in an activity, failure at any stage in the experience life cycle becomes something more than just an inconvenience. Imagine travelling thousands of miles to a remote cabin in the woods only to find you cannot fit into the washroom. This can lead to physical harm or, at the least, convince this consumer that travel is not for them in the future. A positive experience that exceeds expectations will build loyalty and word-of-mouth recommendations.

(2) Setting and meeting realistic expectations.
     The reality is that the industry needs to assure those that have had
     bad experiences in the past that things have changed for the better and
     provide realistic expectations that have not travelled before. The travel
     industry needs to understand what they need to do to meet demand
     and communicate this back to the consumer in a way that establishes
     expectations that will be met by tourism operators. In many ways, this
     is similar to the challenge faced by the alpine ski industry to attract
     women to their resorts in the early 1990s (Williams *et al.*, 1994).

(3) Similar but different.
     People who are looking for accessible and inclusive travel opportunities
     are looking many of the same things as the general population and want
     a variety of these in a diversity of settings Minor differences of intensity
     (preference for lower impact activities) may exist more than anything
     else. Recent research has shown that shopping, relaxation at the beach
     and a mix of dining choices are attractive to this market segment as
     well. They are looking to have equal access, get treated respectfully and
     be able to do this seamlessly with friends and family (Statistics Canada,
     2006).

(4) Incremental opportunities for business improvement.
     Many of the adaptations businesses need to do to ensure inclusive
     environments are low cost adjustments like alternate menus, better
     lighting, clear signs, disability awareness training for staff and desig-
     nated parking. As long as a business clearly communicates any other
     limitations, this may not deter a consumer from patronizing their
     establishment.

(5) Balancing multiple bottom lines.
     Any solution chosen needs to balance environmental, aesthetic,
     economic, social, and cultural concerns to preserve the authenticity of
     the experience. Sustainability will emerge when all these elements are
     considered and stakeholders across interest groups are truly engaged.

Network Analysis

The network analysis methodology provides an effective and scientific
approach to better understand the tourism system. Viewing the destination
as an opportunity for a coordinated strategic plan (Buhalis, 2000) shifts the
scope for action. Network analysis is able to provide unique analysis and
visualization tools (Borgatti *et al.*, 1999, Borgatti *et al.*, 2009) to assess:

- Features in the tourism network and their attributes.
- Ties that exist between these features.

- Structure of the network that emerges from the ties between the features.
- Relational measures of parts or all of the network.
- Roles certain features play within these networks.
- Gaps (*structural holes*) and opportunities (*bridges*) that may not be readily apparent.
- Unique opportunities that may exist that are hidden within the network structure.

Network Terminology

Assets

In network analysis, assets are nodes or vertices in a network graph. They represent entities ranging from individuals to businesses to entire nations. Usually, assets within a network will be at the same scale. If the unit of measure is the nation, all assets will be nations. Mixing scale may lead to erroneous interpretations. Like features in the real world, assets have attributes that help describe their utility such as their accessibility level, revenues, subjective importance to the destination, sector or business type, capacity and geographical location.

When visualizing the network, attributes are used to differentiate assets through the use of size, colour, shape and location (see Figure 9.1). Software like UCINet and NetDraw allows the analyst to assign attribute values prior to drawing the network and make changes in real time to depict network changes like the impact of removing a node from the network. Ties to that node drop off and the connectedness of the network decreases. These tools will help greatly in the dialogue phase discussed later.

In the tourism context, the assets/nodes being examined are businesses or features in the environment that serve as travel experiences such as a

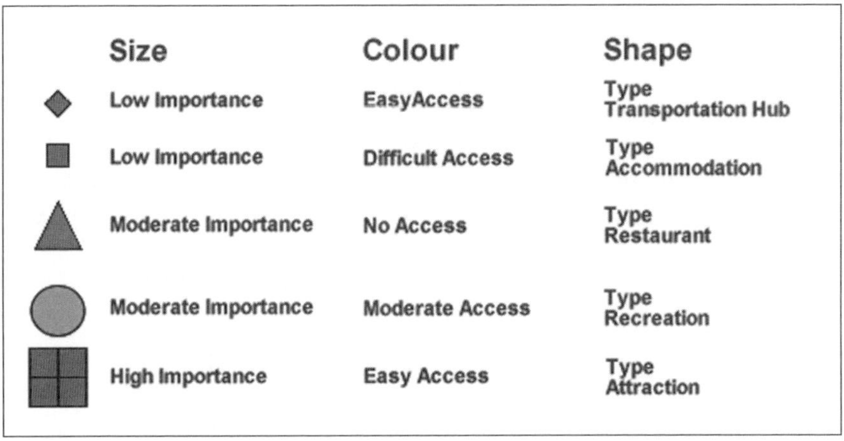

Size	Colour	Shape
◆ Low Importance	EasyAccess	Type Transportation Hub
■ Low Importance	Difficult Access	Type Accommodation
▲ Moderate Importance	No Access	Type Restaurant
● Moderate Importance	Moderate Access	Type Recreation
▦ High Importance	Easy Access	Type Attraction

Figure 9.1 Asset attribute key

hotel, restaurant, monument, store, or beach. These attributes can be used in traditional analysis to report on number of businesses that are fully wheelchair accessible or mix of business types in the downtown core. They can also be used for network measures such as length of accessible paths between museums (the attribute being the specific business type) in an historic district.

Connections (Ties/Relations)

Connections are the ties that connect one asset to another. A network may have a myriad of ties that bind it together producing multiple layers (*relations*) for that network. For instance, two assets might be accessible by a transit connection (blue line in Figure 9.2) but not a pedestrian path. A network can be assessed based on a single relation or by rolling up all possible relations into an aggregated access view. A visitor can get from their hotel to a staging area to a pick up an accessible bus by a walking path only (red line in Figure 9.3). To control public access to the attraction all visitors have to take the bus (blue line in Figure 9.2). Viewed from either mode of transit, the attraction would be considered inaccessible from the hotel. Combining transit and footpaths (red and blue lines in Figure 9.4) reveals the reality that the attraction is in fact, accessible.

Depicting the nature of the connection can be customized just like in the case of assets. Different types of relations can be shown with different colours while varying thickness might represent the relative strength of that tie. In addition, connections can be directional or not, weighted, indicate valence (positive or negative) or some combination of all of these. Depending on the network, the attributes chosen to differentiate ties may vary.

Network relations are also characterized by the role they play in connecting assets in the network (see Figure 9.5). The close-knit ties of a downtown core that share common assets (like parking lots) are the *bonds* that show up in densely packed destination zones. Redundancy (the existence of more path between two assets) of bonds is usually helpful because of the wear and tear that comes about because of their intensity of use. Monitoring for maintenance needs should be done with vigilance when it comes to bonds.

Bridges are the more distant connections like air travel routes which involve national and international organizations and collaboration across

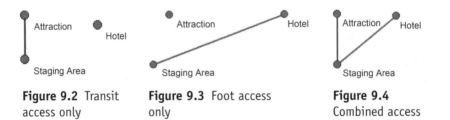

Figure 9.2 Transit access only

Figure 9.3 Foot access only

Figure 9.4 Combined access

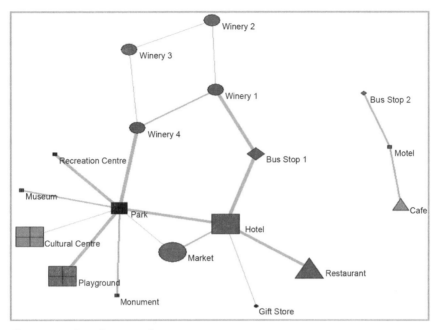

Figure 9.5 Sample network

jurisdictions. Building strong bridges means considering setting up quality of service agreements or considering standards for technology platforms that make it easier for customers to move from one jurisdiction or supplier to another. A standard for video phones in airports will mean someone with a hearing impairment can step off of a plain and have confidence that the device they are using will help them catch their connecting flight or get them to the baggage area.

Lastly, ties connecting assets of similar types are introduced as *bands* in this chapter. A network of bands is flexible and less obvious to consumers and emerges within niche markets. An example of this is the winery tours that are very popular in the Okanagan region of British Columbia. There accessibility however is difficult to ensure or manage because of the highly connected nature of the independent wineries with the tour companies that serve them (and their transportation infrastructure). By taking the approach of 'band management', businesses and transportation options might be more strategically addressed.

Networks are the structure(s) that emerge when assets are tied together. A remote resort may be made up of the resort, a nearby pool and exercise building and a separate dining establishment all connected by paths and roads. In Figure 9.5 the whole networked is mapped to give the reader an idea of the 'big picture'. It is a dichotomous network (non-directional) of ties with varying degrees of strength (line width). Part of the network (the motel connected to the bus stop and café) is disconnected from the larger, connected component.

Network Analysis Measures

The In addition to the attributes of assets and connections (*compositional* information), properties emerge as a consequence of their position in the network (*structural* information). Network properties like clustering of nodes, for instance, highlight hidden opportunities for marketing campaigns. In one district in downtown Vancouver a cluster of aboriginal art, gift shops, unique restaurants, a steam clock and lively pubs are packed into three blocks known as Gastown. This attracts cruise travellers from the port facilities just a few blocks away. Interpretive guides speaking many languages and a trolley bus are available nearby to take visitors safely to this destination. The Gastown cluster is effectively served by a number of complementary service providers resulting in considerable revenues for all of these businesses.

A network is connected if all nodes in the network can reach each other. If they are not, the network is actually a collection of smaller networks. When there is more than one network at a destination, alternate transportation needs to be offered to bridge these gaps. This can be costly and challenging when trying to ensure an adequate level of access. Attaching costs and benefits to nodes and links in the network uncovers measurable financial impacts for alternatives.

Network analysts will often measure how robust a network is by simulating the loss of one or more nodes (*cutpoints*) or ties (*cutlines*) from the network and its impact on the connectedness. There may be critical elements to the network that, if disrupted, could isolate portions of the network to the visitor. Construction activities will often result in the closing down of streets or sidewalks and result in impassable or dangerous paths for some visitors. Rerouting and signage becomes a simple solution if anticipated ahead of time.

In some instances, these disconnects are more than temporary. The gaps (structural holes) between disconnected segments can be seen as problems or opportunities for communities and the industry to take action and build accessibility bridges. A tunnel connecting Richmond with Delta, BC offers a transit option for the many cyclists that take this route.

Density

The density of a network is the number of ties (L) that exist relative to the total number of ties that could exist (g). The formula for determining this is:

Density $_{\text{dichotomous network}}$ = No. of actual ties/twice the
number of nodes present   or L/2g
Density $_{\text{directed network}}$ = No. of actual ties/number of
nodes present   or L/g

On its own, this number is not of great value but it is useful when comparing the variety of choices that might exist in one area versus another or in comparing what is available to the general public versus the accessible travel sector. A dense network usually means greater choice and variety. A ratio of accessible opportunities to total opportunities will also be an indicator of equity (the closer to one, the more equitable the opportunities). The density, like all other measures, can be useful to show changes over time.

Geodesic (Shortest Path)

A geodesic is the length of the shortest path between two points. These are very important to people who cannot walk long distances and should be at the forefront of a network analysis initiative. In the figures below, a typical network (Figure 9.6) has two nodes H and D that are connected by a number of possible paths. An arbitrary walk (H to G to F to E to D in Figure 9.7) has a length of 4 units. However, the shortest path (geodesic) is actually (H to G to A to D in Figure 9.8) is only a length of 3 units. This may represent an insurmountable difference in distance which will deter someone from traveling to D from H. Being aware of this could lead to structural changes or a different marketing and communication strategy depending on the importance of these assets.

The diameter of a network is the length of the longest geodesic between any two points. Like density, this value is not instructive but when used to compare network it can tell you how expansive a destination is. The diameter will tell you the minimal amount of distance required to get between any two points. Tourism planning might create benchmark distance for day tours to use as boundaries within a network.

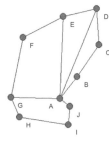

Figure 9.6 Typical
network

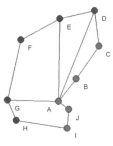

Figure 9.7 Path
(length=4)

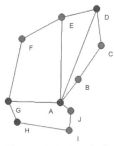

Figure 9.8 Geodesic
(length=3)

Asset Centrality Measures

Centrality is a general measure of how important a node is to the network. This depends highly on how people (or information) move through the network (Borgatti, 2007). It can be used to strategically situate assets and features that are important to visitors. The best centrality measure to use depends on how people move through the destination environment.

Degree

Degree centrality refers to the number of direct ties an asset has to the rest of the network. The most central nodes have the most ties according to degree centrality. Features with high degree centrality are likely to be busy places. In a lot of destinations high profile parks like Central Park in New York or the waterfront in Chicago fill these roles.

Closeness

Closeness centrality depicts how close all other assets are in the network to a target node. While this may not be a busy place, it may be a place that is ideal as a meeting place for people with limited mobility.

Betweenness

Betweenness centrality is an interesting measure that shows how often an asset is passed through to get to other assets. This is measured along the shortest paths between two features. The more times that asset shows up, the more central it is to the network. Assets that have high betweenness centrality are excellent spots to offer basic services like food, washrooms and significant attractions.

Subnet Measures

In large networks, it may be helpful to focus on a core set of key assets or ties. In fact, some analysis cannot be done on an entire network because it is disconnected (a barrier may mean that some assets are unreachable leading to meaningless results). Most travellers, for instance, like to start and end their journeys from their hotel so a closed path of unique features and streets is more attractive than having to retrace their steps. Anchor businesses in a mall and their location with respect to other businesses may contribute significantly to the overall mall success.

A traveller making their way through the network of assets may take a number of paths that define their experience(s). A visitor may wander from site to site, sometimes retracing their steps. The technical term for this is a *walk*. If they start and end at the same place it is a *closed walk* and if every link is traversed, it is a *tour*. A walk can be mapped showing the direction travelled or not. Interpretive tours are a distinct example of a directed walk that provides for a controlled experience at a destination. The length of a walk can either be measured as the number of links or the sum of the actual

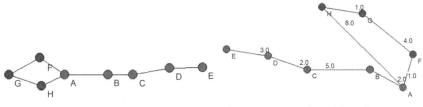

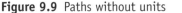

Figure 9.9 Paths without units   **Figure 9.10** Paths with units

length of those links. This information is valuable to people who may have limited mobility.

In the Figures 9.9 and 9.10, the museums are the red nodes (bands) and the lines denote an accessible path between them. The length of the museum band from A to E would be 4 units in Figure 9.9. In Figure 9.10, there are values given for each segment. The length from A to E is (20 + 5.0 + 2.0 + 3.0) 12 units. For ambulatory seniors, in particular, the actual path length may be of great value.

More efficient ways of experiencing a destination include walks where no paths are repeated (*trails*) and begin and end at the same place (*Eulerian trail*) or where the same feature is not visited more than once (*path*). When both of these conditions are met, it is considered a *cycle* – a highly efficient way to experience a destination. The traveler that does a cycle of everything at the destination has completed a *tour* or visits every site just once has completed a *Hamiltonian cycle* (Wasserman & Faust, 1994). These are more than just mathematical entities. They are examples of opportunities to develop seamless experiences for visitors.

Application to Accessible Tourism

The City of Richmond, British Columbia (BC) is a host city for the 2010 Winter Games and has historically seen itself as a travel destination for people with disabilities. For this reason they have been eager to market this opportunity. As founding members of the Accessible Tourism program in the Province, they have taken a leadership role in moving the strategy forward. The following eight steps chronicle universal tourism in Richmond and provide a guide for other destinations to use.

(1) Strategic Plan.
    To establish a firm foundation for the strategic initiative, the right stakeholders were brought to the table. This included government at all levels (federal, provincial and municipal), disability organizations (across all disability types), and tourism associations (Tourism Richmond, Tourism BC and Vancouver Coast Mountain Tourism Region). These organizations acted as the advisory group that helped define the strategic objectives and agreed on the shared vision of 'helping BC become

a premier travel destination for people with disabilities, seniors and others with accessibility needs' and Richmond as a leader in this.

The primary objective for the first phase of the strategy was to raise awareness and take stock of what Richmond already had in terms of accessible and inclusive travel experiences. The partners agreed to adopt 2010 Legacies Now's Accessible Tourism and Universal Parks and Trails guidelines for standards, communications and marketing.

(2) Assessment.
Using the program's checklists and working through Tourism Richmond, Tourism BC and Richmond Parks and Recreation, over 200 businesses were approached and 20 parks were assessed within the City of Richmond limits. Assets in the study included accommodations, dining, attractions and events, activities, transportation, and parks and recreation. Utilizing the Universal Parks and Trails checklists, parks in Richmond were also assessed. All completed checklists were returned to 2010 Legacies Now for further processing.

(3) Data Processing and Reporting.
Data from the checklists were inputted into a customized database that calculated the property's final access rating(s). Park data was entered into a separate program to rate its individual features. Reports providing businesses and parks with specific feedback were automatically produced that went back to them through the DMO. Tourism Richmond, in particular, quickly incorporated this data into their marketing channels and accessibility decals are visible in business throughout the City.

(4) Data Analysis and Visualization.
Data collected from the previous stages was also migrated into the social network analysis software (UCINet) to identify network measures and produce visualizations to be used in the dialogue phase.

The analysis of the Steveston Network (Figure 9.12) focuses on a seven by two block area abutting the Fraser River. Table 9.1 focuses on some of the structural and compositional measures discussed earlier.

The Steveston Village Core (Figure 9.12) is a connected network (only one component) with sparse ties (density = 0.1557) and uniform layout (standard deviation = 0.6314) as a result of the grid layout of the street architecture. This destination has a few cycles (the core is two streets wide and 4 streets long) with linear/acyclic arms. This offers clusters of opportunities for the general public that are closely packed making the diameter large (13) but the average distance is moderate (4.987).

Figure 9.11 BC accessibility icons

TABLE 9.1 Steveston village core network measures

Density	0.1557
Standard Deviation	0.6314
Avg distance between pairs	4.987
Diameter	13

The network measures that stand out are the lack of accessibility at key junctures in the network. While this does not impact the accessibility of the network it does negatively impact the seamless visitor experience. Visitors may become frustrated when central businesses they pass by are not accessible on a regular basis as Table 9.2 highlights.

Overall, the network has relatively low access for people who have greater accessibility needs. While there are few businesses that have no access, there is still a lot that could be done. A critical gap is the lack of public washrooms and limited parking during larger events. Improvements are needed to the path between Pieces and the Cottage Tea Room to mitigate a significant bottleneck on 1st Avenue between Moncton Street and Bayview Street in the heart of the Village core.

(5) Dialogue.
Using reports, network visualizations and network measures a dialogue with Tourism Richmond helped frame the examination of gaps in the Steveston Village Core.

(6) Decision.
Based on priorities and cost benefit estimates, alternatives are being developed. Decisions as to what to improve will be made in consultation with Tourism Richmond's membership and a community access map will be developed for download online.

(7) Implementation
Working with community partners, parks and recreation and private businesses, Tourism Richmond will coordinate a phased implementation of the recommendations that were made in the previous stage.

(8) Monitoring.
Each of the partners that are part of the solution(s) chosen will be assigned metrics to be responsible for and Tourism Richmond will

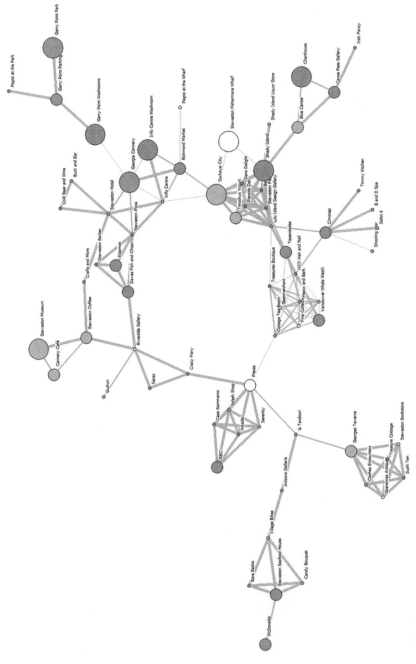

Figure 9.12 Steveston network

TABLE 9.2 Most central nodes (based on betweenness centrality)

Feature	Degree	Closeness	Betweenness	Access
Pieces	10	27.027	46.733	0
la Tandoori	4.286	23.026	30.311	1
Cottage Tea Room	11.429	27.132	28.679	1
Lulu Island Design Gallery	14.286	27.778	28.345	1
Sockeye City	14.286	26.718	25.023	1

TABLE 9.3 Accessibility levels

Category	Average (Standard Deviation)	No.
All	1.521127 (0.808158)	71
Accommodation	1	1
Dining	1.551724	29
Retail	1.357143	28
Activity	1.714286	7
Attraction	2	2
Facility	2	4

coordinate the reporting and communication of these findings to all stakeholders. An Advisory Committee will review the feedback and offer suggestions as to how to proceed from there.

Future Trends

Network analysis is not a panacea for universal tourism but used in tandem with other tools can provide a unique perspective on a destination market. To be truly effective, means will need to be developed that can assess environments in near real time. Dynamic network analysis and agent based systems that can be modelled from collected data will add a predictive capability to help DMOs anticipate trends and provide strategic information that will result in competitive advantage (Buhalis, 2000; McKercher, et al., 2003).

Network analysis will need a great more deal of testing and network measures developed that extend beyond social relations. Network motifs (model dyads, triads and subnets) may serve as feasible means to understand larger networks. Entire regional or national tourism networks could be mapped out to provide local destinations with a broader view of the overall strategic market.

Because no work has been done with this methodology, the opportunities are unlimited at this time. The most beneficial next steps would be to:

- Integrate attribute data more closely with network measures (value of a network based on access levels or importance of a business along paths).
- Integrate revenue figures with network measures.
- Compare customer preferences with structural models (cycles vs linear vs hybrid).
- Identify importance of facilities (parking and washrooms) placement to success.

Conclusion

Network analysis represents an interesting and powerful opportunity to better understand the destination environment for people who have accessibility needs. This market is significant and tourism organizations and governments need easy tools for assessing and monitoring their jurisdictions. A seamless travel experience that is accurately portrayed by DMOs will attract visitors. Destinations that meet or exceed expectations can hope to broaden and deepen their markets and gain first mover advantages while other destinations play catch up.

Network analysis represents the destination more closely and clearly than other methods because it considers how the environment interacts with the experiences offered by firms. Universal standards that are communicated transparently for visitors will give them the confidence that they will be satisfied.

References

Bickenbach, J.E. (2001) Disability human rights , law and policy. In G.L. Albrecht, K.D. Seelman and M. Bury (eds) *Handbook of Disability Studies*. Thousand Oaks: Sage Publications.

Borgatti, S., Everett, M. and Freeman, L. (1999) Ucinet 6.0 (Version 1.00). Natick: Analytic Technologies.

Borgatti, S.P., Mehra, A., Brass, D.J. and Labianca, G. (2009) Network analysis in the social sciences, *Science,* 323, 892.

Borgatti, S.P. (2007) Centrality and network flow, *Social Networks*, 55-71.

Bramwell and Lane (2000) Collaboration and partnerships in tourism planning. In B. Bramwell and B. Lane (eds) *Tourism Collaboration and Partnerships: Politics, Practice and Sustainability* (pp. 1–19). Clevedon: Channel View Publications.

Brandes, U., Kenis, P., Raab, J., Schneider, V. and Wagner, D. (1999) Explorations into the visualization of policy networks, *Journal of Theoretical Politics,* 11, 75–106.

Buhalis, D. (2000) Marketing the competitive destination of the future, *Tourism Management,* 21(1), 97–116.

Buhalis, D., Eichhorn, V., Michopoulou, E. and Miller, G. (2005) *Accessibility Market and Stakeholder Analysis*. OSSATE Project, Guildford: University of Surrey.

Buonocore, F., and Metallo, C. (2004) Tourist destination networks, relational competences and 'relationship builders': The central role of information systems and human resource management. In *ATLAS Annual Conference, Networking and Partnerships in Destination Development and Management* (pp. 377–398). Naples: ATLAS.

Burnett, J.J. and Bender-Baker, H. (2001) Assessing the travel-related behaviours of the mobility-disabled consumer. *Journal of Travel Research,* 40(1), 4–11.

Costa, C. (2001) An emerging tourism planning paradigm? A comparative analysis between town and tourism planning, *The International Journal of Tourism Research,* 3(6), 434.

Daniels, M.J., Drogin Rodgers, E.B. and Wiggins, B.P. (2005) Travel tales: An interpretive analysis of constraints and negotiations to pleasure travel as experienced by persons with physical disabilities, *Tourism Management,* 26(6), 919–930.

Darcy, S., Cameron, B., Pegg, S. and Packer, T. (2008) *Developing business case studies for accessible tourism.* K. Van Asperen (ed.). Gold Coast, Australia: Sustainable Tourism CRC.

Gibson, L., P. Lynch, and Morrison, A. (2005) The local destination tourism network: development issues, *Tourism and Hospitality Planning and Development,* 2, 87–99.

Jackson, J. and Murphy, P. (2006) Clusters in regional tourism: an Australian case, *Annals of Tourism Research,* 33, 1018–1035.

Jamal, T. and Getz, D. (1995) Collaboration theory and community tourism planning, *Annals of Tourism Research,* 22, 186–204.

McKercher, B., Packer, T., Yau, M.K. and Lam, P. (2003) Travel agents as facilitators or inhibitors of travel: Perceptions of people with disabilities, *Tourism Management,* 24(4), 465–474

Miguéns, J.I.L. and Mendes, J.F.F. (2008) Travel and tourism: Into a complex network. *Physica A: Statistical Mechanics and its Applications,* 387(12), 2963–2971.

Neal, J.D., and Gursoy, D. (2008) A multifaceted analysis of tourism satisfaction, *Journal of Travel Research,* 47(1), 53–62.

Novelli, M., Schmitz, B. and Spencer, T. (2006) Networks, clusters and innovation in tourism: A UK experience, *Tourism Management,* 27, 1141–1152.

Open Doors Organization (ODO) (2005) *Travelers with Disabilities.* ODO/Harris, Survey, Chicago: Open Doors Organization.

OSSATE (2006) One-Stop-Shop for Accessible Tourism, Annual Report, 2005, European Commission.

Pforr, C. (2002) The 'makers and shapers' of tourism policy in the Northern Territory of Australia: A policy network analysis of actors and their relational constellations, *Journal of Hospitality and Tourism Research,* 9, 134–151.

Pforr, C. (2006) Tourism policy in the making: An Australian network study, *Annals of Tourism Research,* 33, 87–108.

Ray, N. and Ryder., M.E. (2003) Ebilities tourism: An exploratory discussion of the travel needs and motivations of the mobility-disabled, *Tourism Management.* 24, 57–72.

Scott, N. and Cooper, C. (2008) Destination networks: Four Australian cases, *Annals of Tourism Research,* 35(1), 169–188.

Selin, S. (2000) Developing a typology of sustainable tourism partnerships. In B. Bramwell and B. Lane (eds) *Tourism Collaboration and Partnerships: Politics, Practice and Sustainability.* (pp. 129–142). Clevedon: Channel View Publications.

Selin, S. and Beason, K. (1991) Interorganizational relations in tourism, *Annals of Tourism Research,* (18), 639–652.

Selin, S. and Chavez, D. (1995) Developing an evolutionary tourism partnership model, *Annals of Tourism Research,* 22, 814–856.

Stafford, J. (2001) A growth market: Behaviours of tourists with restricted physical abilities in Canada. Keroul Canada Economic Development Study, Keroul, Montreal, Canada.

Statistics Canada (2006) Participation and activity limitation survey, Ontario, Canada.

Wasserman, S. and Faust, K. (1994) *Social Network Analysis.* Cambridge: Cambridge University Press.

Williams, P.W., Dossa, K. and Fulton, A. (1994) Tension on the slopes. *Journal of Applied Recreation Research,* 19(3), 191–213.

10 Tourism Victoria, Australia – An Integrative Model of Inclusive Tourism for People with Disabilities

Huong Le, Yuka Fujimoto,
Ruth Rentschler and David Edwards

Introduction

In this chapter, we investigate access and inclusion for people with disabilities in tourism. From a policy-systematic analysis conducted at a state level and a case study of Victorian tourism, we conclude that despite the impressive state-wide policy of community oriented inclusion, those policies need greater recognisable impact on the ground (Department of Human Services Victoria, 2007; Department of Premier and Cabinet, 2001, 2005). In particular, while much the tourism practice and research still imagines physical accessibility equates to inclusion, one community used as a case study illustrates consideration for wider community social oriented inclusion. The state-wide policy analysis therefore identified future implications for theory and research on inclusive and accessible tourism in a broader context.

This study explores the benefits of inclusiveness from a stakeholder perspective. It investigates access and inclusion for people with disabilities using a broad state policy analysis in Victoria, Australia. This study provides readers with:

(1) An analysis of the key policy initiatives that impact access and inclusion for people with disabilities in tourism.
(2) A 'gap analysis' which may be used to further enhance strategic development for tourism inclusion.
(3) A case study of Victorian tourism in relation to stakeholder perspectives.
(4) Strategies to foster the concepts of inclusion in all Victorian communities through tourism.

Research on tourism and inclusion is crucial for the following reasons. First, international and Australian studies record that people who are socially marginalised have impaired access to health and community services and have worse mental health compared with people who are socially well integrated (Shaw et al., 1999). Socially marginalised persons in need of assistance often under-utilise support services due to lack of knowledge about availability, stigma and discrimination, geographical isolation, inadequate transport, mobility challenges, cost of services and inflexibility of services (Eichhorn et al., 2008; Daruwalla & Darcy, 2005). These practical barriers are often exacerbated by a lack of services and service providers either inadequately trained or unwilling to address inclusion for people with disabilities (Bi et al., 2007).

Second, inclusion is argued to be of increasing importance to community cohesion and community capacity building in the policy environment. For example, in 1993, approximately 3.2 million Australians, representing 18% of the population were classified as having a disability (Darcy and Daruwalla, 1999, Department of Human Services Victoria, 2007). That figure rose to 3.6 million people with disabilities (19%) and a further 3.1 million with a long-term condition or impairment, but no disability (17%) in 1998 (Australian Bureau of Statistics, 2006). All these statistics indicate that people with disabilities continue to face challenges accessing and being included in community activities. More importantly, by excluding socially marginalised people the quality of life for the entire community is diminished as they do not get to experience the value diversity can bring.

A third element of the policy environment is the sometimes fractious relationship between policy makers and program delivery people which may adversely affect policy implementation on the ground. Such problematic relationships have been reported by Chalip (1995) and as the cause of breakdowns in the links from policy to implementation by De Bosscher et al. (2006). These concerns indicate that policy and implementation analysis ought to be conducted at the macro, meso and micro levels in order to identify the determinants of policy implementation success.

An Overview of Stakeholder Theory

Research used stakeholder theory (Freeman, 1984) to articulate the policy dynamic of the tourism sector. Stakeholders are defined as groups within the sphere of influence of an organization: those who can influence or are influenced by the organization (Jonker & Foster, 2002; Sheehan & Ritchie, 2005). Stakeholder theory arose as an attempt by organizations to consider and address neglected internal and external factors in the strategic planning process (Sheehan & Ritchie, 2005). Freeman (1984) identifies three components of successful stakeholder management as (1) identification of stakeholders, (2) processes of relationships and (3) management of transactions.

Sautter and Leisen (1999) address stakeholder theory in relation to tourism, viewing the role of tourism as a proactive force which benefits the growth of the local community rather than an exploitative force that only benefits affluent tourists. Whether stakeholders are broadly or narrowly defined, all exponents of stakeholder theory agree that organizations have economic relationships within the moral-oriented management context (Sheehan & Ritchie, 2005).

Stakeholder theory is therefore critical to understanding social inclusiveness for service providers such as tourism. Increasingly service-oriented organizations such as tourism operate in close proximity to customers, accordingly, inclusion ought to be a top priority for both economic and socially moral reasons. This study analyses case study data in light of stakeholder theory.

Research Methods

A case study methodology was chosen as one of the research approaches appropriate for the systematic study of a phenomenon (Merriam, 1988). Yin (1994) defines a case study as an empirical inquiry utilised to investigate 'a contemporary phenomenon within its real-life context, especially when the boundaries between the phenomenon and context are not clearly evident' (p.13). Overall, case study methods are suitable for defining the topic broadly, to cover contextual conditions and rely on multiple sources of evidence. A qualitative case study approach was selected as an appropriate way to investigate in-depth the relationship between inclusive policies at a state level and their impacts on practice within the Victorian tourism sector.

Two main sources of qualitative data collection were used: *in-depth interviews* (with stakeholders), and *documentation* (Victorian inclusive polices), to construct a framework for investigating the cases being studied, and to understand how policy influences operations of the Victorian tourism sector. The researchers' field investigations were largely conducted in the Local Government areas of City of Greater Geelong, Mansfield Shire, Surf Coast Shire and City of Warrnambool. These regions are popular year-round tourist destinations. The regions feature a wide variety of accommodation styles and standards and also feature a broad range of cultural, artistic, musical and sporting events throughout the year. Each of these activities contributes to tourism in the regions studied.

Purposive sampling (Neuman, 2000) was utilised to identify and to select respondents to participate in the study. Interviews were conducted with different stakeholders such as managers, volunteers and tourist operators, government officials and festival managers ($N=10$). As accessible tourism has interrelations with other sectors in society such as arts and tourism government bodies, field interviews with key stakeholders reflected powerful change messages contained in the draft policy. These change messages were being accepted progressively across the industry and had been embraced enthusiastically in one community. The findings in this community are detailed in the case study.

Based on the case study findings, we believe that to achieve successful accessible tourism, a whole of community approach is necessary. In other words, disability tourism will only take off if arts, events and accommodation/hospitality work in unison. Interview questions were open-ended and semi-structured. The researchers were particularly interested to hear of disability inclusion awareness and of examples of 'good practice'.

Documentation: Victorian Inclusive Policies. Policy analysis was a significant part of the data collection and analysis. While the Victorian Government has had several policy initiatives, only key policies in Victoria were analysed for the purposes of this research. These policies provided necessary background knowledge of case studies and a foundation for understanding inclusive policy context and their impacts on operations of the tourism sector.

A conceptual framework for policy analysis is employed. This project takes a systems approach to analysing government policy implementation on tourism at micro, meso, and macro level. Specifically, the macro level includes the social ecology and cultural context in which people live: their economic welfare, geographic and climatic variation, degree of urbanisation, political system, and cultural system (De Bosscher *et al.*, 2006). The meso level includes policies developed to effect change and in response to the social ecology. This is the level at which policies may influence implementation. The micro level includes individuals, such as tourists, artists, athletes, and such like. At this level, some factors can be controlled (such as funding provision, targeting of programs and their delivery, sports training techniques and tactics) and others not controlled (personal differences) (De Bosscher *et al.*, 2006; Ashton-Shaeffer *et al.*, 2001). A systems framework was considered appropriate for this study as it allows an implementation construct to be developed to identify drivers of success and barriers at the meso level. In this study, the overall success of policies is analysed at the meso level and of their implementation at the micro level. Analysis of legislation is considered at the macro level. There is some overlap between the three levels as no level operates in isolation. The systems approach to analysis by levels is illustrated in Figure 10.1.

Interview analysis

After a coding process, themes were revealed, and propositions were developed which linked issues. These helped yield patterns and regularities, which then became the themes, compatible with the purposes of the study. Themes were confirmed and refined in relation to what the researchers saw in the data, and relative to the theoretical framework.

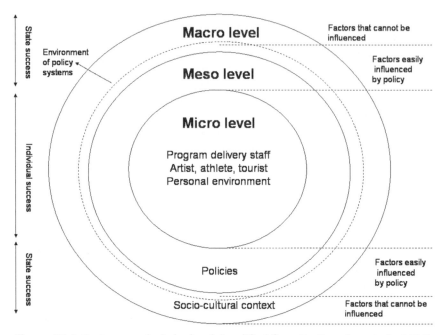

Figure 10.1 Systems analysis by level (modified from De Bosscher *et al.*, 2006)

Victorian Policy Framework: Macro Level

Despite a robust state economy and investment in social capital projects, the Victorian Government recognises that some social injustice and exclusion still exists and seeks to redress this with progressive social policies. The Government has adopted a social policy framework aimed at creating a fairer, more equitable and just society through macro-initiatives. The philosophy underpinning this approach to social citizenship is embodied in a number of key policies including *Growing Victoria Together* (2001), *A Fairer Victoria* (2005) and the *Disability Act 2006*. The Victorian Government's vision is to develop an inclusive community that balances economic, social and environmental actions to benefit all Victorians by expanding their opportunities and improving their quality of life. Of particular importance to people with disabilities in the context of tourism is the Government's commitment to build cohesive communities and to provide socio-economic and infrastructure support for disadvantaged areas and disadvantaged groups.

The new Victorian Disability Act (2006) is predicated on an important paradigm shift and will affect many aspects of community inclusion for people with disabilities, including the tourism sector. The new legislation adopts an 'inclusive model' approach under which people with disabilities have the same rights and responsibilities as other members of the community. Traditional approaches to disability legislation have either taken a medical approach, which situates the 'problem' in the person with a disability and seeks to fix this problem through some adaptive interventions; if the adaptation is not possible, the person is excluded (Fullagar & Darcy, 2004). Or, a social approach which places the disability within a social context and recognises that the extent to which a person is impaired is affected by societal infrastructure and cultural and social conventions, such as building design. The social model locates the barriers to full participation in society and calls upon society to confront and remove barriers (Walsh & London, 1995).

The *Disability Act 2006* takes a fresh approach, which we term a socio-political 'inclusive model' within which people with disabilities have the same rights and responsibilities as other members of the community. We define the inclusive model as the theory that seeks to redress discrimination, and recognises that people with disabilities are an integral part of society. Individuals have a right to participate in all aspects of social, economic and political life to the extent they wish. People with disabilities are to be consulted appropriately, and their personal views respected. We consider this principle as vital for organizations to re-conceptualise the meaning of social inclusion.

The *Disability Act 2006* informs the *Victorian State Disability Plan 2002–2012* which emphasises the importance of people with disabilities being included and participating in mainstream activities in their communities. Moreover, in Victoria people with disabilities have the right to support in the exercise of their social citizenship. We view tourism to be an important conduit for people with disabilities to integrate into their communities and to develop their communities toward social inclusion. Because tourism is such a personal experience it has a unique opportunity to provide a community oriented-natural social setting in which Victorians of all abilities and status can integrate in a manner that is non-political, non-hierarchical, informal and relaxed. If the tourism sector can provide not only physical infrastructures to support people with disabilities to widen their access but social infrastructures for them to integrate with surrounding communities, it would not only increase business opportunities but also act as an excellent exemplar for the inclusion model (Patterson, 2007; Shaw, G. & Coles, 2004; McKercher *et al.*, 2003).

In the reported case study it was evident that an enlightened, whole of community approach to inclusion was not only possible, it paid dividends in many different ways. However, this was not the case in other communities who had not yet seen the potential in disability tourism. In those communities meeting the needs of people with disabilities was still viewed as a 'cost' not as a 'benefit' to business and to the community as a whole.

Victorian Accessible Tourism Plan 2007–2010: Meso Level

The *Victorian Accessible Tourism Plan 2007–2010* is a draft document that sets the strategic direction for the tourism industry to ensure that it provides tourism products that cater for all potential tourists, including tourists with disabilities. It is the result of a collaborative process which brought together key organizations and stakeholders, including service providers and people with disabilities, to draw up a draft plan for the sector. The plan is a work in progress which is being evaluated by stakeholders, including Government. The plan provides some salient advice to tourism operators on their obligations under Commonwealth and State law. The following statement articulates such advice:

> Not only does accessible tourism make good business sense; it is also a legal requirement for all service providers enshrined in legislation in the form of the *Federal Disability Discrimination Act* (1992) and the *Victorian Equal Opportunity Act* (1984). This makes it the responsibility of all businesses to provide a service that does not discriminate against people on the basis of their disability. (Tourism Victoria, 2007: 4)

From our analysis however, despite the Victorian Government's vision for an inclusive community that balances economic, social and environmental actions that will benefit all Victorians by community oriented inclusion, the current *Victorian Accessible Tourism Plan* indicates limited connection to community oriented inclusion as a means to enhance participation by people with disabilities.

The current plan largely equates physical access with inclusion and is more of a business plan/marketing document than an inclusive policy document. This is consistent with the commercially driven nature of the tourism industry. It includes propositions for the development of a positive attitude amongst tourism operators toward people with disabilities, facilitating a change towards more accessible and inclusive business practice by operators and facilitating the provision of accurate and accessible information about tourism product, services, experiences and destinations in Victoria. Despite the above policy initiatives, people with disabilities are not identified as a discrete target group for intervention or implementation strategy. Nor are people with disabilities mentioned in the policy's progress measures. The tourism industries commitment to developing and implementing inclusive tourism for people with disabilities is reflected in the recent work by Tourism Victoria's Reference Group which developed the following policy statement:

Accessible tourism, core values and principles: Accessibility is a concept relevant to more than just infrastructure; it also relates to attitude, awareness, language, services, and information. As a result, access is provided to a diverse community including all societal groups regardless of gender, race, ability or sexuality. (Tourism Victoria, 2007: 8)

Overall, the policy analysis at macro and micro levels indicates that there is a gap between state-wide definition of community oriented inclusion and the tourism sector focus on inclusion as physical access. However, we also observed some improvements into tourism inclusion of people with disabilities and Tourism Victoria's enthusiasm for a more inclusive industry. These new inclusive attitudes were not universally embraced by tourism and hospitality operators.

Evidence from the Field: Micro Level

Field interviews were conducted with government bureaucrats, regional tourism association managers and tourist business operators. Most interviewees believed in the essential need for inclusion in tourism and that the industry needed to embrace a wider definition of disability that took it way beyond ramps, wheelchairs and accessible bathrooms but others were still focused on 'costs for my business'.

Tourism managers and event managers spoke about expanding consumer participation for their respective services; inclusion for people with disabilities was an integral part of their industries' service delivery. Moreover, they understood that drawing a consumer to one service was interdependent with meeting the consumers' wider needs. For example, a regional cultural or artistic event catering for people with a range of disabilities was linked to the need for the regional tourist accommodation and catering businesses being able to also meet those consumers' needs.

The Warrnambool festival operator spoke of how inclusion is seen as providing strong community involvement, and fostering pride:

The inclusion element here is that, whilst it's a tourism strategy, there are strong elements of community involvement and it strengthens our community as a result. We have over a thousand local volunteers, including people with a disability... It's also the fact that the volunteers have a sense of pride in contributing to something that is significant. For inclusion for people with a disability, we work to make the event a 'one in all in' event and accessible. We do an audit of the site to make sure it is accessible to those with disabilities. We have put in hearing aids and signage for hearing impaired.

The Warrnambool festival organization demonstrates in both the design and delivery of its festival that it understands disability inclusion in a most practical manner. All members of the local community, including those with disabilities are welcomed into the organizational process; the festival meets the accessibility needs of a broad range of disability types and the local tourist accommodation outlets welcome guests of all abilities. The local tourism and hospitality industry worked in tandem with the festival organizers to ensure that their premises and staff were equipped to satisfy the special needs of tourists with disabilities.

Several interviewees spoke of organizational cultural change, education programs and the importance of government policy and legislation. But they recognised that it was people who really made the difference. A Warrnambool tourism operator said: *'You can have all the policies you want, but in the end, it's up to individuals to make a difference'*. Within his own business, he had implemented a staff training process designed to change the way his people thought about disability. Another regional tourism authority manager emphasised the importance of education and training: *'... developing a tourism plan for accessibility and inclusion is an important process in itself; ... going through the process, releasing it and making people aware that there is a plan and what it's about is really important'*. He also said: *'including people with a disability makes good business sense; it's a largely an untapped market'*.

This concept of an untapped marketing opportunity was echoed by another tourism manager: *'Government commitment, finances, training, and human resources need to go hand in hand; we need to ensure that we keep building the focus on improving visitor experiences. So if you do that as an organization then you have to think more broadly about the market you're dealing with'*. Local Government also has a vital role to play in community development. A regional local government administrator made the following comments: *'... ensuring that those involved with the provision of services for people with disabilities receive adequate and up-to-date training is an important issue in terms of our community development and local capacity building. Training of participants at all levels should be ongoing and has the power to affect change'*. However, other tourism industry people interviewed expressed concerns about the value of providing services to the disability tourism market. One regional tourism authority manager reported that many of his members did not understand the potential demand for disability tourism and that the concept still had to be 'sold' to the industry. Talking of the concerns of his local tourist business members, this manager said: *'they're mostly small business operators and want to know how they can do it in a way that's not going to adversely affect the bottom line.'* A Government tourism department manager said: *'it's a hearts, minds and wallets issue; disability tourism must be explained to the industry in a manner where they can see the size of the potential market and the value to their business by gaining some of that market.'* He added that: *'small business operators cannot be encouraged to become involved in catering to the disability tourism market on 'feel good', 'feel good' will follow if it makes good business sense.'* Both the regional tourism manager and the government manager were essentially saying the same thing. Tourist business operators need to be convinced of the commercial potential as well as educated about the wider disability issues.

The field interviews indicated that good practice flourishes when there is community recognition that to cater for disability tourists, local events have to be disability friendly and local tourist accommodation also needs to be disability friendly. The best example of this synergy was in Warrnambool. An extensive education process had been undertaken about disability and the cultural change necessary to adopt a more disability friendly approach to service delivery had been undertaken within the festival community and by local hospitality/accommodation providers. Underpinning the efforts of the local businesses was the support of the regional tourist authority and local government. This is a whole of community approach involving not-for-profit festival organizers, commercial hospitality and accommodation businesses, local government, the regional tourist authority and thousands of local volunteers. It shows what can be done to make a town disability friendly.

Implications For Policy and Practice

Policy and the case study analysis provided a platform by which the tourism sector could further their inclusion from physical access to a community oriented integration of people with and without disabilities. The study had implications for theory and for practice. Implications for theory include empowering people in communities with disabilities through social service to build community engagement and integrating people with disabilities into communities. Community engagement develops especially through partnerships between people with disabilities and those in communities and with families (Bradley, 1994; Cheung & Man-hung Ngan, 2007; Wituk et al., 2007). We perceive that the tourism sector, if well managed and adequately resourced, would be able to offer social services for people with disabilities. As mentioned earlier, tourism offers unique social service opportunities for people with and without disabilities to integrate in a relaxed and pleasurable environment. Therefore, tourism could provide a grass roots approach to what community integration processes most beneficial for people with disabilities and most educational for people without disabilities.

Bhattacharyya (2004) postulates three ways to integrate people with disabilities into communities by: (1) educating people willing to help and give to others, (2) providing opportunities for the people with disabilities to share their own perspectives and experiences of needs rather than being defined by their needs, and (3) training and development for stakeholders in communities (such as tourists with disabilities, communities, families members/carers and tourism managers/operators) to meet the needs of people with disabilities for future social integration. This research suggests that volunteering could be another way forward for integration of people with disabilities in communities.

Implications for practice are three-fold. First, policy development allows inclusion policy to be 'refreshed' across departments, in order to better align them with the intent of government community oriented inclusion policy. Second, policy implementation requires integrating diverse groups of stakeholders. In order to implement the community oriented social inclusion policies in tourism, engage a wider range of stakeholders, such as community members in general, people with disabilities and their families, carers, festival organizers and tourism operators.

Inclusion also requires those who choose to become active in the community in diverse ways, such as through programs, administration or volunteering, to have the opportunity to do so. One of the important planks of the Victorian Government's social policies, expressed in *A Fairer Victoria* and *Growing Victoria Together,* is that of involving communities in a consultative manner and building community capacity.

Our stakeholder analysis of developing a community oriented inclusion process for the tourism sector examined critically the means of including people with disabilities in the inclusion planning process. The case study provided one example of practical ways that engagement had occurred in one regional Victorian community. Including people with disabilities as problem solvers for matters related to social inclusion offers a positive future for tourism services to comply with community oriented government policies and values. Making people with disabilities' opinion 'equal' to the rest of communities' opinion means that a holistic-community oriented inclusion process can be established (Bhattacharyya, 2004; Muir *et al.*, 2008). In so doing, the tourism sector can develop a creative and innovative inclusion process. We propose that such participation has important future research and practice implications for the tourism sector.

Conclusion

From our analysis, we recommend that the tourism sector refresh its inclusion policy formation and implementation to align more closely to the state government community oriented inclusion policies. To achieve this goal, we suggest that both practitioners and scholars alike acknowledge the gap in tourism inclusion practice and research which has been more focused on physical access and information than on community integration views and practices. Such an approach will necessitate some cognitive change and wide appreciation of the 'inclusive model' of disability under which people with disabilities have the same rights and responsibilities as other members of the community.

Moreover people with disabilities need their voices heard, received and ideas implemented in the development of inclusive policies and practices for the tourism sector. If the tourism sector embraced a uniform socially progressive approach, it would offer a unique conduit for community oriented inclusion on the ground level. Touring is a pleasurable and relaxing social activity which provides a mainstream approach to community oriented inclusion. In order to ascertain what kinds of initiatives would be most effective, calls for future research into tourism include a stakeholder participative model of inclusion and its impact on future community development and integration.

References

Ashton-Shaeffer, C., Gibson, H.J., Autry, C.E. and Hanson, C.S. (2001) Meaning of sport to adults with physical disabilities: A disability sport camp experience, *Sociology of Sport Journal,* 18(1), 95–114.

Australian Bureau of Statistics (2006) Disability and Disabling Conditions. Available at: www.abs.gov.au/Ausstats/abs@.nsf/b06660592430724fca2568b5007b8619/007014b26d9b2b7eca25693100076c5f!OpenDocument.

Bhattacharyya, J. (2004) Theorizing community development, *Journal of Community Development Society,* 34(2), 5–34.

Bi, Y., Card, J.A. and Cole, S.T. (2007) Accessibility and attitudinal barriers encountered by Chinese travellers with physical disabilities, *International Journal of Tourism Research,* 9(3), 205–216.

Bradley, V.J. (1994) Evolution of a new service paradigm. In V.J. Bradley, J.W. Ashbauh and B.C. Blaney (eds) *Creative Individual Supports for People with Developmental Disabilities: A Mandate for Change at Many Levels* (pp. 11–32). Baltimore: Brookes.

Chalip, L. (1995) Policy Analysis in Sport Management, *Journal of Sport Management,* 9(1), 1–13.

Cheung , C-K. and Man-hung Ngan, R. (2007) Empowering for community integration in Hong Kong, *Journal of Developmental and Physical Disabilities,* 19(4), 305–322.

Darcy, S. and Daruwalla, P. S. (1999) The trouble with travel: People with disabilities and tourism, *Social Alternatives,* 18(1), 41–46.

Daruwalla, P. and Darcy, S. (2005) Personal and societal attitudes to disability, *Annals of Tourism Research,* 32(3), 549–570.

De Bosscher, V., De Knop, P., Van Bottenburg, M. and Shibli, S. (2006) A conceptual framework for analysing sports policy factors leading to international sporting success, *European Sport Management Quarterly,* 6(2), 185–215.

Department of Human Services Victoria (2007) *Disability Act 2006: Policy and Information Manual.* Melbourne: Department of Human Services.

Department of Premier and Cabinet (2005) *A Fairer Victoria.* Melbourne: Department of Premier and Cabinet.

Department of Premier and Cabinet (2001) *Growing Victoria Together.* Melbourne: Department of Premier and Cabinet.

Eichhorn, V., Miller, G., Michopoulou, E. and Buhalis, D. (2008) Enabling access to tourism through information schemes? *Annals of Tourism Research,* 35(1), 189–210.

Freeman, R.E. (1984) *Strategic Management: A Stakeholder Approach.* Boston, MA: Pitman.

Fullagar, S. and Darcy, S. (2004) Critical points against an Australasian therapeutic association: Towards community leisure through enabling justice, *Annals of Leisure Research,* 7(2), 95–103.

Jonker, J. and Foster, D. (2002) Stakeholder excellence? Framing the evolution and complexity of a stakeholder perspective of the firm, *Corporate Social Responsibility and Environmental Management,* 9(4), 187–195.

McKercher, B., Packer, T., Yau, M. K. and Lam, P. (2003) Travel agents as facilitators or inhibitors of travel: Perceptions of people with disabilities., *Tourism Management,* 24(4), 465–474

Merriam, S. B. (1988) *Case study research in education: a qualitative approach* (1st edn). San Francisco: Jossey-Bass.

Muir, K., Fisher, K., Dadich, A. and Abelló, D. (2008) Challenging the exclusion of people with mental illness: the Mental Health Housing and Accommodation Support Initiative (HASI). *Australian Journal of Social Issues,* 43(2), 271–291.

Neuman, W. L. (2000) Social research methods: qualitative and quantitative approaches (4th edn). Boston, MA, and London: Allyn and Bacon.

Patterson, I. (2007) Changes in the provision of leisure services for people with disabilities in Australia, *Therapeutic Recreation Journal,* 41(2), 108–118

Sautter, E. T. and Leisen, B. (1999) Managing stakeholders: A tourism planning model, *Annals of Tourism Research,* 26(2), 312–328.

Shaw, G., and Coles, T. (2004) Disability, holiday making and the tourism industry in the UK: A preliminary survey, *Tourism Management,* 25(3), 397–403.

Shaw, M., Dorling, D. and Davey Smith, G. (1999) Poverty, social exclusion and minorities. In M. Marmot and G. Wilkinson (eds) *Social Determinants of Health* (pp. 211–239). Oxford: Oxford University Press.

Sheehan, L.R. and Ritchie, J.R.B. (2005) Destination stakeholders: Exploring identity and salience, *Annals of Tourism Research,* 32(3), 711–734.

Tourism Victoria (2007) Victorian Accessible Tourism Plan 2007–2010 (Draft). Available at: www.tourism.vic.gov.au/images/assets/All_PDFs/VicAccessibleTourismPlan2007_Draft.pdf.

Walsh, D. and London, J. (1995) *Arts and Disability.* Sydney: Australia Council.

Wituk, S., Pearson, R., Bomhoff, K., Hinde, M. and Meissen, G. (2007) A participatory process involving people with development disabilities in community development, *Journal of Developmental and Physical Disabilities,* 19(4), 323–335.

Yin, R.K. (1994) *Case Study Research: Design and Methods* (2nd edn). Thousand Oaks, CA: Sage Publications.

11 Accessible Tourism in Sweden: Experiences, Stakeholders, Marketing

Lilian Müller

The Development of Accessible Tourism in Sweden

The development of accessible tourism in Sweden has in many respects followed the development in other European countries during the last two decades. Beginning with a growing awareness of the fact that also disabled people has the right to travel and make holidays, continuing with a raised knowledge about disabled people's needs and that this issue is more complex than only the talk about physical access; turning into a wider and deeper understanding of accessible tourism from the point of diversity, design for all and a customer-oriented management.

At the beginning of the 1990s accessible tourism was focused on tourism for disabled people, rather than tourism accessible for all. A number of tourism facilities could provide service and accommodation, adapted in most cases to wheelchair user's needs, as an answer to a growing demand. This development took place in parallel to the changes in the society and disability policies, paying more attention to the disabled people's rights to an independent life. In the Governmental directives for The National Tourism Board in the beginning of 1990s, the Government communicated that the disabled person's right to travel and take holidays should also be taken into account in their work. A holiday guide for disabled tourists was produced by the National Tourism Board, until 1993. After some reorganizations of the National Tourism Board, this message was left out in the following directives, and the Holiday Guide for Disabled was no longer produced. In 1995 Sweden joined the European Union, and one of the many issues that had to be handled in the European Context was Accessible Tourism. In the framework of the initiative Helios, accessible tourism was regarded as one important policy issue, as well as a possibility for development of European Tourism. A number of private and public actors in the European Union's member states initiated development projects on the theme of accessible tourism, and were looking for a Swedish partner. The cooperative association Tourism for all in Sweden was founded within the framework of a transnational project, funded by the European program Employment, the county council of the Swedish region Värmland, and the County Labour Board in Värmland. The idea was to set up accessibility consultancy services for Swedish tourism and at the same time to create new job opportunities for people with disabilities. The Swedish membership in the European Union, and the possibilities to join transnational projects also gave the opportunity for municipalities and regions to start their local development work in this field, which was the case for example in the municipality of Halmstad. By the time more local and regional initiatives was taken, while the activities set up by the association Tourism for all in Sweden was developed and extended, mainly in the framework of European transnational cooperation and networking.

In the year 2000 the Swedish Parliament decided upon the national action plan for disability policies 'From patient to citizen' (Ministry of Social Affairs, 1999). This action plan stated that Sweden by 2010 should be a country accessible for all. In order to put this political vision into practice, The National Board of Housing, Building and Planning developed directives for the *Removal of easily eliminated obstacles* (National Board of Housing and Planning, 2003) in order to improve the accessibility of public and private buildings and open areas. The costs for these actions were not taken into account, but were supposed to be handled within the normal budgets for public and private actors. A big lack of information and know-how could also be noted among the actors. In 2008, with only two years left until the vision should have been turned into reality, there was a lot of work to be done by municipalities, regions, the Swedish state and among the private property owners. The process has been quickened lately by the establishment of the state authority *Handisam (Swedish Agency for Disability Policy Coordination)* that started in 2006. According to the laws and directives, all buildings and outdoor areas that are opened to the public shall eliminate the easily removable obstacles, as defined by the National Board for Housing and Planning. This work, which probably will be significantly enhanced during the coming years, will be of great importance also for the opportunities to offer accessible tourism venues and destinations in Sweden.

Accessible Tourism in Sweden – Strengths and Weaknesses

Sweden can offer a wide range of tourism attractions and activities with a good level of accessibility for all, not at least within nature tourism. But despite a high level of ambitions and consciousness among individual tourism entrepreneurs, there are still a lot of work to be done before one can say that Sweden is a country accessible for all. As the awareness of the demand for accessible tourism are growing among tourism companies, the number of facilities and venues that can present offers accessible for all, are growing. All around Sweden, one can find accommodation, catering, nature experiences, shopping, cultural events, sport arenas, historical buildings etc adapted to meet the needs and expectations from customers with different needs. It's obvious that more and more of the private tourism companies and entrepreneurs are considering accessible tourism as important for being competitive on the tourism market. Tourism for disabled people is turning into the focus on tourism accessible for all. There is still a big lack of knowledge in how to create tourism venues, destinations and offers accessible for all. Many hotel owners are busy adapting a number of rooms for disabled persons' needs, and these efforts are still in many cases focused on physical accessibility; while adaptations of information, communication, and welcoming are not made visible enough. On the other hand, there is a wide-spread understanding of disabled people's needs, and a willingness to do what is possible in order to welcome customers with special needs. The lack of long term strategies is often solved on the spot with *ad hoc* solutions.

The public tourism bodies on national, regional and local level are not coordinated in terms of accessible tourism. The work especially on the national level, is focused on marketing of existing offers. On regional level, the organization, ownership and policy of the Regional Tourism Boards are decided in each region. The ambition to bring accessible tourism forward, is often dependent on the presence of persons with knowledge and experiences in this field. On the local level, there is often a lack of resources that prevents the local public actors to pay special attention to the tourism companies that are willing to adapt their offers. The growing demand for accessible tourism venues has brought the change that many of the tourism brochures often includes some accessibility information (mostly according to the needs of people with reduced mobility).

Actors for Accessible Tourism in Sweden

Another problem that easily can be identified is the fact that there is a lack of cooperation between private and public actors, between municipalities and regions, and between different sectors of tourism. In order to overcome this, the association *Access Sweden* was founded in 2007. The aim of *Access Sweden* is to bring stakeholders and actors together, to build bridges between private and public interests, and to create a platform for development and transfer of knowledge and the practical know-how. *Access Sweden* also acts as the national coordinator for ENAT (European Network for Accessible Tourism) activities in Sweden. The Board of Access Sweden contains representatives from the public and private sector, as well as NGOs like *Independent Living*.

The association Tourism for all in Sweden, since 2002 situated in the region of Skåne, continues the work to develop accessible tourism in terms of development and transfer of knowledge and know-how in transnational cooperation. Being one of the main sponsors of ENAT, Tourism for all in Sweden is an actor that ever since 1995 has been a focal point in Sweden for contacts and cooperation in the context of accessible tourism in European projects and initiatives.

Since 2008, the consultancy and marketing services developed by *Tourism for all in Sweden*, has been handed over to *Svenska EQUALITY* (private company) who runs the accessibility database called EQUALITY and gives support and services to tourism companies, municipalities, regions etc in terms of accessible tourism. Svenska EQUALITY makes accessibility audits and is working in information, communication, marketing and training. Among the Swedish regions and destinations, the works are multifaceted. Some municipalities, such as Askersund and Vellinge, have taken a long-term approach to create strategies for becoming accessible destinations. Among the regions, interesting experiences can be transferred from the work that has been carried out in Skåne. This region in the south of Sweden, has worked with accessible tourism in a business oriented perspective. The aim has been to develop accessible tourism, in order to strengthen the business companies and create new employment in the tourism sector. In cooperation with a German TV producer a film for the German market was produced in 2007, presenting the border region Skåne and Själland as Accessible Öresund (Hermann Hoebel Filmproduktion, 2007). The film was a success, broadcasted in many of the German TV channels, and was presented at the Tourism Film Festival in Karlovy Var, Czechia recently.

At the same time, accessibility has been given attention in all other activities that the region are responsible for. In the natural areas owned and run by the region, a lot of important work has been done in order to ensure good accessibility also to nature environment. The regional company for public transport, *Skånetrafiken,* has also made strong efforts to adapt their service for passengers with different needs and there is an ongoing process to adapt buildings and services to become accessible for citizens and visitors.

Marketing of Accessible Tourism in Sweden – in Mainstream and Target-Group-Oriented Channels

Knowing that of the main reasons for people with disabilities not to travel, was the lack of reliable accessibility information, *Tourism for all in Sweden* created and introduced the EQUALITY concept in 1999. The EQUALITY label is a guarantee for any costumer that the accessibility information shown in the database EQUALITY on internet is collected, measured and analyzed by an external auditor, who have done the work on behalf of the association *Tourism for all in Sweden*. For the facilities and venues that has been audited and marked with the label, the participation in EQUALITY means possibilities to get professional advices on how to handle the continuous improvement of the facility. At the same time to reach important target groups with marketing based on reliable information, and thereby get new visitors. As an EQUALITY-registered facility, a number of services linked to information, support, advising, training and marketing are offered, from the company. EQUALITY is a registered trade mark, and is getting more and more known among tourism companies, public actors and visitors. The idea is to meet the visitor's need of detailed accessibility information, to an extent that is not possible to provide through mainstream channels. Hence it is an important supplement to the ordinary brochures and websites. To reach an even larger public and to improve the service for the tourism facilities, the information in the EQUALITY database was linked to the European web-portal Europe for all (2008) and a booking function was in place in 2009.

Providing accessibility information into mainstream travel channels is of great importance. The region of Västra Götaland has tackled accessible tourism from another angle. In close cooperation with the disability organizations in the region, a new tourism database has been developed with the accessibility information integrated and labelled according to different handicaps. This database covers tourism facilities in the region of Västra Götaland, and there is a possibility also for other regions to use it. The information in the database is based on self-assessment, and the regional tourism board is prepared to support the municipalities and companies with the training needed.

The dilemma of main-streamed or tailor-made information is always prevailing. Ever since the introduction of the EQUALITY label, there has been a discussion about how to present accessibility information. Integrated in the mainstream channels or through tailor made and specialized accessibility information channels? Both from the visitor's points of view, and from the tourism enterprises the answer is probably both! Tourism facilities and venues that are accessible to all visitors have a competitive advantage and should therefore be active to market this advantage to potential customers. To advertise both in the mainstream channels as well as in the target oriented information channels accumulates the possibility to get new customers. Many persons in the core target groups do not always trust the information in the ordinary brochures, and this might be a perception based on own previous experiences. To be able to give accessibility information checked by external professionals is therefore a way to complement and strengthen the basic information given through the mainstream channels.

Accessible Tourism Strategies

There are currently no coordinated strategies on the national level in Sweden, in order to become successful in accessible tourism. The issue is though given increasingly more attention. To realize the Swedish Action Plan on Disability Policies, making Sweden accessible by 2010, is one important tool. Other tools are activities that can give support and inspiration to the tourism enterprises, in example to show good practice and to make it possible to learn from each other. Recently the 'Flag of towns and cities for all' was introduced in Sweden. This initiative was taken by the Design for all Foundation and started in Barcelona. The 'Flag of Towns and Cities for All' offers to municipalities all over the world, the opportunity to join a group of towns and cities that have committed to improve their public space, their facilities, transport, building and services, to improve the quality of life of their citizens and visitors. The goal is to make visible the good practices regarding accessibility and Design for All of the towns and cities involved in the project. To obtain the flag, the actions must be carried out by a local government, and the municipality has to devote at least 2% of their investment budget. There has to be an action plan with tangible results which can be measured each year, and the actions shall be supported by local associations and citizens. The first town to obtain this flag in Sweden was Askersund, located north of the lake Vättern.

Based on the experiences from more than a decade of development of accessible tourism in Sweden, there are some golden rules that could be identified and to learn from, in order to support and speed up the process for accessible tourism for all.

Cooperation: Private/public/NGOs

To make the entire tourism service chain accessible for all visitors, there has to be a close cooperation between the private tourism enterprises, public authorities and municipalities/regions. A successful process also takes into account the participation of non-governmental organizations, who in many ways can contribute to a better understanding of the needs for better accessibility in different terms. Where such cooperation can be found, the results can also be recognized.

Make use of previous experiences and knowledge – don't re-invent the wheel

In Sweden there are many examples of initiatives taken for better accessibility that have been initiated and carried out on the local level, without analyzing what others have done before. The total amount of resources to spend in accessibility adaptations, are often quite limited. To make the tourism industry competitive in the field of accessible tourism has also its time limits – there are many actors in this competition. It is therefore of utmost importance to be efficient when consuming time and money in this matter. To make use of existing knowledge and experiences is one way to become more efficient in the process. The wheel is already invented – and so are many important tools for accessible tourism. Databases, symbols, means and methods to analyze accessibility is some of them. To make use of existing knowledge and know-how also means to consult the experts working in this field. Accessibility is a complex issue that cannot be expected to be learnt in details by all staff members. A transfer of knowledge has to take place, but should be put on the right level and scale.

Provide reliable information

Customers are asking for reliable information. Accessibility information should be dealt with carefully, and routines for quality assurance of the information should be taken into account by anyone that is providing tourism information. Self-assessed information is normally not to consider as quality assured, as long as the informant has not the adequate competence in accessibility. In most cases tourism venue owners do not have this competence. Tourism entrepreneurs are experts in entrepreneurship and the tourism offers he or she provides – but they are seldom accessibility experts! This is the main reason every day tourists can find irrelevant and wrong accessibility information in tourism brochures and on the web. It is also very important to provide the detailed and relevant accessibility information, for those who need it, through target-oriented marketing channels, and at the same time integrate it into the mainstream marketing channels.

Long term strategic planning

Creating an accessible destination cannot be done overnight. Long term strategic planning is needed, as well as a great portion of knowledge, cooperation, and not least patience! One important tool can be to set up an accessibility plan. Such a plan gives an overview of the existing situation regarding accessibility and usability of buildings and outdoor environment for people with specific accessibility needs, and should be the base for which actions that should be carried out in order to improve the accessibility. Cleary identified measureable goals should be set to make it possible to follow the process and improve the plan continuously.

Trained staff

In tourism, the service and welcoming are crucial factors for the quality of the experience. Many high ambitions to create an accessible environment by eliminating physical obstacles, providing accessible information etc have been unfulfilled because of inadequate staff training. No matter how high the level of physical accessibility is in a place, if the staff are not prepared to provide a warm welcome and adequate information and support, the visitors' experience will be negative. The basic knowledge on the specific needs of different people, how to handle difficult situations related to the need or the absence of accessibility and so on is necessary for all employees as well as managers in the tourism sector to undergo.

Experiences from the Municipality of Askersund

Askersund is a municipality with 11,470 inhabitants, situated north of Lake Vättern. In the municipality there is a strong commitment to reach the goal accessibility for all, and to become a destination with a clear profile of being a municipality that works towards an environment designed for all. A detailed accessibility audit has been carried out in 20 of the most important public buildings, and the busiest outdoor routes. From this audit, a detailed action plan for accessibility is being developed, where detailed measures have been identified, and the economic resources to carry out the actions in the plan, have been pointed out in the budget for the coming years. This amount is average to about 10% of the public investment budget per year. Besides the actions set out in the accessibility plan, the perspective of accessibility and design for all will be integrated for all other investment projects.

Besides all the efforts made by the municipality, there are a rapidly growing awareness about accessible tourism among the tourism entrepreneurs. One of the pioneers and an important model, for other tourism companies to follow, is the passenger boat M/S Wetterwik (Figures 11.1, 11.2, 11.3). M/S Wetterwik which can take up to 30 seated passengers with wheelchairs. The ship is equipped with elevator, handicap toilet and hearing loop. When the owners bought the boat a couple of years ago, they decided to invest for better accessibility, thinking why offering a tourism service only to a few people and not to everyone? Spending around €20,000 for the elevator and other adaptations, some might have thought it to be a risky affair. But it proved to be an investment that paid off, already after the first season. Apart from becoming one of the important tourism attractions in Askersund, M/S Wetterwik has also contributed to spread positive effects on accessible tourism in the region.

Receiving many visitors with different specific needs, the demands for improved accessibility has been raised, on other tourism services and attractions, as well as on the community planning. For instance, many disability organizations are now arranging excursions to Askersund for groups of people using wheelchairs, in order to take a trip with the boat. But they also need to eat, to find accommodation, and they want to visit the shops. Some visitors are arriving by car, needing a disabled parking space close to the boat. There is also a need for accessible destinations where the boat can be moored.

The largest forest owning company in Sweden, *Sveaskog*, made their contribution to accessible tourism in Askersund by adapting the island

Figure 11.1 M/S Wettervik, platform lift

Figure 11.2 M/S Wetterwik, Askersund

Figure 11.3 M/S Wetterwik arrives at the island Grönön

Grönön to the needs of people with reduced mobility. In parts of the island a wooden deck was also built, to facilitate the access for wheelchair users. A disabled toilet was also built on the island. Grönön is located in the beautiful archipelago of Vättern, and is a part of an eco-park. Recently the municipality received, as the first municipality in Sweden, the Flag of towns and cities for all. The Flag is an important tool in the continuous work for improved accessibility. It raises the demands on the municipality to take actions that are measureable, and it forces the actors, both public, private and NGOs, to cooperate. To obtain the Flag, the municipality has to fulfil a number of criteria, among them to involve the citizens in active participation. With the available tools and the strong commitment from the municipality and the tourism companies, Askersund has created a strong platform in the development of becoming a destination accessible for all, and the experiences that will be gained along the way will be important for other municipalities and destinations to follow.

Conclusions: Accessible Tourism in Practice

The process of improving accessibility from the human rights perspective is driven in parallel to the discovery that accessible tourism is also a commercial opportunity. In Sweden there are about 1.8 million citizens who are considered to have some kind of disability. Together with families and friends they represent a large part of the population. The improved quality of life that will be gained as a result of the public sector's work to eliminate obstacles in the community planning will also be a driver to increase travel and leisure activities among the target group. Looking at it from the tourism enterprise point of view, all efforts to create accessible tourism facilities will also force the municipalities to expedite the process of creating a society for all.

References

Hermann Hoebel Filmproduktion (2007) *Grenzenlos: Access Öresund* (DVD). Munchen: AK Film.
Ministry of Social Affairs (1999) *From Patient to citizen*: Prop. 1999/2000:79. Sweden: Ministry of Social Affairs
National Board of Housing and Planning (2003, 2004) Removal of easily eliminated obstacles, Directives BFS 2003:19 HIN and BFS 2004:15 ALM. Sweden: National Board of Housing and Planning.

Resources/Web-links

Access Sweden: www.access-sweden.se.
Askersunds municipality: www.askersund.se.
Askersunds archipelago: Grönön: www.askersund.se/turismochevenemang/turismengelska/ontopoflakevattern/moreaboutthearchipelago/gronon.4.18e8fbd11072dbed0b80002410.html.

Flag of towns and cities for all: www.designforall.org/en/dfa/bandera.html.

M/S Wettervik: www.wettervik.se/e_index.html.

National Board of Housing and Planning: www.boverket.se.

Svenska EQUALITY database: www.equality.se/nepsite7/equality/tfa.nsf/mainseek.

Swedish Disability Federation (2008) Statistics available at: www.hso.se/start.asp? sida=291.

Swedish Agency for Disability Policy Coordination: www.handisam.se.

Tourism for all in Sweden: www.turismforalla.se.

Västra Götaland regional accessibility database: www.vastsverige.com/templates/search ____1120.aspx?td=true

12 The Third Sector Responses to Accessible/Disability Tourism

Philippa Hunter-Jones and Anthony Thornton

Introduction

The aim of this chapter is to examine the role of the charitable sector in holiday provision for vulnerable consumers. As it will show, given the paucity of academic tourism research currently existing in this area, to understand this relationship we really need to explore beyond this literature base and dabble in fields of marketing and consumer behaviour research, venturing also into practitioner and trade publications, and literature published by charitable organizations. Two simple questions lie at the centre of the discussion: what do we mean by the term accessible/disability tourism? What role do charitable organizations play in facilitating tourism provision for this community? The chapter begins by addressing the first question and in doing so introduces us to the complex term vulnerable consumer. From here we move into a review of the scope and operation of charitable organizations, both within a general context and also more specific to the Tourism Industry. Methods of data collection, primary and secondary, are subsequently reviewed and the findings discussed. The chapter concludes with suggestions for future research.

Accessible/Disability Tourism

Our first challenge is to ascertain the meaning and scope of the term accessible/disability tourism. If we take a narrow interpretation of this consumer base then this leads us into the domain of the disabled consumer. In the UK, the Disability Discrimination Act (DDA) (1995) defines a disabled person as 'someone who has a physical or mental impairment that has a substantial and long-term adverse effect on his or her ability to carry out normal day-to-day activities' (Directgov, 2008). Further clarification of the scope of this definition is also supplied:

- 'substantial means neither minor nor trivial;
- long term means that the effect of the impairment has lasted or is likely to last for at least 12 months;
- normal day-to-day activities include everyday things like eating, washing, walking and going shopping;
- a normal day-to-day activity must affect one of the 'capacities' listed in the Act which include mobility, manual dexterity, speech, hearing, seeing and memory'. (Directgov, 2008)

From this we can ascertain that the potential UK disabled consumer base is considerable. Indeed the UK Disability Rights Commission (replaced in 2007 by the Equality and Human Rights Commission) suggest there to be in excess of 10 million people in Britain, 700,000 of these children, with an annual spending power of around £80 billion (Family Resources Survey (2003–2004) cited in Disability Rights Commission (2007)). When it comes to the potential market for travel some further facts are interesting: the likelihood of disability increases with age; over a third of the UK disabled population are fifty plus with forecasts indicating that by 2020 this will rise to nearly 60% of this age group; by 2020 depression is likely to be the leading cause of disability (Disability Rights Commission, 2007).

Whilst the needs of the disabled community represents an area of increasing academic research, within the tourism arena there is a notable trend towards interpreting the term in a narrow sense focusing predominantly upon the circumstances of the physically impaired, with an almost total neglect of other equally compromising conditions, sensory impairment, chronic conditions such as asthma and diabetes, progressive conditions, multiple sclerosis for instance and beyond. The tourism research coverage of these latter circumstances, whilst not entirely absent (see for instance Yau et al. (2004) study of mobility and visually impaired tourists), is currently negligible. Authors involved in the debate themselves concur with these observations as Yates's (2007) review of the experiences of disabled tourists illustrates. Arguing that 'disabled travellers remain shadowy figures in existing literature and their voices are rarely heard' (Yates, 2007: 153), she collects and interprets data from people with mobility disabilities to highlight the issues this population faces in accessing tourism experiences. Concluding that research to date has failed to comprehensively review the needs of this consumer, Yates (2007: 164) goes on to argue the need to 'study other disabilities in this context such as unseen impediments like mental-health disabilities' if a fuller appreciation of the disabled population is to be achieved.

But really the scope of this chapter is much broader than considering the disabled consumer alone. Accessible is defined by the Collins dictionary as something which is 'easy to approach'. People are restricted in their consumption patterns by circumstances beyond physical or mental disability, although reaching a true appreciation of compromised tourism consumption is complicated as tourism researcher's use a variety of terms interchangeably: marginalized, compromised, disadvantaged, hidden, sensitive and excluded, to discuss highly complex circumstances (Shaw & Coles, 2004). The uniting feature of much of this work is that really we are talking about a *vulnerable consumer* described by Baker *et al.* (2005: 128) as a state which is 'multidimensional, context specific, and does not have to be enduring' and which includes both perceived and actual vulnerability. Consumer behaviour research provides the key to our understanding of who consumes what, when and how (Blackwell *et al.*, 2006). The inter-disciplinary nature of such research opens up opportunities for exploring interactions, exchanges, experience, needs and desires from a plethora of perspectives (Peter & Olson, 2005). In the tourism arena decision-making models provide one vehicle for extending knowledge of consumer behaviour. Exploring this literature base however, it becomes very quickly evident that related research has commonly focused upon established tourism routes of decision making activity, researching mainstream markets that comfortably 'fit' market segmentation criteria for instance, or revisiting the barriers of time, income and transport which are traditionally recognized as compromising tourism participation.

Economic hardship and disability are most commonly singled out as key factors inhibiting tourism participation. What is noticeable in research though is a tendency towards reviewing one inhibiting factor in isolation, focusing upon poverty alone, or disability alone, or issues linked with the tourism participation of ethnic minorities alone. This approach is problematic as it misses the point that it is really multiple variables which model behavioural patterns; economic disadvantage unlikely to occur in isolation, more likely to be a direct consequence of ill-health for instance. Smith and Hughes (1999) do consider multiple factors in their review of the economic and social circumstances which restrict family tourism participation. Commenting that 'there is evidence to suggest that holidays are widely regarded as a "necessary" part of contemporary life' (Smith & Hughes, 1999: 124), these authors go on to explore the meaning of the holiday to a group of economically deprived respondents who seldom have the opportunity to travel. Focusing upon a holiday trip supported through charitable organizations, these authors conclude that 'for all informants the holiday had a special significance – the meanings were interwoven but focused on "change" of place and of activity (...) the intensity of the meanings are undoubtedly different for this group from those experienced by the general tourist population' (Smith & Hughes, 1999: 132).

Tourism and the Charitable Sector

According to the UK Charities Act (2006), in England and Wales 'charity' refers to an institution which:

(a) 'is established for charitable purposes only;
(b) falls to be subject to the control of the High Court in the exercise of its jurisdiction with respect to charities'.

The Charities Digest (2005: viii) offers us further insights into this by explaining the meaning of the term charitable purpose 'to qualify as a charity an organization must be for the relief of poverty, or for the advancement of education, or for the advancement of religion, or for other purposes beneficial to the community, not falling under any of the preceding heads'. This fourth category is particularly relevant to this chapter as, amongst other purposes, it notes that a charity can exist for the advancement of health, citizenship, human rights and for the 'relief of those in need by reason of youth, age, ill-health, disability, financial hardship or other disadvantage' (Charities Act, 2006).

Questioning the role of tourism and travel as a basic human right, Higgins-Desbiolles (2006: 1197) argues that:

the right to travel and tourism have been incorporated in key international documents including the Universal Declaration of Human Rights of 1948, the International Covenant on Economic, Social and Cultural Rights of 1966, the World Tourism Organization's Manila Declaration on World Tourism of 1980, Bill of Rights and Tourist Code of 1985 and the Global Code of Ethics for Tourism of 1999.

Of these the Manila Declaration on World Tourism is particularly relevant to this chapter as it helps to substantiate why it is important for charitable organizations to be involved in holiday provision. It states that:

Tourism is an activity essential to the life of nations because of its direct effects on the social, cultural, educational and economic sectors of national societies and their international relations. Its development is linked to the social and economic development of nations and can only be possible if man [sic] has access to creative rest and holidays and enjoys freedom to travel within the framework of free time and leisure whose profoundly human character it underlines. Its very existence and development depend entirely on the existence of a state of lasting peace, to which tourism is required to contribute. (World Tourism Organization (WTO), 1980)

Research into charities is a burgeoning area of study. Broadbridge and Parsons (2003a, 2003b) for instance have written numerous papers exploring the charity retailing sector noting particularly the rapid growth of this sector and the increasing professionalism which underpins it, a misnomer for a sector considered to represent the 'voluntary sector'. Both Weightman

(1999) and Chesson (2001) review the work of charities and local authorities in enabling care-recipients to engage in 'normal leisure activities' (Chesson, 2001: 13) through the provision of specialist facilities. Within the tourism academic literature base, a framework provided by Turner *et al.* (2001) differentiates three roles of UK charities in the tourism industry: *outside*, *within* and *above* the tourism industry. Those operating *outside* the tourism industry utilize tourism within their fundraising function. Charities advertise the opportunity to take part in treks, bike rides, mountaineering and other such adventures to the general public. To take part, participants then have to raise a predetermined amount in sponsorship for the charity. This amount usually covers the participant travel costs involved and also a surplus which is then claimed by the charity (see for instance www.childrensadventurefarm.org/event).

Charities operating *within* the tourism industry are exemplified through the burgeoning literature base attached to volunteerism (see, for instance, Anderson & Shaw, 1999; Chen & Chen, 2011; Lo & Lee, 2011). Whilst raising sponsorship may also be a feature of these charities, really it is the opportunity to work in educational, scientific research and conservation activities which are the primary motivations behind volunteer involvement (Turner *et al.*, 2001). Working holidays operated by the National Trust, a UK charity, funded purely through public donations, which protects and conserves urban and rural places of public interest provides one example of this (see www.nationaltrust.org.uk). Charities operating *above* the tourism industry are primarily focused upon campaigning activities and challenging popular thinking in 'areas of government tourism policy, industry practices and education for and about tourism' (Turner *et al.*, 2001: 468). Tourism Concern, a non-industry based organization, established over 20 years ago, involved in campaigns for more ethical, fairly traded forms of tourism, provides one example of this (see www.tourismconcern.org.uk).

A further dimension of charitable work which does not sit so readily within the original Turner *et al.* (2001) framework is linked to the work of charities in supporting vulnerable communities, where vulnerability is linked to poverty, disability/health and wellbeing at an individual level. Much of the material attached to this dimension can be found within the social tourism literature base, a form of tourism 'with an added moral value, which aims to benefit either the host or the visitor in the tourism exchange' (Minnaert *et al.*, 2007: 9). This literature base is currently fragmented reflecting the differing understanding and willingness to engage with social tourism worldwide. In an attempt to capitalize upon, and promote the considerable benefits attached to this form of tourism, the NET-STaR network (www.westminster.ac.uk/net-star) was launched in 2011 within the UK. Supported by funding from the Economic and Social Research Council (ESRC), a goal of this network is to debate the potential of social tourism within regeneration strategy and consider its contribution to policy. But whilst this reflects important progress, the network cannot answer everything. One fundamental question which remains largely unanswered in the existing tourism literatures is what role do charitable organizations play in facilitating tourism provision for vulnerable communities?

Research Methods

To explore this further, two methods of data collection were employed including a literature search and the completion of semi-structured interviews with 20 charitable organizations. The literature search made use of the Web of Knowledge and Scopus databases. Here keywords searched included: charities, tourism, health, leisure, activity breaks, activity camps, activity holidays, non-profit, not-for-profit, voluntary sector, disability, terms used in varying combinations. This initial search supported our earlier observations of the paucity of academic research in the existing tourism literature base. Articles that were uncovered focused most commonly upon conditions arising as a consequence of holiday-taking and also the burgeoning area of health/medical tourism. According to the Charities Digest (2005) there are at least 140 charities in the UK claiming to be involved in some manner with the Tourism sector. We then turned to the materials produced by these organizations, websites and brochure most commonly, to uncover what role, if any, they actually played in facilitating tourism activity. Alongside this, contact was established directly with twenty charitable organizations and semi-structured interviews undertaken to explore the scope and operation of their work, particularly within the context of supporting tourism activity. All organizations contacted agreed to take part in the study.

Findings

Comparing publication materials, websites, brochures and press releases particularly, it became quickly evident that, whilst few charitable organizations were set up with the sole purpose of providing support for holiday-taking, many charities do play multiple roles in this area. Within their facilitating role, charities act as tourism providers and some as tourism campaigners too.

As a tourism provider

Whilst the mainstream tourism marketplace is characterised by an increasing range of holiday options, available within an ever broadening portfolio of destinations, the same cannot be readily claimed for vulnerable consumers. This gap in supply was noted by many of those contributing to this study, their thoughts captured within the comments of the spokesperson for The Royal National Institute for the Blind (RNIB) (www. rnib.org.uk):

> whilst we are very keen to see integration throughout society you really have to make sure support networks are in place for people with particular needs (…). We've found that even with so many holiday options today, many of the people who contact us just can't take advantage of them because they [holiday options and companies] simply don't do anything to help people in need.

Such gaps in provision prompted a number of charities to themselves take on a role in providing opportunities for travel. Two main models of provision existed.

The first model was based around charities owning, or leasing accommodation which they then operated. Examples here included: residential holiday homes (e.g. BREAK (www.break-charity.org)); residential homes (e.g. Autism Initiatives (www.autisminitiatives.org)); holiday homes (e.g. Children with Cancer and Leukaemia Advice and Support for Parents (CCLASP) (www.cclasp.net)); self catering chalets (e.g. Livability (formerly John Grooms Holidays) (www.livability.org.uk)); Scout Holiday Homes Trust (www.scoutbase.org.uk)); holiday bungalows (e.g. Beacon Centre for the Blind (www.beacon4blind.co.uk)); holiday dialysis centres (e.g. The British Kidney Patient Association (www.britishkidney-pa.co.uk)); holiday camps (e.g. Barretstown (www.barretstown.org)); caravans (e.g. Dave Lee's Happy Holidays (www.happyholidays.moonfruit.com)); guest houses (e.g. Corrymeela Community (www.corrymeela.org)); holiday villas (e.g. Christian Lewis Trust (www.christianlewistrust.org)), farms (e.g. www. childrensadventurefarm.org) and boats (e.g. Ellen Macarthur Trust (ellen-macarthurtrust.org)). In contrast to accommodation for mainstream travellers, hotel accommodation was largely absent in this offering, and indeed for the RNIB had been a casualty of the Disability Discrimination Act (1995), which requires mainstream hotel operators to offer more accessible facilities. In some instances the accommodation was offered entirely free-of-charge. In other instances, a fee was payable, often to cover administration, maintenance and cleaning costs.

Not all charities operated an accommodation facility. In the second model, charities funded vulnerable consumers to take holidays in facilities outside the control of the charity. Fundraising activity was a particularly important feature of the work of these charities. Monies raised were used in two distinct ways: direct and indirect. First, they were used in the direct payment of holiday accommodation or transport costs linked to holiday activity. Organizations such as Children's Wish Foundation (www. childrenswish.org), Rays of Sunshine (www.raysofsunshine.org.uk), the Family Holiday Association (www.fhaonline.org.uk) and the Starlight

Foundation (www.starlight.org.uk), for instance, raised funds to support holidays and outings for vulnerable people in need. Second, where an organization had no direct holiday function, monies were used to help vulnerable people with other living costs. Interviews with Age Concern (now Age UK) (www.ageuk.org.uk), Arthritis Care (www.arthritiscare.org.uk), the Multiple Sclerosis Society (www.mssociety.org.uk) and the Disability Foundation (www.tdf.org.uk) all included a recognition that assisting vulnerable people with living expenses might indirectly release, or reduce, the pressure upon personal monies which could in turn be put to some form of leisure pastime.

Regardless of the model adopted, a number of common features of holidays provided by, or through charitable support emerged. First, holidays had to be applied for, although an application did not automatically guarantee success. Success instead was determined by how closely the applicant matched pre-determined criteria. Second, successful applicants usually had to wait a defined period of time, often a minimum of three years, before making a further application for holiday support. Third, in most instances holidays were UK based. Some European options were possible but this was in a minority of cases. Fourth, most of the support was geared towards accommodation provision, or transport costs. There was little funding available to cover spending money or to purchase 'holiday' items, luggage or bathing costumes for instance. Fifth, whilst support often extended to family members, charitable assistance usually followed the patient needs.

As a tourism campaigner

All charities contributing to the study were originally selected on the basis that they had some tourism function. Interview data narrowed this function into two clearly defined groups. Group one consists of those charities with a direct tourism function. The Children's Adventure Farm Trust (www.childrensadventurefarm.ork), Disaway Trust (www.disaway.co.uk), Family Holiday Association (www.fhaonline.org.uk) and Tourism for All (www.tourismforall.org.uk) were the primary charities associated with this function. Group two charities had a much broader remit of activity and were engaged in offering wider help and support to vulnerable people to enable them to live independent and dignified lifestyles. Vitalise (www.vitalise.org.uk), Tripscope (www.tripscope.org.uk) and The Disability Foundation (www.tdf.org.uk) provide examples of this second group.

In the context of this study it is the charities associated with Group one who are particularly important to vulnerable consumers. The purpose and fundraising activities associated with these charities was primarily geared towards enabling vulnerable people to take a break. The common motives behind holiday support were articulated by the Disaway spokesperson:

We try to give people a chance to spend some time away from their problems (…). This often gives them the energy to cope again and, in some cases, an energy to try to change or improve their lives (…). It's also about caring for people. So many [people] on the margins [of society] just get left behind and forgotten about. We try to remind them that they matter too.

These motives echo the previously published evidence that leisure-linked activities can induce positive moods, improve cognitive functioning, reduce depression, improve self-esteem and self-concept and can have a beneficial impact upon various medical conditions (see, for example, Argyle, 1992; Forgas & Moylan, 1987). They also echo the earlier research by Hunter-Jones (2004), who focused specifically upon the contribution of leisure to the health and wellbeing of cancer patients, concluding such enhanced self-image, helped regain independence, contributed to future career prospects and prompted socially responsible behaviour.

Conclusions

This chapter has considered the role of the charitable sector in facilitating holiday activity for vulnerable consumers. This discussion has been developed around two questions: what do we mean by the term accessible/disability tourism? And what role do charitable organizations play in facilitating tourism provision for this community? Building upon both primary and secondary research we are able to conclude that accessible/disability tourism encompasses a broad consumer base. A narrow definition might be linked specifically to consumers who are experiencing some form of disability as defined in the UK by the DDA (1995). However, a more accurate reflection of the marketplace is really offered by opening the debate up to include those who might constitute vulnerable consumers, vulnerable due to health, disability, economic and social factors. Considering which organizations might be well placed to support vulnerable consumers introduced us to the third sector, charitable organizations. As the legal definition of a charity informed us, such organizations exist for a range of purposes, the advancement of health, citizenship, human rights and for the 'relief' of those in need, providing a clear link to the tourism sector.

Questioning what role charities play in facilitating tourism proved quite problematic. From a secondary research position it quickly became apparent that a paucity of research exists considering the relationship between tourism and charitable organizations. Academic sources appear to focus most commonly upon the link between charities and ethical/responsible dimensions of tourism at a community level rather than the health and wellbeing links at an individual level. Primary research has proved far more insightful and alerted us to the key role this sector does play in supporting vulnerable consumers, particularly in relation to providing and campaigning for tourism engagement for as wide a population as possible. Two different models of charitable involvement have been considered, each of which places the needs of the consumer at the heart of their decision-making process.

However, as essential and supportive as charitable organizations are where vulnerable consumers are concerned, there remains considerable work to do in the tourism context. By focusing upon the third sector role in isolation to other sectors, this study has really only addressed the surface of this engagement. What now needs to happen is for research to tackle the issue of multi-sector involvement, ascertaining how that may facilitate greater tourism engagement in the future. One of the problems with sectors working in isolation from each other is the tendency towards re-inventing the wheel. The commercial tourism marketplace is well-placed to provide support to the third sector. Bridging the gap between these sectors represents a considerable challenge, yet one which also offers mutually beneficial opportunities to those prepared to think outside the box. Not only will the tourism industry benefit from an additional source of income, but also possibly an extended season and a contribution to other means of regeneration (Houghton & Rickey, 2011), but the consumer is likely to benefit from greater holiday opportunities too. This must be considered merely as the starting point, though; only when these opportunities extend to include novel locations and accommodation offerings will we be any nearer to including vulnerable consumers within the mainstream tourism sector.

Alongside this there is a definite need for further academic writing in this valuable area. Whilst this chapter did not set out to critique all literature on the subject, rather to provide a flavour of writings, it really was a difficult subject to research. The scope for further engagement is considerable. It is not only in the field of academic writing where opportunities exist, though; indeed more practical suggestions for further work include the need to develop a comprehensive database listing holiday accommodation offerings suitable for different areas of vulnerability. Databases detailing transport choices and funding opportunities would be equally beneficial. One approach to emulate might be that offered by Weightman (1999) whose online UK guidebook of good practice and provision for vulnerable communities provides a useful template for work in this area.

References

Anderson, M. and Shaw, R. (1999) A comparative evaluation of qualitative data analytical techniques in identifying volunteer motivation in tourism, *Tourism Management*, 20 (1), 99–106.

Argyle, M. (1992) *The social psychology of everyday life*. London: Routledge.

Baker, S., Gentry, J. and Rittenburg, T. (2005) Building understanding of the domain of consumer vulnerability, *Journal of Macromarketing*, 25(2), 128–139.

Blackwell, R., Miniard, P. and Engel, J. (2006) *Consumer Behavior* (10th edn). Mason, OH: Thomson Higher Education.

Broadbridge, A. and Parsons, E. (2003a) UK charity retailing: Managing in a newly professionalised sector. *Journal of Marketing Management*, 19, 719–748.

Broadbridge, A. and Parsons, E. (2003b) Still serving the community? The professionalization of the charity retail sector. *International Journal of Retail and Distribution Management*, 31(8), 418–427.

Charities Act (2006) Part 1: Meaning of 'Charity' and 'Charitable Purpose' (c.50). Available at: www.opsi.gov.uk/acts/acts2006/ukpga_20060050_en_2 .

Charities Digest (2005) *Charities Digest 2006* (112th edn). London: Waterloo Professional Publishing.

Chen, L.-J. and Chen, J. (2011) The motivations and expectations of international volunteer tourists: A case study of "Chinese Village Traditions". *Tourism Management*, 32(2), 435–442.

Chesson, R. (2001) Respite: Definitions and policy. A background paper prepared for the MS Society as part of a review of MS Society Holiday Homes. Aberdeen: Robert Gordon University, Health Services Research Group.

Directgov (2008) Definition of 'disability' under the Disability Discrimination Act 1995. Available at: www.direct.gov.uk/en/DisabledPeople/RightsAndObligations/DisabilityRights.

Disability Discrimination Act (DDA) (1995) *The Disability Discrimination Act 1995 (Amendment) Regulations 2003*. Available at: www.opsi.gov.uk/si/si2003/20031673.htm.

Disability Rights Commission (2007) *Number of disabled people in Britain*, Available at: www.DRC/Newsroom/key_drc_facts_and_glossary/_number.

Forgas, J. and Moylan, S. (1987) After the movies: Transient mood and social judgements. *Personality and Social Psychology Bulletin*, 13, 467–477.

Higgins-Desbiolles, F. (2006) More than an 'industry': The forgotten power of tourism as a social force. *Tourism Management*, 27(6), 1192–1208.

Houghton, J. and Rickey, B. (2011) Using tourism to regenerate British seaside resorts. In: *Mapping the territory: social tourism in regeneration and social policy*, NET-STaR – Network for Social Tourism and Regeneration, Seminar 1, 30th March, University of Westminster.

Hunter-Jones, P. (2004) Young people, holiday-taking and cancer – an exploratory study. *Tourism Management*, 25, 249–258.

Lo, A. and Lee, C. (2011) Motivations and perceived value of volunteer tourists from Hong Kong. *Tourism Management*, 32(2), 326–334.

Minnaert, L., Maitland, R. and Miller, G. (2007) Social tourism and its ethical foundations. *Tourism Culture and Communication*, 7, 7–17.

Peter, J. and Olson, J. (2005) *Consumer Behavior and Marketing Strategy* (7th International edn). New York: McGraw-Hill.

Shaw, G. and Coles, T. (2004) Disability holiday making and the Tourism Industry in the UK: A pulmonary survey. *Tourism Management*, 25, 397–403.

Smith, V. and Hughes, H. (1999) Disadvantaged families and the meaning of the holiday. *International Journal of Tourism Research*, 1(2), 123–133.

Turner, R., Miller, G. and Gilbert, D. (2001) The role of UK charities and the tourism industry. *Tourism Management*, 22, 463–472.

Weightman, G. (1999) A real break. *A guidebook for good practice in the provision of short-term breaks as a support for care in the community*. London: HMSO.

World Tourism Organization (WTO) (1980) *The Manila Declaration on World Tourism*. Madrid: WTO.

Yates, K. (2007) Understanding the experiences of mobility-disabled tourists. *International Journal of Tourism Policy*, 1, 153–166.

Yau, M. K-S., McKercher, B. and Packer, T. (2004) Travelling with a disability more than an access issue, *Annals of Tourism Research,* 31, 946–960.

Internet links

This section includes the website addresses of an extensive range of charitable organizations in some way linked to the tourism sector. In addition to these, and acting more as umbrella organizations, the reader is pointed towards the following.

www.charitiesdirectory.com A website offering support (charity listings, message board, newsletter, charity sponsor packages) for UK and international charities.

www.direct.gov.uk The official UK public sector website outlining support and services for UK citizens.

www.equalityhumanrights.com The website of the Equality and Human Rights Commission, a UK non-departmental public body (NDPB), independent of government, but underpinned by public funds.

www.opsi.gov.uk The website of the Office of Public Sector Information (OPSI), an organization which 'provides a wide range of services to the public, information industry, government and the wider public sector relating to finding, using, sharing and trading information'.

www.radar.org.uk The website of the UK's largest disability campaigning network, supported by over 900 individual and organizational members.

13 Accessible Dive Tourism

Caroline Walsh, Janet Haddock-Fraser and Mark P. Hampton

Introduction

This chapter considers the potential for, and limitations restricting, the incidence of volunteer tourism in the context of accessible dive tourism. Whether a person perceives themselves as disabled person or person with disability is defined by perception on the models of disability. The EU uses the term 'person with disability', many NGOs in the UK prefer 'disabled person', referring to the dis-enabling nature of the term. Models of disability can be broadly defined into the Medical or Social Models, each with subcategories. The Medical Model is focused on the traditional perspectives of disability of one who is ill and not fitting with the form of normal body form. A sub category of this is the rehabilitation model, traditionally reinforced between the First and Second World Wars where medical staff worked with services personnel to enable them to be 'normal' again. The Social Model came about in the late 1970s and focuses on the environment being the disabling aspect not the person with the impairment(s).

Accessible dive tourism is an emerging sub niche of dive tourism and has developed from disabled dive tourism. The definition of accessible dive tourism is wider than disabled dive tourism. It also needs to reflect those who face challenges (initially perceived as physical) to access this niche form of tourism. This market has increased in recent years as the number of disabled persons and persons with disability are learning to dive. However, exact data is scarce and difficult to locate on the numbers of disabled divers. Global estimates do not exist and the major dive training agencies such as PADI (Professional Association of Dive Instructors) do not release any figures, but proxy figures can give some order of magnitude. One proxy is the numbers of specialist instructors qualified to train disabled people to dive. The US-based Handicapped Scuba Association (HSA) has more than 2000 instructors and over 4000 members worldwide (HSA website, 2009).

In order to advance our understanding of the potential for accessible dive tourism, we will undertake the following: At the outset we will consider definitions of disability and accessibility. We will then explore the history and scope of disabled-accessible diving in terms of history and size of market. In addition we will investigate and speculate on reasons that may hinder or restrict further development of disabled dive opportunities from a multi-stakeholder perspective. Once we have completed our synopsis of the state of disabled diving as a market, we will then consider the specific case of volunteer opportunities within dive tourism for disabled participants. After understanding that a disabled diver's motivations for participating in volunteer diving (usually for conservation reasons) is similar to the more able-bodied, the chapter will examine the opportunities and limitations on developing volunteerism opportunities for disabled divers. It also makes recommendations that would enable participation in the same volunteer initiatives in marine conservation, natural resource management and poverty alleviation as able-bodied divers. It is hoped that this chapter can help identify some of the barriers to accessible dive tourism, and specifically disabled volunteer dive tourism, and demystify some of the processes involved. The hope is by doing so, it encourages greater involvement and openness to such ventures. Through such inclusive and accessible methods, and by using appropriate expertise, accessible dive volunteer tourism could be an increasing leisure tourism opportunity for more people.

Definition of Disability and Accessibility

'Physically challenged' is a broad category. Within this category are those who are physically challenged due to cultural constraints, those who consider that they are physically challenged because they have a physical challenge to overcome to participate in certain activities and finally, there are the physically disabled by medical condition, illness, accident and so on. 'Physically challenged' is defined in the Oxford English Dictionary as 'Relating to body (or in wider sense gender) opposed to mind, suffering from impairment or disability in specific respect'. 'Physically disabled' is defined by the Oxford English Dictionary as: (1) A physical condition that limits a person's movement, senses or activity; (2) A disadvantage or handicap. Handicapped is itself defined by the Oxford English Dictionary as: 'an environmental or attitudinal barrier that limits the opportunity for a person to participate fully' (either by the person themselves or others). Therefore, physical ability is defined as relating to the body, relating to things perceived through the senses and the ability, skill and talent a person has.

The tourism industry needs to work to overcome moveable physical limits or restrictions that create unfavourable circumstances or conditions for persons with an interest in participating in any form of tourism and to make their participation feasible and accessible to them. These persons may suffer impairment or disability relating to the body in a specific respect and for whom there is a challenge to overcome to contribute to a given activity.

'Accessible' is defined by the Oxford English Dictionary as (1) Able to be accessed; (2) Friendly and easy to talk to; approachable; (3) Easily understood or appreciated. Thus, by inference, accessible dive tourism is able to be accessed by all, approachable, friendly to all, with messages easily understood and appreciated by all.

At least 20% of the UK's working age population has a disability that affects their ability to work (Office for National Statistics, 2007). According UN ENABLE this figure translates to at least 500 million disabled people in the world, of whom 80% live in less developed countries. As such, if these figures are transposed to restrictions on tourism activities, there is the possibility that, in the absence of accessible tourism policies, the industry as a whole is not catering for a potential market opportunity, and needs to consider opportunities to widen participation, and expand its accessibility.

However, there is comprehensive research to demonstrate that attitudes to disability have historically created barriers to leisure, sports, travel and tourism. Such barriers have prevented the tourism industry embracing the opportunities that could potentially be gained from widening access.

History and Scope of the Disabled Dive Market

History

Disabled diving effectively began in the United States in the late 1970s with the formation of the Handicapped Scuba Association (HSA), followed in Europe by the formation of the International Association for Handicapped Divers (IAHD). Disabled diving in the UK started to flourish in the UK in the late 1980s with the formation of the Dolphin Club based at the Diving Diseases Research Centre (DDRC) in Plymouth, and the emergence of specific charities such as the Scuba Trust. With the increase in international travel and increased impetus in disabled diving with the spread of IAHD and HSA training for both instructors and disabled persons, disabled dive tourism evolved from an embryonic base. This, however, was not necessarily *accessible* dive tourism. The reason for this is, particularly from a European perspective, is due to the history and particular development of mainstream diving and, the associated emergence of dive tourism. In the UK and Europe travelling for leisure diving started from a small base of expedition-style adventures that required little, or no, facilities or infrastructure. Diving was broadly a male-dominated activity in these early days often led by instructors who had originally been taught to dive in the armed forces (Ecott, 2002). Equipment was often rudimentary (or even made by participants) and was of a strongly functional/military design with early manufacturers' brands having names like the 'Buddy Commando' etc. In addition, there was a lack of diving equipment (such as buoyancy jackets or wetsuits) that was designed for female divers' anatomy until the early 1990s.

The scuba diving industry has grown rapidly since the 1980s (Garrod & Gossling, 2008) and has also seen a growing market developing for training disabled people. With the continuing growth in the profile of such disabled groups and the increased awareness in dive tourism, it is conceivable, that like other sectors of society, disabled people may increasingly consider participating in dive tourism.

It is hoped that through increasing public awareness of the need for accessible tourism, and the use of marketing tools, coupled with accessible and inclusive practical approaches that all people (regardless of physical ability) with an interest in scuba diving would be able to make an informed choice when assessing the recreational/tourism market about participating in dive tourism. It is about enabling an informed choice in the same way mainstream scuba diving markets itself to other sectors of society whilst providing the practical 'base' to cater for specific needs logistically and scientifically.

Market features

There are two internationally recognised diving agencies that train disabled divers: the US-based HSA and the IAHD in Europe. Other diving agencies include BSAC, PADI, SAA, and NAUI. A recent technical report on diving from the DDRC (Shelly *et al.*, 2002) suggested that that PADI may be the most proactive in disability training and integration. BSAC run a Disabled Awareness Course. Both agencies have Disability Advisors/ Adaptive Techniques Advisors. From the limited and incomplete data available from the relevant organizations' websites the following basic data shows 32 recorded IAHD Instructors in the UK (2003 figures) and 76 recorded HSA Instructors in the UK (of whom one is classed as 'active', one classed as 'teaching' and 74 classed as 'sustaining' their qualifications).

In the US there are 674 HSA instructors and the proportion who are 'active' or 'instructing' is about a quarter of these (HSA website, 2008). IAHD note that they have trained over 4500 instructors in total but do not have figures for those that are now inactive (personal communication with IAHD, 2008). BSAC have designed a Disabled Diver Awareness Course for able-bodied divers to become buddies to disabled divers but it is unknown how frequently this course is run internationally.

Since the later 1970s disabled diving courses run by HSA and IAHD have enabled disabled persons to train as disabled divers, and able bodied instructors to train to work with disabled individuals. In the UK there is one principal disabled diving club – the Scuba Trust – which trains disabled people to dive. Training offered by these organizations tends to focus on adapting and designing dive training techniques which accommodate the impairments of specific groupings. However, these are exclusive groups and do not currently have training or practice sessions with non-disabled divers.

The Scuba Trust has recently changed its philosophy, stating that its focus is training disabled people but that the able-bodied can train alongside (Scuba Trust, 2009). This is a step towards an inclusive approach.

The HSA in the US has used diving as a rehabilitation tool at physical rehabilitation facilities. In Europe the IAHD has largely adopted the 'social model' of disability not the 'rehabilitation' model, promoting scuba diving as an equalising sport, one that divers can participate in equally. From this it is clear that attitudes towards the disabled diver may differ regionally – with greater inherent acceptance and opportunities for recreational tourism diving for the disabled emerging from Europe and for the European market rather than in the US.

It appears that the relatively small proportion of disabled people in dive tourism broadly reflects the general problem of the under-representation of disabled people in leisure and sports in many Western and other societies. It can be argued that this stems from historical social exclusion in society of some groups. Disabled dive tourism has developed out of the growing movement by disabled people to integrate into society, and to take advantage of similar opportunities available to the more able-bodied. However, it has been identified in previous research carried out by Scope (2005) and the Institute for Volunteer Research (2004–2005) that able bodied and disabled individuals do not tend to participate in certain activities together. The groups appear to disengage or avoid engaging with each other due to a lack of confidence and motivation. The lack of confidence and motivation is either in their own ability to interact with the other identified group and/or a lack of confidence in other group to interact in return. There also may be a lack of experience too in terms of meeting the requirements of the disabled diver or understanding their capability. This all adds to the continuation of exclusive groups and activities, and acts to limit opportunities for better integration.

In the United States, scuba diving training of disabled people is used by such agencies as the HSA as a form or rehabilitation activity in rehabilitation facilities. This has meant that that dive tourism of disabled and able bodied people has developed in different spaces (such as different training pools, dive centres or actual dive sites) and at different times. Such separation would hinder integration in a dive site context, as the purposes of able-bodied and disabled divers would be perceived to differ.

In addition, typically, dive resorts such as those located on Egypt's Red Sea coast had initially developed to cater for traditional dive tourists only. However, the latent demand for disabled dive locations has resulted in the HSA initiating dive trips to selected dive resorts worldwide. Interestingly, this growing demand exposes dive resorts to the needs of disabled divers and there is now an impetus starting to encourage dive operators to become more accessible. A similar phenomenon is taking place where European divers of all abilities frequent, for example, Dahab on Egypt's Gulf of Aqaba, and reportedly Eilat. There has also been a movement to bring accessible dive tourism to Aqaba, Jordan. There are other sporadic examples in Southern Europe. This provision occurs at the dive operator provider level but there continues to be a lack of an integrated approach to accessible dive tourism from policy level down through all levels involved in planning infrastructure, services and accommodation. It is not clear at the outset whether such responsibility lies with local authorities, tour operators, hoteliers or instructors. To further understand the disconnect between the opportunities for able-bodied and disabled divers concerning actual dive locations, as well as their interactions requires a consideration of the various stakeholders' perspectives. We consider such perspectives from the policy makers within the tourism industry, dive instructor trainers, diver instructors, and individual participants.

Stakeholder Perspectives on Disabled Dive Tourism

Tourism Industry Policy Makers

In order to identify opportunities attractive to disabled dive tourists, tourism policy makers need to understand not only the individual planning process that divers undertake when selecting, booking and executing dive travel plans but the additional needs of those currently finding difficulties accessing dive tourism. The physically challenged diver looks for destinations (countries, local area within countries), carriers (airlines, boats, trains) and service providers (hotels, activity providers etc) who can demonstrate effective and accurate communication about the current provisions of infrastructure, services and accommodation as well as a willingness to learn to cater for the needs of the whole group undertaking the activity.

A common concern voiced by operators at well-established destinations with existing diving infrastructure, is that it will be too expensive or complicated to adapt current provisions to make them accessible, without necessarily having an understanding of what would be required to make the destination accessible to disabled divers. The counter argument is that there may be economic benefits to increasing the market potential for the site, but also indirect benefits accrued from providing infrastructure that provides societal as well as direct economic benefits, with reputation enhancement opportunities from open access.

The Tourism Provider

Within the tourism industry there is discussion over the degree of perceived adaptations required to incorporate the needs of the disabled diver but further research is necessary to determine whether this perception of degrees of adaptation is correct. There is also a concern, amongst providers in the EU and internationally, that if they provide and fund opportunities for instructors to train with the HSA or IAHD to work with disabled trainees, having invested, they might risk limited demand, or possibly even no disabled trainees. A lack of understanding exists to the image created by dive providers through literature and websites as well as the impact on accessible provisions at dive centre, destination itself as well as travel to and from it. Providers do not understand what is needed to sell their product to disabled divers, or whether particular facilities are required to support them (e.g. equipment, access to and from boats, etc.).

Barry University in the US provides an interesting example that could be used as an example of good practice for others. It runs a leisure undergraduate course for diving professionals that integrates disabled dive training within all aspects of learning about the diving industry. Thus the focus is on dive training for *all* rather than separating able-bodied and disabled instruction. It helps to create the mindset and focus of the instructor towards inclusive and accessible approaches as a norm, effectively bringing this issue into the mainstream.

Such integration can be seen in an example from Thailand where a dive operator – Worldwide Dive and Sail – employs an instructor with a visual impairment not as a role model, but as a normal member of the teaching team (Worldwide Dive and Sail, 2009).

The Instructor

The main concerns voiced by instructors tends to be 'will I have the additional skills required to cope with those divers or dive trainees who don't fit the norm?' and 'Will I make money from training in the same way as I make money training the normal dive trainee?' However, both of these worries can be addressed through awareness training and Continued Professional Development of the instructors, leading to better understanding of disablement and the possible barriers and constraints individuals face, as well as understanding of the extra cost and time that may be required in training and support. This is particularly effective if the instructors are given a greater understanding of the social context of disability within society.

Individual Divers

The personal perspective of the individual depends on the personality and experiences of the individual concerned and how they come to the diving experience, for example, through rehabilitation or leisure choice. Whether or not an individual can participate in accessible dive tourism may further be influenced by their financial situation, economic activity, social capital, and social networks – particularly the mindset and experiences of peers and friends. An example of influence of the personal perspective can be seen in the research undertaken by Natural England (2008) into the constraints affecting socially excluded groups from partaking in activities in the countryside. Those with limited social networks, social capital, a poor financial situation and little economic activity tend not to experience or participate in activities in the countryside. The research findings concurred with the constraints identified in other leisure studies relating to disability. Diving is a relatively expensive hobby and is even perceived by some an 'extreme sport' and thus the inference would be that the same factors influence participation (Ward, 2002). Those connected with such groups such as the HSA tend to experience scuba diving within a rehabilitation context and may then be involved in dive tourism through charitable type opportunities. Thus the negotiation of any barriers is undertaken on their behalf or on a day by day, *ad hoc* basis. However, the negotiation process of individuals outside this sphere relies on whether they have the financial position and experience to do so. Their initial decision to participate in scuba diving also relies on the home community attitude, peer group image, as well as the individual's experiences and personality.

As with able-bodied divers, disabled divers have a variety of motivations to dive. A subset of both groups is interested in diving as part of a wider interest in conservation and a desire to participate as a volunteer in dive tourism projects. Whilst it is recognised that this activity barely exists currently for disabled divers, the next section explores the barriers that currently prevent this development and provides some suggestions as to how these could be overcome – enabling more disabled divers to participate in volunteer conservation and environmental schemes, alongside more able-bodied divers.

Volunteer Dive Tourism and Disabled Divers

Background

UK volunteer organizations involved in international marine conservation often work overseas in less developed countries with an aim to improve and/or monitor the marine and coastal environment for the local population using international volunteers. NGOs in marine conservation such as Coral Cay Conservation and Earthwatch use these volunteers to gather data to assist in natural resource management, marine conservation and in some cases poverty alleviation (Clifton & Benson, 2006). Some also attract local volunteers from that country. The main mechanism for collecting and monitoring underwater environments is through the use of scuba diving. To the authors' knowledge there have been very few experiences of inclusive and accessible volunteer tourism experiences taking place within this context. Many such NGOs have expressed concerns regarding cost, impact on outputs, effects on group dynamics etc as barriers to inclusive and accessible volunteer tourism in this niche sector. Within this section of the chapter we identify the potential barriers as a first stage to breaking them down and enabling greater participation.

The major concerns voiced by such NGOs tend to be over how to integrate disabled divers, and questions over their physical constraints, especially the costs, and the overall cost-benefit analysis arguments supporting integration. In addition, there are questions over group dynamics with the view that there are likely to be negative impacts on group dynamics if the disabled diver needs increased support and whether that might result in a decline in the quality and extent of work produced. In addition, concerns have been raised about the logistics of such dive expeditions. Finally, there are worries over the 'dumbing down' of their conservation activities in terms of coverage and scope, as there is a common view that the disabled diver would be able to achieve less in a given time than a more able-bodied counterpart. Even if they considered accessible dive volunteering, questions remain over how to develop role models such as disabled facilitators and disabled participants.

It is important to explicitly identify constraints that exist in this sub section of dive tourism and assess whether these can be overcome and reduced so that physical ability is not a constraining factor, adversely affecting group dynamics and the desired task outcomes of the NGO. Areas where such physical constraints may exist include logistical/site access, scientific training and education, scientific methodology and the natural environment. The extent to which these physical constraints hamper dynamics and task will depend on the site and its particular details and so cannot be standardised in a simplified fashion. Likewise the extent to which the disabled diver needs support may depend on a range of factors including degree of physical ability, as well as motivation and the context of the receiving environment.

Group Dynamics

In such NGO-led expeditions, volunteers tend to create a 'community within a community'. The effectiveness of the group can depend on the group dynamics, their interactions with each other and outside as well as external factors. However, given the disconnects identified above relating to able-bodied and disabled divers we need to question in this context whether or not the physical ability of individuals could affect group dynamics and thus the task-orientated outputs that are required. It could be perceived that a range of physical abilities would have varying effects on group dynamics and the outputs of that group (that is, how much research and the quality of this research produced). If there is such a negative impact, the disabled diver may not be considered an attractive proposition for NGOs and other such organizations looking for volunteer divers.

The focus for the disabled diver, as for any volunteer, should be on the skills required to practically participate in marine conservation from an on-land and in-water perspective. From this point we can work towards integration/inclusion. Changing the attitude of the group towards considering where the disabled diver can help or participate rather than the mindset of what they cannot do is important for group acceptance. In addition, from a group dynamic point of view, the more the participants dive in a non-volunteer context with disabled divers and understand their equivalency of training the quicker group barriers will be removed.

Cost–benefit analysis

Whilst the actual cost of any modification required to adapt facilities is very site-specific, and may be perceived to be prohibitive, there are a number of principles or concepts that need to be borne in mind in any cost–benefit analysis. These are:

(1) Direct on-site costs (see logistics below) relating to the adaptation of facilities and potentially costs of transport. These need to be balanced against items (2) and (3) below.
(2) Direct benefits accruing from the reduction in the marginal cost (per participant) of expedition infrastructure and volunteer recruiting, as there is potentially a larger group of participants to draw on.
(3) Indirect benefits arising relating to adherence to human rights of the diver as well as societal benefits to the organization and other participants as a result of widening participation.

The cost–benefit case should remain open-minded to the balance of what are largely direct costs against indirect benefits, and the NGOs concerned need to consider the wider scope of 'cost', 'benefit' and 'value' as many need to now in valuing species and conservation projects in any case.

Logistics and Operations

At a practical level, the physical barriers for disabled divers need to be removed to encourage and enable disabled diver participation. These are clearly site and context specific but, in general, a NGO would need to consider, at a site level the logistical elements that are inconsistent with the promotion of accessible marine conservation. These would need adapting to:

(1) enable, enhance and promote accessibility to accommodation and survey sites for all regardless of physical ability;
(2) conform to relevant British and International Building Regulation Standards;

(3) address associated risk assessment and Health and Safety elements associated with changes.

Consideration is required of the carrying capacity of the human and natural environment to incorporate physically challenged divers. Physically challenged divers require two dive buddies. Thus no more than a third of the number of volunteers could conceivably be physically challenged. Alternatively the operator may choose to extend the number of volunteers over and above the norm to accommodate a specific number of physically challenged divers as long as the human and natural carrying capacity is not exceeded.

In terms of concerns about instructor capability it should be possible to promote inclusion in regular training of a HSA/IAHD training course running in parallel where the candidates can gain experience 'buddying' a physically challenged diver, so that they are confident to do this on an expedition. This may aid the process of attracting both physically challenged trainees and divers.

Regarding specific training requirements the following could be undertaken:

- A consideration of the health issues and physical restrictions (movement, etc.) experienced by physically challenged persons and how to adapt marine survey training so that these adaptations would allow them to successfully, safely and actively participate in marine conservation.
- Propose, introduce and teach adapted marine survey techniques to scuba instructors who will teach physically challenged divers.
- Propose how to educate the target group on the extra provisions they need to be aware of when undertaking these activities.
- Raise awareness amongst able-bodied facilitators and participants of these extra provisions as above.

Part of this will involve proposing extra Health and Safety provisions, over and above the provisions, which are already considered by NGOs when considering marine conservation activities. Such training would start to break down the negative attitudes, misconceptions and preconceived ideas about this type of accessible tourism held by the physically challenged stakeholder and the able-bodied participant demonstrating how a precautionary principle can itself be a significant barrier.

Conclusions

This chapter has discussed the emergence since the 1970s of disabled diving, which may be seen as a sub-set of dive tourism. For accessible dive tourism to develop there are a number of barriers currently to the development of integrated and accessible infrastructures, facilities and services to support this niche form of tourism. As the section on accessible volunteer dive tourism in marine conservation showed there are clear costs and benefits to disabled volunteers being included in dive tourism, but what is clear is that the issues are (1) site specific and/or (2) come from a lack of familiarity with dealing with disabled divers. While the cost-benefit argument could be expected to consider benefits beyond the directly financial case, discussions taking place currently within the European Union to develop industry standards for accessibility and appropriate training at multiple levels and multiple stakeholders will also help matters progress. Whilst these standards could be very effective they need to be developed through a participatory type approach involving disabled divers, policy makers and the local tourism providers (Bramwell & Sharman, 1999).

References

Bramwell, B. and Sharman, A. (1999) Collaboration in local tourism policymaking, *Annals of Tourism Research,* 26(2) 392–415.

Clifton, J. and Benson, A. (2006) Planning for sustainable ecotourism: The case for research ecotourism in developing country destinations, *Journal of Sustainable Tourism*, 14(3) 238–254.

Ecott, T. (2002) *Neutral Buoyancy*. London: Penguin.

Garrod, B. and Gossling, S. (eds) (2008) *New Frontiers in Marine Tourism.* Oxford: Elsevier.

Institute for Volunteering Research (IVR) (2004/5) *Volunteering for All: Exploring the Link Between Volunteering and Social Exclusion.* London: IVR.

Natural England (2008), *Diversity Review*. Sheffield: Natural England.

Office for National Statistics (ONS) (2007) *Labour Force Survey Oct–Dec 2007*. Newport: ONS.

Scope (2005) *Time to get Equal in Volunteering: tackling disabilism*. London: Scope.

Scuba Trust (2009) www.scubatrust.org.uk/HTML/home.htm.

Shelly, S., St Leger Dowse, M. and Bryson, P. (2002) *The Report: On data from the 1998–2000, Survey of Scuba Diving for Disabled Divers and divers with other conditions that may affect their diving (injury, surgery and disease)*. Plymouth: DDRC.

Ward, E.H. (2002) Sounding Silent Space: a narrative exploration of scuba diving as a therapeutic wilderness adventure bridging deaf and hearing experience. Unpublished MA thesis. Johannesburg: Rand Afrikaans University.

Worldwide Dive and Sail (2009) *Deaf diving and travel. Liveaboard diving in Indonesia.* Available at: www.worldwidediveandsail.com/deaf+diving/deaf+diving+travel.htm.

Useful Websites

www.hsascuba.com
www.iahd.org
www.un.org/disabilities/default.asp?id=33

Section 3

The Accessible Tourism Value Chain

Chapters in this section:

14 Tour Operating for the Less Mobile Traveller

Andrew Wright

Introduction

In its current form tour operating specifically for people with reduced mobility, is still in its infancy. There are at least 10m disabled people in the UK alone, with 2.5 million of them travelling regularly (Tourism for All, 2008). The remainder do not travel for a variety of reasons, not least of which is because facilities and services are quite limited. This is certainly the perception of many disabled people, who are just not prepared to 'risk it'. An ageing population will result in the number increasing significantly.

Recognising that mobility impaired people rarely travel alone, this really is a huge market to be tapped. There are many issues to be addressed however, before it can be successfully developed. Disabled holidaymakers often find themselves handing over control of their lives to people who are neither well informed nor knowledgeable about their disabilities. There is also an assumption that disabled people are a homogenous group rather than individuals. It is important to recognise that they *are* individuals and that to treat them fairly, they must be treated individually.

This chapter sets out to highlight the difficulties encountered by disabled people travelling overseas. It discusses the specific needs at each stage of the holiday journey, from the decision making process right through to after sales support. Less mobile travellers encompass anyone who has difficulty moving around, either because of their disability, age or temporary injury. It points the way forward for tour operating, based on the pioneering work undertaken by Accessible Travel and Leisure, in the field of 'barrier free tourism'. Case studies have been used to illustrate the rationale behind the conclusion.

The Tour Operation

Marketing and Promotion of the Holiday Product

Reaching prospective clients who are mobility impaired is a difficult task. Particularly as so many do not recognise themselves as being disabled. Unless they are obviously wheelchair users, this is a hard to reach sector.

People often say, 'I'm not disabled, I just need a bit of help.' They are reluctant to use a wheelchair, even temporarily, although this would make life much easier for them and their accompanying friends and family.

Successful marketing is very much a matter of gaining their attention, trust and confidence. Disability exhibitions, journals, and websites are obvious mediums. The terminology and style of advertising is crucial to reach this audience. The growing significance of the 50+ market means it is increasingly being targeted, through retirement shows and lifestyle magazines. This group often have elderly relatives, even if they are fully fit themselves. The government provides extensive advice and online information for disabled people, including holidays and travel, via the Directgov website.

Client Segmentation

Like everybody else, unless extremely independent, disabled people rarely travel alone. Accessible Travel and Leisure's research (Wright, 2008) indicates that 88% travel with friends and family. The holiday choices therefore need to be appropriate for mixed groups.

- Those with spinal cord injuries, usually as a result of accidents, are often quite young and fit. Paraplegics for example may favour a more independent, adventure type break, as they usually have a great deal of upper body strength to compensate for their lack of mobility in the lower limbs. Tetraplegics, however, are far more dependant and therefore require much greater support.
- Older people and those with degenerative conditions tend to favour something more sedate, in a warm climate.
- Friends and family may want nightlife and shopping.
- Paid carers will also need some time to themselves for relaxing, in a suitable environment.
- Temporary disability due to accidents or recent surgery can happen suddenly, and people are often unsure how best to deal with the resulting lack of mobility. This group will be very unused to the situation they find themselves in.
- Accompanying children want kids clubs, swimming pools, entertainments, and excursions to appropriate sites such as theme parks, water parks and zoos.
- Many parents of disabled children often despair of ever being able to take them on a suitable holiday, where their needs can be satisfactorily met.

The Tour Operator as Coordinator

The tour operator's role is to ensure that every element of the holiday journey is successfully addressed. Each piece of the jigsaw must be in place, including adequate insurance and mobility aids. If there is one weak link in the chain the customer can become apprehensive and upset, and the holiday is ruined, not just for them, but also their companions.

The booking stage is crucial in ensuring that the resort/accommodation/ flight chosen are suitable. The client also needs to have sufficient confidence in the sales staff to be able to reveal often quite personal details of their condition and requirements. There is much more to be considered for the disabled client than the non disabled – if the holiday is to be a success.

Elements of the Overseas Holiday Journey

Airport Journey

Disabled travellers may have to consider taking wheelchairs/motorised scooters/crutches/extra cushions/buoyancy aids, as well as suitcases on holiday. Suitable transport to the airport is necessary. Part 3 of the UK Disability Discrimination Act was extended in December 2006, to include taxis, buses and trains, requiring them to make 'reasonable adjustments' to ensure that their services are accessible (Webster & Shah, 2008).

Terrorism activity means that vehicles are unable to stop near the terminal building. If clients are travelling in their own vehicles there is often a long distance to cover before actually arriving at the terminal, and the possibility of assistance. Lone travellers will need to be able to carry their luggage as well as transporting themselves. Current work being undertaken at Liverpool's John Lennon Airport, has seen the number of disabled parking bays adjacent to the main building substantially increased.

Care at Airports and In-Flight

Various surveys (Darcy, 2007), including that undertaken by Accessible Travel and Leisure, (Wright, 2008) discovered that 'flying is the single greatest deterrent for people with disabilities, who are contemplating travelling overseas'. Leonard Cheshire Disability also bears this out (Laidler, 2007). They found that nearly 66% of disabled flyers had experienced problems boarding a plane and 75% felt airports and airline staff didn't meet their needs. Examples of difficulties included a multiple sclerosis sufferer refused assistance at check-in at Heathrow on the basis that if he'd got that far without help, he could continue on his own. Also a wheelchair user was left for hours without their wheelchair in the departure lounge, unable to visit the toilet.

Things should improve under the new European regulations (July 2008), which now make European airports responsible for helping disabled passengers, from arrival at the airport right through to disembarkation and collecting baggage (Able, 2008a). This was previously an airline's responsibility, and was a piecemeal service at best. The new legislation also covers the temporarily disabled and the elderly who have difficulty walking.

The new EU Regulation spells out for the first time, that disabled people have a right to assistance on aircraft (e.g. getting to the toilet) and says airlines should make 'all reasonable efforts' to arrange seating to meet disabled travellers' needs (Equality and Human Rights Commission, 2008). The length of flight a client can undertake often dictates their actual destination. Airline staff are not permitted to assist with any toileting arrangements for health and safety reasons. Therefore clients' bladders will often dictate the length of the journey undertaken.

If clients have booked their holiday with a reputable agent they will usually have a representative waiting for them in the arrivals hall, with accessible transport.

The Resort

Resort Representatives

Individually packaged tours for the disabled are small by nature. To have a dedicated representative in all resorts is a luxury that smaller operators cannot afford. In most resorts however there will be someone with an awareness of disability, to meet and greet customers. In resorts where there is a greater volume of business, for example Tenerife, it is feasible to have a dedicated rep. This is without doubt the Achilles heel of a small, specialist operation.

Accommodation and Surroundings

Accessible accommodation is crucial and this is where clients encounter many difficulties. Often there are steps up to the hotel reception, but no ramp whilst lifts are frequently too narrow to provide wheelchair access. Clients have been known to remove the wheels from their wheelchairs to obtain access to lifts. Doorways can be too narrow and there is often too much furniture in the room. Disabled people usually benefit from plenty of space in bedrooms and bathrooms, providing room for manoeuvre. Beds can often be accessed from one side only. No two people's requirements are exactly the same but different disabilities dictate which side is easiest. Single beds are often too narrow and low. Space is required under the bed if a hoist is needed.

Bathrooms have usually been designed by a non disabled person, with little understanding of the disabled visitor's requirements. Toilets can be the wrong height whilst showers are often fixed over the bath, making them totally inaccessible. The room is designed to look aesthetically pleasing, but is totally impractical. Wheel-in showers/shower seats/bath swivel chairs/ grab rails by showers and toilets, are usually essential requirements. They are often sadly lacking however, or limited at best.

Dining rooms are often accessed via steps and clients – quite rightly – object to being lifted into the dining room as their only means of access. Here again space for manoeuvrability is essential. There are often steps or steep slopes to be negotiated in the public areas of hotels and their grounds.

Swimming pools are well used by many people with limited mobility. Ideally pool water needs to be warmer than for able bodied clients. Although pool hoists are usually an essential requirement, they are often considered to be too expensive or too unsightly to be installed. Ramped pool access is an acceptable alternative.

The surrounding area is also extremely important if the disabled holiday maker is to enjoy the same freedom as the able-bodied. How close is it to the beach, and how flat? Curbs in overseas destinations are notoriously high. Steep slopes make negotiation difficult, and features such as trees planted in the middle of pavements make for tricky navigation. Reliable, accessible transport and understanding and knowledgeable staff are pre-requisites for enjoyable excursions. Vehicles with lifting ramps ensure that several scooters/wheelchairs can be accommodated at the same time. Tourism destinations need to consider where there is adapted transport available? Are the tourist attractions disabled-friendly?

Several destinations and services are emerging globally to benefit from accessibility. For example, the Paralympic Games 2008 accelerated the construction of disabled access facilities in Beijing. The Chinese capital alone has almost one million disabled people. There had been little or no provision made for people with special mobility requirements until recently. China can become a realistic disabled holiday destination if access improves. British Airways responded well to the task of transporting the entire GB Paralympian team, plus their mobility equipment to Beijing in September 2008 (Able Magazine, 2008b). It was recognised that the project 'focussed people's minds on the challenges that disabled travellers experience on a day to day basis.'

Equipment and Nursing Care

Good equipment is the life blood of the mobility impaired traveller. Hiring this in resort avoids transportation and the risk of damage during transit. If they do take their own they need to be sure it can be reliably and quickly serviced if damaged. For example Le Ro in Tenerife and EuroCare Mobility Services on the Costa Blanca are excellent mobility aid suppliers. Both are family run businesses and have a wide selection of aids available for hire, including all terrain wheelchairs for the beach. Equipment can be pre-booked, either via the web or through a tour operator. Zimmer frames/ electric walkers/hoists/scooters/wheelchairs/shower chairs/buoyancy aids/ toilet raisers/commodes/pressure relief mattresses/bath boards and seats are not items that the able bodied need concern themselves with. However they can make or break a disabled traveller's holiday. Supplying equipment in good working order ensures peace of mind. This type of business however has its share of rogue traders. Reputable companies should have a shop front, service centre and be fully registered and licensed.

Le Ro, who also supplies a specialist nursing service, is aware that when clients make a booking they often don't fully inform the company of their specific needs. People are often ashamed and don't want to recognise the extent of their disabilities. It's a question of pride and clients often would like to do more than they actually can. The staff however are all trained nurses and are completely disability aware and experienced to deal with all eventualities.

At many resorts nursing care is available, and a good tour operator will be able to source this. Alternatively many disabled holidaymakers favour travelling with a nurse/carer who can not only attend to their daily needs, but also provide companionship during their stay. Specialist operators will also source a 'sitting service' to give the carer some time off. Attributes and approach of care staff is very important. Customers are on holiday and don't want to see a miserable nurse.

The Next Stage

More Adventurous Travel

Prospective disabled travellers often lack confidence like anybody else. Once they have undertaken a short trip they gain the courage to travel again – perhaps for longer or further afield. They may try more adventurous holidays, such as scuba diving or a safari. Diving is one of the very few sports where they can leave the wheelchair behind, enjoy weightlessness and gain the 360-degree movement they don't have on dry land. Once in the water it is as if the disability has disappeared.

Almost nothing is impossible for the disabled holiday maker on an accessible safari to southern Africa. They can feed elephants, whale watch from land or boat, and enjoy deep-sea fishing. The more adventurous can partake in shark cage diving, bungee jumping, tandem abseiling or tandem paragliding. Tented camping safaris are available for active involvement, using an overland safari truck with hydraulic passenger lift. Removable seating accommodates wheelchairs, making it ideal for game viewing. Accommodation can have accessible bathrooms with roll-in showers, and toilets with grab rails.

Accessible holiday examples

The Haus Rheinsberg Hotel

This hotel in Germany is the perfect venue for a short European break. It is near Berlin and has an excellent transport service. Companions can be provided for sightseeing trips, and an adapted horse drawn carriage is available for local sightseeing. It positions itself as 'a hotel for people with disabilities', and also has barrier free apartments suitable for groups. It has a lakeside wheelchair promenade, water activities, indoor heated pool with sauna and solarium, massage and fitness. Special aid requirements are on request, and there is a physiotherapist on hand.

The Eva Apartments

These apartments in Polis, Cyprus at 4½ hours flying time from the UK, presents an excellent example of a carefully adapted complex, owned and run by a wheelchair user and his family. Every effort has been made to ensure that this property offers a first class holiday centre for the less mobile. All accessible details have been taken care of – right down to the raised sun loungers by the pool. It is a 15 minute walk – or push – to the beach where a long promenade adds an interesting dimension. Access in and around the apartments and resort is generally good and there are ramps where needed. The host family provide accessible transport and wonderful food. Mobility equipment is available for hire.

The Mar y Sol

This Aparthotel in Tenerife has been designed specifically for the needs of disabled holidaymakers. It is set in a totally accessible environment with a wide range of equipment, care and accessible excursions, and is the perfect solution for year round sunshine. Besides the two swimming pools with hoists there is a heated therapy pool with neck showers, water cascades and Jacuzzi. The Terra Lava centre is run by medical experts and provides a wide range of approved therapies and treatments. The resort has a wide, flat promenade along the coast – ideal for mobility scooters and wheelchairs. With its medical staff and facilities on tap, this is the perfect option for the severely disabled.

Cruising

Cruising presents the ideal option, with everything under one roof, in a largely barrier free environment. The holiday starts from when the client boards ship – with none of the stress associated with air travel. Many more cruise ships are accessible with adapted rooms and facilities such as pool hoists. Even gaming tables in the casinos are elevated, to accommodate wheelchairs. Newer ships have more adapted rooms, but often not enough to accommodate the number of prospective clients, therefore early booking is recommended. The many advantages include retaining the same bed each night in familiar surroundings. No taxi transfers are required to/from restaurants, making it much more relaxing for holiday companions. Sight seeing is always possible when the ship is in port. If transfer is by tender then sea conditions plus the accessibility of the tender will determine feasibility. Help is available with embarkation and luggage. Assistance dogs are now welcome on many cruises.

The Way Forward

Accessible Travel and Leisure Tour Operator

Accessible Travel and Leisure (ATL) has gained recognition with the British travel industry as the leading specialist arranging holidays for the disabled, their families and friends. The company has a strong and attractive brand image and was created over 10 years ago, by three wheelchair users, with the vision to offer quality holidays, specifically designed for the less mobile, in a far from perfectly accessible world. The premise was that these holidays needed to be individually tailored to meet clients' particular disabilities and needs. Booking online or through non specialist agents is just too risky for those with essential requirements. The company is dedicated to providing barrier free holidays for all; whether clients need to use a wheelchair, have a modest impairment, or just a temporary injury. The Accessible Travel brand epitomises quality and service and has a caring and supportive staff at its heart. The Managing Director worked in the travel industry for 16 years before becoming disabled, and therefore had the perfect credentials for developing the organization. A factor which gives added confidence to prospective clients.

Ten years ago there was very little for the holiday maker with reduced mobility, and what there was tended to be based on a medical approach. Typically an ambulance or hospital car provided transport and medical staff offered the support, rather than a holiday rep. It wasn't exactly a relaxing break to be enjoyed. The traditional approach to selling package holidays is not appropriate for the disabled market. Holidays for disabled people start from a different perspective because everyone's disabilities, and therefore needs, are different. There is very little that can be packaged together – one size definitely does not fit all. This individual approach however does not lend itself to economies of scale and is heavy on resources and manpower. Mainstream tour operators are rarely able to devote sufficient resources to it, in the interests of economy and their need to cater for the masses. They also have a great fear of being sued. This is why it is essential to have specialist tour operators with an insight into just what it means to be disabled.

ATL sources accommodation and customers are provided with an honest appraisal. They are presented with the facts via brochure and website and decide for themselves whether the resort will make for a good holiday, based on their own understanding of their disability and needs. This is inevitably a more expensive approach, but is money well spent if it leads to a successful holiday. Cost is not necessarily a major factor when clients choose a holiday. Once their trust has been gained they are often retained for life. After sales support is good and satisfaction survey results plus testimonials, bear out clients' satisfaction with the service. This is a field with limited competition. Among the unique benefits of booking an Accessible Travel and Leisure holiday is the fact that all the accommodation and resorts used are personally inspected by ATL staff. They *guarantee* accessible rooms rather than just request them, which is the case with mainstream tour operators. They also provide the airline or cruise company with comprehensive details of client needs and requests, in order to assist with check-in, embarkation, seating etc. They ensure appropriate transport is waiting on arrival. Many clients turn to ATL as a result of bad experiences elsewhere. They may have booked independently via the internet, sometimes via large well-known agents. They have been told they'll get various facilities but have been let down, and they then lose confidence.

The company has progressed over the years and has recently formed partnerships with organizations such as the Stroke Association. A partnership with Advantage Healthcare enables them to offer an in-flight and holiday care service. Packages vary from simple companionship needs through to high dependency complex care requirements. Holidays are all ATOL bonded. Unlike where each element is booked separately and there is no protection in the event of a tour operator failing. ATL works with one of the largest specialist travel insurers for travellers with pre-existing medical conditions. Many travel insurance policies will not provide cover, leading to people travelling overseas without adequate cover. Free Spirit insurance assesses each traveller individually and can provide cover in most cases.

Franchise Operation

In 2007 in order to further develop the company and provide a more individual service for clients, ATL launched an unusual franchise scheme aiming to recruit franchisees as Specialist Travel Advisers. They would either have a disability themselves, or an association with someone who has. On the basis that their insight and understanding of the problems likely to be encountered, plus their probable network of contacts, would make them ideal partners for the organization, the company aims to continue recruiting suitable franchisees UK wide.

Following a comprehensive training programme, advisers visit clients in their own home or workplace, become acquainted with their particular needs and preferences, and advise on the range of suitable holidays available. Franchisees are selected for their interpersonal and business skills.

Several franchisee case studies have emerged. For example *Tracy Mc* represents the Somerset and Wilts area. She was struck with chronic juvenile rheumatoid arthritis at 18 months old. Despite many recurring health problems she had set up several home based businesses previously. As a disabled mum she knows and understands the pitfalls and frustrations of trying to organize a family holiday. 'Because of my own limited mobility I really do understand just what it's like to venture away from the security of home. It certainly helps clients to know that someone from the company has visited all the resorts and accommodation, and checked out any possible pitfalls. I visit clients in their own homes if need be and we can discuss their particular holiday requirements over a cup of tea. This is far better for them than queuing in a high street travel agent or risking disaster by booking on-line, with no guarantee of accessibility of resort or accommodation. I know I can't take people's problems away but I can help them to have a good holiday to look forward to.'

Dympna M is a spinally injured wheelchair user, following a car accident in 1997. She is no stranger to the problems that this presents, particularly with her big passion, enjoying holidays in far flung places. Dympna represents Northern Ireland, where there has been no service such as this available. 'There must be people like me, who love travelling but find it very difficult.' Dympna's first holiday after her accident was with friends to Florida. It was a complete disaster because although she had been assured that she would have grab rails and other aids in her accommodation, these were not forthcoming. Dympna quickly realised that many people's idea of an accessible room simply means being on the ground floor. She was relieved to get home and vowed never to travel again. Several years later she came across the ATL website and since then has had several wonderful holidays – as well as carving out a new career for herself. Most tour operators simply don't have the experience, understanding and above all facilities and accommodation to meet the needs of disabled travellers.

Jan B was the first franchisee to join the company – covering the Isle of Wight. Although Jan is not disabled – with her nursing background and love of travel, she fully understands the many problems disabled people encounter when booking through a high street agent. She was looking for a new career and said 'the personal attention that a franchisee can give to a client's booking can make the difference between a great holiday and a potential disaster. I am able to give support and advice locally and a confidence boost where needed.'

Sue and Nick M are a Plymouth-based husband and wife team covering the West Country. Nick was spinally injured some years ago following a motor cycle accident, and now uses a manual wheelchair. Sue was a nurse working in a busy hospital, and looking for a new challenge that both she and Nick could develop together, drawing on their individual experiences. No one understands better than they do about the many problems disabled people encounter when planning a holiday. 'We've become experts at finding our way around all the numerous difficulties. We first travelled with ATL in 1998. We liked what we saw and have now become part of the operation.'

Conclusion

There are many key challenges to be addressed before holidays for the less mobile traveller become mainstream and they are able to holiday overseas with confidence.

- The world at large needs to *accept* disability rather than being afraid of it. Attitudes must change. Leonard Cheshire Disability's 'creature comforts' campaign is endeavouring to change the way people view disability. The increased coverage of the Paralympic Games, and TV programmes such as BBC's Beyond Boundaries may all help here.
- The impact of the recent EU Regulation, plus an increase in staff training should lead to greater understanding and support at airports and with airlines. It should also help to remove the current conflict between ground handling staff and airlines.
- Legislation needs to continue seeking to provide a better deal for those who are mobility impaired.
- An element of glamour could be injected into marketing literature for the disabled. They have always been the poor relation of the travel and leisure industry.
- The level of accessible accommodation, facilities, and adapted transport needs to increase.
- Develop more adventurous tourism products for the mobility impaired. Use more imagination and focus on what people can do – rather than what they can't.
- Consult disabled people when designing/adapting facilities.
- Mobility impaired people need increased support from those who understand the nature of their disabilities and can accommodate them. Hence the need for more locally based travel franchisees.

If these challenges are met, the product and service development co-ordinated by Accessible Travel and Leisure can be rolled out worldwide, with support from organizations such as OSSATE (One-Stop-Shop for Accessible Tourism in Europe) and ENAT (European Network for Accessible Tourism).

References

Able Magazine (2008a) Flying For Gold, *Able Magazine*, Sept/Oct 2008.
Able Magazine (2008b) Reach for the Skies (July/August 2008) Able Magazine.

Darcy, S. (2007) Improving airline practices by understanding the experiences of people with disabilities, Travel and Tourism Research Association (TTRA) Annual Conference Proceedings. Las Vegas, USA, June 17-19, pp.61-70. Available at: http://www. turismoadaptado.com.br/pdf/trabalhos_e_pesquisas/improving_airline_practices_ by_understanding_the_experiences_of_people_with_disabilities.pdf.

Equality and Human Rights Commission (2008) Your rights to fly – What you need to know, Pamphlet

Laidler, A. (2007) *Now Boarding: Disabled People's Experiences of Air Travel*. London: Leonard Cheshire Disability.

Tourism for All (2008) *Making Tourism Accessible for All*. Kendall: Tourism for All.

Webster, L. and Shah, S. (2008) *Into the Unknown: Disabled People's Experiences of Public Transport*. London: Leonard Cheshire Disability.

Wright, M. (2008) *Report into the experiences of disabled people holidaying abroad*. Gloucester: Accessible Travel and Leisure.

Websites

www.accessibletravel.co.uk
www.chinaview.cn
www.directgov.co.uk
www.ossate.org
www.accessibletourism.org

15 Air Travel for People with Disabilities

Simon Darcy and Ravi Ravinder

Introduction

Tourism around the world has been stimulated by the commencement of low-cost carrier (LCC) operations in various parts of the world. In spite of the apprehension about air travel and associated security restrictions since 9/11, the slowing growth of most developed economies, and ever-increasing aviation fuel prices, there has been no decrease in the number of people flying both internationally and domestically. According to the International Air Transport Association (IATA, 2007), international air traffic increased by 7.6% in 2005, 5.9% in 2006 and back up to 7.4% in 2007. Interestingly, IATA also reported that, taken in total, international airlines were profitable for the first time since 2000 (www.iata.org).

Implicit in the introduction of any lower-cost product or service is the assumption that the product will reach a wider market (Barrett, 2004; O'Connell & Williams, 2005). Given the very low prices sometimes charged by Low-Cost Carriers (LCCs), one could posit that *access* to air travel has improved – certainly that price is much less of a barrier than it used to be. However, are there other barriers or constraints to air travel faced by potential air travellers? This chapter examines the constraints/issues that people with disabilities, in particular, encounter with the airline product, and how this may be exacerbated should they use an LCC. This chapter uses Doganis' (2006) conceptualization of the individual elements of an LCC airline's product elements to identify the areas where such constraints/issues occur.

The Low-Cost Carrier Model

The low-cost airline business model is predicated on an application of Porter's (1985) cost-leadership strategy, wherein the aim is to be *THE* low-cost producer in the broad aviation market. On the one hand, from the supply side, it involves the elimination of, or a reduction in cost in, all of the elements of the (airline) product that do not directly contribute to provision of the core service of air transportation, or increasing revenue. From the airline's perspective, such elements could involve cost reductions in aspects like reservations and booking, checking-in, baggage handling, in-flight services and disembarking. This is done by using price mechanisms to discourage usage or encourage self-service by passengers, which in turn reduces the deployment of resources (primarily staff resources). Reservations, booking and even checking-in is automated (i.e. web-enabled), electronic tickets are used, further, all these processes could be conducted off-site, as it were, through the web. Baggage handling is reduced by levying an extra charge for checked-in baggage, and large penalties for excess baggage are charged. Embarkation and disembarkation is not through aerobridges (thereby saving airport charges), and food, beverage and in-flight entertainment are charged for, and often comprise very basic offerings. These minimal in-flight offerings not only save on take-off weight (and therefore fuel) but also enable LCCs to operate with the ICAO-mandated minimum number of cabin staff (usually three for a single-aisle jet).

LCCs also derive improved yield from their aircraft assets by increasing their seating density (partly derived from operating a single class operation), and also by keeping them flying longer hours than full-service carriers. They, therefore reduce their turnaround times at airports to as low as 20 minutes (usually 25–30 minutes). These incremental savings in on-ground times could result in an extra flight later in the day. A lower amount of baggage handling, food and beverage replenishment and (and the resulting cabin cleaning) enable the LCCs to be ready to operate the next flight within 10–15 minutes of disembarking all their passengers.

On the other hand, from demand side, the aim is to provide a com-moditised or no-frills service to anyone who wishes to partake (what Porter (1985) terms the 'broad' market). Indeed one of the presumptions of this strategy is that a lower cost (and therefore price) would increase demand for the product and/or increase per capita usage/consumption. Low-cost air travel has indeed made air travel affordable to a larger population, particularly in emerging markets. There are also instances of a substitution effect occurring with respect choice of travel mode (Román *et al.*, 2007).

A commoditised product also implies an undifferentiated product that caters to an undifferentiated market. In other words, such products are not resourced to cater for a variety of specific needs – their business model and their service delivery simply does not accommodate such variation. At the same time, low-cost airlines' branding relies on air travel being more price accessible two groups who had previously been excluded. Slogans include 'Now everyone can fly' (AirAsia, 2010), 'Come on, lets fly' (Easyjet), 'Simplifly' (Air Deccan). Indeed, they imply that flying is now within the reach of anyone.

A Note About Language and the Cultural Context of Disability

As Corbett notes 'The power of language is overwhelming' (Corbett, 1996: 2) and language has a significant influence on attitudes and perceptions, and hence policy and practice. This chapter uses person first language where the term 'people with disabilities' is a general term that is accepted when discussing disability in a western context (NSW Government, 2010). It places the emphasis on the person first and foremost and the disability, whatever that may be, second. It does not separate the terms, only placing an order to their use. However, as Darcy (2002a) acknowledges, Oliver (1990) and others deliberately use the term 'disabled persons' as a powerful signifier, indicating that the disabling nature of society produces 'disabled people'. The person first approach to the language of disability has been reinforced internationally with the recently constituted UN *Convention on the Rights of People with Disabilities* and the *International Day for People with Disabilities* (United Nations, 2007). To reflect these enabling language practices, people with disabilities or athletes with disabilities will be used. Further, as a reaction against medicalised terms to describe the 'able-bodied' the term nondisabled will be used to further reflect a critical disability studies or social approach to disability.

Gleeson's historical analysis (Gleeson, 1999) of disability concludes that disability has been a changing social experience due to the economic mode of organization of a society. He goes on to suggest that the experience of disability occurred not only between historical periods but also between cultures within periods. In the context of the 21st century, there is recognition of a difference between Western and Eastern, developed and developing world, medical and social model conceptualisations of disability (Miles, 1982, 1996, 2000). Moreover, in the Australian context there is a difference between European and indigenous conceptualisations of disability (Ariotti, 1999). Abberley (2002) observes that 'It is above all a relationship, between impaired people and society' (p. 6). Eastern conceptualisations of disability are substantially different to liberal Western approaches to human rights that have seen people with disabilities gain rights of citizenship (Jaeger & Bowman, 2005).

With regard to Eastern conceptualisations, Miles (2000) examination of Buddhist, Zoroastrian, Jain and Daoist religious influences in Asia notes, that these view disability outside of European conceptualizations that had been heavily influenced by Judeo-Christian thinking. For example, the Jains of Southwest Asia as far back as the 5th century had protocols and laws against verbally abusing people because of their conditions (e.g. leprosy), which had the effect of reducing the pejorative terms. Yet this 2500-year-old example exists alongside cultures where a social revulsion to disfigurement is one of the few avenues for employment as beggars in many countries.

Zoroastrian Vendidad openly expresses an utopian future which eugenically excludes the 'physically and the morally "undesirable"' (Miles, 2000: 607). It can argued that within Buddhist interpretations of reincarnation, disability is seen as a consequence of actions in a previous life, this is educative or reformist. The influence of religion on culture and, within cultures, provides examples of the complexity in understanding disability within a tourism context.

People with Disabilities, Seniors and the Accessible Tourism Market

Globally there are over 650 million people with disabilities (Fujiura & Rutkowskikmitta, 2001; Mercer & MacDonald, 2007). The Australian Bureau of Statistics (ABS) (2009) show that substantial numbers of Australians have disabilities, and the level of disability in the community increased from 15 to 19% of the population from 1988 to 2009. Australia has an ageing population and the numbers and proportion of older people in Australia is growing dramatically (Australian Bureau of Statistics, 2007). This situation is largely reflected in all Western developed nations with a noticeable difference in Asian countries where ageing is occurring at a faster rate (Altman, 1975; WHO, 2007a). These trends have considerable implications for global tourism (Dwyer, 2005). The World Health Organization (WHO) has reflected concerns of ageing with the recent release of *Global Age-friendly Cities: A Global Guide* (WHO, 2007a). The guide offers directions for urban planners, but also instils accountability through providing a checklist that older citizens can use to 'monitor progress towards more age-friendly cities' (WHO, 2007b). Despite statistical evidence and advances in urban planning, there has been very little research or policy that has sought to systematically investigate the implications of the ageing of the population, subsequent increase in rates of disability and the implications for global tourism (Darcy & Dickson, 2009).

Reedy's seminal book (Reedy, 1993) on marketing to people with disabilities was the first to use the powerful population estimate of 43 million Americans to gain the attention of the US business sector. Similarly, Touche Ross (1993) and Keroul (1995) used estimates of disability in the European and Canadian populations to argue the market potential of the group. The first Australian market study was undertaken by Darcy (1998) where he estimated travel by individuals with disabilities was worth A$473 million, or their group travel was valued at A$1.3 billion. Burnett and Bender Baker (2001) drew attention to the discretionary income of these groups through nationally collected data. It was not until 2002 and 2005 that the US accessible tourism market used a commissioned market research study by the Open Doors Organization, which collected travel patterns of people with disabilities. Through these figures it was estimated that people with disabilities contribute US$127 billion to the economy each year with US$13 billion directly attributed to travel (HarrisInteractive Market Research, 2005). Similarly, Neuman and Reuber (2004) estimated German tourists make a €2.5 billion contribution to the economy where the European Union countries' OSSATE research estimated that tourists with disabilities contribute €80 billion to the economy using gross demand estimates (Buhalis et al., 2005). The most recent Australian estimates by Dwyer and Darcy (in Darcy et al., 2011) are the first to use economic modelling based on the Tourism Satellite Accounts, which estimate that the day trip, domestic and inbound accessible tourism market to be worth A$8 billion to the Australian economy. From an inbound perspective, it has been estimated that 7–8% of international travellers have a disability and it is this group who directly contribute to increased Gross Domestic Product (GDP) to the economy (Darcy, 2003; HarrisInteractive Market Research, 2005).

A number of authors note that tourism experiences for people with disabilities are more than access issues (Shelton & Tucker, 2005; Stumbo & Pegg, 2005; Yau et al., 2004). For people with disabilities a foundation of any tourism experience is having accessible destinations and locating appropriate accommodation from which to base oneself while traveling. Once this is determined in the travel-planning phase then people need to travel to the destination region. A greater proportion of people around the world now use air travel as their preferred mode of travel as it has been democratized through the advent of low-cost airlines (Doganis, 2005). Studies in Australia and overseas (Burnett & Bender-Baker, 2001; Darcy, 1998, 2002a; HarrisInteractive Market Research, 2003, 2005; Turco et al., 1998; Daniels et al., 2005) have shown that air travel creates a series of constraints for people with disabilities.

The applicability of antidiscrimination or disability specific legislation to air travel was first discussed by Reukema (1986) and placed in a leisure travel constraints context by Smith (1987). Yet, surprisingly few studies have specifically examined the air travel experiences of people with disabilities. Abeyratne (1995) presented the legislative responsibilities of carriers for people with disabilities and seniors while Driedger (1987) discuss the accessibility of the components of air travel. A great deal of specific policy has been released by the national government agencies responsible for regulating domestic and international carriers in the USA, Canada, the UK and the European Union. Despite these policies, a review of NewsBank and Factiva databases (1995–2007) revealed many hundreds of articles worldwide outlining the ongoing constraints that people with disabilities encounter with air travel. In the Australian context, the anecdotal accounts have been validated by the Human Rights and Equal Opportunity Commission (HREOC) (2006) complaints cases and Federal Court actions taken by people with disabilities against airports, airlines and the tourism industry generally. This was further developed producing case studies of the constraints faced by air travel from all over Australia (Public Interest Advocacy Centre, 2007).

Given this background, and Darcy's research (Darcy, 2007) through in-depth interviews of this group of people, this chapter examines the airline product as offered by Low-Cost Carriers (LCCs), and highlights the elements of the LCC product/service that poses most problems for people with disabilities. The chapter also posits the airlines' possible rationale for this lack of access. Having done this, the chapter argues for a whole-of-industry approach to provide access to people with disabilities. It is especially important in the context of the rapid growth in airline traffic in India, and the current plans for the modernization of Indian airports, much of which has already started or is being commissioned.

Methodology

This section utilizes the research findings form a larger study undertaken by Darcy (2007) on the air travel experiences of people with disabilities. His research used a modified grounded and phenomenological approach through semi-structured in-depth interviews of fifteen respondents. Their responses were analysed using the NVivo qualitative software package. It is supplemented by complaint cases taken under the Disability Discrimination Act, 1992 through the HREOC (2008).

This section compares the experiences, emotions and responses to the LCC product from the above sources, using the framework used by one of the pioneering airlines – Southwest Airlines from the USA, as described by Doganis (2005). Along the way, the chapter also presents the airlines' rationales for the lack of inclusive management practice. The Southwest model has been adapted and often modified by individual airlines, although it would be fair to say that this model is still one of the benchmarks referred to within the airline industry.

The Low-Cost Carrier Model (Southwest Airlines)

Doganis (2005) lists ten broad elements of the 'simple' LCC product. These are discussed below, with their particular implications for people with disabilities.

(1) *Fares*

Fares need to be 'low, simple, unrestricted (not subject to restriction with respect to advance purchase, and minimum stay away). Cancellations, postponements, and re-routing however are heavily penalized.

The fares need to be point-to-point without interlining or en-route transfers and connections.

The fare sub-elements have provided the opportunity for many people with disabilities to travel who had previously been at an economic disadvantage. Many people with disabilities face higher rates of unemployment and, hence, low or incomes than the general population. Most recent research from HarrisInteractive Market Research (2005) and Dwyer and Darcy (2011) suggest that the majority of people with disabilities undertake them on travel patterns to the rest of the population. The exception to this is people with high level mobility disabilities who require an attendant to travel with them. This group tends to take the simple routings rather than complex multi-stop itineraries.

Two significant issues faced people with disability with respect to airfare pricing. The first is that many airlines practice discriminatory pricing whereby people with disability are charged at a higher rate than people without disabilities (Lazar *et al.*, 2010). This differential pricing is then compounded with the LCC's stringent baggage allowances where many people with disabilities need to travel with extra equipment such as commode chairs and medical equipment such as oxygen and respirators. While some airlines have allowances for designated equipment, policy on baggage allowances for wheelchair users or people with assistive devices such as oxygen, respirators or guide dogs varies from airline to airline. Further, depending on the type of assistance device determines whether it has to go into the baggage hold. Any equipment that goes into the hold may be regarded as baggage and incur additional charges (e.g. charge per bag or per kilogram based on the distance travelled). See Figure 15.1.

As indicated earlier, the LCC model discourages checked-in baggage so as to reduce baggage-handling costs (usually undertaken by a contractor), and also because more baggage incurs a time penalty, which is particularly costly from the point of view of an LCC. Airlines also cap the compensation provisions for any equipment damaged in the aircraft hold. This proves inadequate for high cost disability equipment items. For example, Qantas has a damage cap of US$1600. Most wheelchairs cost between US$2000 for the manual and US$20,000 for power wheelchairs. Due to this, most people with disabilities need to take out their own travel insurance on high cost items.

Since the introduction of low-cost airlines, there has been an increasing requirement for people to provide details about their 'medical conditions'. This has had a series of implications with regard to whether a person meets the airlines 'independent travel criteria' and whether they will be allowed to book with the airline. Virgin Blue domestic service in

Charges for overweight baggage

For any bag you are checking in that is heavier than the free weight allowance of 23kg (51lb), you may need to pay an overweight baggage charge. Overweight baggage charges are payable at check-in.

Overweight baggage charges

Weight	Overweight baggage charges
More than 23kg (51lb) and less than 32kg (70lb)*	£40 or local equivalent at check-in ($60 from any US departure airport)
More than 32kg (70lb)	Baggage over 32kg must be shipped separately as freight or cargo. > More about freight or cargo

* British Airways will waive the heavy bag charge for:

- Gold and Silver Executive Club members
- First, Club World and Club Europe customers on all routes
- American Airlines AAdvantage Executive Platinum members
- Iberia Plus Platinum members
- Mobility aids for passengers with a disability and passengers travelling with their own wheelchair
- Essential medical equipment

Passengers travelling to and from Brazil are entitled to 32kg (70lb) per bag at no extra charge.

Close

Figure 15.1 Excess baggage charges
Source: http://www.britishairways.com/travel/bagchk/public/en_us

Australia introduced such a policy, which is currently being challenged in the High Court of Australia through a class action instigated by a group of people with disabilities who believed they had been unfairly treated by the airline as they have all travel independently with the airline on previous occasions. An extension of the same point has been an attempt by some airlines to indemnify themselves from any responsibility to passengers with disabilities. For example, if one flies Jetlite in India, a 'medical passenger' has to 'indemnify against any liability' and 'hold harmless' the airline for any injury, damage, loss or death.

(2) *Distribution*

Reservations: Most LCCs discourage sales through retail travel agents, and opt instead for distribution through their own website or through

call centres (preferably the former). There have been a series of document constraints with tourism distribution via the web particularly
for people with vision impairments and this problem has been noted
with web-based air ticket sales (Gutierrez *et al.*, 2004). For many people
with mobility disabilities the problem is compounded where after their
bookings are made, they are then asked to contact the airline to ensure
that the airline can indeed facilitate their travel. The Public Interest
Advocacy Centre (2007) and Darcy (2007) report that people with disabilities felt uncomfortable at being 'interrogated' during these calls,
and having to endure some loss of self-esteem in disclosing personal
details. What was worse is that even after this process, a few were
still being refused boarding at check-in based on 'independent travel
criteria', which have been left to the interpretation of reservation staff
who have no training in disability related occupational therapy.

(3) *In-flight services*

Doganis (2005) lists the following elements of LCC in-flight service:
'single class, high density (seating), no seat assignment, and no meals'
(p. 157). The seating density is to increase capacity, and for most able-
bodied people, this is an acceptable trade-off for the price paid, particularly for a short-haul flight. Quite obviously, though, it does become a
major issue for people with any problem with muscles or their limbs, let
alone people in wheelchairs.

Certain categories of people with disabilities may need to be boarded
before the rest of the passengers, especially if they are wheelchair users.
Otherwise, they may need to be assisted on to their seat. This is a
particularly critical part of the flying experience, as in the first place,
the staff assisting in the boarding need to be trained in being able to
efficiently and safely lift an individual onto his/her seat and then make
them comfortable before securing them with the seatbelt. The reverse
process at the destination is equally critical. At the same time, entry and
egress of other passengers has to proceed smoothly without discomfort
to the person with disabilities or the boarding passengers.

From the LCC airline's point of view, this incurs a longer turnaround
time at the respective airports. Many LCCs, even if they do offer pre-
assigned seating, board quickly, because (usually) their aircraft are
smaller, they have only a single class/cabin, and LCCs are particularly
stringent with passengers who arrive late at a boarding gate.

A further problem arises when aircraft are not parked at aerobridges,
and many LCCs opt not to use these to save on airport charges. There
is time taken to transfer the passenger with disabilities through lifts
down the airport to ground level, and then back up to their aircraft
cabin. There are costs arising from staff time as well, particularly during
a period when a quick aircraft turnaround requires an all-hands-on-deck
approach.

Darcy's research (Darcy, 2007) highlights several instances of passengers with disabilities being manhandled, embarrassed and humiliated during the boarding and disembarking process. For people with high support needs, assistance is required to transfer from the wheelchair to the aisle chair and from the aisle chair to the aircraft seat. Even when a full-service airline like Qantas uses a hoist to assist those severe mobility problems, there are reports of being humiliated in the way they were lifted onto it. As Qantas has discovered, the porters assisting people with disabilities need to be adequately trained in disability awareness and this radically improves customer service.

(4) *Frequency and scheduling*

LCCs rely on high frequency of services between two points to realise cost economies. This in itself does not pose specific problems to people with disabilities.

(5) *Punctuality*

LCCs need to operate punctually. Especially when with one aircraft operating a number of sectors during any given day, they would wish to stick to their scheduled times, for reasons mentioned under *In-flight services* above. The major concern here is for scheduling to accommodate the boarding and disembarking of people with disabilities. This is a significant issue where the number of porters allocated to assist people with disabilities has been reduced significantly with the advent of LCC. The operational logistics mean that there are simply not enough porters to assist people with disabilities when punctuality is an issue. There are many documented cases of people being left on board aircraft hours after the plane has landed.

(6) *Aircraft used*

A densely packed low-cost airline also poses problems with respect to the particular seats allotted, the presence of restrictive armrests, and the lack of leg space affecting people with conditions like rheumatoid arthritis. There are even more serious concerns with respect to the lack of accessible toilets and onboard aisle chairs. People with disabilities try to prepare for the worst and use ground toilet facilities before and after they board and many can cope with this alternative for a short-haul flight, but as LCCs contemplate extending their business model to long-haul flights, this warrants some consideration.

Short-haul routes usually involve single-aisle narrow-bodied aircraft, and these pose a greater problem in these respects than a wide-bodied aircraft in being able to accommodate many such conditions. The new Airbus A380 aircraft flown by Singapore Airlines, however, has a couple of seats taken out to accommodate people with wheelchairs; they are also located close to toilets. Will other customers of this aircraft follow suit? Conversely, the British Airways A319 places a restriction on the size of power wheelchairs that can be accommodated. The power wheelchair over 60 kg taken on this aircraft and only one power wheel-chair of this size can be taken at a time. This would mean that if there were a couple who were both power wheelchair users then only one of them could be accommodated at any one time on this type of aircraft.

(7) *Sector length*

Again, the sector length is not an issue of concern, per se, for people with disabilities, but it is the airline's response in catering for longer flights that is the issue, as discussed in the previous two paragraphs. Seat comfort, freedom to move and toilet usage are all concerns that people with disabilities may need to confront on a longer flight.

(8) *Airports*

As indicated in previous sections, a good deal of the onus of care rests with airports – accessible entry and exit to and from the airport, spaces for accessible movement, accessible toilets (including being near boarding gates) and access on to and from aircraft. The use of coaches and/or walk to aircraft parked at remote bays has been alluded to before. In Europe and North America, LCCs often use alternative (or secondary) airports that are cheaper to use because they have smaller runways, minimal facilities within the terminal, and, more often than not, no aerobridges. Some mainstream airports like Changi (Singapore) and Kuala Lumpur International have developed dedicated low-cost terminals within their complexes, once again offering a minimal range of facilities for the passengers. Care need to be taken to ensure that this minimal airport offering does not constrain usage by people with disabilities.

(9) *Staff*

Doganis (2005) indicates that whilst LCCs tend to reduce the number of in-flight service staff to the ICAO-mandated minimum, they need to be paid competitive wages, and be compensated for high productivity. Airline staff (and airport staff) undergoes rigorous training to enable them to cope with a range of situations, some of which could be life threatening to individual passengers or other passengers and crew. It is not unreasonable to expect them to also be trained to handle people with disabilities at least on a physical level (assisting their movement), but also understanding their medical condition and their emotional state. Darcy (2007) features a number of incidents that arise from poorly trained staff or just an inadequate number of staff on hand.

This applies to airport staff as well. One would expect there would be medically trained or paramedical staff at airports. It is not too difficult a task to incorporate specialist training (and facilities) to be able to deal with most contingencies. Coupled with the previously mentioned physical access imperatives, this should make for a more pleasant and equitable air travel experience. However, as previously mentioned disability awareness training is more than medical knowledge. The vast majority of people with disabilities travelling not require medical assistance. What they do require it is well train customer service staff that have had disability awareness training that provides an understanding of the different dimensions of disability include mobility, vision, hearing and cognitive/learning access requirements. Each dimension has different access needs and ways of being assisted. Further, once staff have received disability awareness training they feel far more competent and gain confidence to serve the needs of the group (Daruwalla & Darcy, 2005). When this type of training is part of a broader diversity training by the airlines there is a greater it appreciation of disability as part of a dynamic community.

Conclusion

This chapter highlights several possible 'fail-points' in the service offered by LCCs to people with disabilities. In particular, they are related to fares (and baggage allowances), aircraft used, airport (ground) facilities and services, and in flight services and facilities. Whilst there is a cost involved and a possible loss of efficiency in the provision of these services by LCCs, they may also be construed to be discriminatory. In addition, people with disabilities do travel and as the economic estimates from the US, UK, Canada, Europe and Australia they are already a significant component of domestic and international tourism.

The situation therefore calls for a re-application of minimum standards in line with anti-discrimination provisions of the constitution and relevant legislation. A number of Indian airlines are operating currently with leased aircraft; a number of airports are going through a substantial development phase. It is desirable and more cost-effective to incorporate physical design and operating systems from the beginning by incorporating universal design principles. As research from the construction and building industry shows, there is only a 0.5% cost differential when designing buildings to be inclusive of people with disabilities. Indian aviation has a significant opportunity to strategically position itself to be at a competitive advantage internationally to provide the infrastructure for accessible tourism experiences.

Acknowledgement

The chapter was first presented at the Tourism in India Conference, subsequent to which further literature was added, a series of mistakes/ omissions was corrected and the chapter was rewritten for global rather than Indian-specific relevance (Darcy & Ravinder, 2008).

References

Abberley, P. (2002). Work, disability, disabled people and European social theory. In C. Barnes, L. Barton and M. Oliver (eds) *Disability Studies Today* (pp. 120–138). Oxford: Polity Press.

Abeyratne, R.I.R. (1995) Proposals and guidelines for the carriage of elderly and disabled persons by air, *Journal of Travel Research*, 33(3), 52–59.

Access For All Alliance (Hervey Bay) Inc. (2006) *Survey Into the Barriers Confronted By Tourists With Disabilities – When Making Travel Arrangements, Finding Accommodation and Visiting Tourist Venues*. Hervey Bay: Access For All Alliance (Hervey Bay) Inc.

AirAsia (2010) Fee Schedule. Retrieved 3 October 2010 from: www.airasia.com/au/en/travelinformation/feeschedule.html.

Altman, I. (1975) *The environment and social behavior*. Monterey, CA: Brooks-Cole Publishing Company.

Ariotti, L. (1999) Social construction of anangu disability. *Australian Journal of Rural Health, 7*, 216–222.

Australian Bureau of Statistics (2007) 3101.0 - Australian Demographic Statistics, Sep 2006. Canberra: Australian Bureau of Statistics.

Australian Bureau of Statistics (2009) Disability, Ageing and Carers, Australia: Summary of Findings, 2009 (Cat No. 4430.0). Canberra: Australian Bureau of Statistics.

Barrett, S. (2004) How do the demands for airport services differ between full-service carriers and low-cost carriers? *Journal of Air Transport Management*, 10(1), 33–39.

Buhalis, D., Michopoulou, E., Eichhorn, V. and Miller, G. (2005) Accessibility market and stakeholder analysis – One-Stop-Shop for Accessible Tourism in Europe (OSSATE). Surrey: University of Surrey.

Burnett, J.J. and Bender-Baker, H. (2001) Assessing the travel–related behaviors of the mobility–disabled consumer, *Journal of Travel Research*, 40(1), 4–11.

Corbett, J. (1996) *Bad-mouthing: The Language of Special Needs*. London, Washington, DC: Falmer Press.

Daniels, M.J., Drogin Rodgers, E.B. and Wiggins, B.P. (2005) 'Travel Tales': an interpretive analysis of constraints and negotiations to pleasure travel as experienced by persons with physical disabilities. *Tourism Management, 26*(6), 919–930.

Darcy, S. (1998) *Anxiety to access: the tourism patterns and experiences of New South Wales people with a physical disability*. Sydney: Tourism New South Wales.

Darcy, S. (2002a) Marginalised participation: Physical disability, high support needs and tourism. *Journal of Hospitality and Tourism Management, 9*(1), 61–72.

Darcy, S. (2002b) People with disabilities and tourism in Australia: A human rights analysis. Paper presented at *Tourism and Well Being* – 2nd Tourism Industry and Education Symposium, Jyvaskyla, Finland. pp.137–166.

Darcy, S. (2003) Disabling journeys: The tourism patterns of people with impairments in Australia. Paper presented at *Riding the Wave of Tourism and Hospitality Research*. Lismore: CAUTHE – Southern Cross University, CD-ROM.

Darcy, S. (2007) Flying with impairments: Improving airline practices by understanding the experiences of people with disabilities. Paper presented at *Beating the Odds with Tourism Research!*, Las Vegas, NV. pp. 61–70.

Darcy, S. and Ravinder, R. (2008) 'Last out of the plane': Air travel for people with disabilities. Paper presented at the Tourism in India – Challenges Ahead, Indian Institute of Management Kozhikode Campus, Kozhikode. pp. 500–505.

Darcy, S. and Dickson, T. (2009) A whole-of-life approach to tourism: The case for accessible tourism experiences. *Journal of Hospitality and Tourism Management, 16*(1), 32–44.

Daruwalla, P.S. and Darcy, S. (2005) Personal and societal attitudes to disability, *Annals of Tourism Research, 32*(3), 549–570.

Doganis, R. (2005) *The Airline Business*. London: Routledge.

Driedger, D. (1987) Disabled people and international air travel, *Journal of Leisurability*, 14(1), 13–19.

Dwyer, L. (2005) Trends underpinning global tourism in the coming decade. In W. Theobald (ed.) *Global Tourism* (pp. 529–545). Burlington, MA: Butterworth Heinemann.

Dwyer, L. and Darcy, S. (2011) Economic contribution of tourists with disabilities: An Australian approach and methodology. In D. Buhalis and S. Darcy (eds) *Accessible Tourism: Concepts and Issues* (pp. 213–239). Bristol: Channel View Publications.

Fujiura, G.L. and Rutkowskikmitta, V. (2001) Counting disability. In G. L. Albrecht, K.D. Seelman and M. Bury (eds) *Handbook of Disability Studies* (pp. 69–96). Thousand Oaks, CA: Sage Publications.

Gleeson, B. (1999) *Geographies of Disability*. London: Routledge.

Gutierrez, C.F., Loucopoulos, C. and Reinsch, R.W. (2005) Disability-accessibility of airlines' Web sites for US reservations online, *Journal of Air Transport Management*, 11(4), 239–247.

HarrisInteractive Market Research (2003) *Research among adults with disabilities – travel and hospitality*. Chicago: Open Doors Organization.

HarrisInteractive Market Research (2005) *Research among adults with disabilities – travel and hospitality,* Chicago: Open Doors Organization.

Human Rights and Equal Opportunity Commission. (2008). Disability Discrimination Act Complaints Cases Register and Decisions. Available at: http://www.hreoc.gov.au/disability_rights/decisions/.

International Air Transport Association (IATA) (2007) Business Intelligence and Statistics. Available at: www.iata.org/ps/intelligence_statistics/Pages/index.aspx.

Jaeger, P.T. (2006) Assessing Section 508 compliance on federal e-government Web sites: A multi-method, user-centered evaluation of accessibility for persons with disabilities, *Government Information Quarterly*, 23(2), 169–190.

Jaeger, P.T. and Bowman, C.A. (2005) *Understanding Disability: Inclusion, Access, Diversity, and Civil Rights*. Westport, CT: Praeger/Greenwood.

Keroul (1995) *Tourism for people with restricted physical ability*. Quebec: Keroul.

Lazar, J., Jaeger, P., Adams, A., Angelozzi, A., Manohar, J., Marciniak, J., Murphy, J. Norasteh, P., Olsen, C., Poneres, E., Scott, T., Vaidya, N. and Walsh, J. (2010).Up in the air: are airlines following the new DOT rules on equal pricing for people with disabilities when websites are inaccessible? *Government Information Quarterly*, 27(4), 329–336.

Market and Communication Research (2002) *People with Disabilities: a Market Research Report*. Brisbane: Tourism Queensland – Special Interest Tourism Unit.

Mercer, S.W., and MacDonald, R. (2007) Disability and human rights, *The Lancet*, 370(9587), 548–549.

Miles, M. (1982) Why Asia rejects Western disability advice, *International Rehabilitation Review*, 4th Quarter. Availale at: www.pcs.mb.ca/~ccd/disbookl.html.

Miles, M. (1996) Community, individual or information development – dilemmas of concept and culture in South Asian disability planning, *Disability and Society*, 11(4), 485–500.

Miles, M. (2000) Disability on a different model: Glimpses of an Asian heritage, *Disability and Society*, 15(4), 603–618.

Neumann, P. and Reuber, P. (2004) *Economic impulses of accessible tourism for all* (Vol. 526). Berlin: Federal Ministry of Economics and Technology and Federal Ministry of Economic and Labour (BMWA).

NSW Government (2010) Don't dis me with that language – The disability language A – Z guide. Available at: http://www.northcott.com.au/uploaded/File/The%20Disability%20Language%20A-Z%20Guide.pdf.

O'Connell, J.F. and Williams, G. (2005) Passengers' perceptions of low cost airlines and full service carriers: A case study involving Ryanair, Aer Lingus, Air Asia and Malaysia Airlines, *Journal of Air Transport Management,* 11(4), 259–272.

Oliver, M. (1990) *The politics of disablement.* Basingstoke: Macmillan.

Porter, M. (1985) *Competitive advantage: creating and sustaining superior performance.* New York: Free Press.

Public Interest Advocacy Centre (2007) *Flight Closed: report on the experiences of people with disabilities in domestic airline travel in Australia.* Sydney: Public Interest Advocacy Centre.

Reedy, J. (1993) *Marketing to Consumers with Disabilities: How to Identify and Meet the Growing Market Needs of 43 million Americans.* Chicago, IL: Probus Publishing Company.

Reukema, B. (1986) Airlines are exempt from law on rights of the disabled, *Annals of Air and Space Law,* 11(1), 139–150.

Román, C., Espino, R. and Martín, J.C. (2007) Competition of high-speed train with air transport: The case of Madrid–Barcelona. *Journal of Air Transport Management,* 13(5), 277–284.

Shaw, S. and Thomas, C. (2006) Discussion note: social and cultural dimensions of air travel demand: Hyper-mobility in the UK? *Journal of Sustainable Tourism,* 14(2), 209–215.

Stumbo, N.J. and Pegg, S. (2005) Travellers and tourists with disabilities: A matter of priorities and loyalties, *Tourism Review International,* 8(3), 195–209.

Touche Ross (1993) *Profiting from opportunities – a new market for tourism.* London: Touche Ross.

Turco, D., Stumbo, N. and Garncarz, J. (1998) Tourism constraints for people with disabilities, *Parks and Recreation,* 33(9), 78–83.

United Nations (2007) *Convention on the Rights of Persons with Disabilities and International Day for People with Disabilities.* New York: United Nations. Available at: www.un.org/.

World Health Organization (WHO) (2007a) Global age-friendly Cities: a guide. Available at:www.who.int/ageing/publications/Global_age_friendly_cities_Guide_English.pdf.

World Health Organization (WHO) (2007b) Media Release: *New guide on building age-friendly cities,* Media Release, available at: www.who.int/mediacentre/news/releases/2007/pr53/en/index.html.

Yau, M. K-S., McKercher, B. and Packer, T.L. (2004) Traveling with a disability: more than an access issue/ *Annals of Tourism Research,* 31(4), 946–960.

16 Accessible Public Transport: Vienna City Tourism

Roland Krpata

Introduction

An accessible public transport is an advantage for everyone. Citizens even without mobility restrictions appreciate as much as users suffering reduced mobility a stepless access from all platforms to all vehicle floors. The dispatching time in all stop areas is shorter and enables more comfort and a quicker round trip circulation time on all lines. More comfort, quicker lines, more reliable time tables, shorter waiting times … a win–win–win situation for operators, citizens and tourists was the result of our experiences in Vienna.

Planning and constructing an accessible environment was one of the most ignored subjects for centuries (Figure 16.1). All over the world we were in a similar situation as after the Second World War a new handicapped movement turned up claiming its right on an equal participation on life. Even if most of the European countries have released technical standards and anti-discrimination acts, the awareness concerning accessibility as an important topic is still growing slowly. Unfortunately antipathy and ignorance is still a wide spread attitude.

The Viennese Model

In 1989 the Vienna Lines (Wiener Linien) were one of the first companies opening their doors to the new handicapped movement by starting a dialogue and comparing their offer with the demand of their user groups. First outcome was a demand and measure catalogue. An action plan separated into short term, mid-term and long-term targets. An example for short-term measures was the use of bigger sized letters and information panels to improve the readability of the visual guiding system. For mid-term projects like the lift retrofitting program financial plans and different solutions according to the local situation in old stations had to be worked out. Long-term projects were the development of new low-floor vehicles for all means of transport (Figure 16.2). Finally, some user groups suffering on a reduced mobility mentioned as well a certain demand if there was neither a

Kinderwageneinstieg E2

Figure 16.1 Past situation: old tram

Barrierefreier Zugang ULF

Figure 16.2 Present situation: new tram

product nor a solution available on the market. In some of those cases project managers of the Vienna Lines built working groups with users and solutions were found in research and development projects founded by the Austrian ministry of transport, innovation and technology.

The Vienna Lines, as one of the few remaining companies dealing with all matters of public transport, are still planning, constructing, operating and maintaining an integrated network of bus, tramway and underground lines in Vienna. The owners of Vienna Lines are the citizens of Vienna represented by the municipality. This structure does not allow evasions. User groups or the owners can immediately address their complaints to those who are responsible. Therefore the Vienna Lines considered accessibility in public transport as a challenge and a further chance to improve the acceptance of their services.

An advantage to realize accessibility was certainly delivered by the Viennese Structures. All competences and experiences to find suitable solutions existed at the Vienna Lines. The task was not only the adaptation of several facilities. All adaptations and new developments had to fit to each other. A number of achievements were introduced and those can be examined into details.

Development of New Low-Floor Vehicles

The Vienna Lines are operating the third largest tramway network in the world, after Zürich and Saint Petersburg. On a total network length of 215 kilometres 28 tramway lines circulate in short headways. A milestone in public transport history was the development of the ultra-low-floor tramway vehicle (ULF). In a public private partnership between the Vienna Lines and Siemens Austria the lowest low-floor tramway in the world was constructed (Figure 16.3). A vehicle floor just 19.7 centimetres above the road level allows an almost even access from the stop areas. The remaining gap is covered by a mechanical ramp. Actually there are 191 ULFs in operation; this is equivalent to a rate of 30% of the total number of tramway vehicles. A replacement programme should improve this ratio to 60%. The realisation of a 100% accessible tramway network remains a long-term objective. For economical reasons the long lifetime of old tramway vehicles does not allow an earlier exchange.

In the Viennese bus network there are 84 bus lines operating on a total network length of 650 km. Since 2008 the complete bus fleet is accessible. The shorter lifetime of buses enabled a quicker exchange. All buses are equipped with ramps and liquid gas engines; a further contribution to a clean environment.

On the underground network, the rolling stock of underground line U6 was fixed with an additional ramp profile below the entrance doors to reduce the remaining gap. On the other lines with the development of the

Fahrbahnaufdoppelung im Haltestellenbereich

Figure 16.3 Example of access to a low-floor tram

new V-vehicle the gap between the platform and the vehicle edge is covered by an electrical ramp at the first and the last door (Figure 16.4). On this part of the vehicles there are large sized multi-purpose areas installed to enables a comfortable placing and reversing of wheel chairs, prams or bikes.

Re-Design of Accessible Tramway and Bus Stops

Beside the development of low floor vehicles for all means of public transport the redesign of tramway and bus stop areas was forced in a special retrofitting programme. The key objective was to bring platform and vehicle levels closer to each other. A further target was to improve passenger information at stops and to realize more comfortable waiting areas. Meanwhile the new RBL-system was developed. This computer-aided operational control system enables the operation management to realize an optimal guidance of vehicles in the whole network. In the central control and in four

Überbrückung Bahnsteigspalt V-Wagen

Figure 16.4 Example of access to the new V-vehicle

local traffic control centres the operation managers are informed about the exact position of all vehicles, delays, all kind of disturbances, failures or traffic jams. They are monitoring all services and are able to react immediately on irregularities. A part of this information delivered by the computer aided operational control system was transferred to operational displays in the stop areas and became a part of the new Vienna Lines real time passenger information system. A further advantage was the implementation of traffic light influence programs. Thanks to the permission for realisation of those acceleration programs, public transport was given priority by the municipality. Special road lanes dedicated to public transport accelerate the bus service as well the round trip time of the Vienna Lines. In addition, a new modern shelter in a corporate design should indicate a stop area of the Vienna Lines from a distance. In 90% of our stops the platform edge and the whole waiting area was lifted 15 centimetres above the road level. Short ramps enable at the end of a stop area a smooth passage to pavement or to zebra crossings (Figure 16.5).

The low position of vehicle floors enables a low position in stop areas and this allows a very flexible planning of different types of stops. According to the local circumstances solutions might be found easily. Sometimes an island stop in the middle of a road is suitable. In other cases a usual side

Haltestelleninsel mit Niederflurbus

Figure 16.5 Example of an island stop

stop might be sufficient. A further option is a side stop with a lifted road lane between the stop area and the tramway track.

The Lift Retrofitting Programme

Since 1968, after the Vienna City Council had passed the required resolution for the construction of a new underground system, the network was growing rapidly. During the first construction phase the old Stadtbahn system was adapted to a new underground system realized on the new line U1. A better modal split for public transport by a new underground system should offer an alternative to pollution, noise, traffic jams and on a reduced life quality caused by motor car circulation in the city. Unfortunately accessibility was not really given attention. For handicapped citizens a special car service was organized by the city administration and the underground planning department had given priority to escalators because of their higher transport capacity. Lifts were only built in downtown areas and junctions. In this way the Vienna Lines could improve modal split but not gain the hearts of their users with a reduced mobility (Figure 16.6). They did not accept this unreliable and uncomfortable special car service and felt excluded from public transport. Their perpetual claim on an equal treatment could no longer be ignored.

Meanwhile in 1985 the planning of the second construction phase of the underground network was going on and one of the main targets was to improve passenger comfort by a user-centred equipment standard. In the

Lifts are important in mobility chains for

• wheel chair and rollator users

• elderly persons

• blind and visual impaired users

• mothers with prams ...

Südtiroler Platz

Johnstraße

Margaretengürtel

Retrofitting programs not only in one station.

The whole network must be the target!

Hietzing

Figure 16.6 The lift retrofitting programme

Push - button - divice on a pillar

Good practice: A better accessibility for wheel chair users and blind people

Figure 16.7 Push button device

new architecture of line U3 lifts were implemented in all new and afterwards in all old stations. By this decision the lift retrofitting programme was born.

The planning department of Vienna Lines optimized the lift equipment on the favour of a user-centred design. Transparent lift cabins are moving in solid glass shafts according to the safety requirements of users. Right dimensioning of cabin capacity and a high speed drive system make lifts even more attractive. Lifts in Vienna move rather fast. Minimum speed is 1 m/s, and above 9 m conveyance distances even 1.6 m/s. Cabin capacity differs from 16 to 21 persons according to the circumstances and the proposed passenger figures. Central opening gliding doors are used to reduce stop over time in lift stops. Wider lift cabins are useful if there are more than two lift stops. In stops, not all of users will get off or on. Some might stay in the cabin and for the others it should be enough space for the user exchange and loading cabins should be comfortable for wheel chair users. Tactile push button devices with Braille inscriptions installed on a pillar beside the lift doors are easily found by blind users (Figure 16.7). An acoustic floor announcement in the lift cabin informs blind users about their and the cabin position. Vienna Lines lifts are not comparable with lifts usually installed in residences or hotel buildings. In public transport stations lifts are moving almost all the time. Therefore Vienna Lines lifts are equipped with additional devices to improve their efficiency and reliability. All machine rooms, motors, gears and steering units are cooled down to keep them in order even during the rush hours on a hot day. A lift out of order is just another obstacle. Therefore, in all new stations there are at least two exits and entrances equipped with lifts.

By the lift retrofitting programme not only lifts were implemented in old stations. In station with a single entrance a new second entrance on the other end of the station with additional stairs were constructed and public transport was brought closer to the residences of the users.

Accessible Station Furniture

Toilet facilities for disabled users are also critical for stations (Figure 16.8). The standard equipment for accessible toilets for wheel chair users is defined in standards. The position for all facilities is fixed. But monitoring during the construction phase is recommended. Too many different craftsmen are engaged and if failures appear without being recognised early enough, they are addressed by a team of technicians. At the end all facilities should be placed on the right position.

Ticketing is a challenging area for stations. Ticket vending machines are quite expensive. An exchange into new products is not easy to handle. Ticket systems are imbedded in operational concepts. For this reason the Vienna Lines tried to find an approach by descending each second ticket

Development of accessible toilets

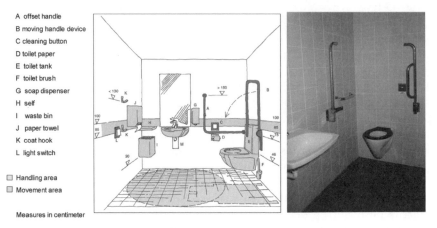

A offset handle
B moving handle device
C cleaning button
D toilet paper
E toilet tank
F toilet brush
G soap dispenser
H self
I waste bin
J paper towel
K coat hook
L light switch

☐ Handling area
☐ Movement area

Measures in centimeter

Figure 16.8 Example of accessible toilets

machine on a lower position (Figure 16.9). This approach offers shorter persons and wheel chair users an access to several modes of payment on ticket vending machines. Electronic ticketing is already realized in Vienna. But not everybody is using this opportunity and the other modes of ticketing should as well be accessible for all. But accessible ticket vending machines according to the Austrian standard B1600 are not produced on the market. Meanwhile there are too many modes of payment and all of them should be offered in a limited area. In addition, producers of ticket vending machines are not very innovative. They just want to sell their range of products.

Visual Guiding System of the Vienna Lines Developed in 1969

Visual impairments call for a clear structured visual guiding system. Meanwhile several typefaces were tested concerning readability and contrast. Helvetica and Frutiger delivered good results. The Vienna Lines are using Helvetica and standardised pictograms to overcome language barriers. In field angle studies the best visible positions for information panels were figured out on platforms, stairs with escalators and passage levels (Figure 16.10).

Thanks to a colour-based logotype structure even illiterate users might easily find their ways. All spot identification panels are white based and all exit panels are kept in black. A different colour is dedicated to all lines. Blue is reserved for Austrian Railway Company lines (Figure 16.11). The primary

Adaption of station furniture

1,2 m

1,0 m

0,8 m

0,0 m

An approach... ticket machines for everyone

Figure 16.9 Accessible ticket vending machines

Figure 16.10 Landstraße – find your way without outside help!

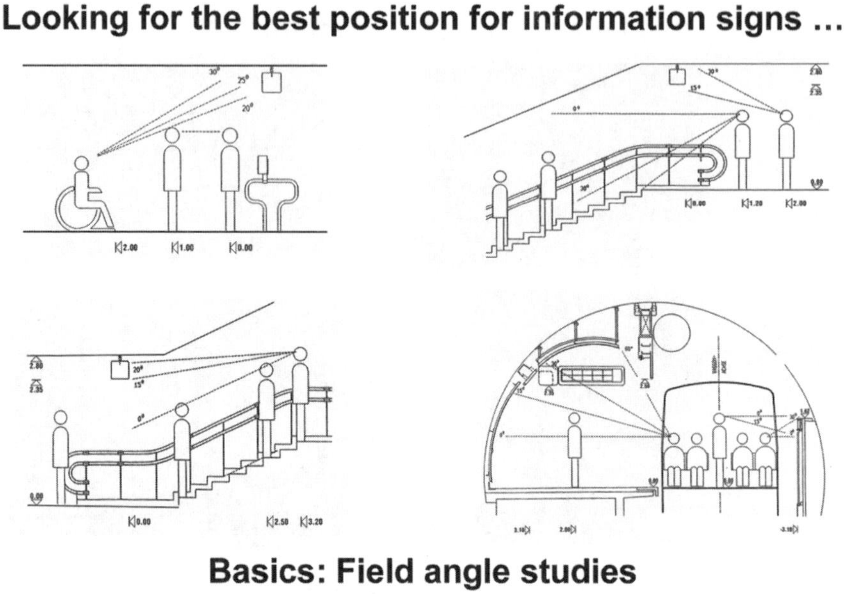

Looking for the best position for information signs ...

Basics: Field angle studies

Figure 16.11 Field angle studies

system level covers line signalisation and the secondary level terminal signalisation. Finally electronic operational displays represent the back-up level and are reserved for disturbance signalisation like one rail operation or replacement of circulation by a different mean of transport.

Architecture plays an important role in accessibility. Nowadays stations are more and more designed like shopping centres with a track connection. Overloaded advertisements are eye catchers in best positions and they are often mixed with hidden passenger guiding systems. As terminals are increasingly designed with an upcoming real estate ideology, orientation problems are welcome and are caused on purpose in order to encourage people to purchase products. The main planning aspect is focused on maximizing the commercial benefit. Travellers are encouraged to first go shopping and afterwards they are allowed to travel. Under such circumstances the best information design cannot work. For that reason the Vienna Lines are still planning their buildings like public transport stations focused on best practice passenger guiding systems. Only a limited number of shops are installed beside the main routes for social reasons.

The best outlines on information design are not a guarantee for best practice application. A strict separation of advertisement from passenger information is as useful as a light single coloured environment to support colour based guiding systems. Obstacles should not harm passenger flows. Modelling methods of passenger flows might be a useful in dimensioning traffic areas on the surface and in stations. Shops should not be placed in places where they introduce an obstacle to flows. They can survive and accomplish a social function even if they are established beside the main passenger flows.

Finally some basic statements on the way to best practice applications.

- The more elements, the more complicate to understand.
- No waste! A panel is not a litter bin!
- Focus on shortness and clarity in information design.
- Focus on strict information and quantity control.
- Focus on functional simplicity and minimalism.
- Focus on a clear structure and subtle outlines.
- A planning competence and experience on applications.
- A planning philosophy based on user group centred design is necessary.

Tactile Guiding System of the Vienna Lines

On the way from a tactile security line along the platform edge to a tactile guiding system the basics for further developments were discovered. Project managers of Vienna Lines built working groups with blind and visual impaired users and mobility teachers. Testing programs with blind users, pilot projects and empirical studies were undertaken and the result of those scientific investigations built the basic of the Austrian standard V2102 and for the tactile guiding system of Vienna Lines. An underground vehicle enters into station with a speed of 50 kilometres per hour. For safety reasons the limit of the dangerous area close to the platform edge used to be indicated for all users by a yellow security line. Visual impaired users could use this signage but blind users had to walk along the platform edge. This risky situation had to change and a tactile security line in a safe distance from the platform edge was required. In 1988 Vienna Lines began, in cooperation with the blind people organizations, to develop proposals. At that time apart of some pilot projects running in Japan no preliminary standards or relevant international examples were known.

Stripe indicators were used as guidelines giving the direction to go and doted indicators were marking turn offs and crossings. For all different platform and stop types lay out patterns were designed. Within the working group all experts agreed in this outlines. Tactile lines should be installed in all areas where the existing orientation aids like handrails, lateral walls or parapets were not sufficient.

In Vienna different tactile indicators on different surfaces were tested before in 1993 and the first pilot project was implemented in the U1 station Taubstummengasse. Gray stripes in a plastic material usually used for marking of zebra crossings were welded on a black tar surface. Tactile security lines of seven stripes, all of them 3 mm high, 3 cm wide and 3 cm apart from each other, realized along two platform edges, were implemented. After a testing phase of three years of practical experience without any significant incident all critical arguments of some members of the board of surveyors were blown away. Their main argument was that members of other user groups might stumble on those indicators grew dump and the permission for construction was grant to Vienna Lines. Consent within the blind people association was built. But some other discussions turned up concerning the lay-out of turn offs and crossings. For that reason in 1997 a further testing program on a test track in Heiligenstadt took place. On this test program, the last doubts disappeared and the basics for the implementation of a tactile guiding system were laid. Meanwhile solutions for several surfaces were found and the financial plan for the implementation of tactile guiding system in the whole network was prepared. In 1998 the retrofitting programme started and in 1999 the Vienna Lines were honoured by the Austrian Board for traffic security with a safety award.

Up to 2009 about 97% of all stations were already equipped with a tactile guiding system. Only in some old Otto Wagner stations certain problems appeared. Those stations were protected by the National Trust and all solutions had to be accepted by this authority. Additionally Otto Wagner used already structured ceramic tiles and designed floor mosaics. For those reasons it took some time to find an agreeable solution for all. But in 2010 the Vienna Lines succeed and a further action plan to achieve 100% is already worked out.

POPTIS – A Navigation System for Blind and VisualLY Impaired Users

The starting point for this project was the existing tactile guiding system of the Vienna Lines. By this system the user group can use safely public transport facilities. But they still need someone who tells them where to go. The intention of the Pre-On-Post-Trip-Information-System (POPTIS) was to support their demand to realize a better orientation in public transport stations (Figure 16.12). The declared objective was the development of an efficient traffic and voyage information system for blind and visually impaired traffic participants, which enables a better use of the existing orientation devices. The target was the creation of a simple constructed tool, which allows them to enjoy a self determined and active participation on every-days life. The basic idea was finally not to create an expensive new product, which they cannot afford. The project team was looking for an innovation based on traditional technologies. Therefore solid and tradable tools like: computer, internet, mobile phone and mp3 players were used.

All trips within the public transport network are collected on the POPTIS data base. Thanks to a clear navigation structure the users might easily find their trips. All trips recommended and alternative routes are

Navigation structure of P O P T I S

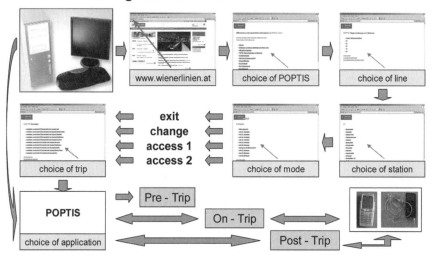

Figure 16.12 Navigation structure of POPTIS

explained according to the demand of blind and visual impaired users. All trips are tested by them and their mobility teachers. The POPTIS data base can be found on www.wienerlinien.at the homepage of Vienna Lines. On the upper left corner you find the access to the barrier free pages. All files on those pages are prepared for screen reader programs just to grant blind users a quick access to Vienna Lines information systems.

Users can navigate the pre-trip function at home on their computers. After having chosen the POPTIS data base, users have to choose a line, a station and an application mode. Within the mode they will find their trip. In the 'pre-trip' function users might prepare all trips in advance by listening to the explication delivered by a text to a speech program. In the 'on-trip' function users might find their trip on trip on a mobile phone like at home if there is already a screen reader program installed. For a quicker approach it is recommended to pre-load the chosen trips at home in order to be able to navigate on your phone immediately. Each move of a trip is explained step by step. If there is something missing users can return and repeat it again. In the 'post-trip' function users can put several trips together. They start with the access trip in the first station, the interchange trip from one to another line in the next station and you finish with an exit trip in the last station. Users can register them on mp3 players or store them on mobile phones. Like that users can store their personal trip collection and use them on trip. For unskilled users mobility trainers might prepare those collections. POPTIS is equally useful for traffic-education of pupils, for the orientation-training of late blinded people, as an advice and guideline for mobility-teachers, as an escort service or a memory-aid for blind and visually impaired traffic participants.

Real-Time Information Accessible Even for Blind and Visually Impaired Users

Until recently count-down information for vehicles approaching, delivered by the computer aided operational control system, was not transferred to operational displays in the stop areas. They also became a part of the new Vienna Lines real time passenger information system (Figures 16.13 and 16.14). Everybody might get the required information about the real time departure time of all lines and all stops, if there will be a low floor vehicle or not, on the homepage of the Vienna Lines www.wienerlinien.at. All this information is integrated in the pre-trip functionality on the computer and in on-trip functionality of mobile phones. The structures developed by POPTIS were well implemented on the barrier free pages and prepared for screen reader programs giving the even blind users in Vienna full access to this information. For wheelchair users the information if the next or the next but one vehicle is a low floor vehicle is still very important.

Real-time-information even for blind traffic participants

at home

www.wienerlinien.at   on trip by mobilephone   or on displays in junctions

Examples for good practice

Figure 16.13 Real time information – inclusive of blind passengers

Good Practice: Real-Time-Information

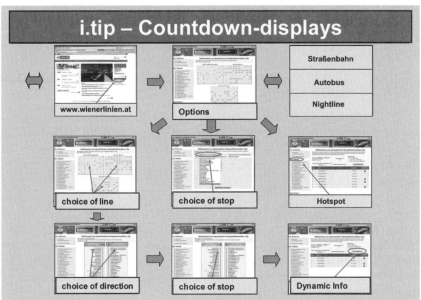

Figure 16.14 Real time information even for blind traffic participants

In junctions with a frequent interchange from underground lines to several tram and bus lines a new information unit were developed. In flat screen monitors the countdown information from the homepage is displayed above an environmental map in which all stop areas are fixed with letters. Those maps below are not north end but they are orientated according to the local situation.

Qando – A Web-Based Route Planner

On the homepage of the Vienna Lines www.wienerlinien.at or on www.qando.at there are web-based route planners. This service is very useful to find the quickest way from one location to another by public transport. This service delivers real time and time table information within the VOR-region. (The VOR-region represents the traffic union of the eastern region of Austria). This service is certainly useful for city tourism. All information is delivered in several languages. Wheelchair users can chose just rides on low floor vehicles. Tourists might get additional information about the cultural surrounding of their hotel, maps, programmes, price lists, the way to the next bus or tramway stop, how and when to move from the hotel to wherever they want to go to within the eastern region of Austria. Qando is available for Java-Mobiles, WIN-Mobiles, Blackberrys and iPhones and enables mobile ticketing by SMS. New releases are planned monthly. Since May 2009 more than 65,000 down loads were recognised. Qando has been honoured by two Austrian awards.

MofA or mobility4all

Plenty of wheelchair users, blind and visual impaired traffic participants are subject to reduced mobility. They are still limited in their choice because they cannot get a driver's licence and they have to use public transport. At the moment their ways in public space before they reach public transport facilities is like a hurdle race. This study intended to deliver a set of basic planning tools to create accessible squares and entrance areas as well as accessible public transport buildings. Key attention was paid on mobility in public space and on a comparison between already realised solutions. New descriptions, observations and classification methods were developed in favour of an accessibility-check including recommendations to solve the discovered problems. The target was the development of a self-assessment tool.

The objective of *mobility4all* was to discover all the obstacles on a trip throughout the mobility chains of several user groups. The accessibility checks were focused on station furniture and public space design. All the tools for the accessibility check like the examination catalogue, check lists and the descriptions, observations and certification methods were defined by a working group composed by experts and users. Experts care about observation and documentation, whilst users with a reduced mobility checked the applications on an authentic test programme in 66 public transport areas and environments. Finally the results of our investigations were delivered beside a failure and best-practice-catalogue more knowledge and planning competence for further projects like the major station of Vienna.

In a subsequent project we intend to use all materials and the experiences made in *mobility4all* to introduce the results of our investigations in regular educational programs on the technical university of Vienna. The experiences shall be useful for the education in construction engineering as well as for architectural and space planning programs.

Quo Vadis Feasibility Study

The intention of the feasibility study of Quo Vadis is to improve communication on board or in stops between the users and the board computers of public transport vehicles (Figure 16.15). Users with a reduced mobility might inform the driver about their demand by a simple handy device. A

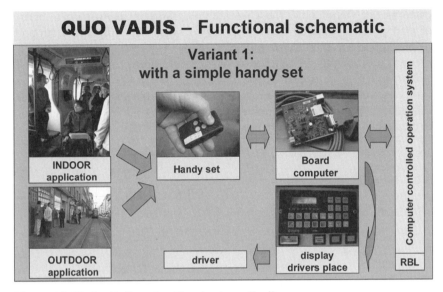

Figure 16.15 QuoVadis – functional schematic diagram

wheelchair user might ask for the ramp at the next stop whilst a blind user might inform the driver on which they intend to get on.

The Quo Vadis feasibility study already finished by a proof of concept and by cost estimation for a system implementation on the whole network. At. the moment in the project of *ways4all* further investigation are on work to improve the simple handy device into a multifunctional device like a mobile phone.

Conclusions: Achievements and Further Developments

The Austrian ministry of transport, innovation and technology has paid attention on the subject of accessibility by several research programs. They started a couple of years ago with an i2-programme focused on intelligent infrastructure and new telemetric solutions in all kind of transport. At the moment they continue with the second call of a research programme called *ways2go*. The main aspects of this programme are the stimulation of innovations and technologies, to broaden the knowledge base for mobility and to develop sustainable and social passenger transport solutions for all. Some key topics of *ways2go* are to figure out knowledge gaps, potentials and hindrances for new technologies, to discover individual and collective mobility behaviours by new observation methods like eye-tracking or shadowing, to control information systems throughout mobility chains for different user groups or to influence strategies towards sustainable mobility patterns. For Vienna Lines those research programs of the Austrian ministry of transport, innovation and technology were a very important support in developing accessibility on public transport. In the *ways2go* programmes Vienna Lines are engaged in a couple of further leading projects like *ways4all, mobility4all, Quo Vadis, Ianus* and *mobikid*.

Those national research programmes are stimulating research centres, universities, industries, stakeholders and small and middle- sized companies to create new applications and products in favour of better living conditions for following generations.

17 Accessible Hotels: Design Essentials

Katerina Papamichail

Introduction

This chapter addresses the most basic and essential points in the design of hotels and other overnight accommodation buildings, in order to make them accessible for disabled people. Designing with the disabled user in mind gives added value to the hotel as all people can benefit from the space standards and many of the features which disabled people need. Customers arriving tired or stressed after a long journey, carrying heavy suitcases, older people and families with small children will all enjoy a safer and more comfortable stay. It is understandable that hotel owners, who are not familiar with disabled people as customers, may have doubts and worries about whether their buildings and facilities are - or can be - made suitable for them. There are many books, guidelines, standards and checklists of user requirements for accessible buildings, with a large variety of information and a great amount of detail. For those hotel owners and architects who are not aware of the design requirements for accessibility, it can therefore be difficult, at the outset, to identify the main priorities and the critical issues – and to create a good solution.

Here we propose a clear, brief and practical guide, which can lead to an effective and economical design, meeting all basic access requirements. It is not an exhaustive explanation of how to cater for *very* particular needs of *all* disabled visitors. For these, further references are included at the end of this chapter (Figure 17.1).

The design of an accessible hotel, requires a 'smart' approach, known as *Design-for-All* or *Universal Design*, in which the needs of the widest range of users are taken into account. Accessible design cannot be achieved without knowing the basic requirements of disabled users, and how to address these in the design solution.

Universal design is the design of products and environments to be usable by all people, to the greatest extent possible, without the need for adaptation or specialized design.

Figure 17.1 Access ramps
Note: A common problem due to lack of information about access requirements. The ramp in the lobby of this hotel was made too short and therefore too steep for an independent wheelchair user, although there was sufficient space to make it longer. The walking surface is not 'non-slip' and may be dangerous

The intent of the universal design concept is to simplify life for everyone by making products, communications, and the built environment more usable by more people at little or no extra cost (Figure 17.2).

The universal design concept targets all people of all ages, sizes and abilities. (*Center for Universal Design*, Raleigh, NC, USA)

The Universal Design principles are:

(1) Equitable Use: The design is useful and marketable to people with diverse abilities.
(2) Flexibility in Use: The design accommodates a wide range of individual preferences and abilities.
(3) Simple and intuitive use: Use of the design is easy to understand, regardless of the user's experience, knowledge, language skills, or current concentration level.
(4) Perceptible Information: The design communicates necessary information effectively to the user, regardless of ambient conditions or the user's sensory abilities.
(5) Tolerance for Error: the design minimizes hazards and the adverse consequences of accidental or unintended actions.
(6) Low Physical Effort: the design can be used efficiently and comfortably and with a minimum of fatigue.

Figure 17.2 Diversity of visitors (2005)
Source: www.ossate.org

(7) Size and Space for Approach and Use: appropriate size and space is
provided for approach, reach, manipulation, and use regardless of user's
body size, posture, or mobility.
(Center for Universal Design, Raleigh, NC, USA; see:
http://www.design.ncsu.edu/cud/about_ud/udprinciples.htm)

It is important to apply Universal Design principles *both* in the case of
new buildings *and* in renovations.

(a) Design of a new building
Following this approach, the aim is to make the building generally
accessible for most visitors while it may also allow for adaptations to
accommodate guests with more extensive needs. Such adaptations can
be foreseen but might not be implemented initially, for various reasons.
For example: support handrails in a bathroom might not be provided
immediately but the wall construction should sufficiently strong to
allow for their later installation; or if a room with a side hung door may
not have enough floor space for a wheelchair user, the adjoining walls
should be made long enough to take a sliding door, as an alternative
solution.

(b) Renovation of an existing building
Every building and every establishment is unique in terms of its location, its surroundings, its design, layout, facilities and fittings. Therefore, in the case of an existing hotel, every renewal or renovation project
will present different problems and possibilities.

244 Section 3 The Accessible Tourism Value Chain

There are several principles for the design of a new accessible hotel. This will give the reader the basic knowledge to understand what would be needed when renovating an existing hotel as well.

Accessible Hotels: Taking Away the Myths

What do we mean by 'accessible' and who are the customers that need accessible facilities? Accessible, in this context, means 'able to be used by disabled people'; but it is a misunderstanding to think that it benefits only them. Accessible facilities will actually benefit all customers, as explained below (Figure 17.2). Disabled customers include:

- Wheelchair users with manual or electric wheelchairs, with or without a helper.
- People with walking difficulties, who may use crutches, a walking stick or a wheeled stroller.
- People with limited use of arms/hands.
- People with low vision or blind people.
- People with hearing difficulties or deaf people.
- People with asthma or allergies.
- People with learning difficulties.

Other customers, who will benefit from an accessible facility, include:

- Very small or very large people.
- Older people, who may be frail, or tire easily, or have any of the above disabilities, due to old age.
- People with long-term health problems, e.g. circulatory diseases.
- Pregnant women.
- Families with small children.
- Persons with a temporary physical impairment, e. g. a broken leg.
- Tired, sleepy and stressed customers.
- Customers with large and heavy pieces of luggage or equipment.

Accessibility does not necessarily increase building costs. There is not a simple linear relationship between cost and accessibility: good access may be achieved without higher costs. Managing costs is most effective when access criteria are introduced early in the building design phase. It will be more expensive to correct mistakes later!

Accessibility may require more space than usual and may result in fewer guest rooms. In general, to accommodate wheelchair users requires some more space, but not everywhere. For example, a small room can be functional for wheelchair users by careful choice of furniture and its arrangement. In design work, space is not a quality in itself: it is the careful layout of space *in crucial areas, with the appropriate form, fixtures and fittings* that leads to a good result. This may result in slightly fewer rooms, but a wide range of customers will appreciate easier access and will be willing to be higher prices due to differentiation.

Hotels don't need to be fully accessible for everyone. A newly-designed hotel can be accessible for all travellers, in most cases, as long as this is *the specific objective* at the beginning of the design process. In existing buildings, there may be circumstances where full accessibility cannot be achieved. But this should not be regarded as a reason to stop *any* improvement work! Every improvement in accessibility is going to be useful and valuable to some visitors. For example, if guestrooms cannot be made wheelchair accessible, other facilities such as the restaurant, conference rooms, public toilet and leisure facilities, indoors and outdoors, might still be made accessible for visitors who use a wheelchair or have other disabilities. Then at least a disabled guest can visit, participate in a conference, have lunch, etc. which is a clear improvement for both the client and the establishment. Also, a hotel that is not fully accessible for wheelchair users can nevertheless be made suitable for people with low vision (e.g. using contrasting colours); people with allergies (use of non-allergenic bedding and cleaning materials) and so on.

The number of accessible guest rooms available should be determined by the appropriate legislation. If there is such legislation, this should be the *minimal* starting point. If not, in general the answer is to follow a design-for-all approach and try to have the maximum number of rooms capable of accommodating wheelchair users, since these rooms will be able to accommodate disabled and non-disabled guests.

A hotel is not less attractive when it is accessible. Well functioning, accessible buildings can be achieved by good designers with very high aesthetic results and should be suitable for all through inclusive design. There are many, many examples of modern, attractive, accessible hotels, youth hostels and other types of overnight accommodation. A skilled designer *who understands access requirements* will be able to incorporate these successfully into his or her design solutions.

Checklist

This section gives an overview of the key spaces and areas where special care should be taken to ensure good access, taking into account the essential functions of the hotel guest.

The essential functions for all hotel guests are:

- reach and enter the building;
- check-in;
- move around – inside and outside;

- sleep;
- attend to one's personal hygiene, bathe;
- eat and drink;
- use the available facilities, for business or leisure;
- evacuate the building safely in an emergency.

In the checklist below some *minimum dimensions* are given for an accessible and well-functioning building design (Figure 17.3). Typically, the requirements of wheelchair users set the benchmarks for the physical layout and design, because these users need more space and the minimum of obstructions.

Access standards used in different countries, or legislation, may vary to some degree. The dimensions given here are based on the experience of working with standards, building projects and observations of buildings in use. In general, and especially in new projects, it is advisable to be generous with the dimensions when deciding on room sizes, corridor widths, door openings and layout, as this will make it easier to cope with unexpected

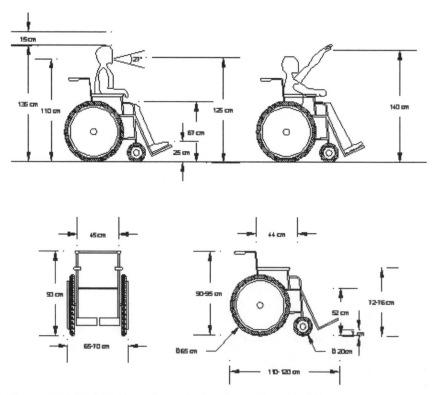

Figure 17.3 Typical dimensions of a hand-powered wheelchair

situations that may arise, either during new construction or renovation work. For example, the builder might 'lose' 5 cm by measuring wrongly or due to the need to add a structural element which had different dimensions or was not part of the original plan.

(1) Designated car parking spaces for disabled visitors
These are required especially for wheelchair users and people with walking difficulties (Figure 17.4).

(a) At least one space per accessible guestroom, signposted and marked accordingly.
(b) Recommended dimensions of parking space: 3.5 x 5 metres. The wider space is required to allow for a wheelchair user to enter and leave the vehicle easily.
(c) At shortest possible distance to building entrance, by level access route.

(2) Access routes and circulation in the establishment (outdoors and indoors)

(a) General (Figure 17.5)
   • Level route, avoiding steps where possible.
   • Clear width: 100 cm. and never less than 90 cm. at the narrowest point.
   • Continuous minimum width, preferably 120 cm.
   • To allow a pedestrian and a wheelchair to pass each other, minimum width: 150 cm.
   • To allow two wheelchairs to pass easily: minimum width 180 cm.

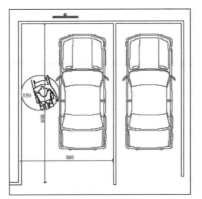

Figure 17.4 Parking bay for vehicles used by disabled driver/passenger

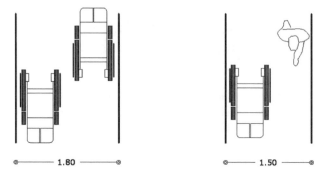

Figure 17.5 Width of corridors and passages must allow sufficient space for wheelchair users to pass freely

- Non-slip and smooth surface; no gaps more than 5mm. wide in the direction of travel (e.g. in joints between paving slabs).
- Well lit routes, including paths, steps and ramps, to aid people with low vision.

(b) Ramps, to overcome height differences (Figure 17.6)
- Recommended inclination less than or equal to 1:20 (5%) with a level rest area every 10 metres.
- Where a slope of 5% or less is not possible, there may be a slope of 7% for a distance of less than five metres; or an 8% slope for a distance of less than two metres. A slope of 12% may be used for a distance of less than 50 cm. Note that users of hand-powered wheelchairs will require assistance to go up or down slopes greater than 5%.
- Add handrails at both sides.
- Two handrails are recommended, one at a height of 100 cm and one at 75 cm, The lower one being for wheelchair users.
- Surface of ramp – non-slip.
- Side protection, 5 to 10 cm high, to stop wheels going over the edge.
- Where there is a door at the top or bottom of a ramp, a level area is required to allow wheelchair users to open door: minimum area 1.50 m × 1.50 m
- Where there is a change in direction of ramp, a level turning area is required: minimum 1.50m × 1.50m.
- Top and bottom of ramp should be clearly indicated with tactile and/or visual markings to avoid people with low vision having accidents.

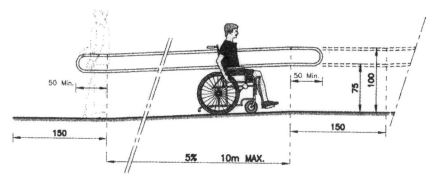

Figure 17.6 Ramp diagram

(c) Steps (Figure 17.7)
Where steps are necessary:
- All steps should have the same length (tread), between 28 and 32 cm, and height (riser), between 15 and 18 cm.
- Top and bottom of steps clearly indicated with tactile and/or visual markings to avoid people with low vision having accidents.
- Provide a landing for every 10 to 12 steps.
- Add handrails at both sides.
- Two handrails are recommended, one at a height of 100 cm and one at 75 cm, the lower one being for shorter people.

(d) Platform lift
In the case of a renovation of an existing building, where there is a difference of levels and it is not possible to build a ramp, a platform lift or stair lift may be installed for visitors using wheelchairs.

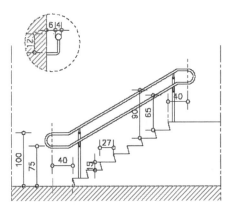

Figure 17.7 Staircase diagram

(3) Main entrance door
(a) No threshold. If there is a threshold: maximum 2 cm in height, so wheelchair users and others may pass without too great difficulty.
(b) Clear width of door opening: minimum 100 cm; larger than 100 cm is recommended, taking into account guests carrying suitcases, emergency evacuation, etc. In new constructions and large hotels the clear opening at the entrance door should be wider than 100 cm.
(c) Recommended door types: side-hung, manual or sliding automatic. In case of a revolving door, have an alternative side-hung manual door, for wheelchair users and persons with walking difficulties who cannot use revolving doors, and to avoid accidents.
(d) Safety markings on large glass doors and windows to make them noticeable, especially for people with low vision, to avoid accidents.

(4) Other doorways
(a) No threshold. If there is a threshold, maximum 2 cm in height.
(b) Clear width of door opening: minimum 90 cm. (In case of renovations, where this may not be possible, a clear width of 85 cm *minimum* will be functional in most cases).
(c) Door handles: lever type recommended (easier to grip), avoid round handles that cannot be used easily by people with arthritis or other problems in using their hands.
(d) Bathroom doors: opening outwards or sliding, to allow more space for circulation in the bathroom and in case the visitor falls behind the door in the bathroom.

(5) Reception and other service areas (Figures 17.8)
(a) Low part of counter recommended for wheelchair users: height maximum 80cm.
(b) Seating provided in reception area recommended (Figures 17.9 and 17.10).
(c) Good lighting at reception counter.

(6) Accessible Lift (Figure 17.11)
(a) Clear space minimum 150 x 150 cm at every lift entrance. For lifts with side-hung outward opening doors, a space of 170 cm opposite the lift is recommended.
(b) Clear width of door opening: minimum 90 cm.
(c) Internal width of the lift 110 cm, internal depth 140 cm, minimum.
(d) Verbal announcement for stops at each floor to inform blind people.
(e) Lift buttons have raised numbers or letters to be understood by blind people. Lift buttons at a height of 90 to 120cm above the floor, so they can be reached by wheelchair users and short people.
(f) Horizontal support handrail in lift at 85 cm above floor, recommended.

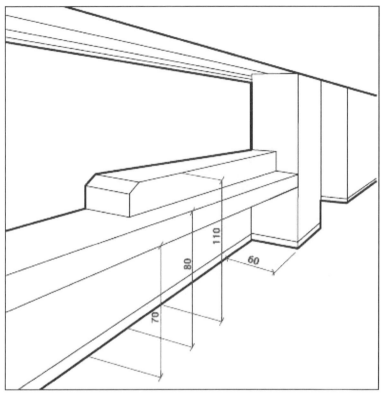

Figure 17.8 Accessible reception desk
Note: Diagram showing the design of a reception counter with two heights and recessed front, suitable both for people who are standing and for wheelchair users

Figure 17.9 Accessible lounge
Note: Seating provided in hotel reception area, with space for a wheelchair user

Figure 17.10 Accessible bar area
Note: The café and bar area allows guests to sit at the low counter while
service personnel are at eye-level with customers, thanks to the lowered floor
behind the counter

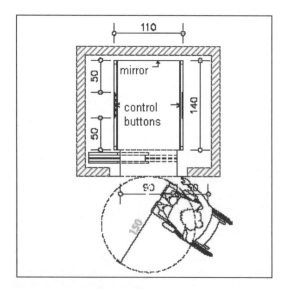

Figure 17.11 Accessible lift
Note: Diagram showing minimum dimensions of lift suitable for a
wheelchair user.

(7) Accessible toilet in common areas (for overnight guests and visitors)
(Figures 17.12–17.14)

At least one toilet should be suitable for wheelchair users.

(a) Door: opening outwards or sliding. Clear width of door opening: minimum 90 cm. (In case of renovations, where this may not be possible, a clear width of 85 cm *Minimum* will be functional in most cases.)

Where the door opens outwards, the space in front of the door should be 170 cm to allow a wheelchair user to open the door towards him/herself.

On the inside of a side-hung door, a horizontal handle slightly less than the full door width will enable a wheelchair user to open and close the door easily (see Figures 17.14, 17.17 and 17.19).

(b) Toilet bowl must have minimum 120 cm free space at the front and 90 cm at least on one side.

(c) A free turning circle of 150 cm diameter in the room is desirable.

(d) Non-slip floor surface.

(e) Washbasin in same room, preferably reachable from toilet. Free space under washbasin: lower edge height over floor 70cm. and upper edge height 80cm.

  • Handrails are placed according to the layout of the toilet room (see Figure 17.14).

  • In a layout where the toilet is placed close to a wall at one side, at the minimum, one horizontal handrail should be fixed to the wall,

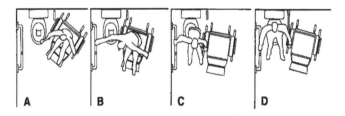

Trasferimento
laterale DX
Right transfer

Figure 17.12 Accessible toilet design – right transfer
Note: Diagram showing lateral transfer to toilet seat from right side

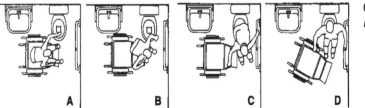

Obliquo SX
Left transfer

Figure 17.13 Accessible toilet design – left transfer
Note: Diagram showing oblique transfer to toilet seat from left side

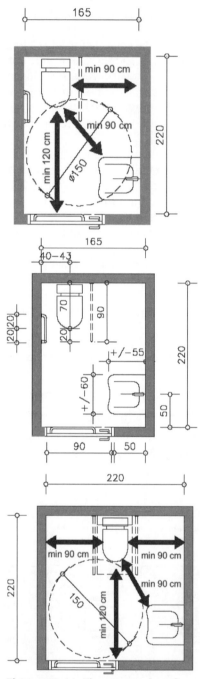

Figure 17.14 Three examples of accessible public toilets

at a height of 80 cm above the floor. A second handrail, which can be raised or retracted, should be placed at the other side of the toilet.

- In a layout where the toilet is placed away from the side-walls, two moveable (raising) horizontal handrails are required at a height of 80 cm above the floor.

To understand more easily why sufficient space is required in front and at the side of the toilet, the drawings in Figures 17.12 and 17.13 show how wheelchair users transfer to the toilet seat, according to their specific situation.

(f) Colour-contrast for doors, door-frames, fixtures and fittings for visitors with sight impairments.
(g) Refer also to General Recommendations, below.
(h) Mirror above washbasin with lower edge 100 cm above floor level and upper edge 200 cm above floor, inclined towards wheelchair user.
(i) Emergency call system recommended.
(j) It is recommended to include a baby-changing table, in the toilet area, where possible.

(8) Bathrooms (Figures 17.15–17.19)

For the accessible bathroom, the requirements are the same as for 'Accessible toilet in common areas', with the following additions:
(a) A shower is preferable to a bathtub. Most wheelchair users cannot use a bathtub. If a bathtub is chosen, provide seating area at one end.
(b) Shower area with level access (no raised shower tray or step-up).
(c) Handrail(s) for support beside the shower or bath.
(d) Height of shower head adjustable, vertically, between 95 and 220 cm.
(e) Provide a fixed or moveable shower chair for wheelchair users and people who cannot stand easily.
(f) Provision of a rubber mat for the shower (or bath tub) is recommended, to avoid accidents.
(g) Provision of clothes and towel hooks at a height of 90 to 120 cm above floor level.

(9) Guest rooms (Figures 17.20 and 17.21)

(a) An *en suite* bathroom is required for wheelchair users. If this is not possible, there should be at least one wheelchair accessible bathroom on the same floor as the guest room(s) for wheelchair users.
(b) Clear space of at least 90 cm At the side of the bed. For wheelchair users, a turning circle of 150 cm, free of obstacles, is recommended. See Figure 17.20.
(c) Top of mattress at height of 45 to 50 cm recommended

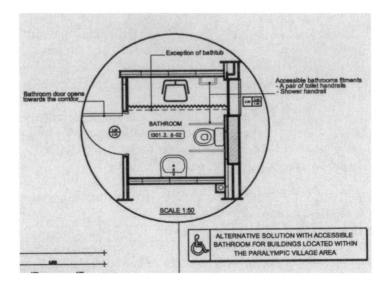

Figure 17.15 Architect's drawing of the adaptable bathroom built at the Athens 2004 Olympic and Paralympic Village
Note: 'Adaptable' indicates a flexible solution, which was foreseen in the design phase. The bathroom may be fitted with a bathtub or, as here, with a roll-in shower for wheelchair users, without moving the toilet or washbasin. Internal dimensions of bathroom: 210 x 220 cm

(d) Non-allergenic bedding recommended.
(e) For a disabled guest with an assistant, twin beds are preferred or a door giving private access to an adjoining room.
(f) Furniture that can be re-arranged is preferable to make more space, as necessary, for individual needs.
(g) Light switches and electrical sockets at height of 90 to 120cm above floor level.
(h) Alternative lower rail in cupboards for clothes-hangers, recommended height 90 to 120cm above floor level.
(i) Vibrating alarm for deaf and hard of hearing recommended.

(10) Dining areas
(a) Level access (with no steps or thresholds), or by ramp or lift
(b) Leave a free passage of minimum 100 cm, preferably 120 cm, between groups of tables and chairs to allow wheelchairs to pass easily.
(c) Choose tables with a central support (leg) to allow wheelchair users to sit close to the table. Underside of tables at height of 70 to 75 cm.

Figure 17.16 Photo of the adaptable
bathroom built at the Athens 2004
Olympic and Paralympic Village
Note: 'Adaptable' indicates a flexible solution, which was
foreseen in the design phase. The bathroom may be fitted with
a bathtub or, as here, with a roll-in shower for wheelchair users,
without moving the toilet or washbasin. Internal dimensions of
bathroom: 210 x 220 cm

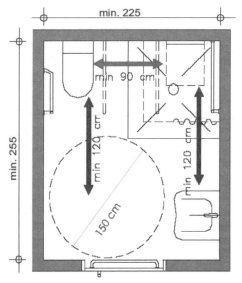

Figure 17.17 Wheelchair accessible bathroom

Figure 17.18 Partial view of a toilet and roll-in shower

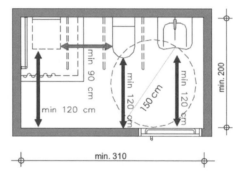

Figure 17.19 Diagram of a toilet and roll-in shower

(11) Outdoor spaces (Figures 17.22 and 17.23)

In areas such as gardens, swimming pools, outdoor resting or dining areas:

- Level access from the building.
- Avoid steps – replace with ramps.
- Well-lit, wide pathways.
- Smooth, non-slip surfaces, with no gaps, for example between paving stones.
- Do not choose plants which are poisonous or cause allergies (or remove them).
- Branches overhanging paths should be trimmed back and have sufficient height not to cause injury.

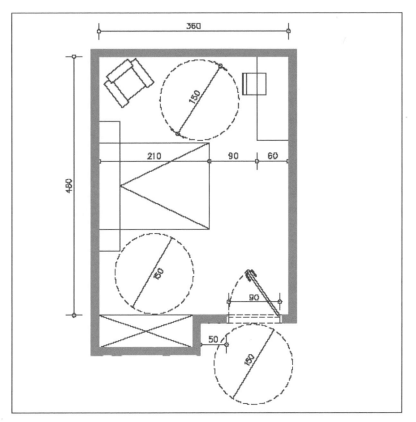

Figure 17.20 Diagram of guestroom layout with double bed

Figure 17.21 Hotel room with twin beds and an extra bed with good circulation space

Figure 17.22 Veranda with level access from dining room, spacious layout of furniture, smooth non-slip floor surface and chairs and tables with rounded edges

Figure 17.23 Outdoor area with level access from dining room, spacious layout of furniture, smooth non-slip floor surface and chairs and tables with rounded edges

- Benches at regular intervals. Leave space at one end for pushchairs, wheelchairs, etc.
- Furniture with rounded edges.

(12) General Recommendations
- No thick carpets – they cause difficulties for wheelchair users and may give problems for people with allergies.
- Furniture with rounded edges.
- Non-reflecting surfaces (tables, floors, etc).
- Colour contrast for doors, door-frames bathroom fixtures and fittings.
- Contrast markings on glass doors and full-height windows.
- Window-ledges at a height of 70 to 90 cm to allow wheelchair users to see outside.
- Good lighting in all areas.
- Signage with large fonts, good contrast. Easily understood pictograms.
- Guest information in large print format.
- Restaurant/bar menus/bar prices available in large print format.
- Non-smoking rooms and non-smoking area in the bar/restaurant/...
- Rooms with non-allergic bedding (e.g. non-feather pillows).
- Emergency call system with vibrating pads (if fire alarm is activated).
- Emergency call system with flashing lights (if fire alarm is activated).
- Emergency evacuation routes (and procedures) for the safe exit of guests with disabilities.
- Audible alarm system.

Conclusions

This chapter, which is based on practical experience and design work, has shown that planning for accessibility is not an unreachable goal or a very complicated procedure if some simple guidelines are followed. Hotel owners should not shy away from the challenge of making their hotels accessible and with a little care, designers can make accessible accommodation that will give good value and better service for everyone.

Acknowledgements

Figures 17.1, 17.9, 17.16, 17.18, 17.22 and 17.23: photographs by the author.
Figure 17.2: OSSATE project www.ossate.org; used with permission.
Figures 17.3, 17.5, 17.12 and 17.13: drawings by the author
Figures 17.4, 17.7, 17.8, 17.10, 17.11, 17.14, 17.17, 17.19 and 17.20: diagrams by Toegankelijkheidsbureau vzw, Belgium, published originally by Toerism Vlaanderen; used with permission.

Figure 17.6: published by Association National de Logement des personnes Handicapées, Bruxelles; used with permission.

Figure 17.21: photograph provided by City Hotel, Ljubljana; used with permission.

Examples of Websites with Guidance for the Design of Accessible Buildings/Hotels

Association National de Logement des personnes Handicapées, Bruxelles (1996). *Une Ville Pour Tous* (in French). Available at: www.anlh.be/?view=rublandid=35andid2=129.

Association National de Logement des personnes Handicapées, Bruxelles (1999). *ACCESSvoiries, Un Espace Public Pour Tous* (in French). Available at: www.anlh.be/?view=rublandid=35andid2=155.

British Standards Institution (2008) *Publicly Available Specification: Guidance on accessibility of large hotel premises and hotel chains.* Available at: www.bsigroup.com/en/Shop/Publication-Detail/?pid=000000000030163227.

ENTER vzw. Belgium (2007) *Accessibility of Hotels* (in Flemish). Available at: www.entervzw.be/assets/files/Hotels.pdf.

Hellenic Ministry of Public Works. (1998) *Designing for All* (in Greek). Available at: www.minenv.gr/1/16/162/16203/g1620300.html.

National Disability Authority, Ireland (2008) *Promoting Safe Egress and Evacuation for People with Disabilities.* Available at: www.accessibletourism.org/resources/accessible-egress-report.pdf .

OSSATE (2005) *Inventory of Accessible Tourism Information Schemes.* Available at: www.accessibletourism.org/resources/ossate_inventory_accessinfo_schemes_public.pdf.

UK Building Regulations Part M. Access to and use of buildings (2000, 2004). Available at: www.accessibletourism.org/resources/br_pdf_adm_2004-2.pdf.

Section 4

Destination Development

Chapters in this section:

18 Wheelchair Travel Guides

Bruce Cameron and Simon Darcy

Introduction

This chapter is based on a travel guide which was first published in Australia in 1995, *Easy Access Australia – A Travel Guide to Australia* (Cameron, 1995, 2000). *Easy Access Australia* (EAA) reflects an individual's need for accessible information during the planning stage and while travelling. The author is a wheelchair user following a swimming accident in 1976. Travelling in Europe, he met one of the Rough Guide's founders and suggested that an access guide to the UK be written. The Rough Guides did not pick up the idea, but EAA was born. The chapter also draws on developments in accessible tourism in the United Kingdom and Europe and several research projects which occurred in Australia during the years 2007 and 2008, covering accessible accommodation (Darcy, 2008; Darcy & Cameron, 2008), business cases for accessible tourism (Darcy *et al.*, 2010; Darcy *et al.*, 2008b), delivering access information about tourism destinations and experiences within a defined precinct of Sydney, Australia. What follows is a discussion of the number of issues that arise in accessible tourism which need to be addressed when designing, researching, writing and publishing a travel guide aimed at meeting the needs of travellers requiring access.

What is a Travel Guide?

Travel guides come in many forms, from brief pamphlets to 1000-page or more documents, TV shows, radio programmes, internet sites and Blogs. They can seek to provide specific information, or to provide general information. Travel guides, like Lonely Planet (2008), Rough Guide (2008), Let's Go (2008), Frommers (2009) and many more, are brands which include a number of titles catering for specific interests; for example Lonely Planet publishes guides for women travellers, families and so on.

Other guides focus on specific, highly specialised topics such as BandBs, Gites in France, travelling with animals, history, cuisine, arts, architecture, music ... the list goes on. A travel guide designed for the access market has one primary objective and that is to provide information so an individual can make up their own mind, i.e. make a positive decision, either to travel, or at least make a positive decision to seek more information.

We need to make a distinction between a travel guide and an access guide. A travel guide is generally much broader in scope providing a range of information across some very large areas, for example *Easy Access Australia* is a travel guide to Australia while *Accessing Melbourne* is a travel guide to the City of Melbourne (City of Melbourne, 2006), and it has a much more focused approach in a smaller defined area. Accessing Melbourne is very much in this style of a travel guide comprising an informative amount of background information. *Access Sydney* (Spinal Cord Injuries Association, 2002) on the other hand is an access guide which is more in the style of a directory offering alphabetical listings of various attractions etc but omitting the interesting and readable background information. Access Guides can be produced for a specific purpose such as for the theme parks on the Gold Coast, Queensland (Warner Brothers Movie World, 2011).

Historically, access guides are compiled without substantial access knowledge and reliance upon the use of symbols or icons to convey the meaning of access. However, the use of the icons is often meaningless, as no definition is offered for the icon. Access information available in Australia up until the early 1990s was very poor, usually comprising loose stores of information held in one of the disability networking groups or disability associations (e.g. ParaQuad NSW). That information was often anecdotal, lacked detail and did nothing to help the individual make a decision to travel. In short there was not an overall strategic approach to what constituted the foundation for access information required to make travel planning decisions. As such, the information did nothing to ease the anxiety that attaches to the travel planning process for people with disabilities and those with access needs (Darcy, 1998).

Some Issues for Travel Guides

Writing an access travel guide requires a number of key issues be resolved or defined at the outset. First and foremost, what type of access information is being included? Most Access guides are restricted to information for people with mobility access needs. This is sometimes referred to as physical access and is usually restricted to people who are wheelchair users or have some other type of mobility disability. Some access guides also provide information for people who are blind or have vision impairment or people who are Deaf or have hearing impairments. Once the decision on what type of access information is to be provided has been made then the publication must decide on the strategic approach to providing the access information.

The most common way to provide access information is through the use of universal icons. Icons are used to convey information about access but they need to be clearly defined. Icons also become incorporated into access information rating systems that convey some type of graded understanding of the level of accessibility of individual properties or destinations.

Rating systems, particularly in respect to accessible accommodation cause problems for the user as they fail to offer sufficient information about the accessible facilities. Mapping or wayfinding systems are another key issue as maps perform two primary functions. Firstly, they put a particular destination into geographical context and secondly, they provide specific information relevant to the access needs of the user. A broader discussion on approaches to presenting access information is now provided.

Iconography

Why use Icons?

Icons or graphics or symbols provide information clearly and simply, examples are parking, toilets and lifts. They provide information in one visual instantly recognisable image. Icons are also used as a warning of danger. People recognise icons, comprehending their meaning quickly, rather than reading text. Icons also speak a universal language; their meaning can be interpreted by people from diverse cultural and language backgrounds, and with intellectual, cognitive or communication impairments. Icons can be effective for those with dyslexia and learning difficulties. So icons convey a meaning crossing linguistic and communication borders.

Icons can be overused when it comes to travel guides and access information. Too often an icon is employed to convey access information but in reality it fails to achieve this aim because the meaning of the icon itself is never defined. An example of this is employing the international symbol of the wheelchair. However, this symbol can mean designated accessible car parking, an accessible pathway and/or a toilet designated as accessible. How is a user who needs the physical access to interpret such a map when the icon can mean three separate things?

Defining Icons for Use

Icons denoting access across a range of dimensions of disability should be specifically defined and used consistently. Many icon's are in circulation and each has an implied meaning. Table 18.1 represents examples employed by organizations in a fairly small geographical area of Sydney, Australia (Darcy *et al.*, 2008a).

An excellent example of how icons can be used clearly and effectively across dimensions of access is seen in a web-based part of the *Visitor Accessibility in Urban Centres* (Darcy *et al.*, 2008a) (see: www.sydneyforall.com). The philosophy of the project was to identify quintessential accessible destination experiences across all dimensions of access. In doing so, the experience is needed to be exemplary for at least one dimension of access and this information had to be clearly articulated to those groups so that an

TABLE 18.1 Comparative analysis of icon use

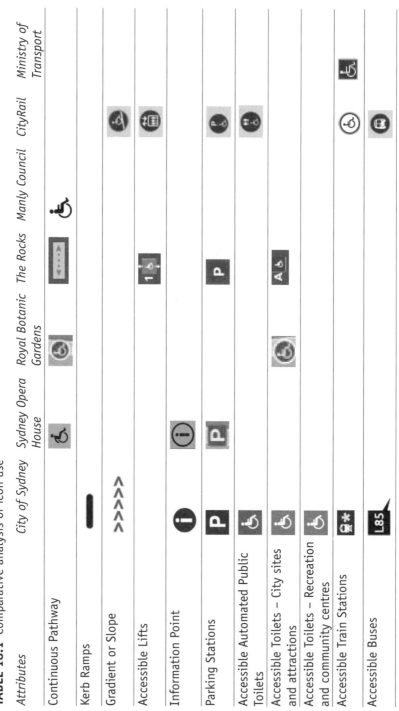

Attributes	City of Sydney	Sydney Opera House	Royal Botanic Gardens	The Rocks	Manly Council	CityRail	Ministry of Transport
Continuous Pathway							
Kerb Ramps							
Gradient or Slope							
Accessible Lifts							
Information Point							
Parking Stations							
Accessible Automated Public Toilets							
Accessible Toilets – City sites and attractions							
Accessible Toilets – Recreation and community centres							
Accessible Train Stations							
Accessible Buses							

TABLE 18.1 Continued

Attributes	City of Sydney	Sydney Opera House	Royal Botanic Gardens	The Rocks	Manly Council	CityRail	Ministry of Transport
Taxi Ranks	[icon]						
Audio Crossing Signals	[icon]						
ATM				[icon]			
Wheelchair Accessible ATM	[icon]						
Public Phone				[icon]			
Wheelchair Accessible Phone / Bus Shelter Phone	[icon]					[icon]	
TTY	[icon]			[icon]			
Assisted Hearing Systems		[icon]				[icon]	
Blind / Low Vision		[icon]					
Tactile Tiles						[icon]	

(Source: Darcy et al., 2008b)

TABLE 18.2 Effective icon definitions

Universal icons will help you decide which attractions provide the appropriate level of access.

	Mobility access is available offering a clear path of travel throughout the venue including an accessible toilet
	A clear path of travel throughout the venue for those who are blind or have low vision
	Audio description is available
	Hearing loop or audio induction loop is available
	Auslan sign language interpretation is available
	Text captions provided for audio content
	Telephone Typewriter (TTY) is available

(Source: Tourism NSW's Sydney for All www.Sydneyforall.com)

informed decision could be made for travel planning purposes. The icon and then definitions are shown in Table 18.2.

The use of icons is effective because each is clearly defined and then employed within the context of the relevant attraction.

Rating Systems

Do rating systems work for accessible accommodation? A distinction needs to be made between rating systems employed to advise on tourist attractions and experiences and those employed to describe accessible accommodation. The level of detail required to assist an individual make a positive decision in respect to accommodation simply cannot be conveyed in a rating (Darcy, 2008). The simplest approach to take is that the individual is best placed to make the decision as to what best suits their needs. Once a rating system is employed, a third party becomes involved and makes an arbitrary decision to assign a rating. The following examples highlight recent thinking from three key areas where development is occurring: Australia, the United Kingdom and Europe.

The Australian Case

In the late 1990s, two icons were employed by the state-based motoring bodies, (RACV, NRMA, RACQ, etc.) to denote accessible

Figure 18.1 Access with Assistance
Source: adapted from AAATourism, 2008

accommodation – 'Access with Assistance' and 'Independent Access'. Each state's motoring body ran the Star Rating scheme and considered access when assessing accommodation for star ratings.

The Independent Access icon was published when a property met the Australian Standard for Access (Standards Australia, 2001) (as assessed by the rating agency inspectors), the Access with Assistance icon (see Figure 18.1) was employed if the property *failed* to meet the Australian Standard for Access. By 1999 when one national Star Rating Agency was formed (AAA Tourism, 2008), the decision was taken to publish all accessible properties with the one Access with Assistance icon. The user was not provided with any of the detailed information assessed by the inspectors.

EAA adopted a forward thinking, utilitarian approach by asking the question, what information would the individual need to be able to make an informed decision to travel? EAA adopted a strategic direction and provided textual information about contact information, access to reception and other facilities and then provided specific detail about the room. EAA edition one (Cameron, 1995) saw 90 full floorplans of rooms, including en suite bathroom, which included detailed measurements. It is important to note that often the featured room would not have reflected the prevailing Australian Standard for Access. This suggests that rooms can be functionally accessible to people notwithstanding the state of the current standard. In 2000, edition two was published featuring some 300 bathroom floorplans with key measurements included such as door widths, bed heights and space for circulation. The example in Figure 18.2 is from Cameron (2000).

Other attempts have been made to seek and provide information on accessible accommodation. Organizations such as NICAN and IDEAS each source information via self assessment checklists, and they publish the responses on their websites (NICAN, 2008 and IDEAS, 2009).

Self Assessment Versus Provision of Information

There is debate about the efficacy of information which is 'self assessed'. Where the term refers to the process, usually undertaken by accommodation

Accommodation – Northern Territory, Darwin
All Seasons Premier Darwin Central, (8944 9000, 1300 364 263,
res@dcentra.allseasons.com.au), Cnr Smith & Knuckey Sts, 4.5star, $199, 4 rooms,
complimentary valet parking, flat access from Shadford Lane through auto doors into
bright foyer and high Reception desk but a side counter is lower. Lift access to rooms
off large atrium.
Room: Door 73ccm, knob 1m, heavy closer, internal corridor 1.5m. Large room with
plenty of space, 1m&1.2m at sides and 1.5m at foot of Queen bed h52cm, limited
space under. Lights, TV (remote) and phone operable from bed. Reachable hanging
space.
Bathroom: Wheel-in shr, hand held rose, lever taps 1m, fold down shr seat h56cm.
Toilet h48cm, c46cm, f80cm.
Other: Commode/shower chair avail (confirm), great views, access to pool and
surrounds, conference facilities and restaurant and bar. No accessible toilet – one is
in the arcade off Smith St.

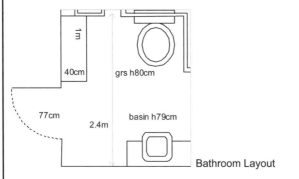

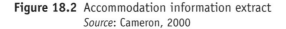
Bathroom Layout

Figure 18.2 Accommodation information extract
Source: Cameron, 2000

managers/providers, of assessing their accommodation access against
a checklist created by a third party (Regional Tourism Organization's,
NICAN, IDEAS, AAA Tourism), often the outlet for the information.

The Human Rights and Equal Opportunity Commission (2008) complaint cases have unequivocally proven that this process has failed to
provide the level of detail necessary for the traveller to make an informed
decision to travel. This failure is partly due to the managers'/providers'
ability to comprehend and appreciate the task at hand. Scrutiny of the
checklists reveals they are based upon the Australian Standards for Access
and Mobility (Standards Australia, 2009), which seeks an indication whether a particular measurement is within the prescribed range of the standards.
Often the actual measure is not provided to the user. In addition ambiguous
terms like 'circulation space' are not clarified for the provider or user. Information Provision offers an alternative to self assessment where specific
measurements are sought for defined key elements of the access. No direct
reference is made to the Australian Standards for Access and Mobility.

What is important is the actual measure. When this is combined with imagery – diagrams and digital photography, there can be a high degree of confidence offered to the user. Research on the preferred room components and presentation formats for people with mobility, vision and hearing disabilities identified the importance of combining Standards Australia measurements with digital photography and a floorplan as the preferred method of information provision (Darcy, 2008, 2010). The research concluded:

> ... it has highlighted the complex level of information required for people to make an informed decision about their accommodation needs. The research suggests that previous attempts to create an iconography or rating system for accessible accommodation are misguided. A radical simplification of the high level of detail presented in the Building Code of Australia and the Australian Standards for Access and Mobility is not possible without compromising the detail required by those using accessible accommodation ....

An outcome of the research was the development of the *Accessible Accommodation Assessment Template* (Darcy & Cameron, 2008) which could be utilised by assessors or providers to generate information which can be relied upon with a higher degree of confidence than previously existed. An example of part of the information generated is presented in Figure 18.3.

The United Kingdom Case

In an approach similar to the Australian system, the UK charity, Holiday Care Service (HCS) developed a system which was in use in 1992 employing a three tiered rating system. The most accessible rating meant Independent Access, the next level meant Access with Assistance and the bottom level involved one or more steps to access (VisitBritian, 2008). HCS has evolved into Tourism for All, UK (TFA UK, 2008), and helped develop the National Accessible Scheme, which has been adopted by VisitBritain where:

> The scheme provides a set of Accessible Standards against which establishments are assessed for their accessibility and awarded a rating. Standards for serviced, self-catering accommodation and holiday parks cover three types of impairment: mobility, hearing and visual. There are four categories for mobility plus an additional accolade 'access exceptional', and two each for visual and hearing impairment with level 1 being the minimum entry requirement.
>
> The standards have been designed to allow people with access requirements and varying disabilities to make an informed choice about where they can go on holiday in the UK.

Format 4   Digital Images combined with Textual and Spatial Presentation
Novotel Sydney Olympic Park
Olympic Boulevard,
Sydney Olympic Park
NSW 2127
Novotel offers 10 accessible rooms, IBIS offers 6 accessible rooms.
Tourist accommodation located at Sydney's Olympic Park, home to Sydney's Olympic venue.
Star Rating: Novotel 4 Stars,   IBIS 3.5 Stars
Reservations:
Freecall:
Phone: (02) 8762 1111   TTY: Nil
Web: www.accorhotels.com.au   Email: h2732@accor.com
              www.novotel.com.au, www.ibis.com.au

Room:
The main door width is 800mm (lever handle at 1m, magnetic card entry, automatic closer not heavy) and
opens into a corridor 1.46m wide (at its narrowest point) before opening into the bedroom. Latch side space
for the door is 480mm.

The rooms are set up with one Queen sized bed at 600mm high, with limited space underneath. Circulation
space is good with 1.32m from the foot of the bed to the furniture, and 1m & 1.7m beside the bed.

TV is operated by remote control and Teletext can be switched on. Tea and coffee making can be reached
while the hanging space in the wardrobe is within reach. The airconditioning control is located at 1m. The
curtains can be opened/closed and desk raised lowered via wind handles!

Bathroom:

The bathroom door width is 840mm, with lever handle 1m high and opens outwards. See Photo 1 - There is
a wheel-in shower with hand held rose, grab rails height 800mm and lever tap. Fold down shower seat
460mm high, 1m x 400mm.
See Photo 2 - Toilet height 480mm, centre to side 460mm, front of bowl to rear wall 820cm, grab rail
height 800mm. Basin height 800mm clearance, lever tap. Light switch at 1.3m.

Floorplan, Photo 1- Roll in shower and Photo 2 – Toilet and Vanity

Photo 1   Photo 2

Figure 18.3 Extract from Accessible Accommodation Template
Source: Darcy & Cameron, 2008

The theory is that properties and attractions displaying the icons *will* have met the National Accessible Scheme criteria. The relevant rating icon is published with information to the property. However, no additional information is published, which raises the concern of the facility being 'not typical' or the individual's needs not being 'typical'.

Typically suitable for a person with sufficient mobility to climb a flight of steps but would benefit from fixtures and fittings to aid balance.

Typically suitable for a person with restricted walking ability and for those that may need to use a wheelchair some of the time and can negotiate a maximum of three steps.

Typically suitable for a person who depends on the use of a wheelchair and transfers unaided to and from the wheelchair in a seated position. This person may be an independent traveller.

Typically suitable for a person who depends on the use of a wheelchair in a seated position. This person also requires personal or mechanical assistance (eg carer, hoist).

Access Exceptional: provides for all levels of mobility impairment listed above with reference to the British Standard BS 8300:2001. Achieves the standards above for either independent wheelchair users or assisted wheelchair users and fulfils additional, more demanding requirements.

Vision and Hearing Rating Icons

Typically provides key additional services and facilities to meet the needs of visually impaired guests.

Typically provides key additional services and facilities to meet the needs of guests with hearing impairment.

Typically provides a higher level of additional services and facilities to meet the needs of guests with visual impairment.

Typically provides a higher level of additional services and facilities to meet the needs of guests with hearing impairment.

Figure 18.4 Visit Britain mobility rating icons
Source: http://www.visitbritain.com/en/Accommodation/Disabled-and-elderly/National-Accessible-Scheme-symbols.htm

Europe for All

Europe for All (2008) is the outcome of a project co-financed by the European Commission, entitled 'One-Stop-Shop for Accessible Tourism in Europe' (OSSATE, 2005).

Commencing in 2005, the OSSATE project recognised the potential of Europe's 50 million people with disabilities and sought to standardise the collation, storage and retrieval of access data on the accessibility of the physical environment, facilities and services offered by tourism providers. In the beginning two EU Member States: Greece and the UK commenced the project with joining partners Belgium, Sweden, Austria, Denmark and Norway.

Europe for All offers owners/managers/operators the opportunity to become part of the scheme by self assessment, detailed information and access audits, via the following:

- Self-assessment forms to be completed by owners and managers of accommodation, attractions etc.
- Photo and Measurement Guides which advise how photos and measurements should be taken.
- Access Audit Checklists, used by trained access auditors conducting on-site assessments.

The documents were developed reflecting a consensus between a 'wide range of experts and user representatives and designed to meet the information needs of tourists with disabilities, older people and families with small children'.

The detailed accessibility information is entered into the 'Europe for all' database, and is displayed to consumers via www.europeforall.com (Europe for All, 2008). Notably the Europe For All information system does not use any icons but presents dimensions and detailed descriptions of those aspects of the venues, that are regarded as 'critical' for disabled visitors to know about when making their decision to visit or stay at any given place.

Mapping

Maps are incredibly important inclusions for travel guides. Maps help the reader put their travels into geographical perspective or context. A traveller without a map will not get very far, a travel guide without a map will not be anywhere near as useful to a traveller. A contextual map would be a basic two-dimensional map placing main features into a context of space. For example a continent, country, states city's and land forms like mountains, lakes, seas, major roads and rivers. A travel guide could then include key region maps.

A specific form of mapping for access guides are Access Maps or Mobility Maps. These maps become very important by assisting travellers navigate their way around, for example a city in which they had no experience. Mobility Maps typically provide information on a city or town. However, they can also be very useful in assisting travellers navigate an accessible path of travel around a University Campus or even a tourist attraction.

Australian examples of mobility maps can be found at:

- Auburn City Council (2005), www.auburn.nsw.gov.au
- Monash University (2008), http://adm.monash.edu.au
- Melbourne CBD (2008), www.melbourne.vic.gov.au where you can download the Melbourne Mobility Map and an Entertainment and Sporting Mobility Map (see Figure 18.5).
- Brisbane City Council (2008), www.brisbane-stories.webcentral.com.au where you can download the Brisbane CBD Mobility Map and Mobility Map – Mt Coot-tha Botanic Gardens.

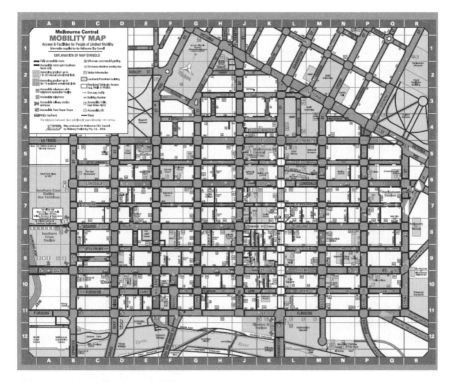

Figure 18.5 Melbourne Mobility Map extract
Source: Melbourne City Council, Melway Publishing, www.melbourne.vic.gov.au

In order to participate in an environment a traveller needs information about that environment and how to most effectively and efficiently way-find in an environment that may have a series of access barriers. Mobility maps provide people with information so that they can wayfind their way around an area as well as locating essential access related features. The Mobility Map should have some basic information about access related features that includes:

- Accessible parking.
- Accessible toilets.
- Accessible path of travel.
- Accessible telephones and TTY phones.
- Street gradients.
- Public seating.
- Taxi ranks, bus and tram stops and train stations.
- Footpath crossovers when they are not part of an extensible part of travel.
- Audio traffic signals.
- Tactile surface indicators.
- Accessible building entries.

Mobility Maps can be very useful for people with vision impairment and can be produced in Large Print or Braille (Edman, 1992), by addressing:

- Size – maps larger than two hand widths can be unwieldy.
- Orientation – some physical feature such as a cut-off or rounded corner indicating North helps in orientation.
- Titling must be consistent so that it isn't confusing.
- Content, such as Tactile Tile location, audio traffic signals and traffic refuge areas, are important, in addition to base information like toilets, transport and telephones.

A Strategic Approach

Major travel guides all follow a structure or format making the guide easy to follow and use. The format followed by EAA was based on the six states and two territories comprising Australia. A General or Introductory chapter sets the scene by including information about the country and would cover such topics as a map, some history, general interest, currency, political system, power system, weather/climate, national transport system, social highlights, tourism contacts and suchlike.

In addition to this information, bearing in mind travellers with disabilities will be interested in generic matters and items of interest, an access guide would seek to include information relevant to their needs. General

Information including contact information of specialist disability organizations and any other matters of national relevance would be included. Examples would be transport, accommodation, equipment hire and attendant care providers.

When structuring a travel guide some logical format must be decided upon. Generally a geographical basis is selected – in the case of Australia, it is the states and territories. The structure adopted follows the following format:

- Brief History.
- Getting there (capital city):
  o air;
  o rail;
  o road.
- Information:
  o tourism;
  o specific interest – disability.
- Transport (Para transport).
- Medical:
  o hospitals;
  o equipment hire;
  o attendant care.
- Shopping and eating.
- Attractions and experiences.
- Accommodation.

Each of these headings requires specific attention to provide information to potential readers in each of the dimensions of access.

Brief History

This section should provide the reader with some generic interesting information, remembering the guide should be readable in its own right. There is opportunity to provide historic information as it impacts upon a destination, for example Sydney hosted the 2000 Olympics and Paralympics. Information about the impact these had on the city in terms of access, may generate some interest by readers.

Getting There

This section is critically important for those with access needs as it must play a large part in reducing the anxiety attaching to travelling to a destination. The information should indicate the accessible options to arrival at the destination (air, rail, road) and include information about the access provision. Contacts details should be offered along with direct links to access information provided by the respective operators (see www.sydneyforall.com).

Information

Direction to information sources relates directly to tourism information but also those sources providing information in respect to access. Examples of these sources would be disability organizations (spinal cord injury, multiple sclerosis, head injuries, vision, cognitive and hearing).

Transport

Once at destination, the availability of transport at destination or Para transport options (Darcy, 1998), enable visitors to explore a destination and experience the cultural aspects of tourism. These transport options would include taxis, buses, ferries, trams, light rail and self drive/hire vehicles. A discussion of the accessible features and links to the operators' information are important inclusions.

Medical

While not critical, having quick and easy access to local hospitals will assist a traveller one day. However, many travellers travel with equipment such as lifting hoists, shower chairs, battery chargers and suchlike. If these items can be hired at destination, then the task of travelling is made easier and often cheaper, thus encouraging accessible tourism at the destination. Closely allied to equipment hire is Attendant Care. Some travellers require assistance for various daily activities such a bathing, dressing etc. If they can be satisfied they are able to achieve the same or similar degree of care at destination, their task is made easier and their decision to travel more likely. Contacts to agencies offering these services should be included but judgement must be carefully exercised to include stable and reputable organizations. Some people receive funding for their care requirements at home. It may be possible for them to take their care funding with them when travelling, this issue could be explored in this section.

Shopping and Eating

These activities have been lumped together as the approach is similar. The sorts of information needed follows the Accessible Path of Travel (Standards Australia, 2001) which takes a visitor from the property entry around the facility, no physical barriers, clear signage, accessible toilets and accessible parking and transport. Accessible shopping requires physical access, but the experience is enhanced by great customer service attitudes. Accessible eating involves physical access to premises, access to (under) tables, legible menus and accessible toilet. Large print menus are useful for people with vision impairment.

Attractions and Experiences

People travel for leisure to experience new things; art, architecture, food, language, climate, culture, the environment, nature – flora and fauna as well as have an adventure. The role of the travel guide is to give the reader confidence the attraction/experience will provide them with the access they need but to also encourage them the attraction is worth visiting. The accessible path of travel is important but can be expanded to the accessible precinct (Darcy, 2005), when dealing with a larger area comprising a number of attractions such as Sydney's Olympic Park. This is where a Mobility Map of the destination is important. One can employ a structure within a structure to write about attractions. Each attraction or experience requires information on Contacts, Access and Content, where the content refers to the reasons why a visitor would attend an attraction. For example consider the extract from EAA (Cameron, 2000), as in Figure 18.6. The example shows how the structure can work combining contact and access information, then interesting information which encourages travellers to visit the attraction.

The Northern Territory Museum of Arts and Sciences, (open 9am–5pm Mon-Fri, 10am-5pm Sat-Sun, with admission free, 8999 8211) is at Bullocky Point, on Conacher St, Fannie Bay, which runs off Gilruth Avenue just beyond the Mindil Beach market area. The museum is a modern building on the side of a hill. A drop-off point is by the front door and parking is nearby. Access to all exhibits is via long ramps (gradient about 1:10). An accessible unisex toilet is on ground level and wheelchairs may be borrowed. A chair-lift is available.

The museum consists of a touring gallery, an excellent collection of Australian artists, a natural science gallery, military gallery, history gallery and Aboriginal art gallery. Exhibited in the natural science gallery are the preserved remains of **Sweetheart**, a 5.1m-long estuarine croc which lived in the Finnis River and took to attacking motorised fishing dinghies that strayed into its territory. Sweetheart died while being captured for relocation: the croc became entangled in the nets used to capture it and drowned. Another highlight is the excellent and informative display of Aboriginal art - in particular the Pirukuparli Poles from the Tiwi islands, which describe the dreamtime story of how death came into the world. Don't miss the Cyclone Tracy Gallery.

After you have visited these attractions enjoy a well earned drink and something to eat at the **Cornucopia Museum Cafe** (8981 1002).

Figure 18.6 Extract from Attraction Guide
   Source: Cameron, 2000

A Word About Alternative Formats

Some travellers will be unable to fully utilize the information contained in a standard printed travel guide for a range of reasons. Some travellers may be unable to read the text because of blindness or vision impairment. Others may be unable to manipulate the guide because of physical disability, for example multiple sclerosis, arthritis or spinal injury. In addition there are some who are limited in their ability to comprehend or process the information.

These users of the guide and potential travellers should not be forgotten and ignored. They can form a body of potential travellers who simply need the information presented in an alternative format or form. Those alternative formats can include:

- Large print version.
- Screen 'manipulatable' – Text or Doc format.
- Audio version – cassette, disc, mp3, mp4.
- Braille.
- Simple English.
- Screen readable.

Web-based sites can present the information in a manner which can be manipulated by the user to suit their own personal needs. A good example is the site www.sydneyforall.com which provides the opportunity for users to change the font size, change the contrast via background colour and font colour and receive text messages where there is an image on screen. Guides can be increasingly downloadable on smart phones and be displayed in a range of media.

Traditional binding is stitching or gluing. Functional guides useable by people with limited grip or hand function need to be considered. Spiral or wire binding while expensive offers a functional option as the guide lays open and flat.

Conclusions

Accessible travel guides are critical sources of information for accessibility requiring travellers. Their primary objective and that is to provide information so an individual can have the information at their disposal to make an informed decision on whether the level of accessibility is adequate for their needs. Accessible travel guides should also provide information to complete the trip travel chain from the tourism generating region, transit to the tourism destination region, transport at the destination, accommodation options at the destination, wayfinding at the destination, accessible destination experiences and transit back to the tourism generating region.

Best practice from Australia for people with mobility access needs can be used around the world to ensure that accessible guides are suitable for the needs of consumers and also that incorporate the right information in the right format.

References

AAA Tourism (2008) Access Information Program. Available at: www.aaatourism.com. au/.

Auburn City Council (2005) Auburn Mobility Map. Available at: www.auburn.nsw.gov. au.

Brisbane City Council (2008) Brisbane CBD Mobility Map and Mobility Map – Mt Coot-tha Botanic Gardens. Available at: www.brisbane-stories.webcentral.com.au.

Cameron, B. (1995, 2000) *Easy Access Australia – a travel guide to Australia.* Melbourne: Easy Access Australia Publishing Pty Ltd.

Cameron, B. (1995) *Easy Access Australia.* Kew, Victoria: Kew Publishing.

Cameron, B. (2000) *Easy Access Australia* (2nd edn). Kew, Victoria: Kew Publishing.

City of Melbourne (2008) Melbourne Mobility Map, Accessible Eating guide and an entertainment and sporting Mobility Map. Available at: www.melbourne.vic.gov. au.

Darcy, S. (1998) *Anxiety to Access – The Travel Patterns of People with a physical disability in NSW.* Sydney: Tourism New South Wales.

Darcy, S. (2008) *Working Paper No. 10: Accessible Tourism Accommodation Information Preferences.* Working paper of the School of Leisure, Sport and Tourism, Faculty of Business, University of Technology, Sydney. Available at: www.business.uts.edu.au/ lst/research/research_papers.html.

Darcy, S. (2010) Inherent complexity: disability, accessible tourism and accommodation information preferences. *Tourism Management,* 31(6), 816–826.

Darcy, S. and Cameron, B. (2008) Accessible accommodation assessment template [software template]. © University of Technology, Sydney and Easy Access Australia.

Darcy, S., Cameron, B., Dwyer, L., Taylor, T., Wong, E. and Thomson, A. (2008a) *Visitor Accessibility in Urban Centres.* Gold Coast, Australia: Sustainable Cooperative Research Centre.

Darcy, S., Cameron, B., Pegg, S. and Packer, T. (2008b) Developing business cases for accessible tourism. *STCRC technical report. Available at:* http://www.sustainabletour ismonline.com/86/growing-niche-markets/developing-business-case-studies-for-accessible-tourism.

Darcy, S., Cameron, B. and Pegg, S. (2010) Accessible tourism and sustainability: a discussion and case study. *Journal of Sustainable Tourism,* 18(4), 515–537.

Europe For All (2008) Europe for All – Better Information for discerning travellers. Available at: www.europeforall.com.

Frommers Travel Guides (2009) *Frommers Australia.* New York: John Wiley. Available at: www.frommers.com.

Human Rights and Equal Opportunity Commission (HREOC) (2008) Disability Discrimination Act Complaints Cases Register and Decisions. Available at: http:// www.hreoc.gov.au/disability_rights/decisions/.

IDEAS NSW (2009) Information on Disability and Education Awareness Services. Available at: www.ideas.org.au/.

Let's Go Travel Guides (2008) *Let's Go Australia on a Budget.* Cambridge, MA: Let's Go , Inc. Available at: www.letsgo.com/.

Lonely Planet Publications (2008) *Lonely Planet Australia.* Footscray, Victoria: Lonely Planet. Available at: www.lonelyplanet.com/.

Monash University (2008), Mobility Maps, visited 12 December 2008 http://www.adm. monash.edu.au/sss/equity-diversity/disability-liaison/mobilitymaps.html.

NICAN (2008) Accommodation and Service Directory. Available at: www.nican.com.au/ search/search.asp.

One Stop Shop for Accessible Tourism in Europe (OSSATE) (2005) www.ossate.org.

ParaQuad NSW Resources. Available at: www.paraquad.org.au/.

Spinal Cord Injuries Association (SCIA) (2002) *Access Sydney, The easy guide to easy access*. Sydney: Spinal Cord Injuries Association (formerly Australian Quadriplegic Association Ltd).

Standards Australia (2009) *Design for access and mobility – General requirements for access – New building work with amendments,* AS 1428.1 (4th edn). Homebush, NSW: Standards Australia.

Tourism for All UK (2008) TFA Directory. Available at: www.tourismforall.org.uk/.

Visit Britian (2008) National Accessible Scheme Symbols. Available at: http://www. visitbritain.com/en/Accommodation/Disabled-and-elderly/National-Accessible-Scheme-symbols.htm.

Warner Brothers Movie World (2011) Guests with a Disability. Available at: http:// movieworld.myfun.com.au/Visitor-Information/Guests-with-a-Disability.aspx.

Web Links

http://www.easyaccessaustralia.com.au/
http://www.europeforall.com/home.seam
https://www.tourismforall.org.uk/
Australian examples of mobility maps can be found at:

- Auburn City Council: www.auburn.nsw.gov.au.
- Monash University: http://adm.monash.edu.asn.
- Melbourne CBD: www.melbourne.vic.gov.au, where you can download the Melbourne Mobility Map and an Entertainment and Sporting Mobility Map (see Figure 18.5),
- Brisbane City Council: www.brisbane-stories.powerup.com.au, where you can download the Brisbane CBD Mobility Map and Mobility Map – Mt Coot-tha Botanic Gardens.

19 Accessing Heritage Tourism Services

Shane Pegg and Norma Stumbo

Introduction

Heritage tourism has become an increasingly important segment of the tourism industry with a significant proportion of domestic and international visitors now looking to participate in cultural experiences as a key element of their holidays (Pacific Asia Travel Association (PATA), 2005; Snowden, 2008; Tourism Queensland, 2003). It has also become an important element of the tourism mix for many holiday destinations where the seaside is not the principal attractant (Prentice *et al.*, 1998). Importantly, the heritage tourism segment represents one of the highest yield tourism groups, ahead of both traditional mass markets and other niche tourism audiences such as the arts. For instance, heritage tourists spend on average 38% more per day, stay 34% longer than traditional tourists, and spend 20% more and stay 22% longer than arts-oriented tourists (Tourism Western Australia, 2006). In terms of locally generated tourist activity in the Australian setting, approximately 10.9 million domestic overnight visitors and 10.4 million domestic day visitors participated in 2007 in some form of cultural and/or heritage activity (Tourism Australia, 2008). Heritage tourism, sometimes also referred to as cultural tourism, is however no different to other sectors of the tourism industry in that it is now starting to feel the full impact of the global financial meltdown of 2008. Recent forecasts suggest that international tourism related travel will decline significantly in the Asia Pacific region in the immediate future (Tourism Research Australia, 2008). This is an important issue for the heritage tourism sector as approximately 51% of all international visitors reported participating in at least one cultural and heritage activity whereas only 20% of domestic visitors did likewise (Tourism Research Australia, 2006). In response, the tourism industry has sought to place a greater emphasis on promoting domestic visits in an effort to generate sufficient business to maintain tourist operations through the difficult times ahead. While there has been much 'doom and gloom' generated to date, the financial crisis has importantly brought with it a greater clarity for many as to how interdependent many markets truly are. Also, for those willing to learn an important lesson, the recent crisis has served to highlight how systematic failure in any one node of the financial network can very rapidly work its way through to service driven agencies (such as those in the heritage tourism sector) operating in the broader economy (Courtney, 2008). Thus, while the financial meltdown of 2008–2009 might have caused a number of heritage tourism operators a degree of short time pain, those willing to rethink the way the way they make strategic decisions, and how they plan under uncertainty, will be best positioned to gain a competitive advantage in the marketplace in the mid to longer term. A line of argument supported by Rumelt (2008), who noted that during hard times, a structural break in the economy, as has occurred globally in 2008, can actually be an opportunity in disguise in that, to survive the harsh economic realities of the business environment, and eventually to flourish, businesses must learn how to exploit it. Perhaps simple enough logic one might suggest but just how can an agency go about doing just that! Well, from the outset it requires an agency to embrace a cohesive strategy (or response) to the challenge at hand. Something that a number of tourism industry leaders have called for in recent times but which, to be frank, have been effectively few and far between on the ground thus far. It is in this context that the argument is presented which businesses in the heritage tourism sector need to rethink how they do business and for whom. The reasoning being that those operators in the heritage tourism sector who do take action will be better positioned to accommodate the newly evolving niche market of accessible tourism. A sector which is now being driven by the tourism needs and wants of the rapidly ageing baby boomer generation and the emergence of the disability market.

Rethinking Service and Product Offerings in the Heritage Tourism Sector

From the outset, it is important to note that one critical condition associated with the heritage sector is that many managers still do not consider themselves to be working in the tourism industry at all. As noted by Garrod and Fyall (2000: 684), 'many still hold the view that they are actually guardians of the national heritage rather than as providers of public access to it'. This is critical point as the underlying philosophy of what managers perceive is their role and responsibilities has a significant flow-on effect not only for how a site is managed but also for what service and setting provisions are made available to various markets that continue to evolve and, in some cases, fragment over time.

Globalization, technological innovations and a changing consumer focus have all served to dramatically change the way that tourism operators need to operate in today's business environment. It has become very evident, for example, that businesses must continuously adopt innovative strategies to improve or maintain their competitiveness in the market place. Managers have therefore been increasingly compelled to develop strategies that will optimize any competitive advantages whilst, at the same time, minimize their operation's vulnerability to external threats and emulation. In particular, it has become imperative that the business (regardless of size) improve services and fulfil the holistic needs of their customers. If operators in the heritage tourism sector are to differentiate themselves and remain distinctive, they must be willing to provide better value (as perceived by the consumer) than do its' competitors. This is particularly important in the heritage tourism sector where the opportunity 'to experience something unique, beautiful, rare, authentic, or of great cultural significance provides a strong appeal for the tourists' (Australian Heritage Commission, 2001: 15). Thus, customer-focused service activities of high perceived value are essential to gaining loyalty and market leadership. This requires businesses to effectively engage themselves in an ongoing process whereby the internal mechanisms of an operation are tailored to meet the changing needs of the customers while simultaneously allowing each to differentiate itself from its competition through it services. Such a process necessitates the identification and adoption of service-oriented activities that are valuable to the consumer, and to do so continually (Solnet & Kandampully, 2008).

As noted by Pine and Gilmore (1998), an experience is, however, not an amorphous construct. Rather it is as real an offering as any service, good, or commodity. This being particular true for the heritage tourism sector where people seek to experience the distinctive natural, indigenous and historic heritage places and the rich stories associated with them (Australian Heritage Commission, 2001). Garrod and Fyall (2000) contended that heritage attractions have been increasingly compelled to provide a high quality service to their visitors if they were to be any chance of competing in the ever more crowded tourism marketplace. They noted however, that visitor access and relevance were critical dimensions often overlooked in such settings because of the heavy emphasis placed on the conservation role by the attraction's management (Garrod & Fyall, 2000).

That stated, it is also an unfortunate reality that in today's service economy, all too many operators choose to simply wrap experiences around their traditional offerings in an effort to better sell them. This is however counterproductive as to realize the full benefit of staging experiences, businesses should be deliberately design engaging experiences that command a fee (Pine & Gilmore, 1998). Something that, to date, has not been well demonstrated by many operators in the tourism industry where much of the focus has remained on the setting, rather the person (Packer *et al.*, 2008). Lusch *et al.* (2007) argued that services were more than simply adding value to products. Rather, effective competing through service had to do with the entire organization viewing and approaching both itself and the market with a service dominant logic. This logic being grounded effectively in a commitment to collaborative processes where due recognition is given to the fact that the organization and its exchange partners (e.g. tourists visiting a heritage attraction) are effectively engaged in the co-creation of value through reciprocal service provision (Lusch *et al.*, 2007). This issue in itself, is of critical importance to operators in the heritage tourism sector as research by Jewell and Crotts (2001) found that not only is the sector quite specialised, but the type of experience sought and the motives and needs that drove tourist engagement were very much discrete to other areas of tourism activity. A notion also supported by Garrod and Fyall (2000: 695), who noted that a changing visitor profile, inclusive of a 'reduced emphasis on the traditional family group, an increased participation by older people in the market, an increased interest in nostalgia, and increased visitor expectations' would all serve to place increased pressure on heritage attractions to better meet consumer interest and demand in the future. As such, it is imperative that the services delivered, and the type and range of opportunities offered visitors to heritage settings, must be suitably blended and balanced accordingly.

Dealing Effectively with a Diverse Range of Clients

As acknowledged by Snowden (2008), clearly one of the greatest challenges today for service-based agencies providing heritage visitor experiences is to meet the needs of their diverse clients and participants. While an important consideration in the inclusionary process is the creation of opportunities for all people, it does not mean however that people must participate in groups characterised by their diversity (Dattilo, 2002; Schleien *et al.*, 1996). Rather, what inclusion should mean to heritage tourism operators is that all people, regardless of ability or disability, should feel welcome and supported to participate in programs or activities of their choosing.

Dattilo (2002) urged service providers to understand that 'choice' means freedom to choose among many available and equivalent options, not between lesser, poor quality, or no options at all. Darcy and Daruwalla (1999) emphasised that the improvement of access for people with disabilities, and the removal of constraints and barriers is not just an issue of providing a legal solution to physical access issues. Indeed, access for tourists with disabilities is affected by a wide variety of intrinsic, environmental, and interactive factors affecting their comfort and enjoyment level (Daruwalla & Darcy, 2005; O'Neill & Knight, 2000; Smith, 1987). Information on accessibility is also of paramount importance. The Barrington Tops National Park information provided demonstrates good practice in integrating accessibility information in the generic provision (Table 19.1). Accessibility icons (Table 19.2) can be utilised to provide this information effectively.

TABLE 19.1 Accessibility information on Barrington Tops National Park

Wheelchair facilities

The following areas in the park are suitable for wheelchairs. We have assessed each facility's difficulty of access for an average wheelchair user:

Easy: Access is free of obstacles such as steps, rough terrain or significant slopes, and may have ramps or boardwalks.

Medium: Access presents some minor difficulties, such as a grassy surface. However, you should be able to get around without assistance.

Hard: Access is via steps or a steep slope, or you'll have to move across a rough surface (with potholes, tree roots, rocks and/or similar obstacles). Assistance will be necessary.

Wheelchair-friendly places

Gloucester River camping ground

Wheelchair access: easy

This is a flat and secluded area suitable for wheelchair-based camping. Wheelchair-accessible toilets are available.

This is a picturesque camping area, providing an ideal base to explore this part of the park. Wildlife includes red-necked pademelons, brush turkeys and lyrebirds. You'll find swimming spots nearby. Walking tracks starting here include Sharpes Creek track and the Gloucester River track. The campground is also close to walking tracks at Gloucester Tops (a short drive away).

Getting there: The campground is on the Gloucester Tops Road.

Facilities: picnic tables, gas/electric barbecues (free), wood barbecues (bring your own firewood), non-flush toilets.

(Source: http://www.environment.nsw.gov.au/NationalParks/parkWheelchairs.aspx?id=N0002)

It is paramount, therefore, that, from the outset, tourism operators have a clear and thorough understanding of issues pertaining to inclusion, diversity, disability, attitudes and common barriers to leisure participation from the outset. Tourist operators must be mindful of the need to facilitate participation in the full variety of cultural and heritage tourism activities by positively encouraging and advocating for inclusion, making adaptations to programs and infrastructure as and where necessary, training staff in welcoming diverse groups, and considering individual characteristics of participants when developing and implementing leisure services.

The Sustainable Tourism Commonwealth Research Centre (STCRC) (2002), in a study of the inbound practices affecting tourism product quality, reported that poor service quality and lack of understanding and appreciation of international service standards and visitor expectations were primary reasons for tourist dissatisfaction with their 'holiday experience.' A notion further reinforced by the STCRC in their report on accessible tourism in which the matter of developing best practice case studies

TABLE 19.2 Accessibility icons

Universal icons will help you decide which attractions provide the appropriate level of access.

	Mobility access is available offering a clear path of travel throughout the venue including an accessible toilet
	A clear path of travel throughout the venue for those who are blind or have low vision
	Audio description is available
	Hearing loop or audio induction loop is available
	Auslan sign language interpretation is available
	Text captions provided for audio content
	Telephone Typewriter (TTY) is available

and assisting industry to better understand what constituted a disability tourism experience were highlighted as being particular priority areas yet to be adequately addressed (STCRC, 2008). The issue was also highlighted in the research findings of Goodall (2006) who, in a review of disabled access to heritage attractions in the United Kingdom, concluded that understanding the nature of stakeholder's interest was critical in terms of an appreciation of their role in the access improvement decision process.

Significantly, the competitive advantage of any tourism operation lies in the uniqueness of its superior service, and the degree to which the organization renders itself difficult to be duplicated by its competitors (Kandampully & Duddy, 2001). An argument supported more recently by Ritchie *et al.* (2008: viii) who, in reviewing the key considerations for visitor satisfaction at various tourist attractions reported that 'overall atmosphere, overall facilities and services at the attraction and overall experiences at the attraction were significant predictors of overall satisfaction and loyalty'. In recognising accessible tourism market as a growing group of discerning and paying consumers seeking out opportunities to participate in various heritage tourism activities, tourism operators have before them an ideal opportunity to seize that competitive advantage. As noted by Tourism Queensland (2003), operators can reach new markets and expand their business if they seek provide memorable (and inclusive) experiences with the emphasis on participant involvement and learning. The heritage tourism sector in particular needs to become more familiar with accessibility standards in general, and the needs of tourists with disabilities in particular (Goodall, 2006). Thus, accessibility audits performed by knowledgeable people with disabilities are a key direction forward in terms of the general improvement of facilities, services and visitor experiences. Parallel with this activity, the heritage tourism sector also needs to significantly improve its customer service training in order to serve those with disabilities and limitations. In this regard, comprehensive programs grounded in the social model of disability need importantly target policy-makers in addition to front-line staff.

Moving Towards More Inclusive Heritage Tourism Services

Much has been written in recent years in terms of why, or perhaps why not, people engage in leisure experiences. Critical issues of perceived barriers and constraints have been well documented in this regard, with most authors generally agreeing that each negatively impacts not only an individual's ability to participate but also their level of enjoyment, engagement, satisfaction, and likelihood of revisitation in that, or in like, settings (Andersson, 2007; Eichhorn et al., 2008; Jackson & Burton, 1999). Research undertaken with respect to nonattendance at heritage attractions has found that these types of settings were often perceived as being formal, formidable and inaccessible places that served to restrict and negate social interaction and active participation, the very elements that many visitors believed to be critical dimensions of a positive leisure experience (Davies & Prentice, 1995). Yet truly inclusive tourism services are those in which everyone, regardless of the presence of disability, has choices, social connections, and supports. In this context, inclusion is defined as a process that enables an individual to be part of his or her physical and social environment by making choices, being supported in their endeavours, having friends and being valued (Bullock & Mahon, 2001; Datillo, 2002).

Clearly, the key tenet of inclusion being expressed is that this process seeks to ensure everyone, regardless of level of ability or disability, has the right to experience an enjoyable and satisfying life. Importantly, and as acknowledged by the Pegg and Compton (2004), inclusive tourism experiences encourage and enhance opportunities for people of varying abilities to participate and interact in life's activities together with dignity and respect. Yet it is clear that many tourism operators, whilst accepting compliance with legislated national requirements such as the Americans with Disability Act (ADA) in the United States or the Australian Standards (1428) guidelines which relate to minimum standards of accessibility to facilities and venues in Australia, often do little to enhance the visitor experience of people with a disability (Darcy, 2002; Devine & McGovern, 2001; Tan, 2002).

An issue identified by Burnett and Bender Baker (2001) who in a study of the travel related behaviours of mobility-disabled consumers found that unfortunately the general response of the vast majority of businesses operating in the tourism sector was mostly compliance with legislated minimum standards of service delivery. This being despite the fact that heritage and cultural visitor attractions also have a public obligation to ensure that their facilities are fully accessible, and that this should be accurately communicated to all tourists (Patterson, 1996). Garrod and Fyall (2000: 691), in discussing the importance of accessibility for such locales noted that 'heritage only has significance to the extent that it benefits people. If people are prevented from experiencing a heritage asset, it can no longer be considered part of their heritage'.

Prentice *et al.* (1998: 6), argued that 'heritage sites were really about producing experiences rather than tangible products, and it was those diverse experiences which are in competition for customers'. Yet it is a fact that many venues still fail to provide appropriately for the distinctive needs of individuals with a disability. For example, while many facilities today utilise electronic visual displays few had incorporated adaptive technologies, such as a speech synthesiser, to assist visitors with a visual impairment. Similarly, while it is true that greater effort has been made operators to accommodate the specific needs of individuals with a hearing impairment it is also true many venues still do not have captioning facilities linked to audiovisual units. Supporting such a notion, Goodall (2006: 71) noted that only 18% of heritage attractions in the United Kingdom had an appropriate levels of service provision for those with a hearing impairment and for those with a learning difficulty the rate plummeted to just 3%. This being despite the fact that such services and aids could become a most positive means of disseminating generic visitor information as well as a conduit for the provision of historic and/or cultural insight into the attraction being visited (Access for All Alliance, 2006). Critically, Goodall (2006: 67) noted that while much emphasis has been placed on the removal of physical barriers in heritage settings in recent years, little attention had however been given to how information and communication technologies could be more effectively utilised as an alternative mechanism through which heritage became more accessible to people. In effect, arguing that technologies such as real-time virtual reality and 3D photo imaging have the potential to becoming a gateway to historic places for people who are not otherwise able to physically get there (Department of Culture, Media and Sport, 2002: 13). Certainly in those cases where modification to the existing setting are either undesirable, because it will substantially degrade the heritage value of the site, or technically or financially not feasible, the adoption of such technologies may lead to a significant enhancement of the visitor experience for an individual with a disability. This is because the majority of individuals with disabilities are more than willing to adapt as best they can to a given setting in order to have a meaningful experience with most fully appreciating that it is often not possible to make a site fully accessible to them (Pottinger *et al.*, 2005).

Conclusions

This chapter has advanced the proposition that heritage tourism operators must change their service philosophies and offerings to better facilitate the development of inclusive consumer-driven services. Key elements of which must include opportunities for self-advocacy, individual choice and control. Importantly, such opportunities will, in turn, facilitate positive and successful interactions between visitors and staff alike (Darcy, 2002; Daruwalla & Darcy, 2005; Goodall, 2006; Pegg & Stumbo, 2008). More particularly, this chapter has also identified the need for heritage tourism operators that presently do not have accessibility mandates or legislation to take direct responsibility for developing such standards and their related strategies. For example, the development of 'zero exclusion' policies would greatly assist many independent operators to develop facilities and programs that are effectively barrier-free and, dare we say, more visitor friendly (Darcy, 1998, 2002; Packer *et al.*, 2008; Turco *et al.*, 1998).

If engaged purposefully in such activity it is clear that these same operators will be better positioned to serve the growing accessible tourist market within heritage and cultural locales. Just as importantly however is the reality that those who make up this market are more likely to be disproportionately loyal to heritage tourism businesses that best serve their needs so they will ultimately derive positive economic benefits from their socially driven actions (Pegg & Stumbo, 2008; Turco *et al.*, 1998). A point also argued by Burnett and Bender Baker (2001) who noted that, as a group of consumers, people with disabilities were very loyal to destination institutions that were sensitive to their needs while not being patronising. Furthermore, they found that people with disabilities would travel a great deal more if they could find disability-friendly destinations, this being particularly true for respondents where opportunities were provided for individuals to receive personal and consistent satisfaction through their involvement and immersion in appropriate and relevant tourism services and settings (Burnett & Bender Baker, 2001). Dattilo (2002) and Darcy (2002) have asserted that the tourism industry needs to provide services that reach all members of the community, that treat everyone fairly, and that help to eliminate any form of discrimination. Moreover, it is argued that the heritage tourism industry has matured to such a point whereby its leading operators must now recognise the need to augment quality (value of service), and hence the service offering, on a continuous basis (Kandampully

& Duddy, 2001). Goodall (2006) argued that the challenge, therefore, for service providers in the heritage tourism sector, and one argued by Schleien (1993) more generally, is that the time has come to adopt a new way of thinking, one founded on the premise that the community belongs to everyone, and everyone regardless of level and type of ability belongs to the community. A critical first step for many operators will therefore be to adopt new ways of thinking and doing such that there be due consideration of not only physical access but also of alternative methods (e.g. intellectual access) of providing tourism heritage services in order to appropriately cater for the full spectrum of prospective visitors as they seek out opportunities for positive engagement in today's experience economy (Goodall, 2006: 57).

References

Access for All Alliance (2006) Wish I could go – Here, there and everywhere! Hervey Bay, Queensland.

Andersson, T. (2007) The tourist in the experience economy. *Scandinavian Journal of Hospitality and Tourism,* 7(1), 46–58.

Australian Heritage Commission (AHC) (2001) *Successful tourism at heritage places.* IAA Conference 2001. Canberra Australian Heritage Commission.

Bullock, C. and Mahon, M. (2001) *Introduction to recreation services for people with disabilities: A person-centred approach* (2nd edn). Champaign, IL: Sagamore.

Burnett, J. and Bender Baker, H. (2001) Assessing the travel-related behaviours of the mobility-disabled consumer. *Journal of Travel Research,* 40, 4–11.

Courtney, H. (2008) A fresh look at strategy under uncertainty: An interview. *The McKinsey Quarterly,* December 2008, 1–9.

Darcy, S. (1998) *Anxiety to Access: the Tourism Patterns and Experiences of New South Wales People with a Physical Disability.* Sydney: Tourism New South Wales.

Darcy, S. (2002) Physical disability, high support needs and tourism. *Journal of Hospitality and Tourism Management,* 9(1), 61–72.

Darcy, S. and Darawala, P. (1999) The trouble with travel: Tourism and people with disabilities. *Social Alternatives,* 18 (1), 41–48.

Daruwalla, P. and Darcy, S. (2005) Personal and societal attitudes to disability. *Annals of Tourism Research,* 32(3), 549–570.

Dattilo, J. (2002) *Inclusive Leisure Services: Responding to the Rights of People With Disabilities* (2nd edn) State College, PA: Venture Publishing.

Davies, A. and Pentice, R. (1995) Conceptualizing the latent visitor to heritage attractions. *Tourism Management,* 16(7), 491–500.

Department of Culture, Media and Sport (2002) *People and places: Social inclusion policy for the built and historic environments.* London: Department of Culture, Media and Sport.

Devine, M. and McGovern, J. (2001) Inclusion of individuals with disabilities in public park and recreation programs: Are agencies ready? *Journal of Park and Recreation Administration,* 19(4), 60–82.

Eichhorn, V., Miller, G., Michopoulou, E. and Buhalis, D. (2008) Enabling access to tourism through information schemes? *Annals of Tourism Research,* 35(1), 189–210.

Garrod, B. and Fyall, A. (2000) Managing heritage tourism. *Annals of Tourism,* 27(3), 682–708.

Goodall, B. (2006) Disabled access and heritage attractions. *Tourism, Culture and Communication,* 7, 57–78.

Jackson. E. and Burton, T. (eds) (1999) *Leisure Studies: Prospects for the Twenty-First Century*. State College, PA: Venture Publishing.

Jewell, B. and Crotts, J. (2001) Adding psychological value to heritage tourism experiences. *Journal of Travel and Tourism Marketing,* 11(4), 13–28.

Kandampully, J. and Duddy, R. (2001) Service system: A strategic approach to gain a competitive advantage in the hospitality and tourism industry. *International Journal of Hospitality and Tourism Administration,* 2(1), 27–47.

Lusch, R., Vargo, S. and O'Brien, M. (2007) Competing through service: Insights from service-dominant logic. *Journal of Retailing,* 83(1), 5–18.

O'Neill, M. and Knight, J. (2000) Accessing the disability tourism dollar – Implications for hotel enterprises in Western Australia, Research Paper, *CAUTHE 2000 National Research Conference* (pp.165–173) Canberra: CAUTHE.

Pacific Asia Travel Association (PATA) (2005) 'QSR' signals growth from emerging markets, *Compass,* September/October, 58.

Packer, T., Small, J. and Darcy, S. (2008) *Tourist Experiences of Individuals with Vision Impairment*. Gold Coast: Sustainable Tourism Commonwealth research Centre.

Patterson, I. (1996) Tourism, travel and people with disabilities: Untapped market segment; Research Paper, *Leisure in the 21st Century: Challenges and Opportunities*. 2nd Gatton International Workshop, October 3-4, The University of Queensland, Gatton.

Pegg, S. and Compton, D. (2004) Creating opportunities and insuring access to leisure and recreation services through inclusion in the global community. *Leisure/Loisir: Journal of the Canadian Association for Leisure Studies,* 1–2, 5–26.

Pegg, S. and Stumbo, N. (2008) Creating opportunities and ensuring access to desirable heritage and cultural tourist services and leisure experiences. In B. Prideaux, D.J. Timothy and K. Chon (eds) *Cultural and Heritage Tourism in Asia and the Pacific* (pp. 250–256). New York: Routledge.

Pine, J. and Gilmore, J. (1998) Welcome to the experience economy. *Harvard Business Review,* 76(4), 97–105.

Pottinger, G., Plimmer, F., Russell, H. Goodall, B., Dixon, T. and Leverton, P. (2005) *Historic environment and tourism: Improving access for disabled people*. Reading: College of Estate Management.

Prentice, R., Guerin, S. and McGugan, S. (1998) Visitor learning at a heritage attraction: A case study of discovery as a media product. *Tourism Management,* 19(1), 5–23.

Ritchie, B., Mules, T. and UzabeagaS., (2008) *Visitor attractions satisfaction benchmarking project*. Gold Coast: Sustainable Tourism Commonwealth Research Centre.

Rumelt, R. (2008) Strategy in a 'structural break'. *The McKinsey Quarterly,* December 2008, 10–18.

Schleien, S., Germ, P. and McAvoy, L. (1996) Inclusive community leisure services: Recommended professional practices and barriers encountered. *Therapeutic Recreation Journal,* 30(4), 260–273.

Schleien, S. (1993) Access and inclusion in community leisure services. *Parks and Recreation,* 28(4), 66-72.

Smith, R. (1987) Leisure of disabled tourists: Barriers to participation. *Annals of Tourism Research,* 14, 376, 389.

Snowden, D. (2008) *Heritage tourism in Australia*. Canberra: Federation of Australian Historical Societies Inc.

Solnet, D. and Kandampully, J. (2008) How some service firms have become part of 'service excellence' folklore. *Managing Service Quality,* 18(2), 179–193.

Sustainable Tourism Commonwealth Research Centre (STCRC) (2002) *Study into the inbound practices affecting tourism product quality in Australia's tourism industry*. Gold Coast: STCRC.

Sustainable Tourism Commonwealth Research Centre (STCRC) (2008) *Accessible Tourism: Challenges and Opportunities*. Gold Coast: STCRC.

Tan, S. (2002) Hotel management attitudes toward people with disabilities in Brisbane. Unpublished Honours Thesis. Brisbane: The University of Queensland.

Tourism Australia (2008) *Cultural and Heritage Tourism in Australia*. Canberra: Tourism Australia.

Tourism Queensland (2003). Cultural tourism. Available at: www.tq.com.au/research.

Tourism Research Australia (2006) Culture and heritage. http://www.ret.gov.au/tourism/tra/Pages/default.aspx.

Tourism Research Australia (2008) *Forecast 2008 Issue 2*. Canberra: Tourism Research Australia.

Tourism Western Australia (2006) *The Heritage Tourism Strategy*. Perth: Tourism Western Australia.

Turco, D., Stumbo, N. and Garncarz, J. (1998) Tourism constraints for people with disabilities. *Parks and Recreation,* 33(9), 78–84.

20 VisitOSLO, Norway: Supporting Accessible Tourism Content within Destination Tourism Marketing

Bodil Sandøy Tveitan

Introduction

Since 2004 VisitOSLO has been involved with accessible tourism through two different projects. VisitOSLO is a limited company based in Oslo, Norway. The organization has shareholders from the city's travel trade and commerce, and co-operates widely with the municipality of Oslo. VisitOSLO promotes the Oslo region as a tourist and congress destination, and runs the Tourist Information Services in Oslo including the official tourist website - www.visitoslo.com. The organization has 26 full-time employees and a great number of seasonal workers during the summer. VisitOSLO has, since 2004, presented information about accessibility at the city's hotels, restaurants and attractions. Integration of this type of information with other general tourist information is very important for VisitOSLO, and in 2004 it was unique in the travel industry in Norway and perhaps also in Europe at that time. The target groups are guests with wheelchairs, walking difficulties, baby prams, trolleys etc., and guests with visual impairments, guests with hearing impairments and guests with asthma and/or allergies.

It is Oslo's intention that visitors to the city find all the necessary information through the website VisitOSLO.com. People with special needs should not have to visit a specialised website for people with their disability. They are to find the information they need in the same site where they find general information about what to see and do in Oslo. By addressing people with special needs VisitOSLO aims to reach new markets and attract more visitors. This case study discusses how information about accessible tourism can be a natural part of general tourism marketing of a destination through advanced information technology and internet. The latest accessibility information on VisitOSLO.com was made possible through the EU-funded project OSSATE (One Stop Shop for Accessible Tourism).

It was after experiencing difficulties in providing reliable information for tourists with special needs for accessibility that VisitOSLO in 2004 entered a pilot project in cooperation with the Delta centre (Directorate for Health and Social Affairs) and Tellus IT (supplier of the destination's information database). The work with the 'Delta project' resulted in a database with detailed information about accessibility. The Delta centre was responsible for and provided the checklists, and VisitOSLO got advice from organizations like The Norwegian Association of the Disabled, The Norwegian Blind Association, The Norwegian Deaf Association and The Norwegian Asthma and Allergy Association. The results were registered in the Tellus database and published on Visitoslo.com free of charge for the venues assessed. The pilot gave us useful knowledge, and in the summer of 2006 we joined an EU-supported project OSSATE. We needed to update the information and in addition to improve functionality for various reasons, including:

- the amount of information provided was huge;
- information was not presented in a user-friendly way;
- the guests' needs were extremely varied and complex.

OSSATE was a collaboration project between different organizations in Europe (both destination management companies and handicap organizations). Together they have created common checklists on different levels, and information about the facilities at hotels, museums and restaurants are presented in a common interface on the website www.europeforall.com. The same information base is used on www.visitoslo.com, but with our own functionality for search. VisitOSLO has gathered the information based on OSSATE's level 2 access audit, which implies that VisitOSLO as an independent party has visited and audited the venues according to a comprehensive checklist provided by the project partners. The results of the OSSATE project were launched on visitoslo.com and europeforall.com in the summer of 2007, and accessibility information for approximately 100 of the city's hotels, meeting facilities, attractions and restaurants is now available.

VisitOSLO's Accessible Tourism Strategies

VisitOSLO is a marketing organization, and being accessible is a way of creating business for Oslo. By marketing accessibility we reach new markets, and as indicated by Buhalis, Eichhorn, Michopoulou and Miller in Deliverable D-6.1 (Buhalis *et al.*, 2005). Based on European figures alone, the total potential travel market for the accessibility segment represents 134 million European citizens with different levels of requirements ranging from severe to low or mild. This includes accompanying friends and family members. A huge market potential in other words, and destinations around Europe have only recently begun to take an interest in this market. As Oslo is a small destination in a European context, addressing these travellers at an early stage is important in order to take a position in the market.

Focusing on accessible tourism strengthens Oslo's brand image as an inclusive, warm and welcoming destination - key values in the general marketing strategy. It is Oslo's objective to be a destination for all, also for people with special needs. Although it is not VisitOSLO's direct responsibility to make sure the city is physically accessible, it is the organization's responsibility to provide quality information about the city's hotels, attractions, restaurants etc. The image of Oslo as a destination for all is also used in bids for international conferences or important events such as the 2011 Nordic World Ski Championships. Because of the increasing awareness of accessibility for all in international legislation, destinations have to be accessible in order to attract conferences to the city.

Focusing on accessible tourism supports VisitOSLO's strategic foundation and goals to:

- Contribute to increase the number of visitors to the Oslo region enabling our shareholders and partners to achieve a higher turnover.
- Provide a professional information- and hospitality function in co-operation with the Oslo Municipality and other partners.
- Promote the importance of the tourist industry motivating the public authorities for continuous support.
- Strive towards quality and ethical awareness in all we do.

By providing information about accessibility VisitOSLO hopes to increase awareness about accessibility in the local travel industry. When destination organizations present this type of information at the same places where the general tourist information is presented, it becomes very clear which venues have potentials for improvement and in which areas they can improve. The information is not 'hidden' in places where only visitors with special needs look. VisitOSLO's approach is to speak a language businesses understand; and demonstrate that there is a market potential by improving their accessibility. Appealing to the ethical aspects of this to the industry has traditionally not led to action. This is especially the case for the accommodation and food and beverage industry, not so much for attractions as they more often are run by or heavily supported by public authorities. However, in times where the economy is going well and the hotels are fully booked most of the time it is difficult to make the industry focus on potentially new markets. But as they say 'it is during the good times you grow the foundation for the bad times …'.

The OSSATE Project: Planning and Implementation and Key Ingredients for Success

For the OSSATE project, VisitOSLO used internal resources for the auditing and planning/organization of the project. A sub contractor, Tellus

IT, was used for the development and technical support with the database and for the transfer of data to Europe for all. Tellus IT has since 1996 focused on delivering efficient information solutions to destination companies in Norway, Sweden and a few other destinations. VisitOSLO's part of the OSSATE project ran from September 2006 to April 2007, while the OSSATE project itself ran from January 2005 to April 2007. The long-term objective of VisitOSLO to join the OSSATE network was to contribute data on accessibility for the city of Oslo and to enhance the revenue structure for both VisitOSLO and 'Europe for All'. The main added value components to join the network can be summarised as follows:

- Promotion of accessibility information about Oslo.
- Dissemination of information to a broader audience.
- Increase in visitors to Oslo.
- Increase in revenues.
- Enhancement of credibility of accessibility information about Oslo.
- Exchange of experiences and best-practice examples between accessibility experts.

As VisitOSLO joined the European group in the last stage of the project, we had to focus on a few tasks where we could contribute. Firstly an analysis of the current scheme was revised within the national and European frameworks. This was important in order for the OSSATE project to be able to expand after the launch of the Europe for all website. VisitOSLO had to look at ways where other organizations or destination companies with already existing accessibility schemes could easily join europeforall.com. Reaching a critical mass of information was a key ingredient for success for the Europe for all website. The main conclusion of the analysis was that the strength of the VisitOSLO scheme was that accessible information was integrated with existing online tourist information. A potential visitor to Oslo should not have to go to a specialist site to find the information needed to plan a trip to Oslo. VisitOSLO also thought that assessing the venues personally, made the information reliable and of good quality. However, the information in the scheme was already out of date and the venues needed to be assessed again. In addition the amount of information provided was huge and the guests' needs were extremely varied and complex. Functionality needed to be improved. VisitOSLO thus had to evaluate the checklists from the European partners to be more suitable for us and decided to update the VisitOSLO scheme with the OSSATE checklists. This would also make it much easier to distribute the information both to visitoslo.com and to europeforall.com.

When it comes to developing the scheme within a national framework, it is an important aspect that the subcontractor Tellus IT, with its database solution for registering tourist information, covers about 60% of all

Norwegian destinations and about the same in Sweden. VisitOSLO's accessibility scheme could therefore in theory easily be adopted by any of these destinations. Accessibility information from all these destinations could also be distributed to the national tourist website www.visitnorway.com, giving Norway a unique position in the market. At the starting point of the project there were no national standard for accessible tourist venues in Norway. However, this is now in progress led by the Norwegian Directorate for Health and Social Affairs and Standard Norge. There are many advantages with national standards, but VisitOSLO has experienced that individual needs require individual information tools. If or when a national standard is in place, one has to look at ways of including this information on Visitoslo. com too.

Within a European framework VisitOSLO, has focused on participation in Europeforall.com. This experience challenged our thoughts on business models concerning distribution of accessibility content. The main conclusion for VisitOSLO was that there is no willingness to pay a fee to be present at portals like Europe for all. This also applies for distribution of general tourist information from Oslo as the marketing budget is limited. However, content can be provided for free and if online booking facilities are distributed together with the accessibility information, a share of revenues is possible. Also, no distribution partners can be given exclusive rights to content from VisitOSLO, as distribution to a wide audience is of strategic importance to VisitOSLO.

Secondly, a live run was performed to test the implementation of the OSSATE checklists and the content distribution to VisitOSLO.com and to Europeforall.com. The OSSATE Level 2 Checklists were developed by the partners before VisitOSLO entered the project. VisitOSLO was the only city in the project actually testing the level 2 independent audits of venues, and an extensive amount of data was personally collected from 42 hotels, 30 attractions and 30 restaurants. This covered approximately 80% of the hotels and all the selected hotels were partners with VisitOSLO. All the major attractions were also covered; all of them participating in the Oslo Pass agreement. A selection of restaurants were covered; with various locations within the city and within various price categories. A member of staff was trained in doing the audits, and collected the information within a period of three months. This happened to be very time-consuming and being that it was a pilot several issues and problems were encountered. After the first few audits, we discovered some problems with the checklists. Some questions were irrelevant and others needed to be changed. This caused some more work since we had to go back to some of the places which had already been audited. However, the changes we had to make were implemented in the final checklists. Some venues also didn't quite understand why it was necessary to make new assessments (the last ones made by VisitOSLO were made in 2004). But after explaining about the project and that this time new checklists were implemented, they were positive about it. Some venues also indicated that they were not accessible, and therefore it was no use being assessed. But after explaining to them that for people with disabilities it is important to know this as well, they allowed us to come after all. Plus we also stressed that the audit did not only check accessibility for wheelchair users, but also hearing impaired, visually impaired etc. When making the various search options for the information presented on VisitOSLO.com, we discovered that some of the searches we wanted to add, were not covered in the questions in the checklists. Therefore we added a few questions only valid on the VisitOSLO.com site. These were marked with special codes, in order not to mess up the feed to europeforall.com. These questions might be included in the next version of the checklists.

A positive result of the assessments was the involvement some of the venue owners showed. At the Munch Museum the inspection was followed with great interest, and they took the opportunity to gather useful information on how to easily improve the accessibility at the museum. A few weeks later, on a visit to the museum, they proudly showed the improvements that had already been made.

A new database was developed for accessibility data in order to implement the level 2 checklists from OSSATE. Subcontractor Tellus IT made a new database for registering accessibility information. These data could easily be integrated with VisitOSLO's regular DMS (Destination Management System) where the rest of the tourist information is registered.

The distribution of content process started with an examination of the technical challenges in distribution of information to different platforms. Due to the strategic decision for VisitOSLO to distribute quality tourist information wherever suitable, it was crucial to have control over the collected information. The idea behind distribution is: 'If the visitors don't come to you – you have to come to the visitors!' This also applies for the general tourist information provided by VisitOSLO – it has to be registered in VisitOSLO's own database. With all types of information available in the same database, it is technically much easier to distribute content to relevant partners. At specialist sites VisitOSLO can include general tourist information about a venue, and at general tourist sites VisitOSLO can include special information like information about accessibility. With all the information registered in one database it is also much easier to be on top of updating the information. Given the global competition situation with time pressure and focus on highest possible revenue, one can not emphasise this time-saving factor enough. Another important aspect to this is that VisitOSLO can easily distribute possibilities for online hotel bookings together with accessibility information. This is important for gaining revenue for both VisitOSLO and partners they exchange information with.

When booking links are distributed together with information, technology makes it possible to share the income of booking made in other channels. This opportunity also makes it more interesting for partners to accept content from VisitOSLO, and hence for VisitOSLO to be visible in other channels.

New Ways of Presenting Tourism Information Data

The main problem from the first project VisitOslo did on accessibility was how to present the large amount of information collected. This did not work very well for the visitors. We tried to make lists where we ranked the most accessible venues first. However, we quickly recognised that the visitors had extremely varied and complex needs. Even people within the same group of disability could have very different needs. Therefore, we decided that we would not rank the different venues, but let it be up to each visitor to decide which venues were best suitable for their needs. Advanced search options turned out to be the solution. See Figure 20.1.

Critical information was identified for five different disability groups:

- guests with wheelchair;
- guests with walking difficulties;
- guests with visual impairments;

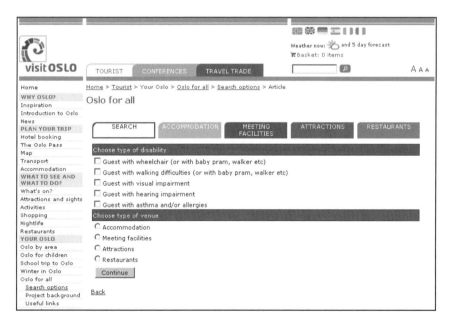

Figure 20.1 Visit Oslo search function

- guests with hearing impairments;
- guests with asthma and/or allergies;

and ended up with a facility to show venues (hotels, meeting facilities, attractions and restaurants) with the following search options:

- free passage from a certain room to another (typically from entrance to bedroom in a hotel);
- level access from a certain room to another;
- available lift or a maximum number of steps;
- evacuation routines;
- a minimum number of adapted rooms;
- special features (attractions);
- handicap toilet (restaurant);
- guide dogs allowed;
- vibrating pads in bedroom;
- induction loop available;
- allergy rooms available;
- possibility to meet special diet requirements;
- no carpets.

In order to be able to make these advanced search options VisitOSLO had to work its way through every point in the checklists and identify which check points had to be fulfilled for each search option. During this work VisitOSLO found that for some of the search options there weren't any relevant check points available. In other words – when the checklists were made it had not been taken into account that the information could be searchable in this way. This was solved by adding the necessary check points only for the VisitOSLO website. Luckily this was discovered before VisitOSLO had started assessing the venues. But a lesson learnt from this could be that in a process like this it could be a good idea to turn the tasks around! Start by identifying how you want to present the information. Then find out what kind of information you need in order to be able to present it the way you want. One thing was to make the information user-friendly by using search options – another thing was to present the huge amount of information at each venue in a user-friendly way. VisitOSLO decided to make it easy to look at only the areas of interest. For example if users are only attending a meeting in a hotel, they do not have to deal with the information concerning the rooms. See Figure 20.2.

As demonstrated in Figure 20.3 when performing any of these searches, users are presented with a list of venues meeting their criteria. When clicking on any of the venues, the criteria are highlighted to make it easier to see exactly how they are met.

Figure 20.2 Visit Oslo search function

Strategic Issues and Problems in Data Integration

There were several challenges and problems on the data integration. The registration system was not possible to fully integrate in the existing database. VisitOslo had to make a separate database for registering the accessibility information, but the results are still easily integrated with the

Figure 20.3 Visit Oslo search function

regular tourist information. However, this makes is more difficult for other destinations to adapt the solution as it is custom-made for VisitOSLO. The integration of accessibility information is not integrated with the VisitOSLO DMS in an ideal way because of restrictions in the existing database. Because of this the information is presented via I FRAME, and therefore it is not very accessible for visually impaired users. This VisitOSLO will have to look into at the next step, and make the content WAI-compliant (WAI = Web Accessibility Initiative). VisitOSLO had a very short timeframe to work within - from September 2006 to April 2007. The main part of the project also ended up taking place at the same time as we were preparing for a new season, meaning it was the busiest time for the staff. This resulted in no time for user-testing, something which would have given us useful feedback on the solution.

Equally, there were challenges in the integration of data on the Europeforall.com. For example, the xml-feed from VisitOSLO is static at the moment. This has to be automatic in order to catch updates etc. The usability, the presentations of venues, search options and profiles at europeforall.com has potential for improvement. In addition more focus is required in information about destinations. People normally choose a destination first, and then they have to find out whether it is accessible or not.

Supporting accessible tourism content within destination tourism marketing can be very time-consuming and expensive. Tourist destinations mostly work with very limited budgets and it is always a question on where to invest the money in order to get the most out it. In most cases the only way to find money for developments of this size, is to organize it in projects and seek project funding. A problem with this is that projects are time-limited, but quite often it is during the end of a project one really have the knowledge to take the solution to a higher level. Another issue is how to keep the information updated after the end of a project period. Doing independent audits of venues takes a lot of time and requires funding on a regular basis. How to cover these expenses are being solved differently at different destinations, but there has traditionally been a trend that venues are not interested in paying for this kind of information. As there is no European standard available, it could make it difficult for people to relate to all the different standards available when comparing European destinations.

Conclusions and Key Success Factors

This process has brought a number of success factors to VisitOSLO. Level 2 independent audits means trustworthy data for accessible tourism and opening to new markets. User-friendly presentation and various search options in critical elements enable a better usability of the data and a more inclusive presentation. Integrated information at VisitOSLO.com – presenting accessibility content in a main stream channel means that it is possible to distribute the information in both the mainstream destination management systems and in all other partner channels.

Developing a European-wide accessible portal – such as europeforall.com – is a good idea, especially catering for markets outside of Europe; not only for markets looking at Europe as one destination, but also in order to quickly find destinations where this type of information is available. The portal and the project have potential of making standardized solutions and search options for accessible tourism on a European level. Comprehensive information about the project is available on europeforall.com – and the work that has been done with common checklists can make it easier for other destinations to gather accessibility information if they don't have this already. In order for a website like europeforall.com to succeed, it is crucial to reach a critical mass of participants and information. However, a European standard when it comes to checklists is not yet in sight. Therefore europeforall.com offers various approaches towards new entries. The results achieved by the OSSATE project would not have been possible without the economical support from the European Union. Funding and cooperation within a network of experts from around Europe within various fields is very important for the success of accessible tourism on a large scale.

A number of lessons for practice in accessible tourism emerged through this process. Firstly there is a need to find long-term solutions for funding that will enable the collection of data and the development of systems. Because of the complexity in people's needs, very detailed and reliable information is required. However, it is of vital importance that it is presented in a user-friendly way through good search options and possibilities for making personal profiles. Adapting user-generated content will come as a natural part of the schemes and should be explored. By using various networks available and by seeking cooperation the network and the information can increase rapidly. Destinations should also learn from each other by making ICT-solutions which can work for many destinations. This saves both time and money, and it is good both for the destination companies and for the visitors who can relate to common interfaces. The information must be easy to distribute to various channels. This applies for the whole database as a white label solution, and for parts of the content where for example a hotel should be able to integrate the accessibility information for their own hotel on their own website. Finally destinations need to take advantage in the fact that the awareness in the industry is rising, but realise that Rome was not built in a day. Even small actions can make a big difference for many people! Shift focus from 'this is something everybody should support' to 'there is business in making a place accessible'. By supporting accessible tourism content there is a large potential for an increase in visitors, and by addressing people with disabilities NOW there is a great chance to take a leading position in this growing market.

Reference

Buhalis, D., Eichhorn, V., Michopoulou, E. and Miller, G. (2005) Market, stakeholder and value chain analysis, One-Stop-Shop for Accessible Tourism in Europe (OSSATE project), Deliverable D-6.1. Luxembourg: European Commission Luxemburg. Available at http://www.ossate.org/doc_resources/OSSATE_Market&Stakeholder% 20Analysis_Public_Version_Fina..pdf

Resources

Accessibility information on VisitOSLO.com: www.visitoslo.com/en/oslo-for-all
Accessibility content from European destinations: www.Europeforall.com
About the OSSATE project: www.ossate.org
Web Accessibility Initiative (WAI): www.w3.org/WAI/
Subcontractor Tellus IT: www.tellus.no (in Norwegian only)

21 Accessible Tourism in Spain: Arona and Madrid

Jesús Hernández Galán

Introduction

Arona, a municipality in the south of Tenerife, and Madrid are two very different tourist destinations, in terms of both character and the products they have to offer. What they do have in common, however, is their importance as tourist destinations in Spain. Of the 59.4 million foreign tourists who visit Spain each year, Madrid receives 6 million and the town of Arona and its surroundings, 2 million. Madrid's importance in terms of tourism is due to its varied cultural offer, especially that of its museums, and of these, those devoted to art, some of which are among the most important in the world. Arona's appeal stems from the sun and the sea, that is, its geographic location ensures it enjoys a warm climate all year round.

Another aspect both destinations have in common is the level of accessibility they have achieved in developing their tourism. Both Madrid and Arona have dealt effectively with the opportunities and challenges posed by the increasing number of people with special needs demanding accessibility. This chapter analyses how Madrid and Arona, each with their different characteristics and tourist products, have approached the concept of accessible tourism.

Arona: Tourist Destination Based Around the Sun and the Sea

Arona lies in the south of the island of Tenerife in the Canary Islands. Its surroundings include the tourist beaches of Playa de Las Américas, Playa de Los Cristianos, Playa de Las Galletas and Costa del Silencio which are especially popular with British, German, Spanish, Swedish and Norwegian visitors (see Figure 21.1 and 21.2). The average stay of tourists in Arona is 10.4 days. In 2006 more than a million and a half tourists stayed there, that is, over 28% of all tourists staying on Tenerife that year.

The development of Tourism for All in Arona dates back to the late 1960s, when groups of Swedish tourists with reduced mobility derived from rheumatic disorders chose Arona as an ideal destination. Its climate and

Figure 21.1 Spanish beach

Figure 21.2 Playa de Las Vistas accessible experiences

waters greatly improved their mobility and on returning home, they themselves began to enthusiastically promote it, leading to ever higher numbers of Swedish tourists heading for Arona. It is now one of the holiday destinations that receives most tourists with reduced mobility in the world.

Arona has developed as a 'Town without Barriers'. While the favourable conditions of its surroundings were major factors in Arona becoming a leading destination for people with reduced mobility, there were clearly others. These included, firstly, the firm political commitment, present from the very start, which has persisted to our days. The town council considers accessibility a basic feature of its tourism services, and examples of this commitment include the Accessibility Plan which is continuously updated and implemented, as well as the fact that included in the five strategic lines the council will develop over the period 2008–2011 is that of Accessible Tourism.

Secondly, the *technical support* provided by the Municipal Board of Tourism is of great importance in that it has a department with two full-time technicians that deal specifically with accessible tourism. Other professionals are also taken on to carry out specific fieldwork on accessibility issues. Among the tasks carried out by the accessible tourism technicians are those of administering subsidies, co-ordination and follow-up of the Accessibility Plan, and advising businesses in the tourist sector on accessibility. They also monitor the levels of accessibility in the area, enabling them to pass on real-time information to the tourists.

Another key factor has been the *collaboration of the tourists themselves*. The Board of Tourism has established a close and ongoing relationship with a group of tourists with reduced mobility who visit Arona once or twice a year and who give feedback on the problems of accessibility they come across when moving around the town and its surroundings. The Board of Tourism meets with them to find out if there are any new actions to be taken and the technicians inform about the actions taken since the previous meeting. The *commitment shown by the business sector* is also an important factor in the development and success of this process. Businesses are gradually getting more deeply involved in improving accessibility in their own facilities and establishments, in response to the ever-increasing demands of the tourists.

Benchmarking is yet another key factor. Arona has studied the experiences of other tourist resorts as regards accessibility, and learning from their mistakes has adopted good practices based on the knowledge thus acquired. In order to be as efficient as possible, before taking specific actions, the accessibility technicians have visited and analysed other destinations such as the Autonomous Region of Valencia and the city of Glasgow.

Training. Arona's Board of Tourism has organized several training courses aimed at raising awareness regarding accessibility issues among the business sector and pointing out the resulting competitive edge to be gained. Specific courses have also been planned for the near future aimed at sub-sectors such as hotels, restaurants and shops, at businessmen and customer care staff, as well as other courses for both municipal technicians and architects and those of construction companies.

Work has also been done in the areas of *tourist information* and *promotion*. The Board of Tourism makes use of its resources to promote accessible tourism and occasionally outsources its activities to companies. Arona has stands at the most important trade fairs, such as FITUR, ITB and WTM; specialised fairs such as Accessible Holiday Show, the Mobility Roadshow,

RehaCare; international congresses such as the International Tourism for All Congress organized by Fundación ONCE in 2007, as well as workshops, seminars and conventions organized by the different Spanish towns and cities interested in accessible tourism. The Board of Tourism seizes every opportunity to appear in the local, national or European press, whether for the general public or specialized. Promotion of accessible tourism is constant on the website and with promo videos. Arona's Tourism without Barriers Guide is constantly updated and shows how accessibility is an added value for a tourist resort. The guide offers detailed information, in three languages and with icons, on the levels of accessibility to the different facilities in the town and its surroundings. The municipal website is aimed at both tourists and tour operators interested in Arona, and provides information on the council's involvement in accessible tourism and the marketing efforts carried out abroad.

Model of Development of Accessible Tourism in Arona

In 2001, the council commissioned Vía Libre, a company belonging to Fundación ONCE, to draw up an Accessibility Plan. This plan was a starting point for raising awareness as to the level of accessibility in the town and its surroundings and helped to define priorities regarding future lines of action. These aspects included town planning, buildings and transport, and although there were no specific actions aimed at tourism, many of the proposals were also applicable in this area. The proposals set out in the Plan are still used as a reference and are updated on a regular basis. A detailed survey of Arona is currently underway and works are being carried out as and when necessary. Actions are thus taken in specific areas already in works, resulting in a concentration of improvements having greater repercussion. Likewise, work has been carried out on info-accessibility, that is, improving accessibility to the website, touch screen and mobile telephony. The Accessibility Plan is no longer an isolated project, but has been incorporated into the framework of the wider-ranging Strategic Municipal Plan.

Accessible tourism is included in the five strategic lines to which the town council has committed itself to developing between 2008 and 2011. The current Accessibility Plan will be further developed to involve the business community even more and to increase the number of actions aimed at eliminating barriers to communication. Funding for the planned improvements comes mainly from the town council's annual allocation. Further funding is available from grants for specific actions given by various bodies, such as Fundación ONCE; the Spanish social services agency (IMSERSO); the regional government of the Canary Islands; the regional agency for services for people with disabilities (SINPROMI); the regional departments of social services and tourism of the Canary Islands; and the national and regional departments for employment (INEM).

Following Arona's lead, other towns are now showing an interest in the know-how acquired by this tourist resort by implementing and running an accessibility plan. Arona is now a reference for competing tourist destinations and has been able to take advantage of its competitive edge in accessibility issues and is pleased to be able to assist all those interested in learning more about its experience.

Arona's Accessible Tourism Facilities and Challenges

Thanks to the plans for removing barriers and an efficient allocation of funds, Arona has been able to carry out several improvements to its streets and squares, on its promenade and beaches, as well as to the council buildings. The zones of Playa de Las Américas and Los Cristianos now have a high percentage of their pavements and promenades free of obstacles. The seven-kilometre-long Promenade of Playa de Las Américas y Los Cristianos is Europe's largest barrier-free pedestrian precinct. The beach at Playa de Las Vistas is the best-equipped, having all the infrastructure and aids necessary for all to enjoy. It has parking spaces reserved for people with disabilities; adapted showers, toilets and changing rooms; a boardwalk connecting the promenade with the edge of the sea and the shaded areas; and personalised attention provided by the Red Cross.

Major improvements in accessibility have been made not only to many of the public buildings, such as the health, administrative, educational and cultural centres, but also to private buildings such as hotels, leisure centres, restaurants and travel agencies. Regarding transport, Arona has four adapted taxis, known as eurotaxis and which allow wheelchair users to remain comfortably and safely seated in their wheelchairs on their journey. These eurotaxis were funded in large part by grants from the Fundación ONCE. There are private coach companies providing vehicles with elevator platforms available both for short journeys and excursions around the island. As for telecommunications, the website is accessible, and information is available by mobile telephone and text phones.

In spite of all the improvements made to date, Arona still faces some important challenges, including the following:

* Raise awareness among the technicians of the public administrations, in order to ensure that they take into account accessibility issues and that new projects include accessibility criteria. The town council would thus be able to achieve results without having to commit its own economic resources.
* Raise awareness within the business community and offer advice regarding how business can collaborate more actively in designing an accessible tourist resort, while helping them to understand how it

leads to improving quality. Results would be achieved faster and more ambitious future projects could be taken on if the whole sector were to provide their support.

- Improve communication between the different departments, resulting in a more efficient use of public resources.
- Create mechanisms to ensure compliance with current legislation, which obliges all companies, both public and private, to remove architectural and communication barriers. This would create the base from which to develop projects to improve the return on investments made in accessibility.
- Increase promotion abroad by arranging visits, attending trade and specialised fairs in order to provide information for tour operators and potential visitors on the accessible facilities available, and to point out the advantages and added value as a tourist destination.
- Publish a regular report for the sector on the relevant statistics and details of accessible tourism. Such a publication would demonstrate the advantages of making strategic investments in accessible tourism.
- Regularly update the information regarding the level of accessibility of the tourist facilities and information regarding the companies offering accessible products and services. This would help to maintain a competitive level within the tourist sector of the town and its surroundings which would, in turn, raise the destination's competitiveness.
- Provide greater variety and amount of accessible public transport within the town and its surroundings, which would result in a greater level of accessibility in the vehicles of subcontracted companies and provide the visitor with more affordable means of transport.
- Raise the level of accessibility to means of communication in all the public funding carried out. This would result in a rapid improvement in the quality of the services provided by the resort by taking into account the communication needs of current and future visitors.

Madrid: A Cultural Tourism Destination

Over 6 million foreign visitors, mainly from the United States of America, Great Britain and Italy, stayed in Madrid's hotels in 2006. The average stay in the capital was two days. The capital's tourist appeal is made up of important art museums, especially El Prado, the Reina Sofía and the Thyssen Museum. Together with the cultural aspects, the city is a business centre and a major venue for conferences and meetings. In this context, it has been endeavouring to make its offer accessible to all, a good example of which is its new Conference and Convention Centre. As a complement to the two aspects above, the hotel sector has also made huge efforts to make improvements to their facilities, making them more accessible to their guests. Over a decade ago, Madrid started working towards making the

Figure 21.3 Accessible Madrid

city more accessible and more welcoming for both its citizens and its visitors. In the mid-1990s, as part of the city's General Plan, a series of works were undertaken to refurbish buildings in the historical centre (Figure 21.3). These works took into account, and emphasised, accessibility criteria and such criteria were supervised and carried out accordingly, with the participation of experts in accessibility. Following the approval of the General Plan, specific municipal plans were drawn up for accessibility to transport, urban areas and buildings.

As regards tourism, accessibility was taken into consideration for the European Year of People with Disabilities 2003. One of the reasons for promoting this initiative was the increasing demand for information on accessible tourism being received – and which continues to this day – by visitors and travel agents, especially from abroad. The project is called *Madrid Accesible* and is run by Madrid's Tourist Board.

The Management Model of Madrid as a City Without Barriers

As in the case of Arona, in Madrid it is also possible to speak of a political commitment to accessibility. There is an *underlying political commitment* by all the departmental heads, and at all organizational levels, to accessibility. Thus, decisions are taken at the highest levels to include accessibility criteria in all new actions to be carried out, to oversee the allocation of budgets for such actions and to co-ordinate the tasks required for developing the targets set. Another important factor is the relationship *with the tourist sector and the bodies representing people with disabilities,* together with the Tourist Board's commitment to collaborating with these stakeholders. To this end, several agreements have been signed between various organizations and bodies, such as ONCE, PREDIF (Platform of Representatives of People with Physical Disabilities) and FESORCAM (Federation of People with Hearing Impairment in the Autonomous Region of Madrid) and there are close ties with all the associations representing the tourist sector in Madrid.

In developing *Madrid Accesible*, several networks have been set up and meetings are held with a view to receiving new proposals from all the stakeholders in accessibility in Madrid. The city's tourism business community is also active and present at all the actions and decisions taken by the Tourist Board, including those regarding accessibility.

The meetings and networks have so far led to the following actions:

- The design and implementation of new tourist products.
- An intensive awareness-raising campaign for accessible tourism, aimed at the city's tourist sector.
- The publication of an online guide of *Madrid Accesible* which provides information of the levels of physical, visual and auditive accessibility to hotels, museums, restaurants and shopping centres. This information is updated regularly, incorporating many new accessible tourist establishments which are increasing in number and raising their level of quality.
- Training: The Tourist Board, in collaboration with the associations of people with disabilities, run training courses on accessible tourism for their own staff, mainly for those working directly with tourists.
- Awareness-raising: Several campaigns to raise awareness on accessibility issues within the hotel sector have been launched. These have been aimed at informing participants as to compliance with accessibility guidelines and they have served as an introduction to the organizations specialising in the matter in order to assist in carrying out the necessary improvements. The Tourist Board, in collaboration with other organizations, has published a guide aimed specifically at the hotel sector which gives advice on the requirements such establishments have to fulfil regarding accessibility.

Since 2003, there has been steady funding for new accessible tourism projects. These budgets come from various sources and steadily increase. Full use is made of grants and public subsidies provided they conform to the projects the currently underway in the area of tourism. Accessible tourism is included under the Four-year Plan and the Annual Action Plans. The city council studies the viability of any new proposal made regarding accessible tourism in order to incorporate it, once approved, into the current Plan. Accessibility criteria have been included in tenders and public procurement documents, for instance, in setting up stands for national or international fairs or for the latest in providing tourist information, a mobile accessible 'tourist office for all'. On occasion, funding has been made available from other departments in order to carry out joint projects beneficial to all. Although each department has its own functions, the experience of joining forces to a common end has proven very positive in carrying out actions related to accessible tourism.

There is a specific Marketing and Communication Plan included in the Accessibility Plan, which ensures that every advance is transmitted to all the stakeholders in the sector. The City of Madrid's website has a section, *Madrid Accesible*, which is used by the Council to promote and disseminate much of the work being carried out in this area and which, concurrently, informs tourists with disabilities of the available products and services when making travel arrangements. Information is available regarding hotels and guided cultural visits to the city. In collaboration with ONCE, a plan with monuments of interest has been made in relief and with descriptions in Braille (Figure 21.4).

Madrid's Tourist Board has started the process towards obtaining the accessibility standard UNE 170001 which certifies the accessibility of the main tourist information office in Madrid's main square, Plaza Mayor. Not only will the office itself be certified as being fully accessible, but also the services it offers and how they are managed. This will lead to new products becoming available and an improvement in the information available to tourists with disabilities.

Figure 21.4 Tourism for blind visitors to Plaza Mayor

Madrid's Accessible Tourism Facilities

The accessible tourism facilities include some notable examples which derive from major actions. These include, for example, Madrid's public transport network which is, to a large extent, adapted for people with disabilities. Another example is the diversification of means of transport which allow for connectivity between urban buses, the Metro, interurban buses and commuter trains. Moreover, Madrid's Tourist Board has included in its *Descubre Madrid* ('Discover Madrid') programme, which has been now been running for several years, a series of guided cultural visits, free of charge, specially adapted for visitors who are blind or visually-impaired, deaf or hearing-impaired, or with physical or intellectual disabilities.

Much of Madrid's cultural offer, mainly that of its museums, has received high investment in universal accessibility, that is, actions that improve both the physical accessibility and the accessibility of communication and interpretation of the works on display. Outstanding examples include the Reina Sofía National Arts Centre, El Prado Museum or ONCE's Museum for the Blind.

Conclusions: Learning from Madrid and Arona

Madrid and Arona are two attractive, but very different, tourist destinations. Neither of them has sought to create new and accessible products and services but rather, to adapt existing ones to ensure they can be enjoyed by all, including people with special needs. The size of each destination, the number of users – both tourists and inhabitants – and the resources available in each case, all play a huge part in their ability to take decisions, set priorities, assess viability, identify accessible tourism projects and to disseminate them. Both Madrid and Arona are examples of tourist destinations which, though based on two entirely different realities, have decided to implement a Management Model of a Town without Barriers, and to maintain said plan.

Each destination has counted on a different dynamic element to implement the process: in the case of Madrid, it has been the council's close and constant collaboration with the various associations of people with disabilities at local and national levels, and the significant resources they provide, above all human resources and know-how, but also funding. In Arona, it has been the actual tourists themselves, the visitors from other European countries, who, together with the local council, have made efforts to implement an ongoing process of accessibility. In both cases, however, it has been the political commitment and the professionalism of the technicians involved that has enabled projects to start and targets to be met.

What can other tourist destinations learn from Arona and Madrid? The following cycle is the key to Arona's position in the ranking of tourist destinations and summarises the strategy that keeps it moving forward: Communication raising awareness though success stories; ongoing assessment of the surroundings, products and services; plan the interventions from the moment they are detected; and take immediate measures.

There are five key action lines in developing 'Madrid Accesible' that are transferable to other destinations including: Provide information on the availability of accessible tourist options; Ensure accessible infrastructures; Design accessible products and services; Continuous staff training and raising awareness-in the sector.

In difficult moments, such as the present one in which an international financial crisis affects all tourist destinations in one way or another, finding a niche in the market is the key to competing for tourists. Both Madrid and Arona have realised this and have made themselves known as tourist destinations that are integrating, convenient and accessible for all. Arona works on the premise that 'there's no such thing as quality if it isn't accessible for all' and all its efforts are headed in that direction. Both Madrid and Arona have now been working for many years planning and investing in accessibility. For the tourist sectors of both tourist destinations it will become increasingly easy to solve accessibility issues or to design ever-more accessible surroundings and services because they have already set up the basic, necessary elements. By having already set off in the right direction, they have a head start over most other competitors, a competitive edge that will allow them to benefit from increasingly profitable investments.

As well as the increasing demand for specialized products and services, there is also a concurrent demand for specific information regarding the accessibility of a destination's products and services. Few tourist agencies or tour operators are able to provide up-to-date information on accommodation and other aspects of interest for the tourists destinations they offer. That's why it is essential that, just as they have done for Madrid and Arona, the business community and tour operators make available all the necessary information they have as to the current level of accessibility in their products and services in order for tourists with special needs, travelling for whatever reason, know in advance the necessary details that will allow them to decide on one product, destination or service over another. Such information must be up-to-date, accurate and detailed. This will enable the business community or public administration to implement plans of action to eliminate existing barriers.

References

Plan Nacional de Accesibilidad 2004–2012: www.seg-social.es/imserso/dependencia/ipna2004_2012.pdf (in Spanish).
La Accesibilidad Universal en los Municipios: guía para una política integral de promoción y gestión: www.seg-social.es/imserso/dependencia/guiaaccesmuni.pdf (in Spanish).

Ley 51/2003, de dos de diciembre (LIONDAU): http://sid.usal.es/idocs/F3/LYN5979/3-5979.
pdf (in Spanish). Also available in English at: http://sid.usal.es/idocs/F3/LYN13769/
LIONDAU.pdf.

Acuerdo de colaboración CERMI-Secretaría General de Turismo de España: http://antiguo.
cermi.es/documentos/descargar/Turismo-accesible/ConvenioSGT-CERMI-dic2002.
doc.

Barometer of the Economy of the City of Madrid (2007) Available at: www.esmadrid.
com/recursos/doc/es/Negocio/ObservatorioEconomico/1258101642_
1642007122232.pdf (in Spanish).

Juncà Ubierna, J.A. (1996) Un Madrid para vivir: Un Madrid Accesible a Todos. *Revista de
Obras Públicas,* n° 3.360, 17–30.

Tenerife Tourist Information (2006) Available at: www.webtenerife.com/NR/rdonlyres/
B212EB9A-2369-44C1-AE26-C982CC777F09/5440/InformesituaciónturisticaArona
2006.pdf (in Spanish).

Madrid City Council: www.munimadrid.es (in Spanish).

Reina Sofía National Arts Centre: http://www.museoreinasofia.es/visita/accesibilidad_
en.html

Madrid Tourist Board: www.esmadrid.com/madridaccesible (in Spanish).

Turespaña. Accessible Culture for All: www.spain.info/TourSpain/Arte+y+Cultura/
Monumentos/¿Language=en.

22 VisitBritain: Leading the World to Britain

Andrew Daines and Chris Veitch

Introduction

VisitBritain, the national tourism agency, is responsible from the promotion of Britain as a business and leisure destination around the world, in partnership with VisitEngland, VisitScotland, Visit Wales, Visit London and the English regional delivery partners . In common with other national tourism organizations, VisitBritain's aims are to increase tourism spend, across the country and throughout the year. This is achieved through the deployment of strategic marketing activity, tailored to VisitBritain's key domestic and overseas markets, and is often undertaken in conjunction with key partners, including the national and regional tourism delivery partners, travel industry partners and non-tourism partners. Increasingly, in line with customer demands, much of VisitBritain's marketing is carried out online.

It is well documented that the world's population is getting older. For many of VisitBritain's key overseas markets, as well as for the UK population, the segments showing the biggest growth as those aged 55 and above. In 1993, those aged 55+ accounted for 12% of all inbound visits to Britain; by 2007 this figure had grown to 17% (International Passenger Survey). Perhaps more so than with previous generations, today's 55+ year olds have travelled during their younger life, and will want to continue to travel in their retirement. However, as these people increase in age, so will the likelihood that their access needs will increase.

Whilst older visitors may form the largest part of those with additional access needs, there are other significant groups to whom Britain's tourism industry must cater for in terms of both tourism marketing and provision of product if it is to maximise the potential of this market, including:

- visitors with permanent disabilities;
- visitors with temporary disabilities;
- visitors who have other reasons why they have additional access needs, for example families travelling with young children.

It is vital that the business visits sector is not overlooked. This is another rapidly growing sector (an increase in value of 109% in real terms since 1979) and one that now accounts for 29% of all inbound spend. A key aspect of the business visits sector is that it is far less likely to suffer from seasonality than leisure tourism. It is therefore imperative that appropriate facilities are in place and information about facilities is readily available to maximise the potential of this sector. Just one person who may be a wheelchair user, or who has other accessible requirements, can affect the choice of a conference or meeting venue for several hundred people. It is not only as a statutory obligation in the UK now (under the Disability Discrimination Act (DDA)), but because it also makes clear business sense.

VisitBritain is working with its partners and Britain's tourism industry to address accessibility in three key ways:

1. Increased provision of information about tourism product, which can form part of VisitBritain's (and VisitBritain's partners') online marketing, as part of the national tourism product database; research by VisitBritain shows that when looking for accessible accommodation, information plays a key role for people with disabilities in their planning and decision making. Therefore the provision of accurate and reliable information is essential for them.
2. Requiring that accommodation businesses of all types, including serviced and self-catering, that participate in the VisitBritain quality assurance schemes have an Access Statement; in Wales, all types of tourism business are expected to provide an Access Statement.
3. Provision of the National Accessible Scheme – one of VisitBritain's quality assessment schemes, allowing accommodation businesses in England to be independently assessed and rated according to their accessibility.

Increased Provision of Tourism Product Information in Relation to Access

A core element of VisitBritain's marketing is the provision of information relating to core tourism product: places to stay, visitor attractions and events. Around 38% of all visits to VisitBritain's websites (visitbritain.com and enjoyengland.com) in the period April 2007-March 2008 result in the retrieval of information relating to specific tourism products. As is the case in many countries, Britain's tourism industry is highly fragmented, containing a large number of businesses, the vast majority of which are small or micro-businesses. VisitBritain consolidates information on these businesses from over 60 partners across the UK, in order to form the National Tourism Product Database (NTPD). The NTPD currently contains approximately:

- 44,000 accommodation products
- 12,000 attractions
- 8000 events

While working with over 60 partners to compile this information can be seen as a complex process, it brings a number of significant benefits:

tourism business typically work with just one organization (usually their local or regional tourist board) to provide information on their product. This is then marketed and promoted via all relevant local, regional, national and international channels. Historically, tourism businesses provided their product information once per year, but now it is assumed that any changes are made as and when they occur.

The opportunity for VisitBritain to participate in a European Commission eContent programme known as OSSATE (One-Stop-Shop for Accessible Tourism in Europe) allowed VisitBritain to work with a number of its UK tourism partners to develop and ratify an extension to the NTPD's minimum data standard in relation to access. The key principle behind OSSATE was the provision of information on the accessibility of tourism products, delivered in a standard format and via online channels. OSSATE delivered a two pronged solution for the provision of this additional information, provided by the tourism business. This method was championed by VisitBritain as a way in which it could allow for and achieve key access information for all product in the NTPD more detailed information, provided by an independent and trained assessor. This approach was championed by, amongst others, VisitOSLO, and is outlined in a separate chapter.

A key motivation for VisitBritain's approach was the desire that all UK tourism businesses should be able to be given the opportunity to state the facts about a number of key accessibility attributes, such as whether there is level access to various areas, or whether printed materials are available in large fonts. VisitBritain and its UK tourism partners would not be judgemental on the responses to these attributes; there are no wrong answers. However, a supplementary benefit might be that these attributes raise awareness of often easy and inexpensive ways of increasing accessibility. Working with Visit Chester and Cheshire, Leicester Shire Promotions and Visit Wales, and alongside other OSSATE partners in Europe, VisitBritain:

- determined the key access information required;
- determined the appropriate balance in providing sufficient information to be useful for visitors with access needs – in particular those with minor disabilities or older people – with a level that would be acceptable to tourism businesses;

- made appropriate technical modifications to principal destination management systems (IT systems used by tourism organizations to, amongst other things, manage tourism product information).

VisitBritain and these partners ran a pilot programme which tested the collection of the additional access information, specifically:

- the quantity of information collected (were tourism businesses prepared to supply this?);
- the quality of the information collected (were tourism businesses able to supply the additional information sufficiently accurately?).

The results of the pilot work were favourable. Across the three areas, approximately 40% of accommodation and attraction businesses completed and returned questionnaires relating to the additional access information. Whilst this number is lower than would be desirable, it is still a significant proportion of the tourism product across those geographic areas. Significantly, tourism businesses were mailed a paper questionnaire, separate to the main annual data collection round (as a result of the timing of the pilot), many tourism businesses saw an additional request for product information as being an 'optional extra'. A subsequent piece of work was carried out in North East England where the accessibility information was incorporated into the standard data collection programme, and a higher proportion of responses for this information was received.

The quality of the information that can be provided by tourism businesses relating to access is naturally an important issue, with inaccurate responses potentially meaning that an individual would be unable to gain access to a building, room etc. For this reason, the OSSATE partners devised a series of straightforward and unambiguous questions, most of which could be answer yes or no. In terms of the quality of the information supplied in the VisitBritain pilot (see Figure 22.1), representatives of Visit Chester and Cheshire, Leicester Shire Promotions and Visit Wales monitored the responses provided by tourism businesses, and found no significant issues.

Following the successful pilot, it was determined that the additional access information should be incorporated as part of the NTPD minimum data standard, requiring that all of VisitBritain's appointed data consolidation partners provide the facility for tourism businesses to supply this information, and that the destination management systems they use are able to collect, store and communicate this information to the NTPD. At the centre, VisitBritain is able to consolidate this so as to distribute this at a national level. This has been in place since July 2008, with an increasing number of data consolidation partners now providing this data. From 2009 onwards, VisitBritain has been able to display this content on its websites, and to distribute it to third party online partners. This has positioned

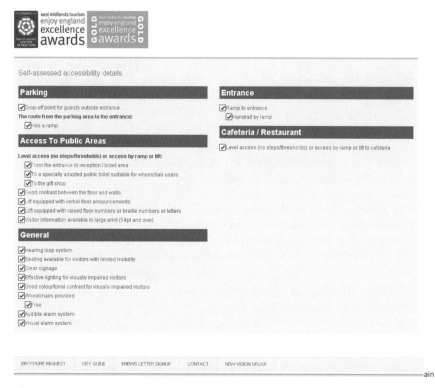

Figure 22.1 Access information supplied in the VisitBritain Pilo

VisitBritain as being the only national tourism organization in Europe to provide this level of access information over such a significant quantity of tourism product.

Access Statements

An Access Statement is an honest description of the facilities and services that are provided by a tourism business for their guests and visitors and shows good customer service for all. Used in conjunction with the additional product information on access collected via the standard data collection programme (detailed above), an access statement allows a tourism provider or operator to give more a more complete picture about the accessibility of their business and enhances the quality of the service they offer all of their customers. Accommodation providers who are part of the VisitBritain quality assurance scheme are required to complete an access statement as part of their assessment. In Wales, Visit Wales encourages all tourism businesses to provide access statements, and is working to introduce a search facility for serviced accommodation, self-catering accom-modation and attractions on its websites based on the product information accessibility fields detailed in the previous section. Details of this can be found on the Visit Wales Industry website at www.industry.visitwales.co.uk/upload/htm/access_search.htm#English.

To help accommodation providers and make completing their access statement easier, VisitBritain has developed an online template to guide them through its completion which they can then save as a document and publish on their website or make available in print for customers to easily access. This is available at hwww.accesstemplate.co.uk/ and examples of access statements can also be found here.

National Accessible Scheme

VisitBritain's National Accessible Scheme (NAS) is a quality assessment programme where accommodation businesses are independently assessed by a trained assessor under a comprehensive series of criteria relating to access by visitors with mobility, visual or hearing impairments. Successful businesses are then awarded with rating, as detailed below. When applying for the NAS businesses receive a Self Survey pack, to help them carry out an audit of their business for themselves. The NAS was developed jointly by VisitBritain and partners from the tourism industry and disability groups to help people identify suitable accommodation more easily, as a logo identifier is used to promote each criteria in the scheme. For mobility there are five different criteria (see Figure 22.2), these are:

M1: Typically suitable for a person with sufficient mobility to climb a flight of steps but who would benefit from fixtures and fittings to aid balance.

M2: Typically suitable for a person with restricted walking ability and for those who may need to use a wheelchair some of the time and can negotiate a maximum of three steps.

M3: Typically suitable for a person who depends on the use of a wheelchair and transfers unaided to and from the wheelchair in a seated position. This person may be an independent traveller.

M4: Typically suitable for a person who depends on the use of a wheel-chair and requires assistance from a carer, and maybe a hoist, when transferring to and from the wheelchair in a seated position.

Access Exceptional is awarded to establishments that meet the require-ments of independent wheelchair users (M3) or assisted wheelchair users

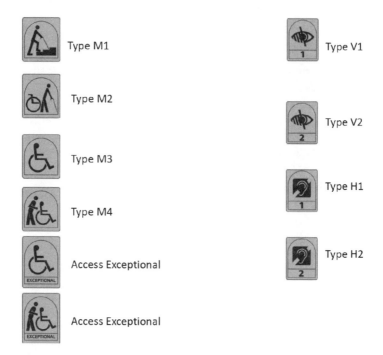

Figure 22.2 Mobility criteria icons

(M4) and also fulfil more demanding requirements with reference to the British Standard BS 8300:2001.

The two other criteria provide key additional services and facilities to meet the needs of visually and hearing impaired guests.

V1: Typically provides key additional services and facilities to meet the needs of visually impaired guests.

V2: Typically provides a higher level of additional services and facilities to meet the needs of visually impaired guests.

H1: Typically provides key additional services and facilities to meet the needs of guests with hearing impairment.

H2: Typically provides a higher level of additional services and facilities to meet the needs of guests with hearing impairment.

The NAS criteria and symbols relating to the gradings for participating businesses that meet the appropriate criteria aid potential visitors not only to find suitable accommodation, but also to provide assurance. Too many times disabled people, especially wheelchair users can be advised that they can be accommodated and arrive to find the main entrance door may be too narrow or there are steps in a hallway which act as barriers for them. As the scheme is independently assessed, those properties that have an NAS grading offer an assurance to users that their requirements can confidently be met.

Product Development

Whilst information has been identified as key to people with disabilities to help with their decision making and planning, it is also essential that the product and services are in place that can meet their requirements. The following are examples of how an attraction and accommodation provider have looked critically at their business and their approach to making changes and what they have done for the benefit of their visitors and guests and of course their business.

Bosworth Battlefield, near Market Bosworth, Leicestershire

Bosworth Battlefield (www.bosworthbattlefield.com) is the site of the 1485 battle that ended the War of the Roses (see Figure 22.3). Located near to Market Bosworth, it is owned and managed by Leicestershire County Council. The attraction was awarded a lottery grant in 2004 and the Bosworth Battlefield Heritage Centre and Country Park now includes the Tithe Barn Restaurant, indoor space for conferences, meetings and education visits and new exhibition space.

Figure 22.3 Guests at a battle re-enactment at Bosworth Battlefield
Image © britainonview/Grant Pritchard

Bosworth Battlefield wanted to attract more visitors, and to increase visitor spend. In order to do this they needed to ensure they offered something for all visitors and to look at how they could increase their visitor offer. Increasing the attraction's accessibility was an important element of this, addressing this from the perspective of visitor needs. To help them understand these needs, they undertook a mystery shopping exercise, involving a range of people including families, older visitors and a range of ethnic groups, previous visitors and people who had never visited the attraction before. They made mystery shopper phone calls and visits to find out where the gaps were.

Tourism businesses often anticipate (significant) financial outlays when first considering improving accessibility. However, small changes can often have the biggest impact. For example, in the gift shop at Bosworth Battlefield, the books for sale were lined up to show their spines as it was thought it made it easier to see titles and to fit more books in. However, the mystery shopping research revealed that it was difficult to pull out the books by the spine. Bosworth Battlefield have now changed the layout and introduced test copies of their biggest sellers so that visitors can easily see what they are buying. The result has been that on some of the books where they have changed from spine to cover-facing displays, sales have increased by 200%.

In the restaurant, pushchairs/baby strollers and wheelchairs were tested to determine how easy it was to manoeuvre them, the outcome being a minor change of layout in order to create greater space. This hasn't reduced the number of covers they can cater for but it also means that visitors (as well as restaurant staff) can get around more easily. Additionally, staff now offer to carry trays to tables.

Another area being actively targeted by Bosworth Battlefield is attracting older visitors, and in particular, the attraction is looking at multi-generational experiences – e.g. children and their grandparents. The attraction now has a grandparent ticket and has introduced activities that grandparents will feel comfortable with. For example, they do not want grandads to feel awkward if they cannot run around! To make sure staff have a high awareness of this, a fact-file has been produced. Regular familiarisation trips are organized for staff at the local tourist information centres, and they are kept up-to-date with upcoming developments and events.

Bosworth Battlefield has an access action plan, as well as access information on the event website (see Figure 22.4). There are lots of changes the attraction would like to make, but that can only be undertaken when a budget is identified - an example of this would be the provision of an adult changing facility. The attraction also continues to test and review their product through a focus group of users that they set up. This group looks at, for example, copy for their promotional leaflets and the design of interpretation boards. In return, members of these groups are invited to events and free tickets are sent to them. The cost of this is minimal and the input the

BOSWORTH

HERITAGE CENTRE | COUNTRY PARK | EDUCATION | FUNCTIONS | BUSINESS | SHOP

You are here: Home > Facilities & Access

Call Now to book tickets
01455 290429

Exhibition
The Battle
Archaeology
Events
Tithe Barn Restaurant
Shop
Facilities & Access
Opening Hours
Contact Us
How to Find Us

SIGN UP FOR
NEWS
JOIN MAILING LIST

Search Site [Go]

Facilities and Access at Bosworth

If you need more information about our facilities or access for people with disabilities, please Contact Us.

Facility	Further Information
	There is a visitor centre on site to assist visitors.
	The car parking charge is £1.50. Coach parking is complimentary when pre-booked as part of an educational visit.
	Parking is also available for disabled visitors behind the Tithe Barn Restaurant.
	The Tithe Barn Restaurant is licensed and offers an extensive daily menu of hearty meals and light lunches using predominantly locally produced ingredients. Food may be served inside the historic barn or outside in the tea garden and patio.
	The gift shop at Bosworth sells a wide range of gifts and souvenirs suitable for all ages, from pocket money items to bespoke merchandise. A pre-order service is also available. Please Contact Us for further details.
	There are toilets located at the Heritage Centre for visitors, we also have the same facilities at Shenton Station.
	There are toilets for disabled visitors on site, we also have the same facilities at Shenton Station.
	Access around the Heritage Centre is suitable for wheelchair users. Access around the Battlefield Trail and Country Park may be difficult for some people. We have one mobility scooter and two wheelchairs that can be used for free by visitors, but pre-booking is highly recommended!
	Assisted wheelchair users are welcome on site. Assistance can be provided for wheelchair users but pre-booking is recommended to ensure staff are available on the day.
	There are low counters in the gift shop and the ticket office.

Figure 22.4 Access Information on the Bosworth Battlefield's website (Bosworth Battlefield's website provides information on the access facilities available at the attraction)

group has provided is invaluable. Bosworth Battlefield's best practice demonstrated: Don't think about access as access. Instead, think about how sales can be maximised by encouraging the widest range of people to visit. Establish focus groups to provide invaluable, honest feedback, for a minimal outlay.

The Hytte, Bingfield, Northumberland

The Hytte (www.thehytte.com) opened in April 2006. A five-star, four-bedroom, self-catering accommodation, it is built in the style of a traditional timber Norwegian mountain lodge with a grass roof. The Hytte's target market includes family groups, walkers and cyclists, holidaymakers with eco-concerns and in particular elderly visitors and families or groups with members who have disabilities or are wheelchair users. The owners, Sonja Gregory and her husband Simon, have strived to make their self-catering accommodation and its grounds as accessible as possible. As a result they have been awarded Access Exceptional under the National Accessible Scheme. They are also graded Level 1 for visually impaired guests and for guests with hearing impairment.

It was decided to make The Hytte fully accessible because they were aware of the pending obligation under the Disability Discrimination Act (DDA) to be more accessible. Also, when they researched the market, Sonja and Simon were amazed that they couldn't find any accessible accommodation listed in various North East England tourism brochures, or at Tourist Information Centres. They were therefore determined to make sure that The Hytte was accessible and they felt that if they were going to do it, then they wanted to do it properly. Accessibility was therefore a key part of their planning from the start and a source of competitive advantage for them.

For advice on being accessible they initially contacted their regional tourist board, on the NorthEast, for advice. Sonja then attended a 'Welcome Host' course (see http://www.welcometoexcellence.co.uk for more information), which she found to be a really good introduction. They then made the decision that The Hytte should be assessed under the National Accessible Scheme (NAS), which they saw as a recognised way to pass on information on accessibility to guests.

Sonja and Simon received the NAS guideline book, which lists all the criteria required to achieve the different NAS gradings. This appeared rather daunting at first, there is advice available from VisitBritain, and it gives tourism businesses the opportunity to decide which level is practicable to achieve. They found the NAS criteria particularly useful when planning The Hytte. If a building is being constructed from, then making it accessible should be no more expensive (and, depending on local legislation, may be mandatory). For example, at The Hytte, Sonja and Simon put standard shower fittings in the shower and wet room, but used an extended rod for the shower so it could be operated higher or lower – an additional cost of just £10. They also put in a standard kitchen and just lowered one of the units so it was accessible for a wheelchair user.

They think The Hytte is special because it is suitable for everyone, but the quality of what it offers plays an important part in the visitor experience too. Sonja and Simon feel there is no conflict between quality and accessibility. For example, they only have small rugs in one of the bedrooms so that wheelchair users can push them under the beds out of the way. When this was explained to the quality assurance assessor, he agreed that shouldn't stop them achieving a five-star rating. They reach their potential markets by advertising on specialist websites, such as Good Access Guide, Disabled Child and suchlike. They have their own website, which is now fully accessible – the majority of The Hytte's bookings now originate on the web. All The Hytte's brochures are in large print – several elderly visitors have said that they particularly liked their leaflet because they don't need to put their glasses on to read it! However, they don't provide a Braille version of their brochure as it wouldn't be cost effective for a business of their size, especially as their website is fully accessible to screen readers, allowing potential visitors with any visual impairment are able to listen to the web content. Word of mouth has also been very good for the business, and Sonja and Simon have received a number of repeat bookings (three groups of guests each stayed twice in a seventeen month period, one group stayed three times).

Sonja and Simon provide full information about their accessibility and all their facilities. The access page on their website has a full floor plan (see Figure 22.5). Their Access Statement provides complete information with descriptions of all the rooms plus door widths, height of beds, turning space, outdoor access, etc. They promote the fact that they have an NAS rating of Level 3 Access Exceptional. One guest making a booking said she thought the place sounded fantastic just from the information given on the website.

Guest feedback forms have let Sonja and Simon know that they are getting things right for their visitors. They also listen to guests' requests and are still learning from experience. For example, one lady asked about a commode, which they did not have. They have now bought one because, if one guest would find it useful, then others will. Another guest mentioned that he found the shower seat hard when using it. As a result, they now provide an inflatable cushion.

Being accessible has proved to be good for business at The Hytte. Their occupancy levels for 2007 were 92.5%, in the previous year they were 85%. It is estimated that about 70% of the groups who have stayed with them have had someone with a disability. One group staying at The Hytte had four wheelchair users. Sonja and Simon believe that being accessible is a key reason for them achieving an increased, high occupancy level in such a short

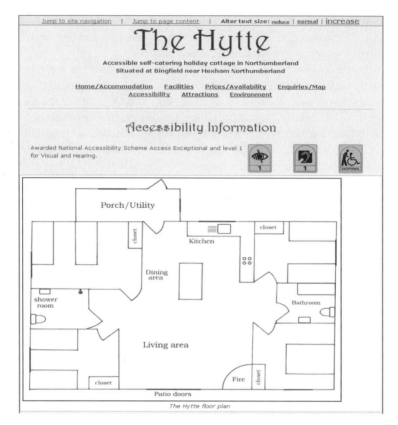

Figure 22.5 Hytte website access information

time from them opening. Sonja and Simon's top tips for businesses wanting to be more accessible are:

- Attend a 'Welcome Host', or similar course.
- Find out more information and plan to be assessed under a scheme such as the NAS.
- Generally become more aware and interested in how accessible other places are (or are not).

Conclusions

These case studies demonstrate that where an accessible approach is adopted by a tourism business the benefits this can offer for both the visitor and of course the business itself by improving the quality of experience. Not only is it important to consider the details of accessibility within the attraction or accommodation but it is also vital to tell potential visitors about these things. Reliable, accurate information is crucial for people with disabilities when planning a holiday, short break or a business visit. It can make the difference between winning and losing customers.

References

Department for Work and Pensions (DWP) (2006) Press release 9th February 2006. Available at: www.dwp.gov.uk/mediacentre/pressreleases/2006/feb/drc-015-090206.asp.

Employers' forum on disability. Available at: www.efd.org.uk/media-centre/facts-and-figures/disability-in-uk.

United Nations (2010) Factsheet on Persons with Disabilities. Available at: www.un.org/disabilities/default.asp?navid=34andpid=18.

United Nations (2010) World Population Ageing. Available at: www.un.org/esa/population/publications/worldageing19502050/.

Useful Websites

Department for Work and Pensions. View more tourism case studies at: www.dwp.gov.uk/employers/dda/case_tourism.asp.

Bosworth Field www.bosworthbattlefield.com

The Hytte www.thehytte.com.

Profit Through Access. Online business access toolkit: www.tourismnortheast.co.uk/site/business-toolkit/raising-quality/profit-through-access.

Think Access. Online access training course www.q-book.co.uk/thinkaccess/.

Tourism For All. UK-based national charity dedicated to making tourism welcoming to all: www.tourismforall.org.uk.

VisitBritain. National Accessible Scheme and Access Statements: www.tourismtrade.org.uk/quality/default.asp.

Section 5

Accessible Tourism Experiences

Chapters in this section:

23 Australia: The Alpine Accessible Tourism Project and Disabled Winter Sport

Tracey J. Dickson and Simon Darcy

Introduction

This chapter provides an examination of the process and outcomes of a project on Alpine Accessible Tourism (AAT) conducted in Australia from 2006 to 2008. The project was unique in that it sought to provide a systematic approach to accessible tourism across all alpine areas in Australia. Alpine areas in Australia are found in New South Wales, Victoria and Tasmania, each area having its own state and local government jurisdictions as well as separate protected-area management agencies. The project was theoretically informed through social approaches to disability, the geographies of disability, destination management and the experience economy. The research design involved a participatory action research framework using questionnaires, in-depth interviews and workshops to develop a systematic approach to accessible tourism within each of the destination precinct areas. The outcomes from the project include an accessible tourism resource kit, disability awareness training, accessible accommodation audit template and wayfinding map. For the stakeholders involved, the project provided a destination management focus through specifically targeting accessible tourism and collaboratively working together through a tightly defined precinct approach to accessible tourism. The outcome for consumers is that the alpine areas involved have consolidated their accessible tourism information, presented it in accessible formats and made it available so that individuals did not have to individually find access information for the infrastructure, facilities and experiences that they sought. While these outcomes have been positive, a major challenge that is still to be addressed involves the ongoing updating and 'ownership' of the knowledge base now that the project has completed.

This chapter presents a case study of the process and outcomes of the Alpine Accessible Tourism (AAT) project conducted in Australia from 2006 to 2008. The project sought to operationalise a destination management approach to accessible tourism that was first designed as a framework for urban tourism accessibility research (Darcy, 2006; Darcy et al., 2008). The chapter first outlines the background to the project, the theoretical approaches that inform the project, the research design and the project outcomes. The conclusion then examines the opportunities and challenges arising from the project with recommendations for the future.

Project Background

This project was initiated by one person's desire to reach the summit of Mt Kosciuszko, Australia's highest mountain. That person, Mr Ron Finneran, was Australia's first winter Paralympian at the 1976 Paralympic Games held in Sweden. Ron went on to become the Executive Director of Disabled WinterSport Australia (DWA) and a tireless campaigner for people with disabilities to be given the chance to access Australia's alpine areas. The project has also built upon the efforts of previous accessible tourism research and practice across Australia (e.g. Cameron et al., 2003; Darcy, 2006). The project aimed to develop community capacity, by building upon existing networks, organizations, skills and resources to provide and promote accessible summer alpine tourism that offered accommodation, activities and dining options.

Darcy has previously defined accessible tourism as:

> ... a process of enabling people with disabilities and seniors to function independently and with equity and dignity through the delivery of universal tourism products, services and environments The definition is inclusive of the mobility, vision, hearing and cognitive dimensions of access. (Darcy, 2006: 3)

As suggested by Preiser and Ostroff's whole-of-life approach to universal design (Preiser & Ostroff, 2001), Darcy's definition should be expanded to include others with access requirements such as families with young children in prams and seniors. Further, the principles of universal design are also beneficial for employers as the environments created are much safer for employees as they do not have 'impediments' or barriers which require lifting in the workplace (Mueller, 2001). Creating accessible tourism environments contributes towards inclusive environments that welcome people across the spectrum of diversity including ethnicity, sexuality and religion (Harvey & Allard, 2005).

Constraints research provides insights into the intrapersonal, interpersonal and structural constraints facing people with access requirements (Daniels et al., 2005; Darcy, 1998; Smith, 1985; Turco et al., 1998). Research for the United Nations (Cameron et al., 2003) has suggested that the structural constraints to participation of people with access requirements are across all aspects of the travel journey, such as:

- Underlying social and cultural constraints that impact upon people's expectation and motivation to travel.
- Information upon which to plan travel.
- Transportation barriers.
- Information and supply of accessible accommodation.
- Diverse accessible tourism experiences at the destinations.

Research from the AAT Project (AATP) reinforces that in Australia's alpine areas there remains a lack of appropriate information upon which someone who has access requirements would be able to make an informed decision to visit the area, despite DWA's 30 years of winter operations. In addition, there is little demonstrated support at any level of government of an ongoing commitment to the resourcing of and development of accessible tourism products and services. However, on the positive side, there is the potential to build upon the positive attitudes of local operators who appear willing to develop their skills and resources to attract the accessible tourism market.

Outdoor Activity Focus

Central to this project has been the experience and networks developed by DWA since its establishment in 1978. In that time, DWA has worked with snow-sport resorts, instructors and volunteer guides to provide opportunities for people with disabilities to access the alpine areas in winter. DWA is also the breeding ground for people aiming to participate in winter paralympic competitions. Drawing upon this extensive experience base has led to a focus for this project, not just on accommodation, but also the need to provide outdoor activity opportunities for people with access requirements.

Rather than setting up separate 'disabled' activity groups (e.g. DWA), the intent of the AATP was to provide training and information to mainstream activity operators to enable them to find ways to adapt their existing products to provide for different access needs. One example is the use of instructors from Riding for the Disabled who trained other operators so they could investigate how they could adapt their existing horse-based activities for a broader market. Other training was provided in challenge ropes course operations, abseiling (rappelling), rock climbing and canoeing. Information was also provided for operators who provide fishing and bushwalking activities. At no time was the aim to make everything 'accessible', rather the challenge was for operators to be skilled enough that they could find ways to make their products as accessible as possible within the confines of their resources, location and the market interest. To that end, it was using 'challenge by choice'.

Ageing Population

Another aspect of the accessible tourism market that influenced the development of the AATP is the growing numbers of seniors worldwide. The World Health Organization (WHO) suggests that the number of people aged 60 or over is projected to more than triple worldwide by 2050. In response to this WHO released the *Global Age-friendly Cities: A Guide* on the International Day of Older Persons, 1 October 2007 (World Health Organization (WHO), 2007). The guide provides a framework that highlights that there are multiple factors, and interactions, that influence whether a person is able to continue to be active as they age (Figure 23.1). Active older people benefit from age-friendly environments by increasing their physical activity, enhancing their social participation as well as being able to contribute to the community and economy through work and volunteering. But, as with accessible tourism, others will also benefit from these environments, including people with disabilities and young children, who will be able move more freely around communities.

The WHO guide includes a range of age-friendly urban features, many of which are applicable to accessible tourism destinations, such as:

- Outdoor spaces and buildings which are clean, have somewhere to rest, age-friendly pavements to avoid tripping and buildings designed to minimise physical barriers.
- Transportation that is available, affordable, reliable and physically accessible.
- Social participation that is facilitated through accessible opportunities, affordable activities, and events and activities that encourage integration and inclusion across generations and cultures.

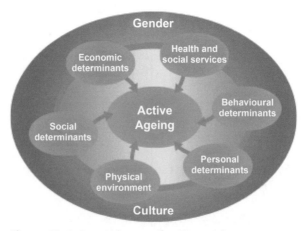

Figure 23.1 Determinants of active ageing
Source: World Health Organization (2007), Figure 3

Informing the AAT Project

Visitor's Journey

In terms of the travel-decision for people with access requirements, a simple model that can be applied is a 'push-pull' model, where the push factors are those internal/emotional things that inspire people to travel while the pull factors are the perceived benefits of visiting a possible destination. Push motivators may include: desire for escape; rest, relaxation; prestige; health and fitness; adventure; social interaction; family togetherness; excitement. Pull motivators may include: the destination's attractiveness; natural features such as beaches and mountains; recreation facilities; cultural attractions; dining opportunities; entertainment; shopping. For tourists with access requirements, the pull motivators will also include how accessible each of these are in relation to their own individual needs as well as the transport infrastructure to and from the destination. The interaction of the push-pull factors will influence the travel decision. In conjunction with the travel experience (to, from and at the destination), these motivators will determine whether that customer develops destination loyalty or whether they are lost to another destination that meets their needs (Figure 23.2).

Discussion of the major phases of the outdoor recreation experience explored in the outdoor recreation and leisure literature could be considered the precursor to most conceptualisations of tourism (Clawson & Knetsch, 1966). Up until this time, it had been implicitly assumed that the on-site outdoor recreation activity was the total experience. More than 40 years ago, Clawson and Knetsch presented a recreation framework for the first time that included pre and post stages of the activity as part of the total experience that involves:

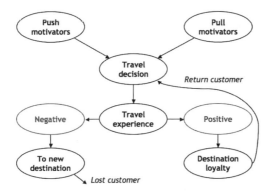

Figure 23.2 Push – Pull travel motivations

- anticipation and planning;
- travel to the destination;
- on-site experience;
- return travel;
- recollection and evaluation.

This framework remained largely unrecognised in the tourism literature until the insights from Otto and Ritchie (1996) who suggested that a tourist's satisfaction is the amalgam of experiences across the journey, then Ritchie and Crouch (2003) who referred to the links in the travel experience chain (p. 213) and Lane who presented the Visitor's Journey (Lane, 2007). As shown in Figure 23.3, Lane's model highlights how a visitor will encounter a range of organizations and businesses throughout their trip, from the process of decision-making, through booking, travel to the destination, time in the destination, leaving, and remembering. Each organization may be either a facilitator or barrier to a positive experience and a visitor's desire to return. This model also reinforces the importance of how the relationships and partnerships between businesses throughout the journey can build upon, or detract from, the overall experience of the visitor.

Understanding this interconnectedness and interdependence of individual businesses in the experience of the visitor is essential in order for destinations to grow their market share, particularly in a niche market such as accessible tourism. To achieve this understanding may require the leadership of destination managers and marketers, such as regional tourism organizations, local chambers of commerce as well as local governments.

Figure 23.3 The visitor's journey
Adapted from Lane, 2007

Destination Competitiveness

Ritchie and Crouch's *Model of Destination Competitiveness and Sustainability* (Ritchie & Crouch, 2003) is widely recognised by tourism researchers and by the WTO as a strategic framework for achieving practical destination management outcomes. Ritchie, Crouch and Hudson propose that the measure of a tourism destination's competitiveness and sustainability is a blend of two dimensions:

- the actual success of the destination is measured by the contribution which tourism makes to enhancing the sustainable well-being of destination residents;
- the extent to which the foregoing level of success has been achieved through an effective deployment of destination resources (Ritchie *et al.*, 2001).

This definition is a strong reminder that the measure of a tourism destination's success is inextricably linked to the contribution tourism makes to the experience and wellbeing of the residents of the destination and vice-versa. For example, a tourism destination that is accessible for people with disabilities and older people will enable the residents of that destination to move around more freely, to actively-age and to be more socially engaged with and within the community. This in itself creates important 'social capital' on which other notions of accessibility can be based. Ritchie and Crouch's model identifies five levels of consideration for destination competitiveness and sustainability. For the AATP this model was used as a framework for analysing the project outcomes. The aspects of the model that were addressed by the AATP are highlighted in Figure 23.4. These elements have been demonstrated as important in the development of the project. As such, it can be seen that it is important to influence multiple levels of the Destination Competitiveness and Sustainability Model in order to support an enduring impact.

The elements that have been impacted by the AATP include qualifying and amplifying determinants:

- Awareness/image.
- Destination policy, planning and development:
  - o   Vision.
- Destination management:
  - o   Marketing; quality of service/experience; information/experience;
  - o   HR/development.
- Core resources and attractors:
  - o   Mix of activities.
- Supporting factors and resources:
  - o   Accessibility;
  - o   Political will.

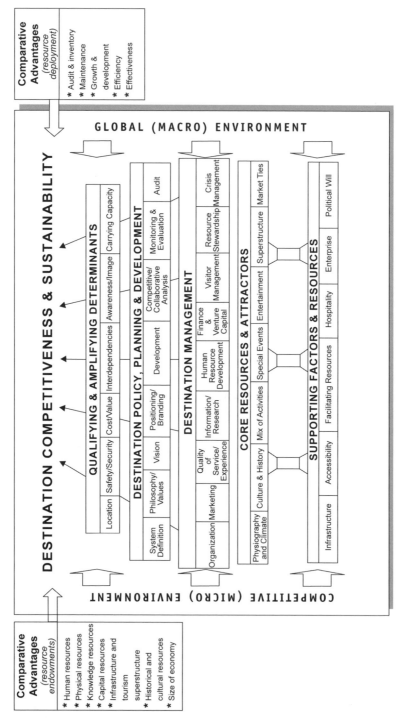

Figure 23.4 Ritchie and Crouch's destination competitiveness and sustainability model
Source: Ritchie & Crouch, 2003, p. 63

These elements form the foundation for the findings and discussion section of the chapter.

The Experience Economy

Essential to the destination's competitiveness and sustainability is the quality of services/experiences. In a tourism context, all tourists want a 'sense of place' from the destination that they are visiting (Stewart *et al.*, 1998; Massey, 1993; Trauer & Ryan, 2005; Lew, 1989). The concept of 'sense of place' has been extended by Hayllar and Griffin's (2005) work on the essence of experiencing urban tourism precincts through a phenomenological perspective. These important concepts can be galvanised by understanding the experience economy as a foundation for developing accessible destination experiences. The emerging experience economy represents a significant shift in production from the goods to service economy as suggested by Pine and Gilmore (1998) who position experiences as the fourth progression of economic values, compared with the previous established order of progression being the extraction of commodities, the making of goods, the delivery of services, and now, the staging of experiences (p. 98). The key differences between experiences and services are that:

- Experiences are meant to be memorable.
- Experiences should engage us in a personal sense.
- Experiences are created: they do not exist on their own,
- Experiences require sophistication to engender a dollar value. (Berridge, 2007)

It is important to note the shift in understanding of experience, from being an ancillary part of a good or service, to positioning experience as the *central component* of the transaction with the purpose being to provide a unique distinction from other goods or services (Berridge, 2007). The experience is central with the service-scape, the backdrop to where the performance takes place (Bennett & McColl-Kennedy, 2003).

Pine and Gilmore (1998) outline the four quadrants that epitomise experiences. Figure 23.5, which is an adaptation of Pine and Gilmore's model, is composed of two axes acting as continuums. The horizontal continuum represents customer participation. At one end of the continuum, participants are passive, meaning that their presence does not affect the performance of the experience at all. At the opposite end, participants are active, meaning that their participation explicitly affects the performance of the experience. The vertical continuum represents connection to the environment. At one end of the continuum, the relationship is absorbing in that the individual is positioned in the experience as an observer, contrasting to immersion, in which the individuals immerse themselves socially

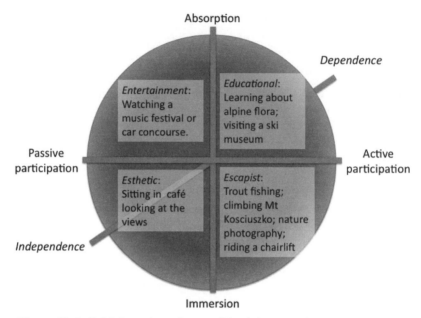

Figure 23.5 Multiple realms of accessible alpine experiences
Source: Adapted from Pine & Gilmore, 1998

and spatially within the experience. The additional dimension is the level of independence of the individual to move freely to and within the destination.

Pine and Gilmore's (1998) Four Es of experience are characterised as:

- Entertainment – passive absorption, such as watching television, attending a concert.
- Educational – active absorption, such as attending a class or lesson.
- Escapist – active immersion, such as acting in a play or climbing a mountain.
- Esthetic (sic) – passive immersion, such as visiting the mountain, but not climbing it.

The creation of experiences involves the balancing of key elements of tangible goods, intangible services and memorable experiences, but recognition that *experience* is an individual interaction and therefore no two people will have the same experience (Pine & Gilmore, 1998). With reference to the earlier discussion regarding the built environment legislation, to realise Pine and Gilmore's (1998) ultimate experience within accessible tourism, tourism organizations need to consider more than simply physical access requirements. Development and provision of accessible destination experiences should be underpinned by a holistic and experiential approach, promoting a whole-of-community enjoyment.

The significance of the Experience Economy theory is that responsibility is placed with the experience creators to act as enablers of a positive experience. Implications for the tourism context across the visitor's journey are that a series of enablers must be put in place by destination managers for tourists with access requirements to immerse themselves in the accessible destination experience. For the most part, however, these enablers are not provided for the accessible tourism market. Instead, there is no responsibility taken by Government departments or the tourism industry to develop knowledge management that integrates the needs of this significant market segment. The result, as documented by numerous studies (see Darcy, 2006), is that individuals are left to discover their own path and to create their own experiences with the inadequate information systems provided by destination managers

An adaptation of Pine and Gilmore's model for an accessible market is the addition of a third dimension, that of independence/dependence (Figure 23.5). Not all people with access requirements need assistance and as such they are looking for accessible tourism experiences that that can enjoyed independently, including accommodation, dining or outdoor activities.

Research Design

Within a broad case study approach (Yin, 2002), the research design for the AAT project involved a participatory action research (PAR) framework using questionnaires, in-depth interviews and workshops to develop a systematic approach to accessible tourism within each of the destination precinct areas. According to Reason (1994), PAR is probably the most widely practiced participative research approach where it emphasises the political aspects of knowledge production. Action research is particularly appropriate in working with stakeholder groups to produce shared knowledge (Zuber-Skerritt, 1996).

The three objectives of the PAR strategy are to:

- Produce knowledge action directly useful to a group of people.
- Empower people at a deeper level by the process of constructing and using their own knowledge.
- Value authentic commitment and processes of genuine collaboration.

A great deal of understanding about access stops at the base unit level. This research project sought to move beyond the infrastructure of access and develop a broader destination management approach, where 'access precincts' encompassed all the base units in an area, space or place of a pre-defined function. Yet, identifying 'accessibility' within a precinct area does not necessarily contribute towards providing the visitor with a tourism experience. Research on disability and tourism has shown that the tourism experiences of people with disabilities are significantly different to that of the rest of the population. While people with disabilities want to experience the same 'sense of place' (Lew, 1989) the tourism industry and destination management responses have not engaged with the group on accessible destination experiences despite the demonstrate market demand. To achieve this, the research design involved four methods:

- Access audit/management information systems.
- Semi-structured interviews with key precinct stakeholders.
- Observation research of precinct areas.
- Workshops.

As stated, this research project developed an access overlay for precinct operations and the marketing of the precinct experience to people with access requirements. This involved taking complex technical information based on the Building Codes of Australia (1996) and the Australian Standards (Standards Australia, 1992, 1993, 2001) and transforming this information into spatial and experiential dimensions (for further information see Darcy *et al.*, 2008).

Case Study Background

Geographical Location

Understanding the spatial influences upon this project is important. The Australian alpine areas of the mainland sit within the Australian Alps national parks. These extend from near the nation's capital, Canberra in the north, through the states of New South Wales and Victoria across 1.6 million hectares of protected areas within 11 parks and reserves. The 650 km Australian Alps Walking Track traverses the length of the Australian Alps national parks (Figure 23.6). These protected areas are located within the most populace region of Australia, which extends from Sydney (three hours north of Canberra) to Melbourne (2.5 hours west of Walhalla) where approximately one-third of Australia's 20 million population live.

Economic Significance of Winter Tourism

The historical and economic influences upon the region include the fact that skiing in Australia began in the 1860s with Scandinavian goldminers in the Kiandra district, near Selwyn Snowfields, using old fence palings to slide down the hill. The first ski club in world was established at this time, called

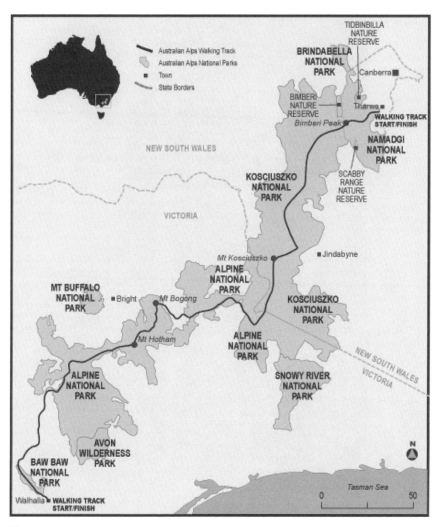

Figure 23.6 Australian Alps National Park walking track
Source: http://www.australianalps.deh.gov.au/parks/index.html

the Kiandra Snowshoe Club (Walkom, 1991). Within the Australian Alps national parks, are located the majority of Australia's 15 alpine resorts where the Australia's snowsport industry is located (Figure 23.7). In 2010, the snowsport industry contributes over a billion dollars to the state economies of New South Wales and Victoria (National Institute of Economic and Industry Research, 2006).

The greatest economic impact of snow-sport or winter sports tourism is seen at the local or regional level, especially for the gateway communities

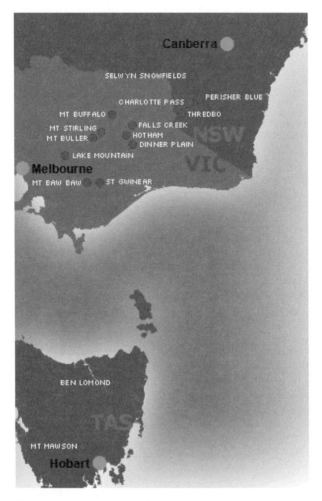

Figure 23.7 Australia's alpine resorts
Source: www.ski.com.au

and local government areas (Table 23.1). Snowy River Shire is the location of most of the accommodation for the two resorts of Perisher and Thredbo and is the gateway to all four of New South Wales' resorts. Up to 57% of the gross regional product for this Shire is a result of winter tourism. In contrast, Alpine Shire in Victoria, the gateway to Falls Creek, Mt Hotham and Mt Buffalo, receives a 20% benefit from winter tourism. Their winter figures appear lower, however these do not include accommodation figures for the resort areas that have been excised from the Alpine National Park.

The importance of tourism to the gateway local government areas is further emphasised through Tourism Research Australia's data (Table 23.2)

TABLE 23.1 Change in Gross Regional Product and Employment by local government area as result of winter tourism (2005)

State/region	Gross Regional Product		Employment	
New South Wales	$m	% of region's GRP	Number	% of region's employment
Albury	42.3	2.5	626	2.8
Snowy River Shire	289.6	57.2	3264	50.9
Tumut	28.4	7.7	557	10.5
Victoria				
Alpine Shire	105.6	20.0	1375.3	20.9
Mansfield and Benalla	48.9	7.6	554.6	5.7

Source: National Institute of Economic and Industry Research, 2006

TABLE 23.2 Tourism profile: Snowy River Shire and Alpine Shire (four-year average to June 2007)

Snowy River Shire (NSW)   Alpine Shire (Victoria)

	International	Domestic overnight	Domestic day	International	Domestic overnight	Domestic day
Visitors ('000)	12	453	np	6	315	214
Visitor nights ('000)	68	1,908	–	39	1,015	–
Spend ($million)	6	367	np	Np	125	15
Average stay (nights)	5.5	4.2	–	6.7	3.2	–
Average spend per trip ($)	462	810	np	Np	396	70
Average spend per night ($)	1,849	193	–	Np	123	–

Quarter returned home	Domestic overnight %	State average %	National average %	Domestic overnight %	State average %	National average %
March	16	27	27	30	30	27
June	16	25	25	29	24	25
September (Winter)	55	23	23	19	22	23
December	14	25	25	22	24	25

Source: Tourism Research Australia, Tourism Profiles for Local Government Areas in Regional Australia (Tourism Research Australia, 2008a, 2008b)

that indicates that for Snowy River Shire, 55% of domestic overnight visitors were there during the three-month period to September (i.e. winter) while for Alpine Shire, 19% of overnight visits were in the winter quarter (again, excluding people who stayed overnight in the excised resorts). Yet winter sports tourism is a fragile industry facing an uncertain future. With climate change emerging as a key challenge, alpine resorts and gateway communities need to look at strategies to 'climate change-proof' themselves. One avenue is to enhance their tourism product and to become year-round tourism destinations targeting people across their life cycle.

Key Stakeholders

Stakeholder theory was developed in the field of strategic management studies where it is acknowledged that the conflicting perspectives of stakeholders need to be managed as part of organizational objectives (Freeman, 1983). In the tourism context, stakeholder theory has been used synonymously in relation to government management of environmental development processes (Sautter & Leisen, 1999). Yet, within the community management context there is a much broader constituency that determines the relative success of tourism within any destination area (Murphy, 1985). As Sautter and Leisen emphasise, collaboration among key players is an essential ingredient in sustainable development (1999). Jamal and Getz (1995) suggest the lack of coordination and collaboration in the tourism industry hinders coordination between stakeholders and we suggest that community involvement in planning and development is critical to the overall sustainability of tourism in a destination region for accessible tourism. As suggested by Leiper, Stear, Hing, and Firth's model of the partial industrialisation of tourism (Leiper *et al.*, 2008), the specific targeting of tourists and collaboration between organizations that specifically target tourists are the defining features of industrialised tourism. To sustainably promote accessible tourism within a destination region, the development of collaboration between the stakeholders is essential giving rise to the potential for collaboration between community development specialists with tourism managers.

An important aspect for the AATP was the focus on the alpine areas' gateway communities and the key stakeholders such as:

- alpine resort management;
- land managers;
- local government;
- regional tourism organizations;
- tourism operators;
- visitor information centres;
- organisations currently working with people with access requirements;
- other interest groups for the target markets.

TABLE 23.3 Alpine areas and gateway communities governance

State	Gateway local government areas	Protected area and land management	Other government agencies
New South Wales	Snowy River Shire Cooma Monaro Shire Tumut Shire	Department of Environment and Climate Change Kosciuszko National Park	Department of Planning Department of the Arts, Sport and Recreation
Victoria	Alpine Shire Mansfield Shire	Department of Sustainability and Environment: Alpine National Park Snowy River National Park Mt Buffalo National Park Alpine Resorts Coordinating Council	Victorian Resort Management Boards Access 5,000
Tasmania	Waratah-Wynyard	Parks and Wildlife Service Cradle Mountain – Lake St Clair National Park	Community Development Division, Department of Premier and Cabinet (Disability Bureau)

Part of the challenge facing many interregional tourism projects, including the AATP, is that Australia is a federation of states where there are three levels of government under the Australian Constitution (Veal, 2002). AATP needed to negotiate the different levels of government, those with responsibilities for alpine areas, the local government of gateway communities and other agencies who may have had responsibility for landholding, infrastructure, planning and development. Table 23.3 provides a sample of the range of the government stakeholders involved with the project. Even though the protected areas are called national parks, they are in fact managed at the state level, not at the national level.

Project Details

This project sought to integrate and build upon the capacity and capability of existing organizations to create a legacy of trained staff, and the production of information and resources that could be used into the future. To achieve this, three key strategies were used:

- Auditing of facilities and tourism opportunities, and the conduct of needs assessments to identify training needs.
- Training and development to address training and development needs.

- Resource development to create an enduring legacy.
- Auditing and needs assessment.

Site assessments using Darcy and Cameron's model were completed for 88 organisations. As of December 2008, only 5 had been uploaded onto websites by individual organisations (5.7%). A further 12 were planning to do so (117.7%), highlighting the challenge of making the information available to the target market.

A survey of tourism organisations was conducted by the University of Canberra to investigate the current level of knowledge, skills and attitudes in relation to accessible tourism. This research drew upon Darcy's previous work and the *Interaction with Disabled Persons Scale* from the University of Sydney.

Training and development

Nine training workshops were conducted over 10 days with 129 attendees across threes states: NSW, Tasmania and Victoria. Topics included: accessibility awareness; sensory loss training conducted by Vision Australia, and an introduction to accessible adventure activities. Two industry workshops were conducted with representatives from state tourism organizations, destination managers and other interested parties. (Sydney, December 2007; Jindabyne, December 2008).

Resource development

A CD based toolkit was produced that brought together a range of fact sheets, tips, tools, techniques and reference websites for businesses to use to help develop their accessible tourism capabilities. Since the completion

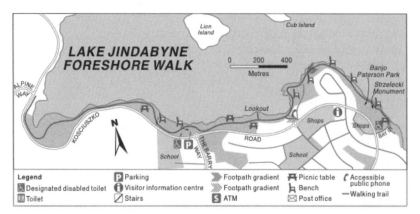

Figure 23.8 Lake Jindabyne foreshore walk from the Snowy Mountains Mobility Maps

of the project the resource has been uploaded onto Disabled WinterSport Australia's website (http://www.disabledwintersport.com.au/).

Mapmakers Cartoscope published Mobility Maps from work conducted on the project, for the Snowy Mountains as well as the Alpine Shire. These highlighted paths of travel, inclines, location of accessible toilets and parking. Examples of short break articles were written to highlight how businesses could work together to co-market themselves and build future accessible tourism experiences.

Discussion

The following discussion of the outcomes of the project are built around Ritchie and Crouch's (2003) Destination and Competitiveness and Sustainability Model (Figure 23.4), highlighting how the AATP built upon different aspects of the model and some of the issues faced in the process (Dickson, 2007, 2008).

Richie and Crouch (2003) suggest that the image of a destination may take some time to change, even after the reality has changed. A low awareness of a destination may mean a slower change in image. Awareness and image are important as they are 'the lens though which tourists perceive all characteristics of a destination and therefore effectively all of the other elements of [the] model' (p. 76)

In the short two-year timeframe of the project it is not possible to measure changes in awareness or image, however the most recent marketing campaign for the Snowy Mountains (Autumn, 2009) included images of older people in the outdoors.

A destination's vision provides the 'more functional and more inspirational portrait of the ideal future that the destination hopes to bring about in some defined future' (Ritchie & Crouch, 2003: 154).

Prior to the AATP commencing, accessibility was already a component of strategies such as the Plan of Management for Kosciuszko National Park (Department of Environment and Conservation, 2006) and the Alpine Resorts 2020 Strategy in Victoria (Department of Sustainability and Environment, 2004), yet there was little evidence that progress was being made. What this project achieved was to offer to land managers and planners some steps to move forward on these strategies without being caught up in the debate about compliance under the DDA. One simple shift has been the focus upon whole-of-life access from young children in prams to seniors, rather than just disability.

The task of marketing is 'to design a product-service combination that provides a real value to targeted customers, motivates purchase, and fulfils genuine customer needs' (Kotler et al., 2003) The AATP produced materials that would enable individual businesses and destination marketers to inform people with access requirements about what accommodation, food and other activities may be available for them. This included reports on facilities, short break stories that demonstrated how accommodation, food and activities could be packaged together and through examples of how individual business may further market themselves.

Ritchie and Crouch emphasise that tourists are buying experiences which are a combination of 'all of the interactions, behaviours, and emotions which each tourist permits their five senses to perceive and experience' (Ritchie & Crouch, 2003: 73). Not just individual experiences but a package of experiences that offered by an array of businesses including transport, accommodation, food and beverage. The AATP emphasised the whole of the visitor's journey and the need for continuous paths of accessible travel. To achieve this requires the communication between tourism providers and managers, working cooperatively, co-marketing and creatively reaching out to the market together.

The information/research component requires effective information systems that can provide timely information to managers about tourists' needs and satisfaction levels. With the access assessments and reports being a key part of the AATP, it was an aim to be able to get these on a central database, such as the Australian Data Warehouse, which would make them available to the broader industry. This would have made the images and reports available for communication mediums such as brochures and marketing campaigns. However in the time of the project this was not achieved and it fell to the individual operators to post the material to their websites. However without an observable demand, many did not see the need, but without the information, the demand could not be generated. This is a classic 'chicken and the egg' scenario, which should come first the demand or the marketing? On the demand side, the only reliable national data available that identifies people travelling who have access requirements was previously collected in 1998 and 2003 (Darcy et. al., 2008). This was not repeated in 2008, despite pleas from the AATP, as there was no interest from the state tourism organizations who influence what data is collected by Tourism Research Australia.

Ritchie and Crouch (2003) suggest that destination management organizations have little control over the education and training that is provided (p. 211), but they can be involved in 'encouraging and stimulating education programmes designed to meet the specific needs of the tourism and hospitality industries (p. 74).

A core component of the AATP was the provision of information and training in accessibility, working with specific disabilities such has vision impairment and developing skills in the provision of outdoor activities for people with access requirements. The AATP partnered, where possible, with existing organizations and people with expertise in these areas, such as Vision Australia, access consultants, and elite outdoor and sporting participants who had disabilities, such as Ron Finneran, Louise Sauvage, Michael

Figure 23.9 Paralympians Louise
Sauvage and Ron Finneran on the
summit of Mt Kosciuszko,
December 2008
Photograph by Tracey J. Dickson

Milton, Kirsty Stafford (*née* Busch) and Stuart Tripp, and elite athletes with
access requirements such as Carla Ziijlstra who had two small children.
Together these people could be examples of what can be achieved when the
tourism industry works together. This was showcased on the International
Day for People with a Disability, 2008 with an 18km hike to the summit of
Mt Kosciuszko (Figure 23.9).

The mix of activities is critical to the destination's appeal, the 'challenge
facing the tourism destination manager is to develop those activities
that take advantage of the natural physiography of the destination while
remaining consistent with the local culture and its value' (Ritchie & Crouch,
2003: 69). Central to the AATP was the development of accessible outdoor
activities. This drew upon Disabled WinterSport Australia's experience
of working with people with disabilities to participate in snow-sports.
Workshops were provided to assist people to develop skills to explore how
to make their activities more accessible in abseiling; climbing; challenge
ropes courses; horse riding; and canoeing.

For Ritchie and Crouch (2003), accessibility is 'the ease or difficulty
confronting tourists in travelling to the destination' (p. 131) and may be a
combination of location, regulation, visas, travel routes and carriers. This
is relevant for those with or without access requirements. For travel to
the alpine areas, private vehicles dominate. For example, 86% of overnight

visitors travelling to the Snowy River Shire use a private vehicle (Tourism Research Australia, 2008a) while for the Alpine Shire the rate of private vehicle use was 92% (Tourism Research Australia, 2008b). The main challenge facing tourists is how they can find out if there are quality and suitable accessible tourism opportunities along the journey and at the destination.

Political will incorporates not only the politicians' support for tourism, but also the influence of community leaders to obtain that support (Ritchie & Crouch, 2003: 71).

In the Alpine regions considered here, winter tourism is a major economic contributor (Table 23.1), so political support is generally there. However, summer tourism is a minor player in the alpine areas (Table 23.2), and in a land driven by a summer beach culture, the political will to promote inland, mountain tourism, is less evident. While the project funding that supported the AATO was substantial, for accessible summer alpine tourism to see a sustainable impact requires an ongoing, long-term, commitment and support from politicians, community leaders and tourism managers alike.

Project Recommendations – Success by Design

Recommendations that have evolved from this project, and that will assist in developing both the demand and supply in the accessible tourism market in Australia's alpine areas include:

- All levels of government must commit to supporting the development of accessible tourism over a prolonged period, not one-off or short-term initiatives. This requires on-going funding at Federal, state and local/regional levels to develop, market, train and support accessible tourism products and services. Not only will that lead to enhanced accessible tourism product, it will also have a flow-on effect for the quality of life of others in the destination communities who have access requirements.
- Local governments need to:
  o   ensure that their communities are accessible and promoted such as through access/mobility maps;
  o   be best practice advocates and examples of accessibility in their local communities, including public building access, recreational facilities and transport.
- Planning regulators need to be aware of and implement, not just the Building Code of Australia, but also the options for universal design.
- Marketing materials need to:
  o   Promote and demonstrate accessible tourism opportunities;
  o   Be accurate and up to date;

o   Get to those who may be travelling with people with different access requirements such as:
  ▪   bus tour operators;
  ▪   school groups;
  ▪   specific lobby/community groups supporting people with different disability;
  ▪   parent groups;
  ▪   play groups;
  ▪   senior citizens groups.
- Tourism providers need to:
  o   develop strategic partnerships with other local operators to enhance the 'Visitor Journey';
  o   be regularly informed about how they can improve access for those with different requirements such as:
    ▪   providing room design information;
    ▪   talking with clients about their access needs;
    ▪   applying universal design principles in maintenance and development plans.

Other strategies that will assist in the long-term development of accessible tourism include:

- Imbedding accessibility into tourism and hospitality training at TAFE and University levels, as well as in other relevant courses such as sport and outdoor recreation training;
- Universal design principles need to be introduced in architectural, engineering, design, urban planning, and building courses.
- The media to be advocates for change by publicising the success of local organizations who are access-aware and highlighting role-models of accessible tourism participants;
- Tourism awards should include an accessibility component.
- Employing people with access requirements will assist in making the whole organization access-aware on a daily basis.

Conclusion

In conclusion, this project has provided an excellent demonstration of the possibilities of a strategic approach to accessible tourism within clearly defined geographic areas (Darcy, 2006; Darcy *et al.*, 2008). By specifically targeting the accessible tourism market and working in collaboration with others in the tourism destination area, accessible destination experiences can be promoted and branded to create a competitive advantage through a strategic approach to accessible tourism (Leiper *et al.*, 2008). While the primary function of these areas has had a winter focus, accessible tourism provides an opportunity for shoulder and off-season use that had not been previously considered. What stakeholders found empowering was that the project sought to build upon current infrastructure, abilities and product through providing a framework to interpret, present and disseminate access information that required no changes to the way that they operated. While the approach required time to attend the workshops and to work with the project team, there were no extra costs involved. Once this investment in time had been made it was efficient for the organizations as they could disseminate information permanently through their own websites and continuously through consumer enquiries. The destination approach then provided those involved with collaborative edge as the destination became an accessible destination area complete with infrastructure and experiences beyond their individual enterprises. However, the excellent foundation that has been developed requires a stakeholder to take ownership of the knowledge base so that it can be further developed, nurtured and disseminated to consumers. This is a challenge that is yet to be realised.

Acknowledgement

The Alpine Accessible Tourism Project was funded by the Australian Commonwealth Government through 'Ausindustry', under the Australian Tourism Development Program.

Resources

Accessible Accommodation and Activities in the Snowy Mountains, New South Wales, Australia   http://www.snowymountains.com.au/Accessible_Accommodation.html and http://www.snowymountains.com.au/Accessible_Attractions.html
Alpine Accessibility Toolkit http://www.disabledwintersport.com.au/Pages/AATP/index.htm
Information on Disability and Education Awareness Service (IDEAS) Website http://www.ideas.org.au/
Tourism Australia Accessible Touring Routes – Marketing Activities http://www.tourism.australia.com/Marketing.asp?lang=ENandsub=0437andal=2571
Training package for the hospitality, tourism, retail and entertainment industries 'You Can Make a Difference to Customer Relations for People with Disabilities in the Hospitality, Tourism, Retail and Entertainment Industries' http://www.disability.wa.gov.au

References

Bennett, R. and McColl-Kennedy, J.R. (2003) *Services Marketing: A Managerial Approach.* Milton, Queensland: Wiley.
Berridge, G. (2007) The experience industry and the experience economy. In G. Berridge (ed.) *Events Design and Experience* (pp. 115–158). Sydney: Butterworth–Heinemann/ Elsevier.

Cameron, B., Darcy, S. and Foggin, S.E.A. (2003) *Barrier-Free Tourism for People with Disabilities in the Asian and Pacific Region*. New York: United Nations.

Clawson, M. and Knetsch, J.L. (1966) *Economics of Outdoor Recreation*. Baltimore: Johns Hopkins University Press.

Daniels, M. J., Drogin Rodgers, E. B. and Wiggins, B. P. (2005) 'Travel Tales': An interpretive analysis of constraints and negotiations to pleasure travel as experienced by persons with physical disabilities. *Tourism Management*, 26(6), 919–930

Darcy, S. (1998) Anxiety to access: Tourism patterns and experiences of New South Wales people with a physical disability/author Simon Darcy. Sydney: Tourism New South Wales.

Darcy, S. (2006) *Setting a Research Agenda for Accessible Tourism*. Gold Coast, Qld: Sustainable Tourism CRC.

Darcy, S., Cameron, B., Dwyer, L., Taylor, T., Wong, E. and Thomson, A. (2008) Technical Report 90064: Visitor accessibility in urban areas. Gold Coast, Qld: Sustainable Tourism CRC.

Department of Environment and Conservation, NSW (2006) *2006 Plan of Management: Kosciuszko National Park*. Queanbeyan, NSW: Parks and Wildlife Division.

Department of Sustainability and Environment, Victoria (2004) *Alpine Resorts 2020 Strategy*. Melbourne, Victoria: Department of Sustainability and Environment.

Dickson, T.J. (2007) *Accessible Summer Alpine Tourism – Quality Barrier-Free Tourism*. Canberra, ACT: Centre for Tourism Research, University of Canberra.

Dickson, T.J. (2008) Evaluation of the Alpine Accessible Tourism Project, 2007-08. Canberra, ACT: Centre for Tourism Research, University of Canberra.

Freeman, R. E. (1983) *Strategic Management: A Stakeholder Approach*. Boston: Pitman.

Harvey, C. P. and Allard, M. J. (2005) (eds) *Understanding and Managing Diversity: Readings, Cases, and Exercises* (International Edition). Upper Saddle River, NJ: Pearson Prentice Hall.

Hayllar, B. and Griffin, T. (2005) The precinct experience: A phenomenological approach. *Tourism Management*, 26(4), 517–528.

Jamal, T. and Getz, D. (1995) Collaboration theory and community tourism planning. *Annals of Tourism Research*, 22(1), 186–204.

Kotler, P., Bowen, J. and Makens, J. (2003) *Marketing for Hospitality and Tourism* (3rd edn). Upper Saddle River, NJ: Prentice Hall.

Lane, M. (2007) The Visitor Journey: The new road to success. *International Journal of Contemporary Hospitality Management*, 19(3), 248–254.

Leiper, N., Stear, L., Hing, N. and Firth, T. (2008) Partial industrialisation in tourism: A new model. *Current Issues in Tourism*, 11(3), 207–735.

Lew, A. A. (1989) Authenticity and sense of place in the tourism development experience of older retail districts. *Journal of Travel Research*, 27(4), 15–22.

Massey, D. (1993) Power-geometry and a progressive sense of place. In J. Bird (ed.) *Mapping the Futures: Local Cultures, Global Change* (pp. 60–70). London: Routledge.

Mueller, J. L. (2001) Office and workplace design. In W.F.E. Preiser and E. Ostroff (eds) *Universal design handbook* (pp. 45.41–45.11). New York: McGraw-Hill.

Murphy, P.E. (1985) *Tourism: A Community Approach*. New York: Methuen.

National Institute of Economic and Industry Research (2006) *Australian Alpine Areas Economic Significance Report*. Melbourne: National Institute of Economic and Industry Research.

Otto, J. E. and Ritchie, J.R.B. (1996) The service experience in tourism. *Tourism Management*, 17(3), 165–174.

Pine, B.J. and Gilmore, J.H. (1998) Welcome to the experience economy. *Harvard Business Review*, 76(4), 97–105.

Preiser, W.F.E., and Ostroff, E. (2001) (eds) *Universal Design Handbook*. New York: McGraw-Hill.

Ritchie, J.R.B., Crouch, G.I. and Hudson, S. (2001) Developing operational measures for the components of a destination competitiveness/sustainability model: Consumer versus maangerail perspectives. In J.A. Mazanec, G.I. Crouch, J.R.B. Ritchie and A.G. Woodside (eds) *Consumer Psychology of Tourism, Hospitality and Leisure* (Vol. 2, pp. 1–18). Wallingford: CABI.

Ritchie, J. R. B. and Crouch, G. (2003) *The Competitive Destination: A Sustainable Tourism Perspective.* Cambridge, MA: CABI.

Sautter, E.T. and Leisen, B. (1999) Managing stakeholders a tourism planning model. *Annals of Tourism Research,* 26(2), 312–328.

Smith, R. W. (1985) Barriers are more than architectural. *Parks and Recreation*, 20(10), 58–62.

Stewart, E.J., Hayward, B.M., Devlin, P.J. and Kirby, V.G. (1998) The 'place' of interpretation: A new approach to the evaluation of interpretation. *Tourism Management,* 19(3), 257–266.

Tourism Research Australia (2008a) Tourism Profiles for local government areas in regional Australia: New South Wales, Snowy River Shire, three or four year average to June 2007. Available at: www.tra.australia.com.

Tourism Research Australia (2008b) Tourism Profiles for local government areas in regional Australia: Victoria, Alpine Shire, three or four year average to June 2007. Available at: www.tra.australia.com.

Trauer, B. and Ryan, C. (2005) Destination image, romance and place experience – an application of intimacy theory in tourism. *Tourism Management*, 26(4), 481–491.

Turco, D.M., Stumbo, N. and Garncarz, J. (1998) Tourism constraints for people with disabilities. *Parks and Recreation*, 33(9), 78–85.

Veal, A.J. (2002) *Leisure and Tourism Policy and Planning.* Wallingford, UK: CABI.

Walkom, R. (1991) *Skiing Off the Roof.* Palmerstone, ACT: Tabletop Press.

World Health Organization (2007) Global Age-friendly Cities: A Guide. Available at: www.who.int/ageing/en.

Yin, R.K. (2002) *Case Study Research, Design and Methods.* Thousand Oaks, CA: SAGE Publications.

Zuber-Skerritt, O. (1996) *New Directions in Action Research.* London: The Falmer Press.

24 Special Needs Customer Care Training for Tourism

Susana Navarro García-Caro, Arno de Waal and Dimitrios Buhalis

Introduction

This chapter reflects the importance of the incorporation of specific training programmes on accessible tourism and leisure. 'These days a fundamental barrier is the lack of awareness of personnel working in the tourism sector. Barriers of attitude can dissuade disabled people from travelling, so the solution to this problem would include training and raising awareness of all personnel on disability issues' (Personal Interview with Maria Nyman, European Disability Forum, 1996). Training contents must not be applied randomly, but should be based on studies of the needs of tourism and leisure clients, in this case, customers with special needs. This chapter offers a proposal for action through the preparation of training content that can be used as the foundation for international training in the sector. This can also be utilised by all universities teaching tourism and leisure courses around the world, as well as business associations acting as liaisons for tour companies involved in the tourism sector. Distance learning applications, through new technologies and the interne,t can enable the distribution of the training to stakeholders globally, without geographical limitations.

Why Train the Tourism Sector on 'Accessible Tourism and Leisure'?

To be successful all training processes must involve the prior study of needs and requirements of the sector. The tourism sector is very changeable and, thus, requires the development of flexible and operative systems. An assessment of the trends and changes occurring in the global environment is also critical in order to adapt the curriculum content of the training to the emerging needs and in order to optimise the use of new training processes and techniques. Training processes should therefore aim to improve the professional qualifications of tourism employees and their ability to operate in a global interactive environment.

The accessibility market covers 3.5 million people with a physical disability in Spain, over 37 million people in Europe and over 500 million worldwide. So it is an important market niche which, if handled according to its special needs, can yield profitable products and services. The ageing European population means that accessibility demand for tourism and holidays will be increasing rapidly in the near future. Thus, it is necessary to adapt facilities and services to the new needs that are emerging and capture this market. According to European Union statistics, there are 100 million people who would travel more if tourism establishments and destinations were more accessible, so new business opportunities are evident. As Spain is the second tourist destination country in the world, adaptation of the tourism service to serve this ever-increasing segment of the market is vital.

After several years teaching courses on accessible tourism and leisure to different sector agents in Spain, it is evident tourism employees receive no training on accessible tourism during their university studies. From 2003, when short training courses began to be taught in different tourism companies supported by associations from the sector, tourism organizations could confirm the importance of training on this issue. Nowadays, very few Spanish universities incorporate accessible training programmes in their curriculum, although different courses and/or seminars on the matter are becoming more frequent. Nevertheless, the contents of such training is not regulated and/or approved by an official body and, hence, there is a great variation in the marketplace. Therefore accessible tourism needs to be developed conceptually and to be incorporated in the educational and training programmes at different levels. This will enable the industry to raise the awareness of employees and to achieve total quality. The development of this book is a step in the right direction for developing the learning material that will facilitate curriculum development.

Employees who are currently working in the sector, as well as students studying for a degree in tourism, hospitality and leisure, should be trained in order to 'care for customers with special needs' and to have some 'knowledge of accessibility issues'. This should incorporate knowledge of the accessibility state of towns and cities, nature reserves, attractions and tourism facilities. In addition, an appreciation of customer needs and some understanding on how to access accessibility information on the urban environment, the public-use buildings (tourism establishments, tourist information offices, businesses, other public and private services, etc) is required. Although previous knowledge of the accessibility is not essential, employees can be trained in these areas. An understanding of the accessibility requirements of disabled guests and a helpful attitude towards understanding the individual requirements of individuals is of major importance though. Starting from the place of employment, accessibility trained personnel can audit the tourism resources at the facility where they work to be duly adapted and to have the necessary technical help or equipment to provide quality service to customers. Accessibility in tourism facilities should be accompanied by appropriate customer care; lack of either of these may cause consumers to be unsatisfied.

The fundamental key to success of accessibility training is to include the perspective of accessibility universally, where accessibility and universal design is part of all training and education modules. Hence not only employees should be training on accessible tourism but also disciplines related to design, architecture, engineering, technical skills and suchlike. Professionals in all these areas need to be made aware of the benefits of accessibility and to be encouraged to examine best accessibility practice and universal design. To achieve this, a dialogue and coordination with all stakeholders must be established and internal contradictions and overlapping avoided. It is necessary to establish a 'horizontal coordination' mechanism, through the creation of sector advisory Councils or Committees on Accessibility that encourage a coherent and coordinated approach when setting up training programmes in different areas. Such representation must be technical and not political, so that the performance of its tasks is really effective. Engaging consumers and other accessibility stakeholders can improve decision making and ensure that best solutions are identified.

Accessibility and its Importance in Tourism Training

Despite the great social advances our society is undergoing, there is still much to be done in the area of accessibility. We live in a culture that has a prototype of person considered 'normal', and everyone who does not fit in with the term is excluded or simply not taken into consideration. This has been so throughout history. This is why, to market a tourism product, marketing campaigns feature people in full use of their faculties, with voluptuous and attractive physiques. However, we rarely see the participation of people with any kind of disability in marketing campaigns. To make progress towards assisting the life of people with some kind of disability, everyone in society needs to work together: politicians, public and private bodies, companies and citizens as a whole. Slowly accessibility is removing architectural, town-planning and communications barriers in our cities. Improvements are being made in employment and training, housing, taxation, social security benefits, transport and many more. It is time to make improvements in leisure and tourism activities for those with disabilities. For this reason it is essential to establish training based on several aspects for current and future employees of the tourism sector. It is also necessary to establish an accessible and sustainable tourism model in which disabled people can enjoy their leisure time and undertake tourism activities that really respond to their interests and meet their expectations. Tourists with functional diversity use means of transport, hotels, restaurants, complementary services, in other words, they participate in the economic and cultural life of the destination. Accessibility is a general improvement for the population as a whole, as it adds value to the destination and/or establishment.

Accessibility and tourism are two related concepts and combining them brings competitive and social value to the tourism market, as well as being an important business opportunity. Tourism destinations and businesses compete in an increasingly globalised and demanding market. The new standards of tourism development are moving towards new fundamental aspects such as quality, sustainability, image, innovation and accessibility. A change of mentality in tourism businesses is needed as the concepts of Innovation and Accessibility are practically new terms for many of them. The process of incorporating these concepts is slow because they are seen as an expense, rather than an investment, that can generate profit – mainly because of the lack of an immediate return on the investment. Practicing accessibility and incorporating universal design can add value to the tourism business and generate new revenue streams whilst increasing the efficiency in operations and management. In tourism destinations and companies, these principles will provide new possibilities in the current tourism offer, opening new market segments, new business opportunities, new job opportunities, and efficient practices. According to the White Paper on Accessibility, the concept of 'universal accessibility' is 'the set of features an environment, product or service should have to be usable in conditions of comfort, security and equality by everyone and, in particular, by people with a disability'.

Difficulties in the Tourism Sector in Spain

According to the Spanish Secretariat General for Tourism, 'training as an objective cannot be considered an independent or isolated fact, but that it participates directly and actively in all integrated processes for the development of society'. The tourism sector in Spain basically faces two difficulties regarding the adaptation for disabled people. Due to the transfer of competences regarding accessibility and tourism to the Autonomous Communities, there is great disparity in legislation and lack of standardisation of accessibility criteria. There are also large gaps in the knowledge, education and training of professionals to provide customer care for disabled travellers.

Hence training is required to enable the sector to deliver suitable products and services and maximise its benefits. Through the specific training proposals in this area, the aim is to participate in raising awareness on this issue, not just from the point of view of civil rights, but from the perspective of the market, which demands more evolved services, such as maximum profitability, capability, quality and sector sustainability. The general objectives pursued are:

- Raise awareness of employees involved in the tourism activity of the importance of considering accessibility in tourism planning and management.
- Provide appropriate care for customers with special needs.

Not only must we deal with physical and communications barriers, but also the social and human barriers in which each of the employees belonging to this sector must participate for the inclusion of disabled people. For this reason, it is necessary to know how to handle their leisure time needs and how to facilitate them to achieve their leisure desires and activities. This can only be achieved through specific training in such a precise area.

Towards an Educational Training System Focused on Total Quality

There is a need, therefore, for the creation of a wide-ranging and integrated education-training system, aimed at the sustainable development of the tourism sector and focused on achieving total quality. To achieve quality, we must focus entirely on the client. Therefore, when creating a tourism and leisure training model we must do the same, identifying employees' needs and being aware of their expectations. According to the book *Educando educadores en Turismo* (Educating the Educators in Tourism), 'Tourism has a great diversity and range of activities, which will be different when training future sector professionals' (Sancho *et al.,* 1995: 45) .For example, the branch of hotel management is different to that of managing travel agencies, airports, etc., but all require specific training courses on special needs customer care, on issues of accessibility, on handling and use of technical aids, and so on. Only in this way we can attain an education model focused on achieving the satisfaction of the end client.

In order to attain this training model, the involvement of national and international bodies, employees and disabled people is important. This allows the development of 'accessible tourism and leisure' modules to be created within the current curricular development on tourism and leisure, as all the countries involved in the tourism phenomenon have to face the challenges with a common perspective.

Training should not only remain within universities and the education sector. Current sector employees must also be trained, and therefore tourism organizations and destinations must make a commitment to adapting their establishment and training their staff. This is complicated and that is why a regulatory body for the training could establish to exchange experiences, organize of workshops and seminars through business associations, create specific publications and manuals for the sector, create training centres, collaborate with educational institutions and disability organizations and suchlike. Above all, government support in the form of providing budget allocations to subsidise accessibility initiatives is fundamental.

Trainers for Accessible Tourism

'The dynamic, fast and innovative evolution of the tourism sector requires adaptation, in these same terms, of tourism education, and a great effort by education professionals in this sector to face the challenges and opportunities of what, without doubt, is and will be the key economic activity of the 21st century' (Sancho *et al.*, 1995). In the last few years, many national and international bodies have made tourism education a priority, supporting many education programmes. However, experience shows that there are few programmes able to prepare tourism education professionals who, ultimately, are responsible for preparing new personnel who must be incorporated in a constantly innovative economic activity.

What is needed to attain total accessibility in the Spanish tourism system is the participation of different professionals, depending on the subject to be taught. On the one hand, it will need the participation of professionals with proven experience in design, execution, maintenance and management of accessible tourism projects who have worked under universal design criteria. The participation of professionals used to using and handling technical aids, providing customer care for elderly people and those with special needs, and professionals who have worked in the training of other employees on this issue will also be required in order to achieve the elimination of barriers and attainment of useful areas for everyone as well as 'correct customer care'.

Training Methodologies, Content and Use of New Technologies

Tourism businesses must invest in physical resources to prepare their human resources. Without the right training policy of human capital, it is impossible for businesses to attain the competitiveness that the dynamism of external organizations demands from them. Training must be systematic, and it must aim to set objectives, provide changes in capacity and increase efficiency so that complete advantage is taken of the investment.

The aforementioned conditions show the importance of developing an education project on accessible tourism in Spain, a tourism destination *par excellence*, which is a tool for the establishment of national education standards, and allows standardisation of knowledge on this issue. To apply this proposal, a national body with associated centres would be necessary to cover the whole country, and these could become examination bodies able to issue certificates and qualifications. To develop this proposal, distance learning methodology could be used and specific courses on accessible tourism and leisure created. It could be done in an eLearning platform that could be distributed via the internet with extensive video and audio software, allowing the development of an interactive and useful learning tool. The system must also provide the possibility of reading files that would effectively be a form of bibliographic access to primary and secondary sources on this new tourism discipline.

The aforementioned conditions show the importance of developing a distance learning education project on accessible tourism that is a platform for the establishment of national and international education standards, and that allows the standardisation of knowledge on tourism issues beyond geographic boundaries. The need for an international body is more than evident and, together with its associated centres, could really be set up as an examination mechanism able to issue certificates and qualifications. The incorporation of a standard test in the programme would be an interesting experience for the students and a way of testing their knowledge.

The objectives that any proposed and developed training programme should pursue are:

- To provide knowledge to employees involved in the tourism activity so that they take into account accessibility issues during renovations and building works, as well as in the design of tourism activities, products and services.
- To provide knowledge to employees involved in the tourism activity on caring for customers with special needs.
- To identify the main barriers to accessibility in tourism destinations and establishments, providing alternatives for improvement.
- To familiarise them with the use of technical aids.
- To disseminate existing legal provisions.

The proposed common training modules for all tourism employees are outlined in Figure 24.1.

Due to the diversity of tourism destinations and businesses, training courses should be adapted to the needs of each of the employees belonging to the tourism sector. With this aim in mind, the following groups are proposed, to which not only the aforementioned modules should be taught, but also specific training given depending on the sector or area of work:

- GROUP 1: HOLIDAY ACCOMMODATION: Customer care managers and staff (reception, reservations, loans, apartments, restaurants, function rooms, etc.) of hotels, hostels, guesthouses, campsites, rural accommodation, apartments and spas.
- GROUP 2: TOURISM TRANSPORT: Customer care managers and staff of city bus companies, discretionary transport, taxis, railways, airlines, water sports resorts and leisure marinas.

MODULE 1. CONCEPTS OF ACCESSIBLE AND DISABLED TOURISM
What is 'accessible tourism'?
Objectives of accessible tourism
Glossary of basic concepts of accessibility
Types of barriers in tourism. Examples
Main types of disability
Customer care for people with disability
Clients with disability as a growing market (future estimates)
Profile of tourists with disabilities: Motivations, type of holidays they choose, perception of personal treatment, role of companions/carers, etc.

MODULE 2. CARE OF CUSTOMERS WITH SPECIAL NEEDS
Basic rules for effective communication.
Common situations and codes of conduct to follow in providing customer care for disabled people.
Basic needs of disabled people in the use and enjoyment of tourism services and infrastructure.
Technical aids available on the market to facilitate the use of infrastructure, means of transport, communication, etc.

MODULE 3. CREATION OF ACCESSIBLE AREAS AND INCLUSIVE DESIGN
Current situation of accessibility in our country.
Examples of good practices applied to the tourism sector by tourism businesses (both on a national and international level).
Examples of the main projects developed by the public authorities nationally and internationally.
Main indicators of accessibility to be taken into account in tourism towns and establishments.
Main laws and legal provisions in tourism towns, bodies and businesses.
Accessibility: another parameter of quality, implementation of global accessibility systems.
Benefits for the businesses and destinations that apply them. A business opportunity.
The WTO (World Tourism Organization) measures and recommendations regarding accessibility.
Application of new technologies for the development of accessible tourism.

Figure 24.1 Accessibility training programme for tourism employees

- GROUP 3. RESTAURANTS, BARS, CAFETERIAS, PUBS AND DISCOTHEQUES
- GROUP 4. LEISURE, CULTURE AND SPORTS ACTIVITIES: Customer care managers and staff at the main tourism resources; theatres, cinemas, museums, monuments, etc.
- GROUP 5. OUTDOOR AREAS: Managers of nature reserves, parks and gardens and beaches.

- GROUP 6. TOWN ENVIRONMENT: In this group we include government staff responsible for the departments of the environment, culture, tourism and leisure in tourism towns. Also, managers of businesses, shopping centres and tourist information offices.
- GROUP 7. MARKET OPERATORS: Travel intermediaries (tour operators and travel agencies).
- GROUP 8. TOURISM ACTIVITY BUSINESSES: Local guides, entertainment companies, vehicle rental firms, passenger transfer companies at the destination, and others.

Although this course is proposed to be developed as a distance training courses, it is important that students receive a classroom session, as this provides an applied focus due to the exchange of experiences and to case studies. The following techniques could be used:

- Presentation of the experiences of companies and destinations that have made a commitment to adapting their products and services.
- Use of role play through real-life situations being simulated. The objective is to imagine the way to act and the decisions each of the people involved should take in different situations.
- Simulation games in order to identify the main barriers.
- Audiovisual presentation of good and bad practices in the tourism sector.
- Disabled people explaining their experience in tourism facilities
- Team work to diagnose a different area of the establishment/destination using questionnaires.
- Exchange of impressions to determine critical areas and steps to be taken for their correct adaptation.

A dynamic and practical methodology is applied allowing students to easily implement the knowledge received in their place of work.

Conclusions

Accessibility must be applied from a cross-discipline perspective affecting several qualifications including architecture and design. The result is buildings and urban areas that are designed for universal use that can be enjoyed by all as well as by people with special needs. Turning to creativity and innovation, as well as searching for technical aids, is essential as the concept of accessibility is compatible with design.

Training future employees of the tourism sector is fundamental if we seek to attain the satisfaction of the end client. For this reason, accessible tourism curriculum content must be standardised and monitored by a body which better controls the contents provided by the different education institutions. Providing specialist courses to current sector employees continues to be essential, as it is clear that there is a lack of information and advice for the business community. In this aspect, the involvement of the government is crucial.

People involved in the training aspects must be aware of the current problems and have experience in creating accessible areas, in special needs customer care, and, at the same time, understand the tourism industry and its idiosyncrasies. The training proposal set out here is designed on the basis of the needs detected in training courses held by Adaptamos Group in Spain over the last five years. Having a national or international body with its corresponding associated centres providing coverage worldwide would be the best way of standardising and creating specific qualifications on this issue. To achieve this proposal, it would be necessary to use distance learning methodology and the Internet to implement an active and useful learning system without geographic boundaries.

References

Alonso López, F. and Dinares Quera, M. (2006) El hotel accesible. Guía para su diseño, organización y gestión (The accessible hotel: guide for design, organization and management). Valencia: Institute for the Elderly and Social Services (IMSERSO).

Di Santo Morales, S, and Grünewald, L. (1997) *La integración de las personas con capacidad restringidas en un medio urbano y rural durante el tiempo libre dedicado al turismo y la recreación: una propuesta educativa*, (The integration of people with restricted ability in an urban and rural environment during free time dedicated to tourism and recreation: an education proposal). Available at: www.tuobra.unam.mx/publicadas/020928220034.html.

Leclerc, A. (2000). *Un mercado en expansión: la experiencia canadiense* (A market in expansion: the Canadian experience). Available at: www.travelturisme/estudios/.

Ortega, E. and Huesca, A.M. (2004) Hábitos y Actitudes hacia el turismo de las personas con discapacidad física (Habits and attitudes towards tourism for people with a physical disability), Madrid: State Platform for Physically Disabled People (PREDIF).

Sancho, A., Fossati, R., Marín, A. and Pedro, A. (1995) *Educando educadores en turismo* (Educating the Educators in Tourism). Spain: World Tourism Organization (WTO).

Sancho, A., Buhalis, D., Gallego, J., Mata, J., Navarro, S., Osorio E., Pedro, A., Ramos, S. and Ruiz, P. *Introducción al Turismo (Introduction to Tourism)*. Spain: World Tourism Organization (WTO).

Further Reading

Tourism Review.com, (June 2008) *Airlines accessible to all? Not Yet*, p.46. Available at: http://www.tourism-review.com/magazine_file.php?id=578andorder=1.

Van Horno, L. (2000) *Turismo para personas con discapacidad, ¿un mercado por trabajar?* (Tourism for disabled people, a market to be worked on?). Available at: www.peru.info/catalogo/Attach/1677.PDF.

Vidal García Alonso, J., Valdominos Pastor, V., Herrera Santos, P.A., Rodriguez-Porrero Miret, C., Rodríquez Mahou, C., Redondo Martín-Aragón, J.A., Poveda Puente, R., Corrales Gálvez, J.M., Barberá i Guillem, R. and Prat Pastor, J.M. (2005) *¡Pregúntame* *sobre accesibilidad y ayudas técnicas!* (Ask me about accessibility and technical aids). Valencia: Institute for the Elderly and Social Services (IMSERSO).

Consumer Eroski (2008) Accesibilidad en las ciudades: analizados zona centro, ayuntamientos, ambulatorios, bus urbano y eurotaxi en 18 ciudades (Accessibility in Cities: City Centre, City Council Buildings, Outpatients Departments, City Bus and Eurotaxi Analysed in 18 Towns). *Consumer Eroski,* April, pp. 32–44.

25 Conclusions: Best Accessible Tourism Practice

Ivor Ambrose, Simon Darcy and Dimitrios Buhalis

In concluding the book, it is timely to reinforce the themes that have guided the examination of best case accessible tourism practice. They were: (1) Policies and Strategies; (2) Networks and Partnerships; (3) The Accessible Tourism Value Chain; (4) Destination Development; and (5) Accessible Tourism Experiences. While not suggesting a linear progression in the themes, there is no doubt an inherent logic to the way that the themes were sequenced and discussed.

Policies and Strategies are required to underpin a strategic approach to accessible tourism as identified in the definition presented in the introduction to this book. While only briefly discussed, the companion book *Accessible Tourism: Concepts and Issues* (Buhalis & Darcy, 2011) fully examined the importance of having well developed national policies in place as a foundation for the development of the underlying infrastructure required for accessible environments, transport and customer service. Only once these are in place can the approaches identified by Ambrose (Chapter 2), Ghijsels (Chapter 3), Neumann (Chapter 4), *Voulgaropoulos, Strati and Fyka (Chapter 5)*, Van Horn (Chapter 6), Darcy, *Cameron and Schweinsberg (Chapter 7)* and Rhodda's (Chapter 8) accessible tourism specific policies and strategies have any foundation on which to move forward. What these chapters contributed were the significantly different approaches taken in each of the nations examined. Each nation had its own cultural context that it had to work within, foundation upon which to build and relationships on which to leverage.

Yet, policies and strategies developed predominantly by governments will remain dormant unless there are **Networks and Partnerships** that bring together private-sector operators across all parts of the tourism system, the local relationships that have an understanding of the 'sense of place' so important for accessible tourism experiences, and the local disability networks of business, government and the not-for-profit sector. As Prescott (Chapter 9), Le, *Fujimoto, Rentschler and Edwards (Chapter 10)*, Müller (Chapter 11), Hunter-Jones and Thornton (Chapter 12) and Walsh,

Haddock-Fraser and Hampton (Chapter 13) outlined, this involves a detailed consideration of the stakeholders engaged in developing accessible tourism products, services and experiences. As their chapters presented, this requires a concerted effort to develop relationships beyond individual organisational goals to meet the needs of tourists with disability. In challenging one of the underlying stereotypes of the accessible tourism market that people with disability do not have the means to travel, the **Accessible Tourism Value Chain** presented the series of supply based transactions required for tourism products, services and experiences that the accessible tourism market requires. Wright's (Chapter 14) entrepreneurial examination provided a model not only to service the needs of tourists with disability but also an opportunity to create niche business opportunities and empower people with disability to be owners/employees within the sector. Darcy and Ravinder (Chapter 15), Krpata (Chapter 16) and Papamichail (Chapter 17) provided examination of service success and failure across the value chain drawing on public transport, air travel and the hotel sectors.

For accessible tourism to be part of a strategic approach to **Destination Development**, requires a conscious decision by destination managers to target the accessible tourism market through collaboration with stakeholders involved in the process. People with disability, and others with access needs, need the same level of service provision from destination managers as the general public. Yet, so often they are let down in the planning phase of their trips through a lack of consolidated information provision, marketing and dissemination across all sectors of the tourism industry, and the city, region and national tourist marketing organisations. Cameron and Darcy (Chapter 18), Pegg and Stumbo (Chapter 19), Tveitan (Chapter 20), Galán (Chapter 21) and Daines and Veitch (Chapter 22) all provide insights on the information strategies, structures and marketing activities, which destinations must put in place to attract customers.

Tourists with disability want the same 'sense of place' and **Accessible Tourism Experiences** in a destination area as any other tourist would expect. Nobody travels hundreds or thousands of kilometres from their home just to stay in an accessible hotel room unless there are experiences that they are seeking. In the case of tourists with disability this involves the development of accessible tourism experiences that satisfy their reasons for travelling in the first place. Dickson and Darcy (Chapter 23) provide a case study of an approach used for Alpine Accessible Tourism, which was based on a premise of providing tourists with disability with accessible outdoor recreation experiences that any tourists travelling to the region would be expecting. To facilitate this objective, they 'packaged' tourism planning information and experience provision together in a single place and worked with local stakeholders to develop a collaborative approach to information collection, presentation, marketing and dissemination. The final chapter in the book by Navarro García-Caro, de Waal and Buhalis (Chapter 24) examined the importance of customer service within the accessible tourism experience development. Research has consistently shown that even if access is not ideal, a 'can-do' customer service approach by operators is valued by tourists with disability and may provide solutions to access constraints experienced. In the chapter, it is strongly argued that disability awareness training should be a foundation for any business specifically targeting people with disability or wishing to maximise business yield.

To conclude the book, we go back to the definition of accessible tourism used in the introduction to reinforce that accessible tourism needs to be part of a strategically planned process, which specifically provides information across all market segments or specifically targets the accessible market. To achieve this outcome, tourism stakeholders need to work together to collaboratively market accessible tourism infrastructure, products, services and experiences. Hence, delivering *Accessible Tourism Experiences* typically depends on a process that incorporates the best aspects of these five themes brought together by stakeholders to show off the best accessible aspects of their destinations. We implore all readers of this book to take the lessons learned from the chapters presented by practitioners and academics and become accessible tourism champions in your own right.

References

Buhalis, D. and Darcy, S. (eds) (2011) *Accessible Tourism: Concepts and Issues*. Bristol, UK: Channel View Publications.

Pollock, A. and Benjamin, L. (2001) *Shifting Sands: The Tourism Ecosystem in Transformation*. London: DestiCorp Ltd.

Rains (2009) slide presentation on 'What is Inclusive Tourism?' online at: http://www.slideshare.net/guest6390726/what-is-inclusive-tourism-scott-rains

Takayama City and UNESCAP Conference Press Release (2009). Available at: http://www.accessibletourism.org/?i=enat.en.news.719

Takayama Declaration – Appendix: UNESCAP (2009). Available at: http://www.accessibletourism.org/resources/takayama_declaration_top-e-fin_171209.pdf

UNWTO (2001) *Global Code of Ethics for Tourism*, A/RES/56/212. Resolution adopted by the General Assembly of the United Nations World Tourism Organisation. Madrid, UNWTO.

UNWTO (2005) *Accessible Tourism for All*, A/RES/492(XVI)/10. Resolution adopted by the General Assembly of the United Nations World Tourism Organisation. Madrid, UNWTO.

UNWTO (2008) *Convention on the Rights of Persons with Disabilities and Optional Protocol (2006)*. Entered into force 3 May 2008. Madrid, UNWTO.